JOHN HUGHES-WILS
historians and comme

With countless others, he is a genuine Cold War warrior. A graduate of the RMA Sandhurst – where he won the Military History prize – and the Army Staff College, he served in both the infantry and the Intelligence Corps, seeing service in BAOR, Northern Ireland, Cyprus, Dhofar and the Falklands, as well as the jungles of Whitehall and Brussels. He retired as a Colonel on NATO's Political Staff to devote more time to serious military matters.

In 1999 Carroll and Graf published his first book, the best-selling *Military Intelligence Blunders and Cover-ups*. In 2002 he was elected Archives Bi-Fellow at Churchill College, Cambridge and is also a working Fellow of the Royal United Services Institute, specializing in intelligence and military history. He was awarded the Gold Medal of the International Napoleonic Society in 2000 for work on *Who Really Murdered Napoleon*? He has led over a hundred battlefield tours and is President of the Guild of Battlefield Guides.

He is a frequent broadcaster on both television and radio, and presented the *What If ?* television series for the BBC. Recent books include *Blindfold and Alone,* on First World War executions (with Cathryn Corns), and *The Puppet Masters,* the secret history of intelligence over the centuries.

He admits to being involved in several of the crises of the Cold War but slept through the Cuban Missile Crisis, as he had just come back from a particularly tiring exercise.

Other titles in this series

A BRIEF HISTORY OF

THE COLD WAR

The hidden truth about how close we came to nuclear conflict

JOHN HUGHES-WILSON

CARROLL & GRAF PUBLISHERS
New York

This book is dedicated to

Lynn

... who knows it better than most.

Carroll & Graf Publishers
An imprint of Avalon Publishing Group, Inc.
245 W. 17th Street
11th Floor
New York NY 10011–5300
www.carrollandgraf.com

AVALON
publishing group incorporated

First published in the UK by Robinson,
an imprint of Constable & Robinson Ltd, 2006

First Carroll & Graf edition, 2006

ISBN-13: 978–0–78671–731–6
ISBN-10: 0–7867–1731–9

Printed and bound in the EU

CONTENTS

LIST OF ILLUSTRATIONS

Cartoons

A 1955 view of the arms race
(*courtesy of Mirror Syndication International and supplied by the Centre for the Study of Cartoons and Caricature, University of Kent*)

A popular western view of the Cold War
(*courtesy of Mirror Syndication International and supplied by the Centre for the Study of Cartoons and Caricature, University of Kent*)

Britain finally wakes up to the reality of communist infiltration
(*courtesy of NI Syndication, London, 2006 and supplied by the Centre for the Study of Cartoons and Caricature, University of Kent*)

Maps

The following maps are courtesy of the author.

ACKNOWLEDGEMENTS

A book like this covers a huge range of subjects. Equally, it does not get written without the help and encouragement of a great many people. Without the resources of the excellent Templeman Library at the University of Kent there would be no book at all. I owe the Librarian and the ever-tolerant staff at Canterbury a huge debt of gratitude.

My friends and colleagues in the Study Group on Intelligence all contributed in their various ways, chief among them Christopher Andrew, Richard Aldridge and Rupert Allason. John Montgomery, Librarian of the Royal United Services Institute, was as always patient and helpful, and excelled in chasing down obscure titles.

The majority of the manuscript was typed by Lynn, who also contributed by asking probing, and occasionally completely unanswerable, questions, thus helping to turn the indulgent vaguenesses of the original text into a book.

Although life is hard for independent publishers in the early years of the twenty-first century, Constable & Robinson did more to assist the process of authorship than many others. In particular, a wide subject like the Cold War needs a special breadth and expertise in the full editing process. Mary Sandys did the painstaking labour of copy editing and Beckie Hardy and Claudia Dyer of Constable & Robinson were at all times patient and helpful.

I thank them all. Their contribution has greatly enriched the book: any errors are my own.

Finally, I apologize to all those who feel that some particular aspect of the Cold War has not been covered as deeply as they would wish. Any book on the Cold War is by definition a miracle of compression. Things like the Non-Aligned Movement, the Bandung Conference, and such fascinating details as how CENTO, SEATO and Strategic Air Command came into being and conducted their business, all spring to mind as fascinating byways that deserve more attention.

Sadly, on a subject that encompasses the whole globe, and absorbed half a century of the developed world's geo-political energies, there is only room for the commanding heights of the story to emerge above the fog of recent events, as memory slowly turns into history. However, maybe one day there may be a full 'official history' of the Cold War.

I do not envy the author . . .

J. H-W
Ringwould, Kent

HOT WARS, RUMOURS OF WAR AND PROXY WARS TIMELINE 1945–91

1945   Greek Civil War

1946   French Indochina

1947   Palestine and Israel

1948   Communist takeover of China

1948   Berlin Airlift

1948   Malayan Emergency (until 1960)

1950   Invasion of South Korea

1953   Berlin Riots

1953   End of Korean War

1954   Dien Bien Phu

1954   Algeria (until 1962)

1955   Hungarian Uprising

1956   Suez

1958   Chinese Offshore Islands Crisis

1960   Congo (until 1965)

1961   Berlin Wall goes up

1962   Cuban Missile Crisis

1963   Second Cuban crisis: JFK assassinated

1965   US fully in Vietnam

1967   Six Day War

1968   Tet Offensive, South Vietnam

1973   Yom Kippur and Oil Crisis

1974   Dhofar War, Oman

1974   Angola and Mozambique (until 1991)

1974   Ethiopia, Somalia, Eritrea (until 1991)

1975   Fall of Saigon

1979   Soviet invasion of Afghanistan

1980   Iraq-Iran War (until 1988)

1981   Poland Solidarity crisis

1982   Israeli invasion of Lebanon

1983   Cruise missile/Able Archer panic

1989   Berlin Wall comes down

1990   Kuwait

INTRODUCTION

As the Cold War fades and memory gradually turns into history, what was at one time taken for granted – what was even a way of life for many – becomes a curiosity to others, and particularly to those born after 1980.

For those who lived through the Cold War the invisible ideological struggle between east and west became the constant background to their lives, like some disagreeable wallpaper. Most ordinary folk managed to avoid thinking about it as they went about the everyday realities of their day-to-day existence: going to work, raising their families, running their homes. Occasionally some crisis would erupt and intrude into the newspapers or news bulletins to make people think, before fading away. *Very* occasionally a real crisis would explode into the headlines to threaten their very existence. Frightened people would then become aware that nuclear Armageddon and the death of everything that they held dear really was only a heartbeat away. At times like the Cuban Missile or Berlin crises, the world held its breath. The threat of a nuclear shooting war was always out there, somewhere.

For those who actually fought the Cold War it meant living with a constant state of war. Like George Orwell's perceptive comment in *Nineteen Eighty-Four* – 'war is peace' – that is exactly what the Cold War became. Nuclear bomber crews were on wartime alert, and bombers and tanks stood at readiness, for decades. Aggressive submarines roamed the sea lanes of the world and generations of young men prepared their guns and missiles for the battle that could come at any moment. For the intelligence collectors the Cold War was virtually indistinguishable from the real thing. To the combatants on both sides the Cold War was a constant – if usually bloodless – battle. For these warriors-in-waiting the Cold War meant that a state of war became a fact of life. The Cold War did not only deform lives, it deformed whole societies, as well as costing a fortune.

Considering its all-pervading impact there are surprisingly few general narratives on the Cold War. There have been some ground-breaking television series and some excellent coffee table books. There are also innumerable *detailed* studies of the events that made up what we call the Cold War, as well as thousands – if not millions – of works at every level on individual aspects of that curious conflict. From journalism to cartoons, from individual articles to whole magazines devoted to weapons and strategy, plus in-depth analyses of politics and proxy wars – the literature of the *detail* of the Cold War is immense. But, astonishingly, there are very few books on the whole story of the Cold War aimed at the general reader.

This *Brief History of the Cold War* seeks to address that deficiency. If journalism is the 'first draft of history', then the time is now ripe for the 'second draft' as an accessible narrative and commentary on the extraordinary tale of a conflict that, for half a century, shaped the lives of millions of people all over the world, and sometimes scared *everyone* very badly indeed . . .

I

FIRST FROSTS

THE BOLSHEVIKS DECLARE WAR

The Cold War started much earlier than most people realize. As far as communist Russia was concerned it really began on 25 October 1917 (7 November in the new-style calendar), the day the Bolsheviks mounted their coup at St Petersburg and seized power in Russia, long before Churchill made his famous 'Iron Curtain across Europe' speech in 1946.

To say that the Bolsheviks were surprised by their new-found elevation to supreme power in Russia is an under-statement. Reared on theorizing, arguing and dreaming of the wondrous day of the Revolution yet to come, this tiny handful of fanatical revolutionaries were astonished to find themselves suddenly in charge of a huge empire spanning eleven time zones. On 26 October, realizing that he was head of a revolutionary government with supreme power and really could order anything by decree, Lenin confided to Trotsky (in German) *'Es schwindelt . . .'* ('It takes your breath away'). A modern colloquial translation would be 'I'm gobsmacked!'

Not everyone shared the Bolsheviks' delight. From the very start the 'Red' conspirators found themselves surrounded by hostile forces both within and without their ruined and fragmented nation. It was a challenge to which they rose without hesitation. For these professional revolutionaries, raised on that half-baked mixture of Hegelian philosophy, Dickensian social observation and dated mid-Victorian economic theory that we know as Marxism, this elemental struggle against the 'dark forces of imperialism and capitalism' was their very life.

They not only expected trouble with foreign governments; as good Communists, they positively encouraged it. The reason was simple: as lifelong students of Marx and Engels, Lenin and his fellow revolutionaries were class warriors to their very core. They therefore 'knew' that foreign governments would automatically oppose their new regime, because every foreign government was dominated by the ruling class, the *bourgeoisie*. Revolutionary Marxists everywhere understood that they were engaged in a war between the classes, from whatever country. The *bourgeoisie* was their class enemy at home and abroad. Marx had said so.

The result was that, on the day that they seized power, Lenin and his Bolsheviks automatically declared a *de facto* ideological war on the imperialist and capitalist '*bourgeois* scum' (in Lenin's own words) who ran *every* foreign government. To them, this class conflict was pre-ordained and inevitable, making any deed against the *bourgeoisie* permissible in the sacred name of the Revolution. Spreading the Revolution to the 'oppressed peasants and workers of all lands' justified any action on their part, however immoral. Anyway, Lenin and his fellow Bolsheviks argued, morality and 'normal diplomatic relations' with foreign governments dominated by their hated 'class enemies' was a *bourgeois* concept. The Party played by different rules. For example, the Bolsheviks dealt with an attempted British banking coup to buy up all the Russian banks and their assets in the confusion of the Revolution by the simple expedient of nationalizing the banks and all their assets without compensation. The British were stunned at this simple act of robbery – or 'expropriation for the good of the Russian people', as the Bolsheviks called it – but there was very little they could do about it.

The British fought back as only they knew how. The British Secret Intelligence Service (MI6) supported and mounted an undercover sabotage network among the Bolsheviks, especially the Navy, from early 1918 onwards. Russians were well bribed with British gold to report on their Party overlords' plans, to flood coalmines and scuttle ships to prevent them leaving port. Any worthwhile centre of opposition to the Bolshevik usurpers was supported and encouraged by the British: anything to bring the Reds down. At the heart of this secret anti-Bolshevik crusade was a Captain Cromie, the naval attaché in Petrograd, armed with a fighting fund of £1,000,000 in gold coins and clear orders from Manfield Cumming, the original 'C' of British intelligence, to destabilize the Reds' revolution by any means. On 1 July 1918, a British Special Operations force even raided the house in Ekaterinburg being used as a prison to house the Imperial family in an attempt to rescue the Czar. The plot failed and only one daughter, Tatiana, was spirited away to England. A vengeful Lenin ordered his Baltic Praetorian Guards to 'dispose' of the original guard force and then, on 25 July, to kill the Czar and all his family.

The British struck back in this undercover war. Their Consul in Moscow was Robert Bruce Lockhart, in reality an undercover intelligence officer of the British Secret Service

(MI6/SIS). He was ordered by London to raise the stakes. Helped by an adventurous spy called Sidney Reilly, code-named 'ST 1' by MI6, the British now backed a plot to kill Lenin. On 31 August 1918, just a month after the murder of the Czar, a woman called Dora Kaplan, a member of the Socialist resistance to the Bolsheviks, fired two shots at Lenin, hitting him in the lung and neck. In retaliation, a few hours later, Bolshevik guards burst into the British Embassy in Petrograd. Cromie resisted and shot three of the invading Reds before being gunned down and killed. The Bolsheviks rifled the Embassy looking for evidence of British Secret Service plots. The British government protested, demanding an investigation and apology. Should none be forthcoming, the British 'threatened reprisals'. The Bolsheviks ignored the threat and arrested Bruce Lockhart as a British agent and spy.

The other undercover MI6 agents in Moscow and Petrograd went to ground. Reilly escaped by the skin of his teeth and fled back to England. The British retaliated by seizing Maxim Litvinov, the Bolsheviks' official representative in London, and the new regime's first major overseas spy, as a hostage. A stand-off ensued. In the end Litvinov was exchanged for Bruce Lockhart. But what this bitter little secret 'war of the envoys' did was to confirm to the Communists that the west was not only an implacable enemy but would stop at nothing to attack and overthrow them. 'What we are facing,' declared Lenin, 'is a systematic, methodical and long planned . . . counter-revolutionary campaign against the Soviet Republic.' The Soviets in their turn swiftly nailed their own colours to the mast. The first Communist International – or 'Comintern' – met in Moscow in the spring of 1919 to declare its intention to carry the revolution to the four corners of the world and to overthrow the *bourgeoisie* everywhere. The mould of a bitter

Cold War between east and west was firmly cast as early as the beginning of 1920.

Even as the Bolsheviks were beginning this underground intelligence war against the 'western capitalists', their new Central Committee was hastening to improvise its authoritarian bureaucratic dictatorship. Lenin's first task was to 'construct the new Socialist Order'. Not everyone agreed. The Bolsheviks' internal and external foes were descending from every direction, determined to snuff out the forces of this dangerous 'Red Menace' once and for all. From Archangel in the north to Vladivostok in the east, the enemies of the Revolution – and thus the mortal enemies of the Communist Party of the USSR – now openly attacked Russia's new oligarchs in an attempt to throw a *cordon sanitaire* around the contagion of Bolshevism.

Lenin and his fellow Kommissars (the Bolsheviks didn't like the word 'ministers' – it sounded too *'bourgeois'*) were thus immediately plunged into a real war virtually from the start. The Russian Communists' war against the *bourgeoisie* and the rest of the world really began on that first day of their revolution. For a war it certainly was. Once Lenin had secured his home base, he and his fellow Reds had to fight off the 'White' counter-revolutionaries, who were armed, supported and trained by foreigners, especially the British and the Americans. Three separate anti-Bolshevik White armies drove deep into the Russian heartland, with advances in north Russia, south Russia and Siberia. The Whites received plentiful and open support from their western friends. In January 1919 there were no fewer than 180,000 non-Russian troops inside Russia's borders, all determined to end the Bolsheviks' rule by armed force.

There were military contingents from the British, American, Japanese, French and Czech armies as well as sizeable detachments from Greece, Serbia and Italy. At one point a British naval squadron under Admiral Sir Walter Cowan actually sailed into the Baltic, where they caught a Soviet naval squadron in the act of bombarding Tallinn, the Estonian capital and a centre of anti-Bolshevik resistance. Cowan ordered his squadron to open fire and in the resulting battle sank several Red ships before the remainder fled.

Perhaps the most daring British attack on the Bolsheviks was the action of a British secret agent called Augustus Agar who was waiting to be extricated from Russia by the Secret Service. While moored in his speedboat in the Gulf of Finland, Agar noticed how close he was to the Kronstadt naval base, earlier one of the bastions of the Revolution. He begged a torpedo boat from Admiral Cowan's blockading squadron and managed to sink the Soviet cruiser *Oleg*. Recognizing the possibilities now open to him, Cowan then moved in to launch a British naval bombardment on the Soviet fleet moored in Kronstadt, sinking two battleships and wrecking the submarine base. Significantly, this British attack provoked a mutiny among the Russian sailors, chafing under the restrictions of the Bolsheviks, which was only suppressed by bitter fighting between the Bolsheviks and the Kronstadt garrison. Agar was awarded the Victoria Cross from the hands of King George V, the only member of the British secret service ever to receive this prestigious award.

The truth is that Lenin and the Bolsheviks spent their first three years of power fighting a shooting war against 'imperialists' and well-armed foreign invaders. What we now call the 'Cold War' between Russian communism and their international enemies started out as a very hot war indeed. Over 8 million people died in the Russian civil wars between 1918 and 1922, including over 1,000 British and American soldiers and more than 900,000 Russian and foreign fighters. All were dedicated to overthrowing Lenin and his Party by force. This

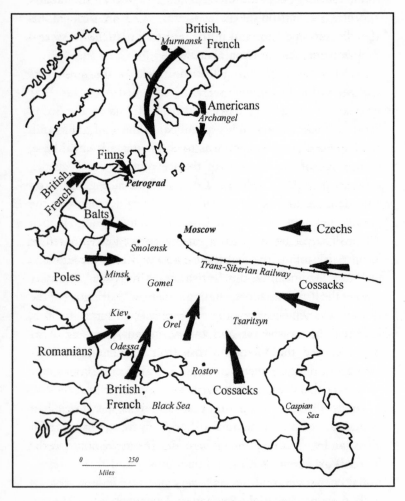

The Bolsheviks at bay, 1918–22

was no tacit or discreet support either. Kolchak's White
Russians in Siberia, Denikin in the Ukraine, and even the
Don Cossacks in the Caucasus, depended heavily on western
support; and the 100,000 British, French and American troops
that landed at Murmansk, Vladivostok and Odessa were a
tangible reminder of open hostility by the Great Powers.

In 1919 Winston Churchill urged Lloyd George's reluctant
cabinet to even stronger efforts:

> . . . It would be better to risk a few thousand men . . . than to
> allow the whole fabric of Russo-Siberian resistance to Bolshe-
> vism to crumble. What sort of peace would we have if all
> Europe and Asia from Warsaw to Vladivostok were under the
> sway of Lenin?

Churchill's prescient words carried little weight with a tired
British cabinet worried about their own Red Revolution at
home. It was the war weariness of the Allies after the blood-
letting of 1914–18, the disorganization and corruption of the
'White' royalist Russians, and the ruthless determination of
Bolshevik leaders like Trotsky, that eventually saved the
Revolution from defeat at the hands of the hundreds of
thousands of enemy troops on Russian soil. More importantly,
it was the civil war that helped to transform the Bolshevik
party from a tiny splinter group of squabbling revolutionaries
preaching 'people's democracy' in some Utopian socialist
paradise into a brutal and ruthless dictatorship holding down
a shattered empire by brute force.

By 1922 it was all over, and the invaders withdrew, leaving
Lenin's heirs to their ill-gotten gains. But the allied occupation
of Russian territory had sowed fatal, and permanent, seeds of
distrust between east and west which blossomed into real
enmity. The message to the new Soviet rulers of Russia was

unambiguous – the *bourgeois* and capitalist foreigners in the west were, at best, not to be trusted under any circumstances; at worst, they were implacable enemies of Soviet communism. The long Cold War had begun.

These early chills became institutionalized surprisingly quickly.

The regime of the Soviets clearly needed some force to ensure its survival against the threats and plots that abounded on every side. Lenin turned to the cold figure of his own 'sea green incorruptible', Felix Dzerzhinsky, a Pole and a genuine fanatic. Formerly a candidate for the Catholic priesthood, Dzerzhinsky had long before the war turned instead to the heady conspiracies of the Bolsheviks and was briefly imprisoned by the Czar's secret police, the Okhrana, as a dangerous revolutionary. In 1917 Lenin – a close personal friend – gave him the task of 'safeguarding the gains of the revolution' and protecting the safety of the Party's leaders. Dzerzhinsky obliged by setting up a ruthless force of secret policemen, Marxist sailors and thugs obsessed by 'revolutionary purity' called the Cheka ('the Extraordinary Commission for Combating Counter Revolution and Sabotage') to move against the Bolsheviks' enemies. Dzerzhinsky was quite clear as to his Soviet masters' aims: 'We stand for organized terror . . .' and 'The Cheka does not judge – it strikes!'

Following the attempt on Lenin's life, any restraints were swiftly discarded. Despite having no legal authority to order, let alone carry out, executions, Dzerzhinsky's secret policemen launched a campaign of terror, killing, torturing and jailing anyone suspected of being an enemy. Everywhere traitors to the glorious revolution, real and imaginary, were hunted down. One turned out to be very close to home indeed: Roman Malinowsky, leader of the Bolsheviks in the Duma and one of

Lenin's closest lieutenants, was exposed as a long-term agent of the Czar and the White Russians. He was executed by the Cheka. From 23 members in 1917 the Cheka had swelled to 37,000 by the beginning of 1919. Soon the number of executions exceeded the capacity of mere pistol and rifle; Dzerzhinsky ordered the Cheka to begin mass executions with machine guns. As with their counterparts in France 130 years previously, some kind of revolutionary bloodlust took over. At one stage there were so many condemned that they were just tied together and dumped into the sea off Kronstadt to freeze and drown. The Cheka's 'Red Terror' was very real and very bloody. It was the Cheka who set up the first camps of what became known as the Gulag on Solovetsky Island as early as 1922. One estimate of the Cheka's victims places the total at over 250,000 between 1917 and 1925, and it is thought that over 1,300,000 Russians were held in labour camps. Lenin and the Revolution had found their 'organ for defending the revolution', at least within their new kingdom. The new Revolutionary secret police struck terror into the Russian population as surely as Ivan the Terrible's murderous Oprichniki three centuries before. After the collapse of communism, KGB records revealed that the early Bosheviks were often little better than bloodthirsty monsters in how they treated their captives. Captured White officers were sometimes fed feet first, alive, into furnaces; cages of rats were attached to suspects' bodies to force the beasts to gnaw their way out through their victims' stomachs; and, in Kharkov, victims' hands were flayed off in one piece to produce 'gloves' of human skin. Dzerzhinsky's men were brutal and uncompromising, and rightly feared. Lenin's Chekists were to exercise a terrifying stranglehold on all levels of Russian society for seventy years. To this day secret policemen and intelligence officers in Russia are still referred to as Chekisti.

But, above all, Lenin and his fellow Bolsheviks were obsessed by the prospect of *foreign* plots against their Bolshevik
regime. Dzerzhinsky was ordered to act against dangerous
foreigners as well. His fanatical determination to stamp out
resistance recognized few diplomatic restraints. As early as
1918 his Chekists were raiding French and US diplomatic
buildings inside Russia to arrest foreign spies and enemies of
the regime. Nowhere was safe. To trap anti-revolutionary
activists outside Russia Dzerzhinsky set up 'The Trust', a
clever and well-run 'sting' operation designed to ensnare
foreign plotters and White Russian counter-revolutionaries
far from Moscow's control.

The Trust claimed to be a secret anti-Bolshevik underground
working out of Moscow and Petrograd under the very noses of
the Party. It set up fake banks and encouraged anti-Bolshevik
groups to meet in secret. In fact, it was a gigantic trap designed
to keep an eye on the million or so White Russians and Czarist
émigrés and their foreign backers. Czarist officers and counter-
revolutionaries were tricked into believing that they really
were in touch with the Russian anti-Bolshevik underground,
when in fact they were walking into the arms of what was later
to become known as the KGB. The Trust's greatest success was
the trapping of the British arch-spy Sidney Reilly, who was
lured back across the border from Finland in 1925, convinced
by his MI6 handlers that he was in touch with a genuine
counter-revolutionary plot in Moscow. Instead, he ended up in
the Lubyanka, where he was interrogated and executed by the
Cheka, an early high-profile victim of the Cold War between
east and west.

From their successes in stamping out opposition in Russia
the Cheka took their underground war overseas. Although
western intelligence agencies were deeply suspicious of the
Trust, they had no comprehension of just how thoroughly they

had been duped. By 1924 the Cheka had in fact completely penetrated most of the west's attempts to get in touch with dissidents inside Russia, and in many cases were actually using foreign Secret Service funds from blown western intelligence operations to subsidize their own. If nothing else, the Cheka was cost-effective. However, the west, and Britain in particular, were in no doubt as to where they stood. The Bolsheviks told them. On 9 May 1925, Lenin's successor, Josef Stalin, specifically named Britain as the 'Imperialist foe' and 'the principal adversary', and warned of the determination of the Cheka – now renamed the OGPU – to snuff out all threats to the Revolution.

The bitter underground spying war continued and climaxed in the infamous Zinoviev letter of 1924. The letter, which was a White Russian forgery, purported to be from Grigorei Zinoviev, the Head of the Communist International, or Comintern, and incited British socialists and would-be revolutionaries to mobilize 'sympathetic forces' to work for the communist cause, to stir up agitation in the armed forces and to overthrow the Westminster government. It was allegedly intercepted by Britain's SIS and, despite the express wishes of a Labour Prime Minister, deliberately leaked to a right-wing newspaper by the Secret Service and published just four days before a general election. Headlines such as CIVIL WAR PLOT, and MOSCOW'S ORDERS TO OUR REDS had the desired political effect. Unsurprisingly, the socialist Labour Party lost the election by a landslide and the 'Red' cause and its supporters were thoroughly discredited in the eyes of the outraged British middle classes.

The Zinoviev letter made the already sour relations between London and Moscow even more acid. Within three years the British police were openly raiding a Soviet trade mission in London in an effort to expose the Bolsheviks' 'Red plots'. A similar undercover trading and spying organization, AM-TORG, survived in America unscathed, thanks to a man called Armand Hammer, who would spend the rest of his days acting – very profitably – as the Soviets' 'agent to capitalism' in one way or another. But Hammer was the exception. By the late 1920s the undercover 'intelligence war' between east and west had became a bitter fact of life. Any Soviet or Marxist organization in the west, or their sympathizers, was now automatically suspect to the authorities. In fact, it can be argued quite forcefully that the west's secret services' obsession with Bolshevism and the underground struggle against the Reds during 'the dark valley' between the two world wars was partly responsible for the democracies' failure to recognize the growing threat of Fascism.

Once joined, the underground battle against the Red Menace was a struggle that would continue for the next eighty years, with little quarter given on either side.

2

THE VIEW FROM
THE FROZEN STEPPE

MUTUAL LOATHING

After they had consolidated their successful revolution, the Bolsheviks' foreign policy was shaped by three main factors. First, there was the inheritance of the historic Czarist-Russian expansionism from the previous century – the Bolsheviks had effectively put the old Russian Empire 'under new management'. Second, Lenin's ruling circle held deeply embedded ideological notions that a fundamental clash between Marxism and capitalism was inevitable. Last, but by no means least, the new Russian leaders simply had to *survive* in a sea of enemies. Nobody in the early 1920s expected them to do so, even the Bolsheviks themselves, assailed as they were on every side by enemies within and without. From their stolen battlements in the Kremlin, Lenin and his heirs looked out on a dangerous world.

Overshadowing this whole view from the new Russia of the

1920s was the bitter memory of western intervention on the side of their Czarist enemies during Russia's civil war from 1919 to 1922. This early struggle for continued existence by the hard-nosed clique around Lenin crystallized into a continuing world view of the Union of Soviet Socialist Republics which placed it implacably at odds with the western powers. Like some zealous counter-reformation bishop, Lenin believed that he was fully authorized by his own secular faith – Marxism – to use any means possible to bring about a socialist Utopia. From such fanaticism naturally flowed a suspicion of anyone who disagreed with him and confrontation with his *bourgeois* neighbours.

Given the Bolsheviks' pathological suspicion of the liberal values espoused by Woodrow Wilson's 'Fourteen Points' at the Versailles Peace Conference of 1919, it now seems obvious to us that dangerous ideas like individual freedom, free trade, open markets and self-determination were the very last things that Lenin and his Party wanted to see, let alone tolerate, inside the new Russia. Marxist communism meant *planning*; planning meant control; control meant ordering people to do what the Party ordered. And failure to obey the Party had to be punished. The twisted logic of Marxism ensured the rise of a police state far more harsh than any Czar's: at least until the state 'withered away'. In the Marxist paradise of revolutionary Russia, the state showed little sign of withering away. In fact, the 'dictatorship of the proletariat' had turned out to be the dictatorship of the Bolsheviks and their Communist Party. It seemed that, to ensure proper social control, brutal repression was the order of the day. It was all very confusing for revolutionary Marxists . . .

The Red tyranny of Lenin and the Bolsheviks was to prove Bakunin's chilling prophecy of 1870 only too accurate: 'Take the most radical revolutionary and place him on the throne of

Russia with dictatorial power and within a year he will be a greater tyrant than the Czar.'

The irony was that for many in the west, socialism, Russian style, seemed to offer real hope. A generation worn out by the upheavals and losses of 1914–18 and constant social strife looked approvingly to the 'new Russia'. Here, surely, was the answer to the ills of capitalism with all its inequalities and problems? The Bolshevik – now communist – rulers of Russia turned gratefully to these new friends in the west (whom Lenin called 'helpful idiots') for both support and help. They, only too willingly, obliged. The result was that from the mid-1920s onwards the Kremlin was able to mount a sophisticated campaign to take over and control many of the 'progressive organs' in the west. The Kremlin recognized the ideological nature of the struggle between capitalism and communism long before the west had woken up to the reality of the threat. For the hard-nosed and committed early Cold War warriors of the USSR, the left in the west was a very soft target for communist Russia's message.

Foremost in the vanguard of seekers after this 'new truth' were, surprisingly, many western intellectuals. While ill-informed down-trodden workers and their semi-communist trade union leaders in the west could be forgiven for supposing that Stalin's USSR offered a genuine model of a workers' paradise, the so-called intellectuals and academics who visited the Soviet Union (under carefully controlled secret police guidance, naturally) had no such excuse. Blindly, a generation of starry-eyed thinkers like H. G. Wells and Beatrice and Sidney Webb, the founders of the left-wing Fabian Society, were either duped or refused to acknowledge the brutal excesses of Stalin, Lenin's heir. Somehow the great intellects of the left seemed to be able to overlook the blatant bureaucratic terrorism, the slaughter of the better-off peasants and the deliberate engineering of famine in the Ukraine, in order to better eulogize their own vision of some new Jerusalem of socialist joy. Rarely can such a totalitarian nightmare have been so wilfully misrepresented to so many by so few. Gullible fools on the left flocked to praise the achievements of Russia's new communist regime. One famous scientist, J. D. Bernal, stands as an example for many. His mistress asked him if he would murder her if Stalin and the Soviet Communist Party ordered him to. He replied that he would – 'but only very reluctantly'. The result was that in the late 1920s and early 1930s the brutal excesses Stalin perpetrated in forging his totalitarian dictatorship found western apologists only too easily.

Such simplistic comradeship from the Revolution's friends in the west was confused, however, by inter-governmental tensions – which were anything but fraternal – on both sides. This diplomatic frost kept the post-Revolutionary undeclared diplomatic war smouldering between the new Russia and its neighbours. In 1926 the Soviet 'Trade Unions' – under Communist Party control – offered millions of pounds to support Britain's coalminers, who were heavily involved in the General Strike. This obvious interference in Britain's internal affairs (almost as interfering as Whitehall's own attempts to destabilize Bolshevik affairs within Russia) caused outrage. The British Security Service (MI5) had plenty of clear evidence that the Bolsheviks' representatives in London were blatantly engaged in subversion and spying. The subsequent police raid on the Russians' trade mission in May 1927 further embittered relations between Moscow and London, and on 26 May 1927 Britain broke off all diplomatic ties with the Kremlin. Although the new Labour government restored them in 1929, from the mid-1920s onwards Whitehall regarded Moscow as a dangerous and destabilizing menace.

American opposition to Russia's communist regime was even more clear-cut. From the very start, Americans had considered the Bolshevist USSR as little more than an anti-democratic revolutionary oligarchy holding down the Russian people by force, and by force alone. This clear-thinking recognition of a harsh reality – whilst uncomfortable to old-style diplomats accustomed to presenting the international world in delicate shades of grey – was backed by a hard-headed conviction that Soviet-style socialism was totally incompatible with American ideals of a free market economy. Lenin's own rhetoric did little to help. In 1918 he had addressed a call to arms to American workers, in which he called their President, Woodrow Wilson, the 'chief of the American multi-millionaires and the lackey-slave of the capitalist sharks'. Such language was hardly calculated to foster international cordiality.

Unsurprisingly, the USA flatly refused to recognize the USSR in the 1920s as anything other than an aberration and a pariah state. Even the new Soviet ambassador to Mexico was banned from travelling across American soil to take up her new job. The American press supported this hard official anti-Soviet line, openly opposing the USSR and broadcasting its failures. Headlines such as FAMINE STRIKES RUSSIA, HUNDREDS DIE IN UKRAINE RIOTS and SOVIET PARTY IN CHAOS AS TRADE, INDUSTRY TOTTER could hardly improve relations with the Bolsheviks' regime, especially as they were so very obviously true. The USA's awareness of communist and Bolshevik subversion in the 1920s was only too accurate, however much it made European socialists wince. Red scares were not confined to Europe as the Comintern and its agents in the USA tried to subvert the weak US labour unions in a determined effort to undermine their ideological foes. This atavistic clash placed the USA implacably in the battle-lines of the Soviet Union's enemies from the start, and both sides knew it. For Russia and for the USA the struggle was ideological from the beginning.

PUNCH, OR THE LONDON CHARIVARI—FEBRUARY 20, 1918.

THE LIBERATORS.

First Bolshevik. "LET ME SEE; WE'VE MADE AN END OF LAW, CREDIT, TREATIES, THE ARMY AND THE NAVY. IS THERE ANYTHING ELSE TO ABOLISH?"
Second Bolshevik. "WHAT ABOUT WAR?"
First Bolshevik. "GOOD! AND PEACE, TOO. AWAY WITH BOTH OF 'EM!"

The western view of the Bolsheviks
(Unknown artist, published in *Punch*, 1918)

It was against this backdrop of subversion, distrust and diplomatic conflict that a single major event changed virtually everything. In 1929, the Wall Street stock market collapsed and the world's economic system collapsed with it. As demand fell, unemployment soared and 'free capitalism' stood discredited. The impoverishment of the *bourgeoisie* went hand in glove with falling share prices and bankrupt bankers begging in Wall Street. Socialists everywhere hailed the vindication of Marxism, as its great ideological enemy appeared to be on the verge of final meltdown. Banks were going bust, millions were ruined, soup kitchens fed thousands in New York. Marx had been right all along. A glorious new socialist world order beckoned from the ruins of the old. Capitalism and democracy had been shown to be failures. Socialism was the hope of the future.

The great liberal democracies of the west reacted in different ways to this threat to their economic and social stability. While Britain and France tried desperately to cope with the Great Depression by Parliamentary methods, German democracy voted in a new Bismarck to act as their strong leader in a time of trouble. The new Chancellor, Adolf Hitler, was to prove somewhat stronger than many of his German voters had bargained for. 'Democracy is the source of Germany's troubles,' he bawled in a hundred speeches, along with steady rants about the Versailles '*Diktat*', the lack of work and discipline, the Jews and, above all, too much political confusion in post-war Germany. 'Just how many political parties does a working state really need?' he asked. One of his first acts, after having swiftly established himself as dictator of a one-party state, was therefore to lock up all the Communists and their socialist camp followers. Marxist stringency was not the only way to impose order on confused citizens or – God forbid – unsympathetic opposition. Mussolini looked admiringly on. For many, as trade dried up and millions became unemployed, Fascism seemed to offer as viable a solution to the ills of the west as democracy or communism.

America's response to the Great Depression was to introduce 'Government' money – taxpayers' money – as a new source of capital in order to revive a stricken economy, to the outrage of many of the great magnates of capitalism. But in a dark decade, where the song 'Buddy, Can You Spare Me a Dime?' reflected the hopelessness of mass unemployment, unfettered capitalism seemed to have little more to offer for most folk. As part of his 'New Deal', America's new President, Franklin Delano Roosevelt, also reconsidered the USA's position on Soviet Russia, and in 1933 for the first time recognized the new USSR. One of the very first American diplomats to be sent to Moscow was a young State Department officer, George F. Kennan, a man who was to have a long influence on American perceptions of the Cold War. From his new Moscow office, Kennan soon realized that the ideological chasm between east and west was gaping wide and was effectively unbridgeable. He warned Washington that 'There can be no possible middle ground or compromise between the two systems . . .' He also observed that the Soviet Union was root and branch opposed to the west's traditions, values and political systems. The more he observed of Russian communism at first hand, the more Kennan realized that the enmity between capitalist west and the communist east was implacable and ideological at its core and must inevitably lead to conflict. Events like the 1933 show trial of six British Metropolitan Vickers engineers working on a Soviet building contract did little to ease the tense climate of suspicion surrounding Anglo-Soviet relations. All westerners were potential spies and counter-revolutionary to Stalin's Russia.

However, Kennan's perceptive analysis of the true nature of the ideological conflict underpinning all relations with Stalin's USSR found little favour in the Great Depression of the mid-1930s. To many in the west, Russia instead appeared more than ever a beacon of hope in a collapsing, discredited world. There seemed to be no hunger in the planned socialist economy of the USSR. Everyone had a job, industry was booming under the Party's 'Five Year Plan', and Soviet propaganda cinema showed cheerful peasants gathering yet another bumper harvest under sunlit skies as burly men toiled over hot steel in modern industrial foundries to meet the Party's norms. To the unemployed and hungry of the west, the Soviet Union often seemed a genuine workers' paradise. Communism worked. You only had to look at the newsreels. Beneath the surface of this new diplomatic and ideological rapprochement, however, an ugly new phenomenon began to take root.

Nations have always spied on each other. But in the 1930s, Stalin's intelligence services began a new and deadly assault on an unprecedented scale to spy on those they perceived as their enemies. From the start Britain and America were on the receiving end of this secret intelligence war.

3

STALIN'S SPY WARS

THE UNDERCOVER WAR

The recruiting of spies and informers was deeply entrenched in Russian thinking and had been part of the fabric of Russian life since the days of Ivan the Terrible, whose black-cowled Oprichniki (secret police) had terrorized Russia in a way not seen since the Inquisition had terrorized Spain. The 'Special Office of the Czar', secret police, informers, spies and fear of all things foreign had all been deeply embedded in Russian culture long before Stalin took over the Communist Party on Lenin's death in 1924.

This national xenophobia reinforced Stalin's own personality and coloured all his thinking. It is no exaggeration to say that Stalin's suspicions of foreigners shaped the foreign policy of the USSR from the 1920s until his legacy at last faded in the 1970s. Russia's Cold War against the west can even be simplistically described as *Stalin*'s Cold War, so closely did it mirror the dictator's own view of the world around him.

Stalin was in many ways the catalyst for the Cold War. His ruthless extermination of any rivals meant that all Russian policies were rooted in the office and the personality of this new Red Czar. As a result, his reign as communist dictator effectively determined all relations between east and west for a quarter of a century. The reactions of Stalin, the Vozdh (which can, ironically, be translated as Führer), shaped everything within and without the Soviet Union. His personality is one of the prime keys to understanding east-west relations in the twentieth century and especially during the Cold War.

Stalin was born Josef Dzhugashvili, in 1879, to a poor cobbler's family in Georgia. Expelled from an Orthodox seminary, he soon turned to the more secular faith of the Bolsheviks. He became an underground organizer for the Party and soon figured on the Okhrana's wanted list as a Revolutionary suspect. Arrested on at least seven separate occasions, he was exiled to Siberia. He seems to have escaped, possibly to emerge, astonishingly, as secret agent 'Josef Georgi' on the Okhrana's books. Stalin ('Man of Steel') was contemptuous of the 'toothless' handling of dissidents by the Czar's jailers. 'Our prison is little more than a revolutionary training camp and university,' he said scornfully in Siberia, similar to what was said of the British government's handling of the Provisional IRA sixty years later. Being imprisoned actually 'helped the movement'. When he came to power many years later Stalin would make it his business to ensure that anti-Soviet dissidents, guilty or not, did not share his own comfortable experiences of incarceration under the Czar. Stalin's political prisoners were either worked to death or shot. Escapees were to be, in his own words, 'hunted down like wolves'.

Before 1914, Stalin visited London to attend the Party Congress, possibly spying as a double agent or as an enemy of revolutionary splinter groups opposed to the Bolsheviks.

This was where he first met Lenin and in 1912 the cobbler's son from the Caucasus was appointed to the Bolsheviks' Central Committee. Although he did very little during the 1917 Revolution, Stalin's administrative skills, long access to Party records and extraordinary memory made him the classic indispensable bureaucrat. In 1922 Lenin appointed his *éminence grise* General Secretary of the Communist Party. It was a serious mistake, as Lenin realized on his deathbed, when he tried vainly to warn his colleagues of Stalin's true nature. But by then it was too late.

From 1925 the 'First Secretary' moved to take over the Party machine, removed his arch-rival Trotsky, and effectively became dictator of Soviet Russia. Although Stalin did not invent the Communist Party's repressive apparatus – the Bolsheviks' fanatical secret policeman Dzerzhinsky had moved swiftly to exterminate any enemies of the Revolution once the Communists had seized control – the new Party leader transformed the Cheka and the OGPU into an even more brutal enforcer of his own personal power. The midnight knock of the secret police became a very real terror for millions of Russians. The Czar's mild despotism seemed but a pale shadow of the Communists' savage rule.

As Lenin had warned, Stalin turned out to be an iron-willed, ruthless opportunist. Within four years he had transformed the Party's bureaucracy into his personal power base. From this controlling position he ensured that the old dream of World Revolution would remain just that, and one by one he ousted all his old Communist Party rivals. They either died or, like Trotsky, fled abroad. Now securely at the Party's helm, Stalin concentrated on making the USSR a secure, strong bastion of 'socialism in one country' with himself as dictator. His enemies died or fled to be hunted down by the assassination squads of the Cheka.

The price paid for this seizure of power was as bloody as any exacted by a despotic Roman emperor, as the self-made Georgian cobbler's son imposed his own personality on his stolen fiefdom. The dictator's suspicion, fear and contempt for his clever but weak-willed rivals (Trotsky always treated Stalin as 'that dull mediocrity' – a serious error of judgement) ensured an imperial tyranny familiar to any reader of Edward Gibbon. Within the new socialist-communist Russia, secret police and informers abounded. The Party reigned supreme, the courts were rigged, and troublesome political rivals and critics were silenced by the executioner's bullet or consigned to the slave labour camp. Terror, purges and fear ruled Russia under Stalin, and all roads led back to the Russian leader's personal cruelty, suspicion and paranoia. 'If you have a man who is a problem,' he once famously said, 'kill the man. There: no problem.'

From 1929 to 1953, for nearly a quarter of a century, this 'pock-marked Caligula' (in Boris Pasternak's memorable phrase) was the cold-blooded, ruthless, unscrupulous tyrant who directed and personally shaped every aspect of life in the Soviet Union and, more importantly, its relationships abroad. Russia's communist dictator sent over 30 million of his fellow Russians to their deaths, far more than Hitler or Himmler ever dreamed possible. The result was that it was Stalin and Stalin alone who effectively decided Russia's policies towards the west. Stalin truly was the 'continuity man' of the Cold War and, in many ways, its chief architect.

The results of such personal paranoia at the top of a single party dictatorship were only too predictable. A generation of Soviet diplomats from 1925 to 1970, mindful of the old communist maxim: 'Sniff out; suck up; *survive*!', echoed the Great Leader's prejudices. His secret services spied on every-thing and everybody; and Stalin's own dislike of 'clever foreigners' – amounting to an inferiority complex – drove him to the obsessive collection of intelligence on everybody. A 'Georgian dwarf' with a foul mouth and rough manners Stalin may have been, but he was determined not to kow-tow to every 'foreign son of a bitch'. For the latest ruler in the Kremlin, the key to survival was intelligence on every possible threat at home and abroad. Stalin lived by intelligence on friend and enemy alike.

Stalin had, very early in his struggle for power among the post-Revolutionary Bolsheviks, learned to try and see his adversaries' hands. Internal spying on and telephone tapping of Kremlin 'colleagues' in the 1920s seamlessly became part of the USSR's foreign policies as well. Conspiracy ruled. As a matter of routine all foreign embassies were bugged, diplomats suborned, secret documents stolen and military secrets pursued on a scale never before seen. Confirmation of the fact that this vast bureaucracy of intelligence was directed by Stalin personally comes from his ace agent-handler in London, Y. Modin, speaking after the dictator's death: 'We almost never went looking for information at random. [For example] Stalin badly needed to know exactly what transpired between Churchill and Roosevelt when they met, so our agents abroad were directed to find out at all costs. His highly authoritarian style produced excellent results.'

With such a personality at the helm, and with such a heritage of conspiracy to guide him, it is little wonder that Soviet Russia's intelligence net was wide. Communism had to spy to survive.

By 1930, mindful of spying disasters caused by its attempts at cooperation with the various national communist parties in the early years, the OGPU/NKVD began to shun open contact, at least in public, and concentrated on a much less obvious campaign of recruitment behind the scenes. Young potential

agents were identified, talent-spotted, groomed and then allowed to fade back into the fabric of their own societies to
make their careers without any obvious taint of Moscow
Centre or communism. The process could – and often did –
take years: but the payoff was one day having an ideologically
sound, committed agent of the USSR in a position of power.
Not for nothing was the KGB's watchword *I serve the Soviet
Union*!

Long before the Second World War, far too many westerners had chosen to do just that.

The Soviets had planted their spy seedlings early.

In 1921 a promising young Petrograd physicist called Peter
Kapitza was sent to Cambridge University on a Soviet scholar-
ship. His father had been a Czarist general, so such magna-
nimity at the time on the part of the Cheka seems unusual, to
say the least. But the brilliant young physicist was a plant. His
brief was to infiltrate the British scientific laboratories of the
day and steal industrial secrets for Moscow.

Kapitza succeeded beyond the Soviets' wildest dreams. By
1930 he was acknowledged as a leading theoretical physicist,
fêted on all sides and elected a Fellow of Britain's prestigious
Royal Society. Then, in 1934, he went back to Russia 'for a
holiday'. He never returned. Slowly the truth filtered back:
Kapitza had effectively defected back to the USSR. Visitors
reported that he now had a purpose-built laboratory in Moscow, four times the size of his Cambridge facility and with over
a hundred assistants, many of them with PhDs.

Tellingly, it later emerged that the Soviets had started to
build their wonderful new laboratory for Kapitza in 1933 – a
year *before* he 'went back on holiday'. After he had gone, the
British admitted that Kapitza's field of expertise was atomic
and nuclear physics. Although MI5 played it down at the time,

for obvious reasons, they later grudgingly confirmed that when he went back to Moscow he carried most of the secrets of Rutherford's Cavendish Laboratory in his head.

His case was not unique. A year before Kapitza's arrival, in 1920, one Francis Meynell, an anti-establishment journalist from a privileged English family and a natural rebel, had acted for a while as an illegal courier for the Cheka/KGB. Meynell's flirtation with the left and radical socialism eventually petered out, but it became the model for Moscow's conspiracies. It also made the Soviet spymasters aware of the vulnerability of radical British idealists to ideological penetration. It was the *intelligentsia*, not the communist parties, who offered the best return as the Soviets' preferred tool to penetrate the west. Another advantage was that the Soviets did not have to try very hard to recruit their spies among the smart leftists in the liberal democracies. Their gullible recruits were already lined up, waiting at the gate, positively begging to be admitted into the Kremlin's conspiracies.

In many ways, the willingness of the intelligent young idealists of the 1930s to choose Marxism as their new creed now seems distinctly odd. The intellectual weakness, rotten economics and Marx's inability to understand human nature are nowadays only too obvious. Even odder perhaps was the social background of some of these early committed Cold War warriors. For they were not the horny-handed sons of toil so beloved of pure Marxist theory, with natural backgrounds of deprivation and hardship. On the contrary, many of them emerged from the very heart of the upper reaches and leisured classes of the establishment to which they belonged. In many cases, privilege, not hardship had nurtured them; and money – a lot of money – had educated them.

These ideological communist fellow travellers came from all levels of society. In Britain, even the King's cousin Lord (Louis)

Mountbatten, egged on by his new 'best friend', a homosexual Soviet agent called Peter Murphy, had become a secret communist sympathizer at Cambridge in 1920. By the end of the 1920s nearly two-thirds of prominent British Communists were from Oxbridge or the fashionable chattering classes, champagne socialists and the *bien pensant* section of the media.

Part of the reason for this was the impact of the Great Crash of 1929–32 and the subsequent depression which changed many thinking observers' views of how their society should be organized. It was clear to any intelligent soul that the old order had failed, and failed in the most conspicuous manner possible. The old Victorian certainties collapsed. Traditional politicians of left and right had no answers, Britain's antique industrial base was equally bankrupt, social unrest was everywhere, and the generation who could have led Britain to a bright new future now lay mouldering in the graveyards of France and Flanders. Capitalism seemed bankrupt in every sense. It was hardly surprising that radical new solutions beckoned to the impressionable young.

In Britain the Communist Party, above all, seemed to offer the ideal forum for youthful anti-establishment rebellion and idealism. Lytton Strachey's response, in 1923, to Bertrand Russell's question: 'So, why are you a Socialist? Did you hate your father, your childhood or your public school?' – best sums it up. Strachey replied, 'A bit of all three.' On to this fertile soil of intelligent young misfits, scornful of the ruined societies of their parents and keen to change the world, fell the Communist recruiters' seeds.

Once again, Peter Kapitza's Cambridge was to the fore. A Cambridge don, Maurice Dobb, was co-founder in 1931 of the first communist cell in Cambridge. Prompted, as we now know, by the Comintern (as advised by Litvinov) the Cambridge cell blossomed. David Haden-Guest and John Cornford turned a tiny clandestine debating group into a cell of political activists promoting their version of a better world.

The result was that by 1933 Cambridge was clutching a viper to its bosom. Over thirty young Fellows and under-graduates were by then actively promoting Moscow's aims and ambitions. Among this group of dedicated Communists were Guy Burgess, Donald Maclean, Anthony Blunt, Alan Nunn May and Julian Bell. Kim Philby, although not an overt Communist, was also recruited by the Soviet secret service while at Cambridge. Behind them in the shadows stood the Comintern's fellow travellers and support troops: James Klug-mann, Douglas Springhall – the National Organizer of the CPGB who would be jailed in 1943 for spying for the USSR and who subsequently emigrated to Russia – and champagne socialists like Clemens Palme Dutt, ever ready with advice, guidance and a fashionable bed for the night. The group was further bonded by the thrill of the forbidden. At a time when homosexuality was illegal, yet another underground conspi-racy merely seemed an extension of an existing secret lifestyle for many of the ex-public school recruits to the Party. For many of the communist faithful adolescent protest, socialism and sexual freedom walked hand in hand.

The process of recruitment is depressingly familiar to us nowadays. Once the ardent young communist sympathizers had identified themselves as friends to the Party they might be invited to a glass or two of sherry in the private rooms of a like-minded don. This 'talent spotting' might be followed by a visit by a suitable assistant from the Communist Party HQ in King Street for a cosy chat in a pub, or a walk by the river. Then would come the final pitch, tightly controlled by the Comin-tern's men or Moscow Centre and their Resident GPU-NKVD Director, or, more likely, his number two. This was a charis-

matic Austrian Jew called Arnold Deutsch, who, like so many
clever Jews at the time, had elected to substitute Lenin and
Marx for the God of Abraham and Moses. These secret
meetings might take place at the Soviets' safe house at 3
Rosary Gardens, South Kensington or more likely during a
discreet walk in the park. Deutsch was a man of outstanding
personality and an equally outstanding agent handler. Years
later Philby described him as 'a marvellous man', and was, like
so many of Deutsch's other conquests, star-struck by the spymaster's intellect and personality until the day he died. The
KGB archives later revealed that the industrious Deutsch had
recruited no fewer than twenty Britons to spy on behalf of
Soviet Russia before he was ordered back to Moscow in 1937
at the height of Stalin's terror and purges.

The latest starry-eyed recruit to the cause of World Socialism
would then go back burning with a sense of mission, relishing
his privileged opportunity to build a better world and really
'work for peace'. Such methods worked nearly every time. The
Jesuits would have been proud to emulate the Communists'
success in binding impressionable youth to their cause for life.
The result was that by the mid-1930s the USSR had effectively
infiltrated its ideologically committed foot soldiers deep inside
the foundations of the British establishment. Similar processes
were at work in the United States, France and Germany, as well
as a host of other countries. All concerned were under no
illusions about the undercover purpose of these new agents for
the cause. Moscow's instructions to its secretive overseas
minions were absolutely explicit: '. . . all legal Parties are
now under the greater responsibility in respect to the creation
and strengthening of an *illegal* apparatus.'

By the mid-1930s Moscow's new secret army of spies were
only too ready to burrow like moles into the fabric of western
life.

4

WARM NEW FRIENDS?

HITLER AND STALIN

From the Kremlin this Soviet spying offensive seemed wholly justified, for by 1935 the USSR had ample reason to believe itself threatened. Japan to the east and Nazi Germany to the west posed clear – and openly declared – challenges to the USSR. Japanese leaders talked openly of 'clashing swords with the USSR on the fields of Mongolia', and Hitler's 1925 *Mein Kampf* actually laid out a detailed blueprint for Nazi colonial aggression eastwards to seize 'the new soil of Russia and her subject border states'.

By 1934 Hitler had renounced the Treaty of Versailles and was openly preaching war. In the Far East, Japan's 'protectorate' in Manchuria had been formalized despite the pleas of the League of Nations. But the League was powerless to enforce its will, even more so when criticized nations, like Italy and Japan, just withdrew their membership of the Geneva talking shop. International security was everywhere breaking down.

Mussolini was on the rampage around the Mediterranean. In Berlin, Nazi Brownshirts openly sacked Soviet offices, contemptuous of Kremlin protests. Anti-communism became official German state policy. In every capital talk of war was in the air. The truth was that the Kremlin had every good reason to be uneasy. In the circumstances, the Kremlin could be forgiven for believing that an intelligence attack was its best form of defence to forestall an onslaught to come. But from the west, still suspicious of the motives of the 'Third Communist International' and its dreams of world revolution, this intelligence offensive seemed merely to confirm the USSR's malign intentions. The diplomatic war between Soviet Russia and the west spluttered on.

Proof of Soviet growing alarm at these events became more tangible. In the two years from 1934 to 1936 an increasingly nervous Kremlin raised the Soviet military budget no fewer than *eight* times. Thousands more military aircraft and tanks were ordered from already over-burdened factories. Workers' norms were increased. The Red Army was brought ever more closely under Party control (with ultimately disastrous results, as the events of 1939 in Finland were to prove). Thousands of Party members were accused of spying or backsliding, and were purged in a series of highly visible (and sometimes highly risible) show trials at which 'Socialist judges' sometimes had to prompt the hapless defendants to remember their forced 'confessions' of treachery to the Revolution – and, of course, Comrade Stalin. Innocent or guilty, the end was invariably the same: some nameless secret policeman's bullet in the back of the head in a shower room beneath the Lubyanka.

Overseas, in what looked like a panicky search for allies, the Comintern suddenly changed the political line and instructed its parties overseas to back the socialists, previously their mortal enemies on the left. In France the Communist Party, on instructions from Moscow, suddenly sided with the broad left in an anti-Fascist crusade to avoid splitting the socialist vote and letting the Fascists get into government. In Britain, Moscow's network of undercover spies was exhorted to work even harder for the cause and to report the slightest sign of the British government trying to cut a deal with Berlin. The peace of the world depended on their efforts for the socialist cause in its holy anti-Nazi crusade. It is no exaggeration to say that, from the mid-1930s on, the growing Nazi threat to the USSR dominated Stalin's and the Kremlin's thinking. In desperation, the USSR looked for new friends among old rivals.

Soviet long-term intentions never changed, however, and not everyone was fooled. For example, following Pierre Laval's curious Franco-Soviet pact with Stalin in 1935 (in which France seemed to become an ally of the Kremlin against Hitler's increasingly warlike Berlin), a cheerful Ambassador Potemkin openly admitted to the French Minister of War, 'Soviet Russia was born out of the First Great War. A Soviet Europe will emerge from the Second.' This extraordinarily prescient declaration could only have come from someone with a true insight into Stalin's long-term motives. The 'dark valley' of the 1930s may have been a dangerous and unstable time, but true Communists never forgot their real aim.

The smouldering ideological conflict between east and west, communism and the western states, finally burst into flames in one of Europe's most backward nations. In 1936 the Spanish Civil War erupted to disturb the holiday from war which Europe had enjoyed since 1919. Within months both Nazis and Communists had shown their hand. Germany and Mussolini's Fascist Italy intervened to support the rebel General Franco against the legitimate Socialist government. Moscow sided equally openly with the Republican government. Arms, money and manpower were mobilized by both sides to support their 'clients'. For the next three years, Spain's civil war took the bloody internecine course of most wars of its kind.

Brother slaughtered brother as men of goodwill were terrorized into ever-greater excesses. On the ground, 'Red' atrocities were matched by Fascist brutality. The world was appalled by newsreels of the indiscriminate bombing of Guernica by Hitler's Kondor Legion, with its bloody warning of the horrors of Rotterdam, Warsaw, Coventry, Hamburg and Dresden still to come. Public opinion in the west was no less shocked by the Communists' desecration of Christian churches and cemeteries on the orders of the Kremlin's pro-consuls in Madrid, determined to stamp the Kremlin's Marxist truth on what they saw as an ideological struggle. Soviet control even extended to 'show trials' of alleged renegades within the ranks of the Spanish left. Spain's communist Partido Obrero de Unificación Marxista (POUM) was purged as thoroughly as Stalin's own Red Army. *Pravda* was uncompromising and unapologetic: 'In Catalonia the elimination of Trotskyists and anarcho-syndicalists [i.e. the radical left's opposition to Moscow's Bolshevism] has begun; it will be pursued with the same vigour as in the USSR.'

To back the Soviet cause, GPU-NKVD death squads of the Russian secret police stamped their iron control on any dissent in the ranks of Stalin's Spanish warriors. In return, Fascist units shot communist commissars taken prisoner out of hand. In 1937–38 it looked as if Europe's Cold War between bolshevism and capitalism was about to come to a head.

From 1937 events in Europe accelerated, taking on a dreadful momentum of their own. In rapid succession, and seemingly encouraged by a British government led by Chamberlain and Halifax (who turned a blind eye to Nazi excesses in the fond but foolish hope that by appeasing Hitler they could prevent another European war), Hitler was allowed to run amok, annexing Austria and stealing half of Czechoslovakia in a humiliating western climbdown.

Stalin's worst fears seemed to be confirmed. Clearly the capitalist west was prepared to give Hitler anything as long as they didn't have to fight him. Democracy was gutless and would cheerfully allow Hitler a free hand provided they kept out of any nastiness. The USSR was therefore on its own in any future fight against the Fascists.

In the face of such Nazi aggression and western pusillanimity, an alarmed Kremlin stepped up its preparations for what seemed now to be an inevitable clash of arms between east and west.

The Kremlin redoubled its preparations for a hotter war to come.

Without exception, all those who wield dictatorial powers eventually fall prey to a crippling *déformation professionelle*. However good their original intentions, those obsessed with staying in power eventually lose their patience with dissent – from any quarter. As contradictory voices wane, the leader's paranoia increases. Threats abound on every side, even from old friends or allies. Soon a paradox emerges: the more such leaders surround themselves with 'yes men' and see the world only as fearful minions represent it to them, the more real the threats seem. This iron rule of the debilitating effects of too much power can be seen today in Downing Street, in any Whitehall office, or even in many a newsroom or fashionable salon in Washington, DC. Thus it was with Stalin, only more so. In his case, the process was reinforced and accelerated by an over-concentration of power multiplied by his own dark defects of character.

Harrison Salisbury saw the problem clearly: 'Nothing in the Bolshevik experience so plainly exposed the defects of Soviet power monopoly as when the man who held that power [Stalin] was ruled by his own internal obsessions.'

Stalin's 'obsessions' – his fear of foreigners, his cynicism and personal isolation – drew him and thus his USSR into a serious error. Seeing the world only through his own black-tinted glasses, he made the classic mistake of judging all others by his own deeply corrupt standards. It was obvious to Stalin that capitalist western governments were conspiring against the socialist USSR. Not only was this a basic tenet of Marxist dogma but his spies in the west reported that the nervous democracies were now preparing to appease the German dictator behind Russia's back. All western statesmen were clearly as devious and ill-intentioned as he was himself: and finally, there could never be any respite from his eternal battle with dark forces in the outside world. To Josef Stalin, all politicians of the 1930s were self-seeking, unscrupulous rogues.

Such a worldview may seem an unduly pessimistic one – for most of the time, anyway – when applied to men like Franklin Roosevelt, Neville Chamberlain and Winston Churchill. But in all fairness to the Soviet dictator's suspicious mind, in one case he was spot-on accurate: Adolf Hitler. Stalin immediately recognized another warped personality where ideology, dogma and ruthless *realpolitik* collided with personal and national ambition. It frightened him.

Hitler fascinated Stalin as much as Stalin fascinated Hitler. It may be that only brutal dictators can fully understand their fellow tyrants. Stalin had, however, good reason to be wary of Hitler's Nazi Germany. For, alone of the 'capitalist' western powers, only Germany appeared to have the capability and the declared intention to assault Russia's communist paradise. Only Nazi Germany seemed implacably resolved on attacking the USSR. By the end of 1938 it was as clear to the now-nervous ruler in the Kremlin as to the frightened western powers that something would have to be done about Germany. After the final dismembering of Czechoslovakia in the spring of 1939, it was clear to all that a new German war was only a matter of time. As the summer of 1939 wore on, talk circulated in nervous western chancelleries about a possible new alliance between the democracies and the USSR against the growing menace of Nazi Germany. Feelers were put out and delegations despatched. Stalin himself encouraged secret talks to explore such an unlikely diplomatic accommodation. For once, the western democracies and the USSR seemed to share a common interest. No one was looking for a war with Adolf Hitler in 1939.

Not everyone was convinced of this new policy line from Moscow. Any doubts about the existence, before 1945, of what was later to become known as the Cold War can be dispelled by a telling document tucked away in the British Foreign Office files.

In the spring of 1939 Whitehall received a discreet brief on Soviet affairs from a Reuters correspondent who had covered the Metropolitan Vickers trial of British engineers accused of spying on the USSR, one Ian Fleming, who was later to work for British Naval Intelligence and who would become the world-famous author of the James Bond novels. Fleming alerted the Foreign Office in quite unequivocal terms of the dangers posed to the west by the USSR, possible ally or not. Anticipating Hitler's war, he warned: 'the threat of a territorial world war should not blind us to the ideological struggle which will have to come one day . . .'

And, in a later paragraph: 'Russia would be an exceedingly treacherous ally. She would not hesitate to stab us in the back. Stalin fears a too-powerful Germany. This fear would be sufficient inducement for him to co-operate [with western allies] who he knows have no territorial designs on Russia.'

Some ambitious FO mandarin (who obviously didn't want to rock the pre-war Whitehall boat) has scrawled in an unknown hand *take this out* against 'Stalin would not hesitate to stab us in the back.'

What Fleming's perceptive and accurate 1939 analysis confirms is that, despite the modern belief that the Cold War was a purely post-1945 phenomenon, experienced observers who were untainted by naïve idealism, political ambition or government policies were quite clear between the wars that the USSR and the west were *already* locked in a deadly underground struggle. In fact, little had changed from the 1920s when, despite the early Soviets' overall economic and industrial weakness, they were rightly seen as a threat from social unrest, sabotage, subversion and spying. The Bolshevik threat existed at all times between the wars and was divorced from any particular military capability. It was always a clash of ideologies.

Despite the peace feelers from the west in 1939, Stalin himself recognized this. As a committed Marxist he 'knew' that 'imperialist contradictions' must one day run their course and that eventually the capitalist powers would destroy each other. Marx had said so. However, by mid-1939 Stalin became convinced that France and Britain's real diplomatic aim was not to conclude an alliance with the USSR against Germany but merely a trick to divert Hitler's aggressive tendencies and encourage him to look eastwards at the USSR. The western powers were obviously behaving with typical *bourgeois*-capitalist duplicity. Something must be done quickly to protect the USSR from such double dealing and buy time to confront the challenge of a resurgent and dangerous Germany. In the middle of dilatory negotiations with the west, Stalin suddenly ordered an astonishing diplomatic *volte-face*.

The political landscape was turned on its head in August 1939 when Stalin, anxious to buy time for his purged and weakened armed forces, dismissed feeble (and reluctant) offers of an alliance between Britain and France with the USSR to oppose Nazism. Instead, in a decision that sent shock waves round the developed world, the communist dictator decided to ally himself with Hitler, his declared arch-enemy. He ordered his Foreign Minister to conclude a Russian-German Friendship Treaty. Communism and Fascism were to get into bed together. It was as if Satan and St Michael had concluded a pact of mutual friendship and then gone down to the pub to celebrate.

To say that the Molotov-Ribbentrop pact of August 1939 stunned observers is a gross understatement. The amazing news sent ripples of well-justified alarm through London and Paris. The diplomatic and international consequences were obvious – and worrying. The new 'party line' of friendly neutrality between those committed ideological foes of Nazism and communism had now freed both parties – for the time being – from worrying about each other. It therefore allowed a delighted Hitler a free hand to fall on those he chose. More importantly, it laid Poland open to attack like a tethered goat in a jungle clearing.

A mere three days after the signing of the Soviet-German Non-Aggression Pact, Hitler's legions invaded Poland across the Oder. With the Molotov-Ribbentrop pact and Hitler's subsequent aggression, the whole edifice of western 'appeasement' collapsed. To contain the Nazis, Britain and France declared war on Germany – a hopeless gesture, as poor Poland was quite beyond salvation. Two weeks later Stalin's Red Army joined in, invading from the east to feast on his share of Poland's carcass. On 27 September, after twenty days' bombardment, Warsaw fell. The light of an independent Poland was extinguished for over half a century.

The balance of the underground diplomatic war was now completely realigned. The USSR and Germany were *allies*, in peace and now in war. For the Kremlin's Cold War intelligence assault on the west, however, it made not a jot of difference. The USSR's secret spying onslaught on the west remained 'business as usual'. Not just for the men from the Lubyanka, either: the British in their turn were actually preparing to mount a major series of sabotage attacks inside the USSR as an attack on 'Hitler's Communist ally' when events over-took them in May 1940.

The Russo-German Non-Aggression Pact of August 1939 did however cause a profound sense of shock to many Soviet sympathizers and communist fellow travellers in the west. Many of those who had turned a blind eye to Stalin's internal excesses in the 1930s on the grounds that the USSR was a staunch bulwark against Nazi Germany and a 'noble social experiment' were now appalled by the Kremlin's duplicity and hypocrisy. Further Soviet aggression against Finland, Estonia, Latvia and Lithuania merely reinforced this revulsion against the Soviet Union in particular and communism in general. Liberal-minded social democrats who in the past had been apologists for the 'workers' paradise' now openly rejected Stalin's USSR. The years 1939 to 1941 were to mark the low point of Marxist-Leninist appeal to thinking men and women everywhere.

Not for one group, however. Behind the scenes Stalin's secret army of spies worked on diligently for the Kremlin. Along with open Party members such as Harry Pollitt ('the boneless wonder of King Street', as one cartoonist cruelly depicted the confused leader of Britain's Communist Party), they tied themselves into intellectual knots to follow every twist and turn of Stalin's new 'party line'. Such egregious efforts to square Soviet *realpolitik* with communist theory convinced few. A cynic might observe that the real truth about

SOMEONE IS TAKING SOMEONE FOR A WALK

A contemporary view of the Hitler-Stalin pact
(David Low, published in *Picture Post* and *Collier's Magazine*, 21 October 1939)

these ideologically committed traitors was that they didn't really care about any change in Moscow's line. Hating their own countrymen more than any mere foreign communist tyranny, they simply spied on for their Kremlin master unabashed, any moral ideals now totally ignored and discredited. So much for 'Socialist principle'.

But if nothing else Stalin's shifting diplomacy had won time for the Soviet workers' paradise. In the spring of 1940, the all-conquering Nazi legions were free to turn on the west. In May Hitler unleashed his Wehrmacht again. Within a month France was consumed and Britain besieged alone on its island. The result was that by the winter of 1940 a curious stand-off ensued. The isolated British could not attack Hitler's victorious armies, now master of the European continent; and Nazi Germany, its Luftwaffe thrown back in the Battle of Britain, could not invade the British Isles.

Ironically, this stalemate now permitted Berlin to do the very thing Stalin feared most of all. In November 1940 Hitler dusted off *Mein Kampf* and ordered his victorious generals to prepare for Operation Barbarossa, and 'kick in the door of Bolshevism to bring the whole rotten edifice crashing down . . .' On 22 June 1941, Germany unleashed its 180 divisions, 3,000 aircraft and 5,000 tanks against the Soviet Union. Three million soldiers advanced across Russia's western border. Within three months the Wehrmacht was within striking distance of Moscow.

Suddenly, thanks to the Germans, the Kremlin's long running Cold War with the west had become very hot indeed.

5

COOL NEW ALLIES?

THE THREE-SIDED WAR

The German assault on Russia changed everything. Churchill, the arch-enemy of communism 'in all its loathsome forms', now had a co-belligerent in Britain's struggle against Nazi tyranny.

We now know that Churchill had not been surprised by Hitler's assault on Stalin. As early as 16 May 1941 the Enigma code breakers had alerted him to the Nazi invasion forces gathering in eastern Europe. A month later he had warned both Roosevelt and Stalin of the storm to come. (Stalin suppressed the warnings, calling them 'capitalist provocations'.) On the very eve of the invasion Churchill discussed the attack with his secretary Sir John Colville, who was surprised to learn that the Prime Minister intended to side with the USSR, come what may. Colville pointed out that for Churchill, the avowed anti-communist, this would be seen as a dramatic *volte-face*. Quoting from the Book of Kings, he said it would be 'bowing down in the House of Rimmon'.

In a much-quoted reply, Churchill growled that he only had one purpose – the destruction of Hitler – and that 'his life was much simplified thereby. If Hitler invaded Hell he would at least make a favourable reference to the Devil.'

Churchill's relief at the USSR's engagement – albeit enforced – in the war was matched by the delight of the all-too-numerous communist fellow travellers lurking in the political undergrowth in the west. Since the Molotov-Ribbentrop pact and Britain's war with Germany, the reputation of communism and Communists had suffered badly. Communist Russia as the Nazi's *ally* had done little for the reputation or the cause of world socialism. Now, with Comrade Stalin and millions of innocent Russians suddenly fellow victims of Nazi aggression, it became the duty of every right-thinking person to support the USSR in its hour of need. Everywhere communist fellow travellers emerged from the woodwork to support 'Uncle Joe' and his heroic Red Army, fighting 'single handed against the tyranny of Fascism'. Socialist sympathizers and spies could now openly campaign for the Soviet cause. Overnight, treachery had suddenly become patriotism. The wider war effort justified all. Well-orchestrated rallies in Trafalgar Square demanded 'Second Front Now!' Moscow's cause was everybody's cause.

One group in particular, however, remained strangely shy. They had every reason to, because Stalin's secret spying war continued uninterrupted, even on his new ally. Although privately they admitted their treason to close friends – and in the drunken homosexual Guy Burgess's case sometimes to anyone who would listen – the Soviet secret service's moles planted deep in British society so long ago stayed hidden. Now they were able to justify the long-term investment in them by the Soviet secret service. From their positions of access inside key British institutions such as the BBC, the Foreign Office,

MI5, MI6 and the secret code-breaking establishment at Bletchley Park, the NKVD's 'Famous Five' spied for the USSR with prodigious success. In a bizarre twist, their flow of intelligence was so great that at one time Stalin and Moscow Centre actually stopped reading their best spies' traffic, suspecting that 'the Magnificent Five' were really a British counter-espionage plant. At times it seemed, literally, just too good to be true. A crack team of undercover NKVD-KGB men was despatched to Britain to follow the Famous Five and report back if they were in fact British intelligence double agents. After blundering around wartime London for a week, the Russians became a standing joke in their ill-cut suits and gangster hats. Some couldn't even speak English. Moscow Centre hastily recalled them. Blithely ignorant of this bizarre twist in their story, Burgess, Maclean, Philby, Blunt and Cairncross carried on their treacherous work for a disbelieving and unappreciative Mother Russia.

No one better exemplifies the impact of Stalin's spies – long before the post-1945 Cold War era – than James Klugmann. Klugmann, like so many Communists at the time, was of Jewish descent. Before the war he had been a contemporary at Trinity College of Guy Burgess, Donald Maclean and John Cornford, and a dedicated member of the Cambridge communist ring. He had also been an open member of the Communist Party and had made little secret of his desire to see the glorious dawn of a peasants' and workers' paradise in Britain too, and the establishment of a communist state. His views were well known to Britain's secret police – the so-called Special Branch – and to MI5, the security service. The coming of Hitler's war then placed Klugmann and his ilk in a quandary. In 1939 he was slavishly supporting Moscow and the Communist Party line. With Stalin as Hitler's unlikely friend and ally, Klugmann's only course was clearly to stay out of the war as much as he could. But Hitler's invasion of the USSR in June 1941 changed all that. For 'Uncle Joe's' fight was now Britain's fight too. Klugmann could then become a soldier and be as loyal as the next man: loyal – that is – to the *Soviet* cause.

As a Communist well known for his radical and dangerous views, Klugmann was unlikely to be an immediate choice for the undercover secret work of the Special Operations Executive in their campaign to 'set Europe ablaze'. However, something very convenient happened: Klugmann's personal security file at MI5 mysteriously went missing. To this day there are many who believe that one of his communist friends already working in MI5 'lost' the incriminating P File and claimed that it had been burned in the Blitz. It could have been his friend Anthony Blunt or someone else. It might even, by some unlikely stroke of luck, have been a genuine error. Whatever the reason, Klugmann could now masquerade as 'a bit of a sympathiser with the Communist cause when he had been an undergraduate'. In 1941 that was good enough for the harassed and overworked British security vetters. So when the dedicated Communist volunteered for service he was willingly accepted. One of his friends actually met him in Whitehall and, on hearing that he was now employed by the Intelligence Corps and SOE, said, 'My God! How can that be? You used to be a red hot commie . . .' Despite this, Klugmann was posted to SOE Cairo, where he was able to change the future course of the Cold War, and consequently the course of world history.

SOE Cairo was responsible for processing all reports coming out of the SOE operation to support the Yugoslav partisans engaged in a guerrilla struggle with the occupying Germans. The Yugoslav resistance was a murky, confused affair of tangled loyalties, with many of the groups jockeying for post-war advantage. Every report coming from the SOE teams in-country came across the pro-communist Klugmann's desk.

At the time the British were favouring the non-Fascist nationalist Cetnik bands of the anti-German patriot Mihailovich, who were undoubtedly the most effective enemies of the Germans. The smaller communist resistance partisans led by Tito were fighting an entirely separate war. Sometimes they would attack the Wehrmacht; but just as much of their efforts seemed to be dedicated to fighting Mihailovich's rival partisans in an internal power struggle to take over and rule Yugoslavia after the war. Tito's Communists were not above ambushing and killing the nationalists, attacking their villages and even betraying their fellow guerrillas to the Germans. Moreover, Tito's communist partisans took their orders direct from Moscow.

Something very curious then happened, which was to change the course of the war and the shape of post-war Europe. Someone, somehow, managed to change the British position from supporting Mihailovich to supporting the communist partisans. We now know that the individual in question was Moscow's man, the dedicated communist Major James Klugmann. As SOE Cairo's staff officer with specific responsibility for reading and screening all material coming out of occupied Yugoslavia and for preparing digests and briefs for London, Klugmann distorted the picture, sometimes quite literally. For example, in 1943 the Germans put up posters of both Mihailovich and Tito, offering 1,000 gold marks for the capture of the two guerrilla leaders: by the time an example made it back to London, only Tito figured as the Wehrmacht's 'most wanted'. In true Soviet style someone had airbrushed the individual out to alter the truth.

A more serious example occurred in October 1943, when Mihailovich's men attacked the Belgrade–Sarajevo railway and destroyed four bridges. They then assaulted the Nazi garrison at Visigrad and briefly occupied the town. By the time these incidents were reported back to London they had been mysteriously credited as 'attacks by Tito's communists'. The small SOE office in Cairo had no means of double-checking what came in and what was reported back, and anyway Major Klugmann was a trusted intelligence officer. Even direct reports from the SOE's Colonel Seitz in-country had been altered before they were put in front of Brigadier Anthony, the ranking SOE officer in Cairo, who dutifully added his own comments and sent the reports from Yugoslavia back to London. Puzzled analysts at Bletchley Park, who were decoding the original signals from the Balkans, were baffled by seeming inconsistencies; but then, in the ruthless compart-mentalism imposed by the secret world of signals intelligence, they just assumed that they were not seeing the whole secret picture.

Fed this regular diet of reports from SOE that it was the *communist* bands led by Tito that were causing the most havoc, plus unsubstantiated reports coming back as gospel from SOE Cairo that Mihailovich's Cetniks were 'little better than Nazi collaborators' (which for some anti-Serb groups was true), Churchill ordered that the British SOE effort in the Balkans should in future be diverted to Tito and his communist partisans. Starved of arms and supplies from their British backers, by 1944 Mihailovich's units were withering on the vine.

Konstantin Fotit, Yugoslav ambassador to Washington from 1935 to 1944, revealed the whole disgraceful saga after the war. But by then it was too late. Yugoslavia had gone communist and was firmly under Moscow's sway. Like the obedient Communist that he was, Klugmann, by his treachery and lies, had done his duty for his Russian communist masters and changed the course of history in eastern Europe, with consequences that we live with to this day.

The Cambridge spies were not the only treacherous maggots hatching out in Britain during the Second World War. Modern access to the intercepted Soviet coded cable messages of the 1940s (the so-called 'Venona' traffic) identifies numerous communist blowflies feeding off the British secrets to pass on to Moscow during the early years of the Second World War. Many of these still remain unidentified, but they undoubtedly existed. By 1940/41 no fewer than thirty-seven Britons were secretly spying for Moscow, from 'Reservist' (an unidentified colonel in the Royal Artillery, wounded at Dunkirk) to 'Intelligentsia'. 'Intelligentsia' stands revealed by the secret Venona cables as none other than Professor J.B.S. Haldane, a distinguished academic and nephew of a Lord Chancellor. Haldane, an open communist sympathizer suffused with an ideologue's zeal and an academic's intellectual arrogance, had turned up in the trenches in the Spanish Civil War; and despite his supposed intellect he was somehow able to ignore the twists and turns of the Party line during the Molotov-Ribbentrop fiasco. This brilliant fool was so subservient to the Communist Party that he actually sought its approval before publishing a book on Air Raid Precautions to ensure that its contents were ideologically pure and acceptable to the Party. For committed Communists, apparently, even building an air raid shelter was dependent on political instructions from Moscow. Such contemptible intellectual cowardice seems to have been a common factor among the British communist traitors recruited to spy for Stalin in the 1930s and 1940s. The great academic brains of the left allowed the Party – which in fact meant Moscow and Stalin – to dictate their thinking for them.

Another Moscow lackey outed by Venona was the Honourable Ivor Montagu. The GRU code-named him (rather obviously) 'Nobility'. Montagu, yet another Cambridge man, was a committed Communist. He visited the fledgling Soviet Union in 1925 and came back enormously impressed by the Socialist marvels his Russian hosts had permitted him to see. Like so many other gullible intellectuals, the naïve young aristocrat promptly became a dewy-eyed convert to Marxism and supported the communist cause all his life. His treachery was especially important to Moscow, as by 1940 Montagu had unrivalled access to high political secrets and could act as both a liaison officer to Moscow's so-called X Group of British spies and a talent spotter and recruiter for the cause.

Perhaps the deadliest foot soldier in Stalin's undeclared war on Britain was another treacherous academic revealed by the decoded Venona traffic, Dr Alan Nunn May. Also a Cambridge man, Nunn May visited the USSR in 1936 and was closely associated with the CPGB before the war. By 1942 he was working on the atomic project at the Cavendish Laboratory in Cambridge, and by 1943 he had been seconded to Canada as part of Britain's top scientific team building the first atomic bomb. Nunn May's post-war arrest and interrogation revealed that the treacherous British scientist actually handed mineral samples of uranium 233 and 235 to his Soviet controller to be flown direct to Moscow. Stalin's 'third front' (the USSR's undeclared intelligence war against the west) had never borne such vital fruits.

Such pro-Soviet conspiracy was not confined to Great Britain. In the USA, 349 resident Americans have been identified by Venona as communist agents during the Second World War, and another 139 are known to have spied for the Kremlin who are not mentioned in the Soviet spy cables. This staggering 488 known traitors proves beyond doubt that Stalin's paranoia, suspicion and distrust even of his wartime allies far exceeded the normal intelligence operations undertaken by states. Nearly 500 known spies hints at many others as yet uncovered. If Alger Hiss in the State Department, and perhaps even Harry Hopkins at Roosevelt's elbow in the White House, were serving the Soviet Union, then just how many others were too?

The Kremlin's intelligence assault, even on its supposed friends, is evidence of a deeper distrust and hostility. Even at the height of the struggle against Nazi Germany in early 1943, a senior British diplomat admitted the truth about the Soviets: 'We are quite wrong in expecting any response to efforts on our part to conciliate the Soviet Government and get its confidence.'

The truth was that the Kremlin had never faltered in its Cold War attack on the west and its secrets from 1921 to 1945. Even Hitler's invasion of the USSR and the subsequent alliance between Britain, America and the Soviet Union made little difference to Moscow Centre's efforts to spy on the west. The Great Patriotic War was merely an interlude in a much wider struggle. Stalin's Cold War of 'unarmed aggression' against capitalism continued unabated throughout the war years. For the NKVD the only difference between spying on the Nazis and spying on Russia's allies was that they were actually shooting at the Germans. Friend or foe, all that mattered was satisfying the voracious appetite of the suspicious dictator in the Kremlin.

There is clear evidence that even during the war Churchill himself remained intensely suspicious of Stalin and his communist motives, ally or no ally. In October 1943 he admitted that it might be a mistake to hammer the German army into oblivion. 'We mustn't weaken the Germans too much,' he mused to an astonished Alan Brooke and the Chiefs of Staff. 'After all, we may need them to fight the Russians.' And in Cairo, on the way to the Tehran Conference in late 1943, he warned Roosevelt that 'the real problem is Russia . . .' From

1944 onwards British concerns about the post-war ambitions of the Soviet Union increased to such an extent that a bitter bureaucratic war erupted in Whitehall. On one side were the optimists of the Foreign Office vainly trying to sell the post-war world as they would wish it to be, who believed that a diplomatic deal with the USSR was possible. Pitched directly against them were the cynical realists of the War Office, led by the Chief of the Imperial General Staff himself, who viewed the Soviet Union and Comrade Stalin as dangerous, tricky and mendacious Mongols. The British Foreign Office clung to its view of Russia as a peacetime ally, despite the mounting evidence of continued Soviet intelligence gathering. Eventually the realities of the continuing Cold War were reflected in a vicious policy debate inside the British establishment until even the ever-optimistic diplomats cracked. Sir Owen O'Malley, late of the Budapest Embassy, and an experienced critic of all things Soviet, openly challenged the FO's Pollyanna view of the post-war world. Instead he emphasized the 'sinister nature' of many Soviet aspirations and accused his less-experienced colleagues of 'Alice in Wonderland policy formulation' in the face of inevitable Soviet land grabs. Even Churchill was muttering darkly about 'Operation Unthinkable', the plan for a war against the Soviet Union. By 1945 most of the military and virtually all the American policy makers heartily agreed that the post-war Soviet Union would represent a threat to the west. One key policy maker, however, did not.

The over-confident Roosevelt dismissed such *realpolitik* notions as colonialist delusion on the part of the old imperial war horse Churchill. He was convinced that he could 'handle Uncle Joe', even going so far as to try to arrange a secret bilateral summit with Stalin in Alaska behind Churchill's back. Challenged about this, he deliberately lied to the British premier, denying that he would ever even contemplate such a thing. Churchill's rage when he later discovered the truth was incandescent. An intemperate prime ministerial telegram had to be withdrawn at the last moment to prevent a major breach of Allied relations.

Until his death in April 1945 Roosevelt seems to have believed that he could manage the Communists and that he could negotiate any problem with the Russians. But he was wrong, and badly wrong at that. Instead it was 'Uncle Joe' who played off Roosevelt against Churchill at Yalta in January 1945 and contrived to wring every concession he could out of the weakening American President. Not everyone was fooled by Stalin's cynical manipulation of the gullible Roosevelt, however. By 1944–5, senior American strategists were harbouring deep suspicions about the USSR's real motives and goals, and warning of trouble to come from the Russians after the war. That this suspicion of a post-war USSR went right to the top of the American establishment is only now fully emerging. The distinguished physicist Professor Joseph Rotblat resigned from the atom bomb project (one of only two to do so for moral reasons) on being told in *early 1944* by General Leslie Groves, the Manhattan Project's overall boss, that 'the real purpose of making the bomb is to subdue the Soviets . . .'

The result of this changing perception in the west – seeing Stalin's Russia as more threat than ally – inevitably had its effect. By 1945 the anti-Soviet factions in London and Washington found common cause as they considered the potential threat posed by the advancing Red Army. Gradually the Allied intelligence effort against Germany began to shift its emphasis. By the end of the war both Bletchley Park and the American sigint community were intercepting and sharing numerous signals from German intelligence reporting on the strength of the *Soviets*' armed forces. The result was that by the time

Nazi Germany was defeated the western allies were effectively running a full-blown intelligence operation against their own wartime ally, using all the German enemy's resources as well: sigint, captured documentation and prisoners of war.

The Soviets were only too well aware of these developments through their remarkable spy network. In the circumstances they had every reason to be suspicious of future western intentions following the imminent and inevitable collapse of Nazi Germany. The news that Himmler's deputy, General Wolff, was actually trying to negotiate a secret deal with the British and the Americans to form a common front against the advancing Russians can hardly have inspired an atmosphere of trust. Senior representatives of the German High Command actually contacted Alan Foster Dulles through Major Waibel of the Swiss secret service in April 1945, offering a deal. The SS reported directly back to Hitler in his Berlin bunker on 15 April with the news that it might be possible for a weary Führer to fight on after a German surrender in northern Italy. Whether this was a clever plot to destabilize an already slightly mad Hitler or a real effort to stop the fighting in Italy, thus freeing up von Vietinghoff's Army Group to turn on the Russians, will probably never be known. But it goes some little way towards explaining why Stalin was as suspicious of his allies' motives as they were of his.

Harry Truman, who succeeded as President after FDR's death in April 1945, shared these concerns about the Soviets from the start. Unlike Roosevelt, he had a clear view of what American power was and how it might be needed to contain Soviet military adventures. By the war's end the Soviets, well armed and trigger happy, were deployed across eastern Europe and the Far East. If there was any doubt about the Kremlin's real intentions, the Russians soon made their feelings clear.

On 29 August 1945, just two weeks after VJ Day, Red Air Force fighters closed in on and shot down a clearly marked US B-29 over Korea which was parachuting supplies to Allied prisoners of war. The Soviet authorities were unapologetic. Korea was in the USSR's new zone of influence. The 'Yankee bomber' had been invading Moscow-controlled airspace.

According to the Russians, wartime allies or not, the USA 'was committing a hostile act.'

6

GROWLERS

THE VICTORS FALL OUT

By the end of the war, the Red Army stood victorious in Berlin amid a Germany in ruins. Thirty million displaced persons were on the move across Europe, trying to rebuild their shattered lives among the wreckage of the most destructive war the world had known. The victors and wartime allies now turned to the problems of building a new and peaceful Europe and the political problems of the peace.

At the end of the Yalta Conference in February 1945 Churchill had toasted Stalin and Roosevelt. Looking forward to the post-war world, he said, '. . . it was as if we were standing on the crest of a hill with the glories of great future possibilities stretching before us . . . In the modern world the function of leadership is to lead people . . . into the broad plains of peace and happiness . . .'

Despite the British leader's pious hopes, a year later Stalin was openly re-arming to confront his wartime enemies. In

early 1946, on the eve of elections for the Supreme Soviet, the
Soviet leader made an openly bellicose speech, in which he
threatened: 'The development of world capitalism proceeds
not on a smooth and even progress but through crisis and the
catastrophe of war . . .'

This uncompromisingly Marxist speech alarmed many in
the west. It was even held to be a 'delayed declaration of war
against the US' by some observers. A pragmatic alliance based
on a shared war had, within a few months, begun to dissolve
into what we now call the Cold War. A baffled US State
Department consulted its long-standing Soviet expert, George
Kennan. This experienced observer of the Kremlin scene sent
back a famous 8,000-word reply known as the Long Telegram. In it he reported accurately and clearly his view of
Moscow's aims and intentions. Little had changed in the
Kremlin since his first posting in Moscow well before the
war. His analysis of what makes the men in the Kremlin tick
has never been bettered:

> The Kremlin's neurotic view of world affairs stems from the
> traditional and instinctive sense of insecurity . . . The Soviet's
> Party Line is not based on any objective analysis of the
> situation beyond Russia's border: it has little to do with the
> situation outside Russia: it arises mostly from inner Russian
> necessities, which existed before the recent war and still exist
> today . . .

Kennan warned the US administration to prepare for a
battle with its erstwhile ally. He foretold an 'unremitting
struggle between the USSR and the West, made even more
likely by the Communist view that such a conflict was not only
inevitable', but according to the Holy Communist Gospel of
Marx, was 'pre-ordained'.

Kennan also highlighted the major flaw in US policy. The Grand Alliance against Germany had rallied round the standard of strategic *military* policy, and military policy only. Agreement on post-war political arrangements had in fact been studiously ignored by the policy makers despite Churchill's Clausewitzian warnings. In a Utopian detachment eerily reminiscent of President Wilson's initiatives in 1918, the dying Roosevelt positively encouraged indecision about the post-war world, contenting himself with 'amiable sentiments about freely negotiated settlements'.

An increasingly worried Churchill plead the cause of the Poles and the other peoples of eastern Europe, to no avail. The American President was resolute to do nothing, adamant for apathy. From late 1944 until his death in April 1945, Roosevelt allowed Europe's future politics to drift in a sea of inertia, while a smiling Stalin looked silently on, measuring his chance of carrying Russia's borders ever further westwards on the bayonets of the Red Army. After all, in 1815, as Stalin announced to an astonished American diplomat, 'Czar Alexander had got to Paris . . .'

The new balance of power in Europe in the late summer of 1945 therefore came as a profound shock to the western powers, particularly the United States. America's perfectly justified pride in victory was tinged with a genuine perplexity about the USSR's post-war motives. The habitual self-righteousness with which America goes to war seemed to be challenged by this ruthless Soviet exploitation of victory: surely the Russians were the good guys? The truth was that for the first time the USA and the USSR were confronting each other across an armed border. Those great ideological enemies capitalism and communism were, by early 1946, now standing eyeball to eyeball. The USSR still had 3 million men under arms: the Americans alone had the atom bomb. 'A blind and sterile confrontation', in Kennan's words, was inevitable. The Cold War, as we now know it, had begun. But, as Kennan kept pointing out to the deaf and blind in Washington, nothing had ever really changed: in reality an ideological war had been going on ever since the Bolsheviks took over in the Kremlin. The US tendency to oscillate between idealism and military intervention and isolation was now confronted by a harder-edged and ruthless enemy, seemingly determined to push as far west as possible.

If there were any lingering post-war doubts about the in-grained hostility of the Soviet Union they were dispelled once and for all in September 1945 when Ivor Gouzenko, a clerk in the Soviet Embassy in Ottawa, decided to defect along with his young wife. His revelations about the extent of Soviet spying on their supposed allies came as a profound shock to the west. As a GRU cipher clerk Gouzenko had deep access into many of the Russians' intelligence secrets. The senior GRU resident in Canada was unmasked, along with dozens of others suspected of spying for Stalin throughout the war. Most damaging of all, Gouzenko fingered the USSR's nest of atom spies working in North America, including Alan Nunn May and many other traitors. As the realization of the extent and depth of the Soviets' intelligence war against the west gradually emerged, Britain – and America even more so – began to rethink their relationship with Stalin's Russia. It seemed that 'Uncle Joe' wasn't quite so friendly after all.

America's real problems with its late ally had evolved partly out of naïvety and a misplaced idealism about the USSR. What the State Department never seemed to realize in the immediate aftermath of the 1939–45 war was *Russia's* absolute priority, Soviet-led or not. After two disastrous wars, the Kremlin's main aim was to see a weak, unarmed and non-threatening

Germany at all costs. It suited the USSR to keep an iron control of its own occupied zone of Germany because, from their point of view, the Allies were at best being weak over the defeated Germans, and making potentially alarming moves towards their former enemies at worst. The Soviets had some cause to be concerned. In Bavaria, America's General Patton was openly criticizing the Red Army as 'a scurvy race, Mongolians and permanently drunk . . .' while turning a blind eye to thousands of ex-Wehrmacht and even SS men heading west, away from the advancing Russians. Oberst Gehlen, the head of the Wehrmacht's 'Eastern Armies' intelligence bureau, had been whisked to Washington to tell the Americans everything he knew – which after four years of war was a lot – about the Soviet military machine. There were even rumours that the Americans intended to set him up in a comfy office near Munich with his old staff, plus his invaluable secret files on the USSR, and were going to invite Hitler's intelligence expert to continue his spying on the Soviet military, but this time for the Americans. The wartime allies were falling out.

Operation Paperclip, the plan to loot the Nazis' technical and industrial secrets, had turned into a vicious free-for-all amid the chaos of post-war Germany, with the Americans invading the British-occupied zone to grab defence material and the Soviets removing whole secret nerve gas factories back to Russia before anyone else could get their hands on them. Operation Big was little better. US scientific teams snatched the complete top-secret German nuclear pile at Haigerloch, scientists, papers and all, to make sure that no one could pass the information on German nuclear advances to anyone else, British or Russian. Off the coast of Lithuania and the Baltic States, the British Secret Intelligence Service had already begun an undercover campaign to ship Lithuanian 'freedom fighters' secretly back to their homeland to stir up resistance against the occupying Red Army. Fortunately, from the Soviets' point of view, Kim Philby of SIS had betrayed the lot, and most of them were rounded up on landing and quietly executed by the NKVD-KGB. The USSR was under no illusions about *its* wartime allies. Or its late enemy, either: the Kremlin looted no less than $13 billion from Germany in punitive reparations back to the USSR as well as asset stripping eastern Europe after 1945.

Clumsy diplomacy made things worse. At a hastily called summit of foreign ministers in Moscow in December 1945, Byrnes, the new US Secretary of State, failed to coordinate a joint policy line with his British counterpart, Ernest Bevin. Ill-prepared and over-confident, the American tried to 'cuff it' at a high-level policy meeting with Molotov about the future of Europe. As Byrnes pointed out, they were 'allies, after all'. The result was a diplomatic disaster, so much so that the British delegation actually complained about the State Department's 'amateurish diplomacy' and the respected *Economist* magazine summed up the conference: 'Byrnes produced the show and Russia stole it.'

The US Secretary had signed a wishy-washy agreement with the Kremlin in the teeth of protest not just from his British allies, but also (it later emerged) from within his own US delegation. Stalin in the Kremlin purred with satisfaction over a basket of territorial and political concessions wrung without demur. As a result, an angry President Truman ordered a complete review of post-war foreign policy towards Russia. He had earlier been much vexed by Stalin's virtual annexation of Bulgaria. In an aside to an aide as early as Christmas 1945, he admitted that 'the only thing they [the Russians] understand is divisions'. From now, on Truman declared, 'I am tired of babying the Soviets . . .' By the spring of 1946, America's line hardened towards its erstwhile ally.

As *Newsweek* observed, 'The soft glove approach toward the Soviet Union is now being abandoned.' A tougher US line emerged, inspired by Soviet totalitarianism in eastern Europe, a continuing Soviet occupation in Iran, and fresh territorial demands on Turkey. We now know that Truman's concerns were real. By early 1946 he was convinced that the Soviets were out 'to confuse the West and expand their power'.

Public opinion slowly caught up with events on the ground in Soviet-occupied Europe, and hardened. By June 1946, doubtless inspired by Churchill's famous 'Iron Curtain' speech of March, a poll indicated that 60 per cent of Americans believed that the Kremlin was bent on world domination. The wartime Grand Alliance had totally collapsed. Two clear blocs were emerging: east versus west. Suddenly a US-USSR clash seemed a dreadful possibility. It was a confrontation that would shape the next half-century and – occasionally – terrify millions. The Cold War as we now know it had emerged as an unpleasant fact of life for ordinary people.

The principal area of disagreement – and the cockpit of any confrontation – was the shattered continent of Europe. In particular, Germany posed a problem from the start. Despite refusing to endorse US Treasury Secretary Morgenthau's plan to reduce Germany to a pre-industrial agricultural economy, the US and Britain had allowed the victorious Russians to cart off as much of Germany's heavy industry as they could during the summer of 1945. Egged on by the French (who had been admitted to the diplomatic top table on the fiction that France had been one of the victorious powers and who were only too keen to keep Germany weak), the Soviets were determined to keep Germany under their heel. An occupied, defeated and impoverished Germany suited Soviet diplomatic concerns very well indeed in 1946.

The Iron Curtain: the heart of the Cold War

The other two occupying powers, the US and Britain, were not so sure. How, reasoned diplomats and economists alike, could Europe ever recover from the most disastrous war in history without economic activity? And, like it or not, Germany was the economic hub of Europe. Germany's future was crucial to any final settlement of the Second World War. On 6 September 1946 at Stuttgart, US Secretary of State James F. Byrnes made a speech that changed western policy and sent a shudder through Poland and the USSR, the most recent victims of German aggression. The west called for nothing less than the rehabilitation of Germany. Byrnes invited his audience to 'help the German people to win their way back to an honourable place among the free and peace-loving nations of the world'.

That was the very last thing some of his listeners wanted to hear. Memories of German aggression were still fresh in too many minds. 'Not in our back yard, you don't,' said the Russians and clamped down even harder on their occupied Soviet zone. A re-unified Germany was never going to be on any Soviet agenda.

From the viewpoint of those who had recently suffered from the attentions of a strong Germany, a weak, divided Germany was a safe Germany.

7

THE EUROPEAN ICEBERG

THE COLD WAR BEGINS

Stalin, not unreasonably, particularly feared any idea whatsoever of a strong revived German state. After all, these were the very people who had invaded Russia three times in his lifetime and had very nearly prevailed.

In particular he feared that the Germans' technical abilities, their industry and their inevitable economic power, would one day again threaten the USSR. He privately forecast to a colleague that German recovery would only take twelve to fifteen years 'and then we will have to have another go at it'. However, pragmatic as ever, the Russian leader realized that Germany could not remain crushed and neutralized forever. He therefore tried to stamp his own vision on to post-war Europe, to control the defeated Germans and contain any future threats to the USSR. The Kremlin demanded a compliant and disarmed Germany, a Germany kept well under their thumb, with no nonsense about democracy. Democracy would be what Comrade Stalin said it was.

His erstwhile allies did not agree. The nation that had bred Goethe and Beethoven had somehow to be readmitted into the comity of nations. As a result, post-war Germany became the great problem between east and west at the very heart of the Cold War. A conference to hammer out a final peace treaty failed to come to any agreement. The wartime allies could not agree over many things, but Germany was always top of the list. The 'Truman Doctrine' of spring 1947 further closed Stalin's options and divided the victors still further. The American President's declaration of 'support for the free peoples of the world' and his public denunciation of communist policies in eastern Europe as the 'imposition of the rule of minority on the majority' finally ruled out any Soviet dream of a united Germany subservient to Kremlin influence. In the Soviet-occupied parts of Europe, 'free people' was a contradiction in terms, and the Kremlin intended to keep it that way, however much the west protested.

As the disagreement hardened it was clear that Stalin had failed. By 1946 Soviet policy over post-war Germany was in ruins and the western allies frustrated and suspicious. Politically, east and west were now at daggers drawn. As 1947 dawned the battle-lines of the Cold War had been clearly drawn for all to see.

The post-war split widened. In the summer and autumn of 1947 the Allies pressed ahead with their own political initiatives. General Marshall's plan to pump 1 per cent of the USA's GDP into Europe to boost post-war reconstruction electrified European leaders. For the truth was that the problems of Europe's lacklustre post-war economies did not stem only from the destruction of factories and railways. A lot of trade had actually dried up, and there was far too little commerce to generate wealth. This was one area in which America now was not only impelled to act out of morality but also out of enlightened self-interest. Sound economics dictated American generosity as much as any other factors. The US Congress threw American taxpayers' money at Europe's problems, and Europe's finance ministers rushed to take advantage of this largesse. But to the Kremlin the American plan represented a clear economic and political threat to Soviet control over their newly conquered satellites. A furious Stalin denounced it as 'American interference in the internal affairs of other countries', and insisted that the Czechs withdraw their request for US economic aid. He unleashed his secret agents to destabilize the plan. The US ambassador in Moscow described the Kremlin's angry reaction as virtually 'a declaration of war by the USSR . . .' To lead this anti-western campaign, Stalin ordered a new Cominform (Communist Information Bureau) into action 'in the vanguard of Socialism'. To many observers the Cominform looked suspiciously like a revived Comintern, still bent on carrying the Socialist revolution to the 'ignorant toiling masses enslaved by world capitalism' by undermining the west. To economic control of eastern Europe was now added communist ideology backed by the naked threat of force.

Communist fellow travellers and sympathizers throughout Europe reacted swiftly to their master's call to undermine the Marshall Plan. In France, the Fourth Republic was suddenly hamstrung by a sudden series of strikes coordinated by the communist leaders of the Confédération Générale du Travail and 'secret soviets' were formed around the country to challenge American influence. Civil war seemed a very real possibility. In Italy, where the Communist Party was the biggest outside the USSR and its allies, the political see-saw teetered dangerously towards the left and Moscow. An increasingly alarmed America countered this wave of pro-communist subversion by unleashing its own campaign to influence Italy's internal affairs. Ten million Italian-Americans were mobilized to 'write to the good folks back home', and money was pumped into 'black-bag' payments to any Italian (and many other) political parties opposed to the Communists. Even the Pope was discreetly encouraged to ask the Church to mobilize to prevent the 'Godless Atheists' and 'church smashers' of the Spanish Civil War from gaining power. A network of 18,000 Italian 'civil committees', one in every parish, rallied to the anti-communist cause, supported by covert – and sometimes not so covert – aid from the newly formed CIA.

American money, pressure and influence worked. In Italy the Christian Democrats won the election to stay in power as an anti-communist bulwark for over a quarter of a century. In France the Communists over-reached themselves by resorting to open sabotage. The deliberate derailing of the Lille–Paris express and the death of twenty innocents caused outrage. Throughout Europe the internal communist threat subsided, and Marshall Aid and US money in unprecedented quantities began to flow into Europe.

The Marshall Plan was more than just charity. Only a small percentage of American aid actually came as hard cash. Most came as goods and products. The main financial incentive was a cleverly managed conversion fund, by means of which European companies exchanged low-cost goods and services for high-value aid using US-backed dollars as the convertible medium. Thus European companies could buy American goods at beneficial rates. Bomb-damaged plant could be renewed for a song and, in return, American companies could sell their products to a new mass market. It was effectively a financial transfusion to bring the sick European patient back to life. Everyone benefited, except the USSR and its sulky satellites, forbidden by Stalin to enjoy Marshall's $14 billion bonanza and forced to join Moscow's pale alternative gesture,

Comecon. Thanks to America, by 1948 a new Europe was emerging from the ashes of the war and the Red Czar in the east had suffered another major defeat. However, the Marshall Plan did have one unintended effect. It solidified and advertised the division of Europe between east and west.

The next flashpoint was, almost inevitably, Berlin. As the four occupied zones of Germany had solidified after 1945, Allied insistence on a post-war solution to Germany's status intensified. Every approach foundered on the rocks of the Kremlin's intransigence. Frustrated, the western powers looked for their own solutions. A conference of the western allies met in London in early 1948 to discuss Germany's future and was promptly betrayed by Stalin's western spies. Later, at an Allied Control Commission meeting, the Soviets confronted the western allies with their 'perfidy over the German question', quoting verbatim from the secret London discussions. Then they walked out, leaving the stunned US and UK commissioners open-mouthed.

This chain of events had two major consequences. Firstly, an alarmed west hastened to 'proceed with the . . . establishment of an Atlantic Security system', the forerunner of the NATO alliance. Secondly, it encouraged the Soviets to bring pressure to bear on the west.

Berlin was the obvious target. More than a hundred miles inside the Soviet-occupied zone, the German capital had since the end of the war been jointly administered by all four occupying powers, each with its own sector. Access through the Soviet zone that lay to the west was only by agreed 'corridors' on land, via canals and in the air. The result was that 2 million Berliners were daily hostage to the Soviet authorities' goodwill. During the spring of 1948, Soviet co-operation changed to Soviet delay, which soon turned to Soviet interference. Tension increased throughout the summer as the western allies hastened to set up an autonomous German government in their own sectors of Germany's traditional capital. The move was inevitable as part of the post-war rehabilitation of Germany, and was in fact the embryo of what was later to become the West German state. Events came to a head on 18 June 1948 when a new currency, the Deutschmark, was unilaterally introduced throughout the western-occupied zones without Soviet approval.

Retaliation was swift. Within a week, Moscow ordered all land routes into Berlin to be blocked. It was tantamount to a declaration of hostilities: 2 million Berliners and the western garrisons were now cut off, marooned deep inside Soviet territory.

The west's response came equally swiftly. American generals clamoured to thrust armoured columns up the *autobahn* corridors to battle their way into the beleaguered city. But Truman would have none of this direct head-to-head confrontation. A shooting war with the Russians was not the aim. Relieving Berlin was. However, sixty B-29 atomic bombers were despatched to forward airbases in the UK (albeit without their bombs) to show that, if need be, America meant business. To back up this obvious threat, President Truman ordered a massive relief airlift to the besieged city. Despite the obvious difficulties (a Dakota DC3 could only transport 2.5 tons and Berlin needed 4,500 tons of fuel and food a day to survive) the Allied Commander-in-Chief, General Lucius Clay, mobilized every transport aeroplane he could lay his hands on to fly supplies into Berlin.

For once Stalin had badly underestimated both his opponents' will and their capabilities. Political determination, the Americans' logistical skills and the courage of the thousands of RAF and USAF transport pilots – plus hundreds of 're-mobilized' civilian contractors – broke the Soviet blockade. At the

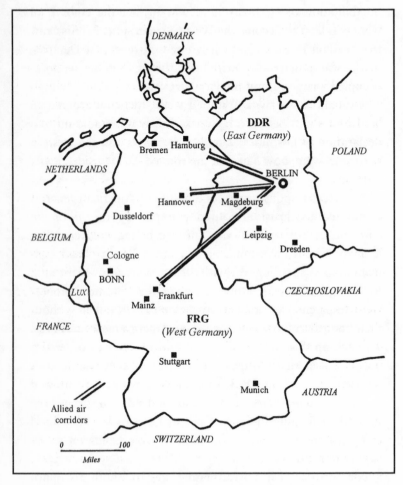

Divided Germany

West Berlin airfields and even on the city's lakes, transport aircraft were soon landing every ninety seconds and turning round in quarter of an hour.

Civilian morale rose as the supplies poured in and by the winter of 1948/49 the Allies were airlifting in over 4,500 tons a day, to the delight of the Berliners and the dismay of the Soviets, who could only look up glumly from their roadblocks as the Allied airborne armada thundered overhead. Holding 2 million people to ransom made Soviet policy look inept and stupid and the USSR and the communist cause deeply unpopular around the world. To make matters worse, the Allied counter-blockade of the Soviet zone hit East German industry hard. Steel plants, dependent on West Germany's coking coal, closed down. Industry in the East began to slow down and dry up. Soviet economic plans were in danger of collapse.

By May 1949 it was all over. Western technological superiority had bested communist brute force. The blockade was lifted and, as a public sop, another round of sterile talks on the future of Germany opened. Both sides knew they were a sham. Germany was now effectively divided into eastern and western zones. The west was stronger now, united by fear of Soviet capabilities and intentions. If anything the Soviets' Berlin blockade had spurred the west into working together to put together the alliance which would soon become NATO.

Nowadays we take the NATO alliance for granted. For over half a century, the Atlantic alliance has been the bedrock of 'the west' and NATO a recognized 'brand name' in articles, books, broadcasts and the general public consciousness. Until the collapse of the Soviet empire after 1991, 'NATO' invariably evoked positive responses in countless opinion polls. For fifty years, western democracies huddled safely underneath its umbrella, secure from the threat of Soviet expansionism.

It was not always thus. At the end of the Second World War the Americans wanted only to 'bring the boys home'. Troop levels were reduced from 12.1 million men under arms in 1945 to 1.7 million in 1947 (corresponding Soviet figures were 11.3 million to 3 million). Disengagement from the messy affairs of troubled Europe was official US policy in 1946.

It is rare for a single moment in world affairs – apart from war – to change the course of history. Such a moment occurred early in 1947, a moment seen by many as marking the start of the Cold War as much as any speech by Churchill. In March 1947 Britain officially informed its American ally that it could no longer afford to maintain its support for the Greek Royalist army, which was engaged in a war against Greece's Communists. Two crippling world wars, a worldwide depression and the loss of all its gold meant that Britain was bankrupt. Even bread was 'on the ration', a hardship unknown even during the blackest days of the war. Britain and its Empire were broke.

This moment, described by Sanche de Gramont as 'the moment the US took up the mantle of world leadership', electrified Washington. Over the weekend, lights burned late in government offices. By the following Monday morning the world had changed. America would bankroll anti-communist aid to Greece. America would now become fully engaged in maintaining the security of Europe. American arms, money and political assistance started to flow, and the Truman Doctrine was born.

By the end of 1947, it was obvious to every observer that Soviet aims for post-war Europe differed radically from those of Britain and America. The breakdown of an Allied Standing Conference of Foreign Ministers in December 1947 signalled the end of any hopes of an Allied deal on Europe in general and Germany in particular. From the debris of their political plans, the Allies looked east to a devastated eastern Europe, still firmly under the Red Army's iron fist. Things looked bad, and dangerously bad at that. The view was not encouraging else-where either. Further north, new tensions loomed. The 78-year-old Finnish President had been brusquely summoned to the Kremlin in February 1948 and *ordered* to sign a 'friendship treaty' with the USSR. Norway too felt threatened. In a series of meetings in March 1948, the Norwegian government made it clear that should the Russian Bear think of moving further west in the Nordic region, Norway would resist. Would the British – and, more importantly, the Americans – come to little Norway's aid, if it were attacked?

From this approach events moved swiftly. Control of the Norwegian coastline would open the North Atlantic to the huge Soviet submarine fleet. Those countries who formed the loose pact of the 'Brussels Treaty' could not realistically fight any Soviet adventurism in Scandinavia on their own. Europe needed to stick together. Behind the scenes the United States began a vigorous campaign to encourage the Europeans to integrate even more. Europe had caused the United States quite enough problems over the previous forty years. Organizations like the shadowy American Committee on a United Europe (ACUE) and other discreet CIA offshoots offered bribes and offices to the founding fathers of the European Union, in the hope that Europe would band together inside the Atlantic camp. Now that a real threat seemed to be looming there was a clear chance of establishing a concrete Western alliance.

There were other, more discreet, motives behind the found-ing of NATO, which nowadays are rarely admitted. France, in particular, wanted to keep any revival of Germany's fortunes on a tight rein, a point of view shared by the Soviet Union. Both nations had suffered once too often from the attentions of a strong Germany. NATO would keep any resurgence of German power under international lock and key. Britain too had its own motives: in its enfeebled economic and military state, its government was only too anxious to lock the USA into Europe at all costs. Any alleged post-war threat from the Soviets and the emerging Cold War served these hidden agendas admirably. Whatever their motives, the Europeans threw themselves enthusiastically behind any new alliance.

Encouraged by those giants of the post-war foreign policy, Britain's Ernest Bevin and America's George Marshall, talks were opened in 1948 at ambassadorial level. A year later, on 4 April 1949, the North Atlantic Treaty Organization was formally agreed. The new defence alliance had twelve members, from Iceland to Portugal, from Alaska to Ankara. Its principal brief was very simple and very clear: in Article 5 of the North Atlantic Treaty, all the signatories agreed to come to the aid of any one of their members who was attacked. An attack against one would be deemed an attack against all. As only one country, Soviet Russia, appeared to have any designs on any of the signatories, the message was quite obvious to everybody. NATO was clearly a defence alliance to oppose any Soviet ideas of further territorial expansion.

The new alliance faced a serious problem from the outset. The west's principal supply of good intelligence had dried up. In the autumn of 1948 the American and British signals intelligence operators were stunned to discover that they could no longer read or decipher Soviet military communications. For years they had been listening to, and understanding, much of the Red Army's operational-level traffic and a great deal of diplomatic material besides. Suddenly the airwaves were full of incomprehensible rubbish. The reason was simple – western intelligence had been betrayed.

The culprit was a traitor in their midst. The Soviets had recruited a little known American spy called William Weisband. He worked for the US Army Security Agency as a cipher clerk and he had much of interest to tell his Soviet spymasters. Of particular interest was the revelation that the capitalists had been eavesdropping on the Soviets for years. Moscow made its plans accordingly and on Friday 29 October 1948 a completely new one-time cipher pad system was introduced across the Soviet armed forces. Intelligence dried up at a stroke. Against the biggest threat in their history the US and its allies were now virtually flying blind.

NATO confronted two other challenges from the start: it lacked armed forces, and no one really knew what to do about occupied Germany. The first was rapidly addressed as new international HQs and staffs were formed and the USA re-engaged with Europe, stationing troops and aircraft on the continent as a highly visible symbol of American commitment. Sorting out the political future of Germany, on the other hand, was a problem that would take much longer.

The USSR viewed these proceedings with mounting suspicion. Whilst it was quite clear from the start that NATO was a defensive organization and nothing more, Soviet policy makers could not grasp such a simple truth. To them, NATO was anti-Soviet. That much was obvious. If it was anti-Soviet, it must therefore be hostile to the USSR; *ergo* NATO was manifestly an enemy of Soviet Russia. The Kremlin's baleful gaze now turned on this 'new enemy' with a vengeance. Once again the KGB's usual 'other means' were mobilized in support of Moscow and the wider 'Socialist Cause'. The usual pro-communist fellow travellers and liberal writers throughout the world were instructed to do everything in their power to rubbish the new alliance, obstruct its formation and warn of dire consequences should it ever become fact.

It was all to no avail. Frightened by the Red Army, by Stalin's bellicose statements and policies, by events in Berlin, and by the evidence of the Kremlin's oppressive regime in eastern Europe, the European sheep huddled together into a protective alliance with the American sheepdog prowling and growling on the perimeter.

NATO was a fact. A further humiliation for the USSR followed when the western zones of Germany were given a draft constitution of their own, completely divorced from East Germany. A new Federal Republic of (West) Germany had come into being and was even – cautiously – being mobilized as an ally of the west. Stalin's cherished aim of keeping a single neutralized and unified Germany as a buffer state had collapsed.

Moreover, at home, behind the Iron Curtain, Stalin had his hands full. In the spring of 1949 things were not going well in the various workers' paradises. Nationalist tendencies were getting out of hand. Czechoslovakia had been seized by what amounted to a Moscow coup and its moderate premier silenced by a mysterious suicide. In Poland, Gomulka seemed to be questioning the whole idea of Poland being controlled from Moscow; and Tito, more in sorrow than in anger, had withdrawn Yugoslavia from Moscow's control and gone it alone as a 'nationalist-communist'. (In this he was helped by the knowledge that Yugoslavia shared no common border with any Red Army troops and so didn't risk a sudden invasion of well-armed 'peacekeepers'.) Even committed and innocent communist leaders came under Stalin's increasingly suspicious gaze. Contact with foreigners meant communication with spies and imperialist agents.

A clear example was needed to bring the socialist satellites to heel. In Hungary, Láslzó Radik – a good Communist whose only crime was to have fought on the communist side in the Spanish Civil War – was arrested, tortured into confessing to ludicrous crimes at a short trial, and hanged '*pour encourager les autres*'. He was one of many. A collective shudder went through the satellites of eastern Europe in 1949.

Stalin may not have been able to control the west, but by the end of the 1940s he could certainly ensure that the Red Army's iron rod and the Kremlin's bloody writ kept eastern Europe to heel like a whipped puppy.

8

NEW BOMBS, NEW WARS

THE NUCLEAR DIMENSION

The potential of nuclear power was well known long before the Second World War. The dropping of the American atomic bomb on Hiroshima, on 6 August 1945, saw it become reality. It also demonstrated several other factors: nuclear power was hideously destructive, it was hideously expensive, and it was very hard to use effectively. The Manhattan Project had cost $30 billion (about $300 billion at 2005 prices). Money, scientists, knowledge and rare raw materials were needed to harness atomic power successfully. But the economic power of the victorious USA (48 per cent of the world's economic activity in 1946 was taking place in the US) was now matched by a monopoly of the bomb.

America's possession of the atom bomb accelerated competition between east and west. Through his remarkable network of secret agents Stalin was only too well aware of the Manhattan Project to develop a nuclear weapon. His spies had brought him nearly every detail of the Allies' most secret project.

THURSDAY, AUGUST 9, 1945   "BABY. PLAY WITH NICE BALL?"   (Copyright in All Countries)

1945 – the reality of the nuclear age strikes home
(David Low, published in the *Evening Standard*, 9 August 1945)

However, mere knowledge was not enough. Developing and building atomic weapons required more than just theoretical physics. Stalin was under no illusions that he was involved in an arms race to break the power of the American nuclear monopoly. The mushroom clouds over Hiroshima and Nagasaki spurred Russia's scientists, now under the direct control of Lavrenti Beria, head of the secret police, to even greater efforts – or else. Their very lives depended on it. In January 1946 Stalin personally summoned Igor Kurchatov, manager of the Soviets' lacklustre atomic programme, and ordered him to build a bomb 'at any cost'. Billions of roubles were suddenly made available, slave workers redeployed, and costly investments made in the electro-chemical, mining, metallurgical and power industries. Whatever happened, Stalin was determined to match the USA's monopoly and build his own atom bomb.

As early as 1946 western thinkers and strategists such as Bernard Brodie were musing on the role of this new wonder bomb. Could it be that the role of these potent new weapons was really not to *win* but to *deter* future wars? Could the atom bomb have meant the end of war? How could America's nuclear monopoly best be used? Fellow academics and strategic thinkers nodded sagely. While the ivory-tower thinkers of academia debated this fascinating new subject, Stalin's scientists worked furiously to actually do something: namely, build an atom bomb for their master. Stalin never wanted to *deter* war. He wanted the USSR to be able to *fight* wars armed with the most powerful weapon possible. Just like the USA, in fact.

America was far too complacent about its ownership of the bomb. Senior experts and intelligence analysts had assured the President it would 'take years' for the Soviets to develop a bomb. General Groves, leader of the Manhattan Project, estimated it would take twenty years. In fact, it took just five.

The Soviets were greatly helped in their atomic project by captured German physicists, but also by their western spies and fellow travellers, who virtually handed all the Allies' atomic secrets to Stalin on a gold plate. Maclean in the British Embassy in Washington, Nunn May in Canada, Klaus Fuchs in Oak Ridge and Los Alamos, all saved Russia billions of roubles and years in nuclear development. Yet again, Stalin's 'Third Fighting Front' and 'other means' (spying on friend and foe alike) had scored a major intelligence success on Moscow's behalf. Soviet nuclear scientists, spurred on by an impatient Beria and with free access to virtually all the latest western technical breakthroughs, redoubled their efforts.

As if to rub home their ability to strike anywhere at any time the US Air Force flew the B-50 Stratofortress 'Lucky Lady' non-stop round the world in March 1949 to demonstrate their air refuelling capability. The message was clear: America alone had the bomb, and could drop it anywhere on the planet.

On 20 September 1949 Stalin's overworked scientists finally succeeded. A US B-29 on a routine sniffer flight over the North Pacific off the Vladivostok coast detected unusual levels of radiation in the upper atmosphere. Follow-up checks confirmed the readings and other checks proved that the USSR had achieved the unthinkable: they had detonated a Soviet atomic bomb. 'Joe 1', as it was code-named by the Americans, came as a profound shock and changed the balance of power completely. The USA no longer had a monopoly of nuclear weapons. Fears of an 'atomic Pearl Harbor' suddenly became a genuine possibility.

One effect of this new nuclear capability on the part of the USSR was to spur the US into developing as quickly as possible a 'super-bomb' based on the fusion – not fission – of uranium atoms, to counter Russia's new atomic parity. A hydrogen bomb would be even bigger and more destructive than those that had brought destruction to Hiroshima and Nagasaki. The very first atomic test at Alamogordo in the New Mexican desert had in fact been a plutonium device (the key to a hydrogen bomb), so the scientists knew that it could be done. While the American Committee of Atomic Scientists argued among themselves, and Oppenheimer's team talked earnestly of 'limiting totality of war and thus eliminating the fear, whilst raising the hopes of mankind', more robust souls argued strongly for continued nuclear development. Teller wrote in his minority report: 'Those who oppose the development of the hydrogen bomb are behaving like ostriches if they really believe that they are going to promote world peace.' Eventually an irritated President Truman put a stop to the scientists' wrangling and ordered the National Security Council to develop the 'super-bomb'. The US could compete in any arms race with the Soviets. America raised the stakes. A lethal game of nuclear poker had begun.

Stalin's friends in Washington soon alerted him to this new threat. As usual, Beria and the NKVD/KGB turned to their friends and agents in the west to do all they could to undermine this new development. Moscow spymasters dusted off their old files on western fellow travellers with a view to slowing down and obstructing any western nuclear developments, 'in the interests of peace', naturally.

Soviet agents of influence were ordered to infiltrate peace movements in the west and promote anti-nuclear activity. For example, in Britain, the pre-war Peace Pledge Union was re-mobilized for the first Hiroshima Day in 1950 and the British Communist Party was instructed to discreetly influence the British Peace Committee, using it as a front for Kremlin subversion and propaganda. Stalin's fellow travellers rushed to oblige their master in Moscow.

But Truman had been influenced in his decision to build a hydrogen bomb by two other developments that, when added to the Soviet threat, began to look suspiciously like a communist campaign for world expansion. In October 1949, Mao Tse-tung's communist Chinese had established their People's Republic in the world's most populous nation; and on 25 June 1950, North Korean communist forces invaded South Korea.

The communist takeover in China caught the US administration completely on the hop.

Roosevelt, who had armed and supported Chiang Kai-shek's nationalist Kuomintang forces against the invading Japanese during the war, regarded China as an ally. Following the surrender in August 1945, US aeroplanes had actually airlifted KMT units in an attempt to limit communist advances in the immediate post-war months. Roosevelt had even pushed for China – by which he meant Chiang Kai-shek's nationalists – to be one of the 'Four Global Policemen' with a permanent seat on the UN.

Unfortunately for the Americans, their policy was destabilized by Chiang Kai-shek himself, who, in an over-ambitious bid to snuff out the 'Red Menace' once and for all, turned his KMT forces against Mao's Liberation Army of Communists. At first all seemed to be going well, but Chiang over-extended himself and dispersed his forces. Tied down by Mao's guerrillas, the nationalists' Kuomintang army was gradually worn down during 1947. A year later Chiang's army fell apart following disastrous defeats in Manchuria and the north-eastern provinces.

By mid-1949 the KMT were everywhere in retreat and Mao's victorious Communists moved to seize power. By October 1949 it was all over. Chiang Kai-shek and the fragmented rump of his defeated army fled to the island of Formosa (Taiwan) and Mao Tse-tung's People's Liberation Army became masters of a new communist People's Republic of China. To make the new China's position crystal clear, China's new ruler proclaimed a policy of 'leaning to one side', formalized in early 1950 by a defence pact between the Communist Parties in Moscow and Beijing. There was now a Bamboo Curtain as well as the Iron one. American policy in the Far East was in tatters.

The debacle in China did not go unnoticed by that acute observer of communist affairs, George Kennan. In 1949 his State Department Planning Staff had expressed concern for the region, writing, 'The area is the target of a coordinated offensive by the Kremlin.' To dedicated anti-Marxists like Kennan, worldwide communism was monolithic. The Comintern and the 1920s still cast a long shadow.

While we now know that this was not entirely true, Ken-

nan's staff cannot be faulted for their views because at the time
it looked as if virtually every country in Southeast Asia was
vulnerable to a communist takeover as European empires there
collapsed. The French were bogged down against Ho Chi
Minh in Indochina; an attempted communist rebellion in Java
and the Dutch East Indies had been suppressed only with
difficulty; and in Malaya the British were struggling to contain
a Marxist guerrilla insurgency. Overshadowing all was the
victory of Mao's communism and the establishment of the
PRC, which seemed to offer a simple blueprint for wars of
national liberation and peasant uprisings everywhere. To
western strategists in the late 1940s, it looked very much as
if the dominoes were falling one by one before a coordinated
communist onslaught. It really did seem to Washington that, if
they failed to act, communism would triumph throughout the
region. Two days after the North Korean invasion of South
Korea, American policy suddenly displayed itself once more as
implacably opposed to any more communist expansion in
Asia. On 27 June 1950 a US battle fleet sailed to block the
straits between Formosa and mainland China, and US forces
were fully committed to defending their South Korean allies
against the communist invasion.

In Korea the Cold War had suddenly become a hot war.

Korea had been left high and dry after the Japanese surrender
of their colony in 1945. The Yalta Conference had agreed to
divide the country into US and USSR zones – rather like post-
war Germany – and the 38th parallel had been chosen off the
map as an arbitrary demarcation line between the two. As with
Germany, both sides sought to stamp their respective systems
on their new clients. The indigenous inhabitants in many cases
objected to being told what to do by their new overlords, and
both the US and the USSR found it necessary to suppress

nationalist dissent. In the north the Red Army put down anti-communist uprisings with their usual crude efficiency. In the south the Americans imposed a strict control over political life and manoeuvred a pro-western moderate legislature into power. Divisions between the two halves of Korea became increasingly wide. Things came to a head when a UN commission visited the peninsula in May 1948 to oversee free elections. The communist North refused to accept external observers and Syngman Rhee was elected President in the South. In view of the electoral vacuum in the North, the UN then recognized the southern regime as the lawful government of *all* Korea. North Korea swiftly retaliated by declaring a 'Democratic People's Republic', which in its turn claimed suzerainty over the whole country. Korea stayed divided.

The final catalyst for conflict was North Korea's communist leader Kim Il Sung. We now know (thanks to Khrushchev) that Kim actually sought permission from Stalin before ordering the attack on South Korea. We also know that the last thing that the cautious Man of Steel in the Kremlin wanted was an open showdown with a nuclear-armed USA. Stalin in his turn hedged his bets by consulting his fellow Communist in the region, Mao Tse-tung. Both finally gave the green light to Kim Il Sung for his surprise attack, believing his assurances that a short sharp war could conquer South Korea without American retaliation. A unified communist Korea seemed an achievable goal. Having now got permission to fight from his communist masters, Kim prepared for the first overt communist challenge directly against western interests by means of a shooting war.

The west's response to the invasion, however, confounded both Moscow and Beijing. The US lost no time in pressing the UN for action, quoting the pre-war League of Nations' failure to act against aggressors as the principal cause of the Second World War. President Truman sincerely believed that if the

aggression was not stopped in its tracks the world faced a third
world war. The 'unprovoked attack had to be stopped to
ensure international peace'. An untried UN endorsed this view
and, crucially, authorized UN forces to help the South Koreans
– now in serious danger of being over-run – and defeat the
aggressors in an armed demonstration of collective security.
The UN's decision to mount a 'police action' was made much
easier by the absence of any Russian veto. (Stalin had unwisely
withdrawn Malik, the USSR's UN representative, as a symbol
of his boycott of the UN because communist China was not
represented.) Britain, Australia, Turkey and ten other nations
eventually sent contingents.

Within three days, more than 90,000 North Koreans had
captured the South Korean capital of Seoul and were driving
south. Truman ordered US aircraft to harry the North Korean
invaders from the air to try and slow the communist advance,
while on the ground the first US forces were hastily committed
to the battle direct from Japan. At a hastily improvised road-
block near Osan the Americans' lightly equipped Task Force
Smith had its first bruising encounter with the North Korean
army's T-34/85 tanks. To the GIs' horror their bazooka and
anti-tank rounds literally bounced off the well-armoured Soviet vehicles. The baffled and outnumbered Americans were
forced to retreat to survive.

Inadequately armed, continually outflanked and vastly outnumbered, the US Army suffered a series of humiliating defeats
as, with their Republic of Korea (ROK) allies, they were driven
back into a last-ditch defensive position around Pusan in the
very south-east of the peninsula. From the perimeter of this
100 x 30-mile enclave, weary South Koreans and shocked
Americans looked out on the all-encircling invaders spoiling
for the final assault. Everywhere else, Kim's communist forces
ruled. Unthinkably, defeat in Korea looked like the outcome of

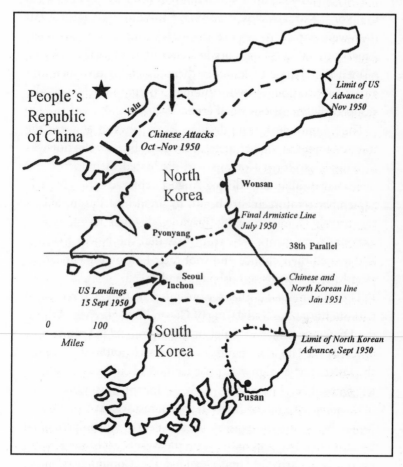

The Cold War turns hot: Korea, 1950–3

the first open shooting war between east and west. A communist victory seemed assured.

Only airpower and a shrinking perimeter saved Pusan. As the North Koreans closed in for the kill during August 1950 they were forced to expose themselves and mass into what Americans call a 'target enriched environment'. This gave the airmen the chance to hammer their targets in the open and airpower, combined with limited counter-attacks, finally stopped the victorious northerners.

The Communists now decided to dig in and squeeze the trapped forces in the perimeter. However, by now the tide was turning. The North Koreans had dissipated their forces and their piecemeal attacks during August achieved little. By early September reinforcements began to flood into Pusan, led by the British Commonwealth Brigade, the first of many UN national contingents. The truth was that the North Koreans had missed their chance and shot their bolt by the end of the month. Kim's surprise onslaught had failed.

They had made another serious mistake: they had reckoned without the genius and daring of General Douglas MacArthur, the US Commander-in-Chief in the region. MacArthur, now officially the UN Commander, was an arrogant and conceited showman but a highly experienced, bold and above all intelligent soldier. His counter-stroke at Inchon must rank as one of the most inspired counter-attacks in history. At dawn on 15 September 1950 an invasion fleet of nearly 300 ships landed US amphibious forces halfway up the west coast of the Korean peninsula, nearly 200 miles behind the Communists' main battle lines. MacArthur's decisive boldness achieved complete strategic and tactical surprise. It could have won the Korean War. By the evening of D Day 13,000 US Marines and support troops were driving ashore and pushing deep inland. A tactical airfield was quickly set up by engineers as only the US knows how and US ground attack aircraft began drenching the counter-attacking enemy T-34 tanks with napalm. By 29 September Seoul was recaptured by US and South Korean forces in savage house-to-house fighting to winkle out the last-ditch communist snipers. The North Korean forces, dug in around Pusan 150 miles to the south, had been taken in flank and rear as the US-UN divisions drove to seal off Korea from west to east. The invaders were completely cut off. Surrounded, running out of supplies and ammunition, under attack by advancing US forces out of the Pusan perimeter and harried from the air, the panicked North Koreans broke and fled. North Korea's invasion of the South collapsed in ignominious flight or surrender.

By early October, MacArthur's victorious US troops had crossed the 38th parallel and advanced north in hot pursuit of the defeated North Koreans. On 19 October Kim's capital, Pyongyang, fell to the UN and MacArthur ordered a general advance north to the Chinese border on the Yalu River to occupy the whole Korean peninsula.

MacArthur's victory had, however, roused anxieties among North Korea's discomfited communist backers. His triumphant advance had awoken the sleeping dragon. While Stalin remained adamant that the USSR should stay out of any direct confrontation with the west, Mao had more pressing concerns: the US-UN forces were advancing dangerously close to Chinese territory. Moreover, a complete North Korean defeat would send the wrong signal about China to other Communists in the region. By mid-October, we now know, Mao had already taken the decision to intervene if necessary to warn off the US-UN forces. On 25 October he ordered a token unit of 'volunteers' over the Yalu to engage the Americans and signal China's intentions. The Chinese came out of the hills, pasted an isolated American unit, then faded back into the hills as suddenly as they had arrived. The American 6th Division correctly identified their new opponents as 'Chinese communist forces' and reported this ominous development.

More warnings trickled up the US staff chain: on 8 November, B-29s bombing the Yalu River bridges were attacked. One of the attacking aircraft was a MiG 15 jet fighter. Yet, despite this clear evidence of Chinese involvement, the US intelligence staff ignored the warning. The war was as good as over in many American minds. But the truth was that MacArthur had over-reached himself when he ordered the general advance to the Yalu. Victory had seemed only a matter of time. 'Home for Christmas!' was the US motto. But the triumphant American force was running into a gigantic trap. On 26 November, more than 350,000 'volunteers' of the People's Liberation Army struck back across the Chinese border.

Within six weeks all the UN's gains had been wiped out as the outnumbered and overwhelmed US forces suffered a serious mauling at the hands of the PLA. Their lines shattered and suffering heavy losses, over-extended US divisions once again went into what was described as 'bugout mode'. MacArthur's forces were driven back in a long and bloody retreat in conditions reminiscent of Sir John Moore's epic 1809 retreat to Corunna. At Kunu Ri the whole US rearguard division was caught in a classic ambush by Chinese forces in the hills overlooking the road and barely escaped with their lives. All their vehicles and equipment were captured and the 2nd Division lost over 3,000 men; they were virtually wiped out by the Chinese.

Now the Chinese and North Koreans again flooded south. Northern forces re-occupied Seoul, the South Korean capital, and at one point looked unstoppable. The massive communist Christmas onslaught shocked the Americans and the UN allies alike. Only airpower, lack of supplies and low mobility finally wore down the Chinese advance. As January wore on, what the communists failed to do, the hardships of the Korean winter completed for both sides as ill-prepared American, British, Korean and Chinese soldiers froze to death in semi-Siberian conditions. The fighting petered out. The arrival of the charismatic Matthew Ridgeway as the US Commander on the ground in January turned the situation round for the UN; but the stark fact was that by March 1951 both sides were digging trenches where it had all started, along the 38th parallel. The Korean War had reached stalemate.

Having succeeded so spectacularly in military terms, the flamboyant MacArthur now over-reached himself politically. In the words of a US news reporter 'the sonovabitch just got too big for his britches'. As the Chinese continued their attacks in early 1951, he proposed raising the stakes and calling for a risky escalation of the war. In public he advocated that the Taiwanese Chinese nationalists should attack mainland China and that the US fleet should blockade the Chinese coast. More dangerously, he called for a free hand to bomb the Communists' bases north of the Yalu in mainland China. While militarily this might have made sense, politically it was a disastrous notion. Whatever MacArthur's regional obsessions (he had been effectively acting with almost plenipotentiary authority in the Far East since 1945, and clearly believed he was above Washington's control), his proposals ignored America's real strategic aims, however much military sense they made. Washington told MacArthur to shut up. The President himself warned his Viceroy in Japan not to publicly dissent from US government policy again and to toe the administration's line.

MacArthur, seemingly believing himself unsackable by a mere president or chiefs of staff, ignored orders and openly called again for the bombing of mainland China, with atom bombs if need be. This time Truman sacked his arrogant

Commander-in-chief on the spot. Korea was a limited war, and it would stay that way; the President said so in a famous address to the American people on 11 April 1951, the day he relieved his famous general of his command. Spelling out the core of US Cold War policy, he said:

> What we are doing in Korea is to *prevent* a third world war . . . We do not want to see the war in Korea extended. We are trying to prevent a world war – not start one . . . But you may ask: why can't we take other steps to punish the aggressor? . . . bomb China itself? . . . If we do these things we would be running a very grave risk of starting a general war . . . And what would suit the ambitions of the Kremlin better than to have our military forces committed to a full scale war with Red China?

The stunned 'American Caesar' came back from Asia to parades and public adulation. But his rueful final address to a joint sitting of Congress only served to emphasize the importance of political primacy over mere soldiers. Clausewitz would have approved.

The events of 1950, and those which had led up to the armed clash between east and west, now crystallized strategic thought in Washington. All doubts – and any hope of peaceful post-war co-existence with the Soviets – were finally swept away. Acknowledgement of the new geo-strategic reality was encapsulated in Truman's National Security Council Policy Paper 68 of 1950, which stated baldly:

> . . . within the past thirty-five years the world has experienced two wars of tremendous violence . . . two revolutions – the Russian and the Chinese – of extreme scope and intensity . . . the collapse of five empires – the Ottoman, the Austro-Hun-

garian, German, Italian and Japanese – and the drastic decline
of two major imperial systems, the British and the French . . .

The paper went on to address America's global aims in the face
of a world dominated by two 'continental sized superpowers',
the USSR and the USA. NSC 68/50 was to become effectively
the blueprint for the next thirty years.

During the spring of 1951 another development occurred,
unique in the history of the Cold War. The air war in the north,
and particularly along 'MiG Alley' on the Yalu River, began to
hot up. The communist air attacks on US aircraft became
increasingly aggressive. Swarms of the latest Soviet MiG 15s
pounced on the slower American F-80s and F-84s. These new
MiG jets were heavily armed, fast and manoeuvrable. They
should have been – they were powered by a version of the
latest Rolls Royce jet engine which the Attlee government had
unwisely given free to the Soviets 'to improve trade relations'.
F-86 Sabres engaged these new attackers and it was noted that
some of the MiGs were quite clearly flown by more experienced and better trained pilots than their usual run of adversaries. Nicknamed 'Honchos', these better-flown MiGs baffled
the US Air Force pilots. But not their signals intelligence
officers, because they knew that the Honchos were talking
to each other and their ground controllers in *Russian*.

In fact, the Red Air Force had drafted in a team of Second
World War fighter aces to try and match the USAF's air
superiority over Korea. It was the only time in the whole of
the Cold War that the US and Soviets ever engaged in pro-
tracted open combat. The deadly secret was kept. Although
USAF aircrew were suspicious at the time, the Pentagon denied
any direct Russian involvement and the Kremlin said nothing,
while the USA and USSR battled it out at 30,000 feet in the icy
skies over North Korea. The aerial confrontation became more

and more savage. On 23 October 1951, a force of over 100 MiGs swooped on a half-squadron of B-29 heavy bombers heading for the communists' new airfield construction in the North. The F-86 escort was completely outnumbered and nearly 50 MiGs broke through to hit the bombers. Five went down. By the end of the month the USAF had lost 13 B-29s and the Superfortress was withdrawn from day bombing, escorted or not.

Confirmation of this deadly secret duel only emerged after the collapse of communism. Kremlin records show conclusively that from spring 1951 onwards no fewer than twenty-four Russian Air Force fighter regiments were rotated through Korea to 'gain experience'. The pilots were given Chinese uniforms and taught 200 words of basic Chinese to complete the fiction. In the end, however, it was the fighter pilots of the USAF who won the secret aerial war over Korea with a 6:1 kill ratio over the MiG 15s. Many of the downed MiGs were piloted by Russians.

Despite a huge offensive by over 400,000 North Korean and Chinese in April 1951, the UN lines held – thanks partly to a spirited defence by the British on the Imjin – and both sides settled down to the rituals of trench warfare. In such a stalemate UN technical superiority came into its own. Huge artillery barrages, reminiscent of 1914–18, destroyed any Chinese attacks. Such 'meatgrinder' tactics were reflected by American air superiority as the allied bomber offensive dropped over 600,000 tons of bombs on the North to try and smash it into submission. Ironically this pounding from the air had the effect of actually *strengthening* Northern morale. In an echo of the Berliners' defiant graffiti during the Second World War ('our walls may break, but our hearts will not'), Kim Il Sung actually rallied his North Koreans to be proud of their resilience in the face of 'Yankee terror bombing'. It was a powerful lesson and a forecast of the limitations of air power. The USAF would have done well to heed it for the future. We now know that wars cannot be won by airpower alone.

By the autumn of 1951, it was clear that the war in Korea was going nowhere. The Communists' invasion to seize the South had failed. MacArthur's drive to the Yalu to unify Korea by invading the North had failed. Politically and geographically, there were no gains to be made by either side. The peace talks at Panmunjon ground on for another two years, to no avail.

Ironically, it was something akin to MacArthur's recommended strategy that helped to end the conflict. In 1952 Dwight D. Eisenhower was elected US President.

Like so many American presidents before and since, Eisenhower's simple 'country boy' image masked a military and political operator at the highest level. A professional army officer before the Second World War, he had endured the boredom of peacetime garrison life and had slowly climbed the ladder of promotion, winning good reports from, among others, Douglas MacArthur. By 1942 Eisenhower was working direct to General Marshall, the US Army Chief of Staff, who formed the view that 'Ike' was a clever, hardworking officer, with unusual patience and diplomatic skills. The 52-year-old Eisenhower found himself, to his own (and many others') astonishment, appointed by Marshall as overall Allied Commander of Operation Overlord. As the Supreme Allied Commander in the west, he confirmed the 'people skills' he had demonstrated as commander of the Torch landings in North Africa. He possessed a sharp intelligence, an ability to smooth out any bickering between allies, and the firmness and tact required to harness a multi-national team of strong-minded senior officers to do his political masters' bidding. He insisted on 'unified command', accepted responsibility, and had proved himself an outstanding leader at the highest military levels. It was as good a training for a US President as any and he had avoided the messy and damaging compromises that went with long service on Capitol Hill. Eisenhower owed nobody anything.

Comparisons with his old boss, MacArthur, are inevitable. Eisenhower had the same drive, grace and charm to make a coalition work. Yet he was a more politically aware figure than MacArthur, the 'American Caesar', could ever be. Above all, 'Ike' knew the Soviets, his late allies in war and now his opponents in peace. As President, Eisenhower had the experience and skills to lead his country at a critical moment in its history. He also had the flexibility to know when – and how – to cut a deal for survival. He would prove a worthy Cold War foe for the Kremlin.

Seeing no signs of progress, and determined to bring the boys home, America's new President raised the stakes for the Chinese, threatening action against mainland China and ostentatiously moving nuclear weapons into the region. Moreover, the war in Korea was also hurting China in terms of both money and manpower. In just one wave of abortive attacks in June 1953, three Chinese armies launched a massive attack on well-defended UN positions with trench lines of 1914–18 depth and complexity. They were swiftly stopped by a massive and sustained barrage of 2.7 million artillery shells and suffered over 100,000 casualties for no tangible result. Even the Chinese could not continue to take losses on this scale. China's primitive peasant economy was buckling under the cost of the war. Over 450,000 Chinese 'volunteers' had died in the fighting so far, plus 2 million North Korean soldiers; and every bullet and truck supplied by the USSR had had to be paid for in hard cash. 'What price Chinese blood?' Mao is alleged to have grumbled to Stalin. Stalin shrugged and went on taking Beijing's money. Sino–Soviet relations cooled.

But by the early summer of 1953 Stalin was dead and the Kremlin in disarray. With no prospect of any progress, communist will cracked. On 27 July 1953 an armistice was signed. Neither side could claim victory.

However, the Korean War did change the Cold War landscape. It institutionalized it even more; it encouraged the continuation of an arms race, and it raised the worst case spectres of a 'nuclear Pearl Harbor' and a 'Korean War in Europe' in the minds of politicians, press and public, let alone the ever-alarmist military. However, there were some beneficial side effects too. The US and its allies could claim that they had resisted communist aggression in the region and had 'contained China'. The UN had shown that, unlike the League of Nations, it had teeth and had 'saved' Korea. China could take credit in the communist bloc for standing up boldly to the imperialist-capitalist aggressors. Taiwan now had guaranteed American defence. The Japanese economy had boomed.

The only losers were the Korean people, in both North and South. Over 5 million Koreans had been killed or maimed for no discernible purpose.

Kim's Korean adventure had been futile. We still live with the consequences.

9

DEATH OF THE ICE BEAR

EXIT STALIN

By the time of Stalin's death on 5 March 1953, the world had come a long way in eight short years.

From the ashes of 1945 a new West Germany based on the British and American zones was showing all the signs of becoming a new nation, both politically and economically. Across the Elbe, East Germany and the rest of eastern Europe remained under their conqueror's heel militarily, politically and economically. Two competing power blocs had crystallized to confront one another: Soviet and western policies were at loggerheads everywhere, and now both sides of this confrontation had the atomic bomb.

The death of the 'Father of the Russian People' had a major impact not just inside the USSR but worldwide. Stalin's reign of terror had returned in the last years. In 1951 he had been heard to mutter enigmatically, 'I don't trust anyone. Anyone. Not even myself.' Visitors reported him as distracted, endlessly doodling sharp-fanged wolves on his blotter. He suffered dizzy spells and nervous doctors tried to treat him. Everywhere, the dark soul of the old bloodstained tyrant saw traitors and plots. After his death his successor, Nikita Khrushchev, reported that the old man had been genuinely terrified that the US would attack the USSR. 'When I'm gone, the Imperialist powers will wring your necks like chickens,' he is supposed to have told the Politburo, and in 1951 he had summoned the leaders of eastern Europe to the Kremlin to prepare them for war. As 1952 wore on, those around Stalin had begun to feel ever more nervous. Signs of new terrors to come abounded as the morose dictator began to threaten his closest aides of thirty years.

**A Cold War cartoon of 1952 showing the
Soviet view of the division of Germany**
(Unknown artist, published in *Krokodil*, June 1952)

Whether as a consequence of Stalin's re-awoken fears or as a pragmatic policy to soothe an increasingly alarmed and confrontational west, the USSR's external relations and policies appeared to mellow in Stalin's last two years as he himself became more withdrawn and even more suspicious. Discreet indications were leaked to the west that the USSR would look favourably on moves to end the stalemate in Korea. Most important of all, in March 1952 the Kremlin proposed a new re-unified Germany. It could even be re-armed, said the Russians, provided that it was declared a neutral state. Stalin also hinted that he would consider a summit with President Eisenhower. In Britain such moves found an echo in Churchill's thinking. In one of his first statements to the House of Commons after being re-elected he had told them that he and Britain's Foreign Secretary Anthony Eden were:

> committed to the idea of a supreme effort to bridge the gulf between the two worlds so that each of us can live its life, if not in friendship, at least without the fear, the hatreds, and the frightful waste of the Cold War.

Churchill hoped that once again the memories of Yalta and Potsdam might be mobilized in the cause of international harmony. Those two conferences had recognized the realities on the ground of Germany's defeat in eastern Europe. Perhaps now there was a chance to move the process forward at last and find some end to the seemingly intractable armed stand-off between east and west. They should at least talk to Stalin. But such Kremlin overtures were not always welcome in western chancelleries. Washington, in particular, was suspicious and saw them as mischief-making designed to derail western plans for Germany or a Soviet diplomatic trick to buy time. But some senior US and UK policy makers felt that the Soviet line might really be softening. Eden, an experienced Foreign Secretary, wrote, 'this could be a serious, but very dangerous, attempt to settle the German question . . .'

No one will ever know Stalin's intentions for sure.

The old man was by now half senile and very deaf. Although his cunning and his grip on all power still stayed as strong as ever, in Politburo meetings he would ramble, his mind straying back to Lenin and distant memories of the glory days of the 1920s. Most of the time he sat morosely silent, glowering at his supposed colleagues and advisors. As Stalin's paranoia grew, his manner became increasingly threatening even to Beria, his Chief of Secret Police. Occasionally he muttered dark threats about plots. His doctors were suddenly arrested on the baseless grounds that they were poisoning Comrade Stalin. As the consultants and professors were mainly of Jewish extraction, *Pravda* named it a 'Jewish doctors' plot'. The chief interrogator of the wretched Jewish medics now languishing in the bowels of the Lubyanka was told to extract confessions from his innocent victims or literally 'lose his head'. To those who remembered them it looked like the beginning of a return to the terror-filled days of the 1930s, with their purges and show trials. Those closest to him trembled at the dictator's whims. Who could feel safe?

Nature – or an assassin – put an end to their fears.

On 1 March 1953 Stalin appears to have suffered a stroke at his dacha. The anxious Praetorian guards of the MVD-KGB were too frightened to wake 'the Boss' next morning or even to enter the Great Man's bedroom. By mid-day the domestic staff became worried. All day on 2 March Stalin stayed in his room unattended and alone, while his terrified personal staff whispered outside. Eventually, at 11.30 p.m., the duty KGB Special Attachment officer was deputed to knock and enter on the pretext of bringing 'urgent correspondence'. He found the Man of Steel on the floor paralysed, dribbling and unable to speak. The Red Czar had been lying for hours in a pool of his own urine. Panic-stricken, the staff placed him on a couch and promptly sent for the Chief of the Secret Police rather than a doctor. In dictatorships such inhumane priorities seem normal at times of crisis.

Beria was eventually run to earth in his latest mistress's arms. He rushed to Stalin's dacha, where he found Georgi Malenkov, incongruously clutching his new shoes under his arm, 'in case they squeaked' and disturbed their master. Quaking, the two men tiptoed in, to meet the furious glare of their mute and paralysed leader. They fled. Outside the door, to Malenkov's astonishment, Beria calmly told the staff that 'It's all right. Comrade Stalin is sleeping – everyone can stand down.' They disappeared to their beds, puzzled by this extraordinary turn of events. Stalin was left alone again, with his natural heir standing guard. Did Beria act as Caligula to Stalin's Tiberius and finish the vengeful old despot off? We will never know.

This bizarre state of affairs continued until 9.00 a.m. the following day. By the time the doctors were finally called in, the old man had been semi-paralysed and in a coma for at least nineteen hours and possibly much longer. A strutting Beria now dictated events, warning the frightened medical team that their lives depended on Stalin's survival. But by now Stalin was past medical care. He lay comatose on a couch surrounded by an exhausted group of doctors and key members of the Politburo. Occasionally he would show some spark of life and glare at the whispering group around him, who swiftly composed themselves into suitably obsequious poses of respect and muttered the usual sycophancies. It was to no avail. The old man gradually sank into unconsciousness. The vigil continued all night, broken only by the arrival of his drunken son shouting, 'You've killed my father, you bastards!' before he was quickly hustled away.

The old tyrant finally breathed his last on the evening of 5 March 1953. A shattered Politburo dispersed to come to terms with the succession and the consequences of Stalin's passing. The dictator who had guided Russia for quarter of a century, and ensured that the Cold War became a reality, had gone. All Russia was stunned when the news broke. Strong men and war veterans wept openly in the streets, crying, 'What shall we do now?' Even more astonishingly, prisoners in the Gulag actually broke down and mourned their chief tormentor's demise. In the west, hurriedly convened conferences debated the same question. The chief architect of Russia's long hostility to the west, the builder of the system that had brought bloodshed and misery to millions, had gone forever. Who would fill the vacuum? And what would it mean? Could the USSR and the west now end their Cold War?

Within a month the dam burst inside the USSR. As Stalin's powers were shared out among the Politburo to prevent another over-concentration of power, new policies emerged. Georgi Malenkov called for new discussions with the west, saying, 'There is no disputed or unsolved question which cannot be settled by peaceful means . . .'

It looked as if a new era was dawning.

Key parts of the Stalinist repressive mechanism were dismantled. Beria was arrested, allegedly by a pistol-wielding Marshal Zhukov during a cabinet meeting, and tried by a secret kangaroo court of his frightened Politburo colleagues. The ambitious secret police chief was despatched as he had despatched so many of his victims during his long reign as Stalin's enforcer: gagged, protesting his innocence, and with a bullet into the forehead to shut him up for good. The new collective leadership of the Communist Party meted out equally summary justice to the others involved in framing the victims of Stalin's last purges. The hapless Kremlin doctors were quickly released from their torture cells and the 'Jewish doctors' plot' exposed in *Pravda* as a lie and a fabrication of the secret police.

In the north and in Siberia hundreds and thousands of prisoners were quietly released from the Gulag to return home. The dictator's brutal and drunken son, Vasily, was found guilty of misappropriation of state funds and dismissed from his post as an Air Force general. Everything now depended on the USSR's new policy line towards the west: and, perhaps more importantly, the west's reaction to any olive branches offered by Stalin's heirs.

Malenkov emerged as *primus inter pares* in a new collective leadership. He had built a reputation as a practical manager rather than a committed political ideologue. By the summer of 1953 he could point to a series of Soviet initiatives that boded well for east-west 'co-existence', as he put it: the Korean armistice, cooperation at the UN, and new talks with Turkey and Iran to solve regional disputes. Russia's milder new leader now looked to the west for a constructive response.

Churchill was the principal advocate of some kind of rapprochement to end the Cold War arms race between east and west (his famous 'Jaw-jaw is better than war-war' dates from this period). Now Europe's eldest statesman advocated early cooperation with Russia's new leadership to hammer out a final settlement over Germany and to offer confidence-building measures to ease Soviet fears of an aggressive NATO. However, events in eastern Europe and suspicions in both Washington and Moscow meant that Churchill's efforts to support Eisenhower's initial call to 'give peace a chance' were to come to nought. The hard-nosed men in Washington and the US media were not really interested in rapprochement in 1954. For them, communist weakness clearly spelled an American opportunity and America was not only the dominant

A 1955 view of the arms race
(Victor Weisz, published in the *Daily Mirror*, 21 March 1955)

power but unwilling to listen to advice from mere Britons, however eminent. Britain no longer sat at the top table. Truman and Eisenhower had long ago repudiated Roosevelt's and Churchill's wartime agreement to cooperate in the nuclear field, and relations between Washington and London were cool. By the end of 1954 Eisenhower and John Foster Dulles had openly spurned Churchill's suggestions to embark on their own policy of brinkmanship with the USSR.

Despite changes in the Kremlin, the Cold War was going to continue.

10

THE PEOPLE SPEAK

IDEOLOGY AND PROPAGANDA

The new, seemingly softer, line from the Kremlin was greeted not just by suspicion in the west but by a very real fear of disorder in the east. Sudden changes make dictators very nervous. With their great leader and protector now safely embalmed in the Kremlin wall, many of the hardline communist leaders in the satellite states suddenly felt vulnerable. Dictatorships and police states seem surprisingly safe, provided everyone toes the line.

No single eastern bloc leader appears to have felt as vulnerable as Walter Ulbricht, the arch-communist dictator of the East German Soviet zone. He had spent the war in Moscow and was arguably the most Stalinist of all the eastern party leaders. On Stalin's death, this insecure Stalinist 'sub-contractor' decided to enforce new 'work norms' and to crack down on dissent to show that, Stalin dead or not, he and the Party were still in charge.

The results of such traditional communist 'labour relations' were predictable. In a fury of outrage, the 'oppressed workers' rose against their 'employer' – the East German Communist Party. Hundreds of thousands of East Germans took to the streets to demand less work for more money in the time-honoured manner of trade unions everywhere. The difference was that the workers of the workers' paradise had some really serious grievances against the Party. Ominously, they also demanded free elections. Order broke down, factories emptied, and unofficial workers' committees challenged their Party bosses.

The reaction of the East German communist state was equally predictable. Within days Soviet tanks were patrolling the streets. Striking workers were gunned down by the militia and the secret police enjoyed an orgy of arresting strike-leaders and other 'enemies of the state'. To the Kremlin's alarm, the wave of unrest swept across the Soviet empire. Czechoslovakia erupted in rioting and even, astonishingly, political prisoners in Siberia went on strike. The uneasy triumvirate who had inherited Stalin's crown, Molotov, Malenkov and Khrushchev, had firm ideas about such anti-Party shenanigans. They moved swiftly to snuff out any anti-communist dissent. A firm line was obviously required. Moscow and the Communist Party everywhere clamped down hard. The brief thaw was over.

The Americans in their turn contributed to the continuing hostility between east and west. The new President Eisenhower, spurred on by his hard-line anti-communist Secretary of State John Foster Dulles, moved from a policy of 'containing' communism to one of 'rolling back' communism. With hindsight we can see that this was a missed opportunity, but at the time anti-communism was rife in the United States. The Red Menace had become a national obsession following the extraordinary saga of Alger Hiss's appearance before the House Un-American Activities Committee (HUAC) in 1948. Hiss was an east coast Ivy League lawyer who had worked for both the White House and the State Department under Roosevelt. Questioned for the HUAC by an ambitious young lawyer called Richard Nixon, under pressure Hiss eventually revealed that he had spied for the USSR. He went to a Federal penitentiary for four years.

The Hiss case was not the only reason for good Americans to fear communist infiltration. From the spying revelations of the KGB Archive we now know that many of America's fears were only too justified. Although they didn't know it at the time, Americans had many open and public reasons to be suspicious of communist infiltration from the late 1940s on. Given the trial of Ethel and Julius Rosenberg (atom spies who had gone to the electric chair for betraying nuclear secrets to the Russians), Stalin's sabre-rattling over Berlin, the revelation that Klaus Fuchs had given Britain's nuclear plans directly to the NKVD-KGB, and the detonation of the first Russian atomic bomb, it was hardly surprising that a surge of nervousness infected American society with a very real fear of 'Reds under the bed'. Communist agents and their sympathizers seemed to be everywhere. For many Americans, as for many Europeans of the right, 'anti-communism' became an easy slogan for explaining the troubled world in which they now lived and for understanding the complexities of foreign affairs. Anti-communism seemed to offer a simple solution to many of the world's ills. Ambitious political opportunists moved to cash in on this new wave of popular feeling.

Chief among these were the Director of the FBI, J. Edgar Hoover – ever-anxious to increase his power and puff up his agency's budget – and an obscure senator called Joe McCarthy. Hoover contributed directly to the Red Spy fever sweeping the USA in a public statement:

> Communism is in reality not a political party. It is a way of life,
> an evil and malignant way of life. It reveals a condition akin to
> a disease that spreads like an epidemic, and like an epidemic. A
> quarantine is necessary to keep it from infecting this nation . . .

McCarthy was, however, the real catalyst and promoter of
the extraordinary panic, sometimes amounting to a psychosis, that overcame many sensible Americans in the late 1940s
and early 1950s. At the beginning of 1950 McCarthy had
been looking for a headline-grabbing issue for his re-election
campaign. Now out of power for twenty years, Republicans
were desperate for votes. Someone suggested: 'How about
going for the Commies, Senator? That'll git you on the
news . . .' The equation was simple: left-wingers equalled
closet Communists. Communism equalled un-Americanism.
Were the Reds not threatening the nation's very existence?
The idea was simple, media-savvy, and wholly dishonest.
McCarthy went for it.

Overnight McCarthy became a fervent and very public anti-
communist. Everywhere he looked, he claimed, Communists
were undermining US life 'like cockroaches'. Suddenly the
lacklustre and semi-alcoholic senator was a national figure,
his campaign supported alike by Republicans anxious to get
back into power, big business and scared Middle Americans.
The media cooperated enthusiastically with the frenzy. Cardinal Spellman of New York publicly urged Americans to hunt
down 'the Communist enemy within'.

In vain did the incumbent Democrat President Truman try
to dismiss McCarthy's attacks:

> Not a single person who has been judged to be a Communist or
> otherwise disloyal remains on the Government payroll
> today . . . We are not going to turn the United States into a

right wing totalitarian country in order to deal with a left wing
totalitarian threat . . .

In vain, and too late. Scenting a chance for the Republican
Party to discredit the Democrats and win votes, Senator
John Rankin, a Mississippi racist bigot of the worst stamp,
co-opted McCarthy to join his Un-American Affairs Committee. (Shortly after he had discovered his new cause, a
female admirer asked McCarthy how long he had been an
anti-communist crusader. McCarthy winked and said,
'About two weeks, ma'am!') The Congress asked their
new Witchfinder General to 'ferret out those who threaten
the American way of life'. Armed with his new notoriety
and power, McCarthy went looking for 'Commies'. The
artistic community, and Hollywood in particular, became
his target.

Artists and writers have invariably been the most susceptible
to liberal ideas in any society. Change, novelty and provocative ideas have ever been the life-blood of the arts. It was
therefore hardly surprising that many of Hollywood's finest
had flirted with politically radical ideas at some stage. Within
two years half the American artistic/liberal establishment had
been blackened as communist fellow travellers (and thus
obviously traitors and anti-American) by being hauled before
the HUAC for what was effectively a televised show trial. The
other half was collecting information for the FBI on 'the Red
Menace in our midst' and informing on their colleagues to the
HUAC. McCarthy's bullying questioning at the HUAC gave
writers, artists and intellectuals an unenviable choice: to inform on their friends and colleagues in public, or to plead their
right to silence (guaranteed by the Constitution and the Bill of
Rights) but never work again. To many, the HUAC proceedings smacked of Stalin's show trials of the 1930s, albeit

without the bullet in the back of the head. It was decidedly not American democracy's finest hour.

Nonetheless, the stampede of anti-communist paranoia across America was very real. From 1947 to 1954 a kind of collective hysteria seems to have gripped its people. Using what the FBI later admitted were exactly the same methods as the KGB, Hoover went after the 'Commies'. It made him and the FBI look like 'big heroes'. Actors were hauled in and pilloried for alleged communist links or for the briefest youthful flirtation with Marxist ideas, and American informed on American in a way that was positively Orwellian. As in Ancient Rome, professional informers abounded. A paid informer called Harvey Mastow worked undercover for J. Edgar Hoover's FBI and the HUAC; he testified at 25 trials and over 180 investigations, and later admitted cheerfully that he had made most of his testimony up. 'It sure is a great racket,' he told a thoughtful House Committee of Investigation, '. . . being a professional witness for the Feds . . .'

Howard Hughes led the Hollywood witch-hunt to seek out the 'liberals, pinkoes and communists' preposterously supposed to be planning to overthrow the US government. Everyone was questioned. Ronald Reagan, at the time an actor and president of the Screen Actors Guild, said:

> There has been a small group within the Screen Actors Guild that has consistently opposed the policy of the Board of Officers, as evidenced by the vote on various issues. That small clique has been referred to – has been discussed – as more or less following the tactics we associate with the Communist party.

Decent men went to prison or into exile for refusing to testify before the Senate. A group called the Hollywood Ten defied the House Committee, demanding their constitutional rights and giving as good as they got. The following exchange between the courtroom interrogator and screenwriter John Howard Lawson catches the flavour of the times:

Q: Are you a member of the Communist Party?

A: It's unfortunate that I have to teach this committee the basic principles of Americanism . . .

Q: That's not the question. The question is, are you or have you ever been a member of the Communist Party?

A: I am framing my answer in the only way that an American citizen can . . . absolutely invades my privacy [sic] . . .

Q: Then you deny it? You refuse to answer the question? Is that correct?

A: I have already told you that I will offer my beliefs, my affiliations and anything else to the American public, and they will know where I stand as they do from what I have written . . .

Q: Stand away from the stand! Officer, take this man away . . .

The Hollywood Ten went to jail for contempt. Many other careers and reputations were destroyed overnight. Some even committed suicide.

Not everyone bent the knee. To his eternal credit, Gary Cooper, the star of *High Noon* (and the rightest of Republicans), flatly refused to allow his friend Carl Foreman, a noted socialist and sympathizer with left-wing causes, to be kicked off the film set. However, this was unusual. Eventually all the studio bosses, without exception, capitulated to the HUAC's open bullying. Anyone in Hollywood with the slightest accusation against them just did not work again. Even Gene Kelly, star of *Singin' in the Rain*, was blacklisted (he dared to give parties for liberal causes) and was only saved because Louis B. Mayer just had too much money invested in MGM's biggest star. The black singer Paul Robeson became a particular target. In 1949 he had dared to sing in Moscow. New York was less friendly on his return. A hostile crowd greeted him at a concert, jeering and chanting: 'Go home, Commie-loving nigger!', 'Go back to Russia!', 'Commies, Niggers, Jews, you got in but you won't get out.' And 'Hitler didn't finish the job, but we will!' Robeson was lucky to get out alive as the concert degenerated into a riot. Racial hatred and the politics of anti-communism had begun to merge. Robeson was black-listed and his right to a US passport removed.

Even such American icons as Edward G. Robinson, Walt Disney, Dorothy Parker and Danny Kaye fell under the deepest suspicion. An actor called John Garfield sarcastically informed the public in a radio broadcast that the HUAC had told him that 44 per cent of Broadway plays were supposed to be subversive. 'What next?' he asked his audience. 'Censorship?' He was promptly blacklisted. As the wave of hysteria mounted, libraries were told to check their shelves for 'subversive literature'. The US Information Service was accused of secretly holding dangerous, subversive books in its libraries. There were book-burning parties. Things got worse and worse. A man whistling the 'Internationale' in a lift was hauled in for questioning by the HUAC as a possible subversive. A fellow American had informed on him.

As the wave of anti-communist hysteria mounted, other politicians on Capitol Hill jumped on this vote-winning bandwagon. As ever in a democracy, where the people went their political leaders rushed to follow, in order to better lead them. The House put forward the McArran Bill, for the better regulation of the alleged 'enemy within'. This extraordinary measure proposed detention without trial for suspected subversive American citizens and would have given the Federal government the legal power to set up six concentration camps.

The First Amendment to the US Constitution seemed to count for nothing. President Truman refused to go along with the tide of political hysteria. He promptly vetoed the Bill, and was equally promptly vilified by the mob in the media and on Capitol Hill. In 1952 the would-be president General Eisenhower was able to beat his Democrat opponent with the stick of being 'soft on Communism'.

> The future of this country belongs to courageous men, it belongs to those who know that freedom's fight must be forever, relentless, uncompromising and fair. It belongs to men who today are ready to bear spiritual and intellectual arms against an alien army of communist ideas . . .

The nadir was reached in the spring of 1954, when McCarthy, trying to widen his net, dared to accuse Dean Acheson, the Secretary of State, of being a Communist. He then turned his attention to General George C. Marshall – Roosevelt's revered Chief of Staff of the Army – accusing him of being a 'secret communist', because he had supported the Red Army's plans in 1944–5! To his eternal shame, Eisenhower never denounced this *canard*, despite having once been Marshall's *protégé*. We now know from Herb Brownall, Eisenhower's Attorney General, that Ike detested McCarthy and all he stood for but was hampered in his dealings by the oldest political problem of all: he needed the votes. The new President's attitude was summed up in an aside to an aide: 'I'll not get into the gutter with these guys . . . in my experience these things usually take care of themselves.'

Instead it was left to the courteous Judge Walsh, Army Counsel at the 1954 hearings, who, hearing the drunken McCarthy's ever more wild accusations, turned on him scornfully during a live television broadcast and asked, 'Senator . . .

have you not done enough? Have you no sense of decency, sir, at long last? Have you left no sense of decency?' A stunned and befuddled McCarthy could not reply. It was a watershed moment. McCarthy's power collapsed as his fellow politicians fought to distance themselves from this embarrassing colleague.

A proposal for a Senate motion of censure soon followed, and shamefaced senators realized that McCarthy's personal witch-hunt risked bringing their great chamber into disrepute. His bubble burst, McCarthy sank back into the swamp of malevolent mediocrity from which he had emerged, never to be heard from again. He died in 1957 of chronic alcoholism. The Black List slowly faded out. Kirk Douglas led an open revolt against the studios by insisting that the blacklisted Stanley Kubrick's name appear in the title credits of *Spartacus*. And in a final delicious irony, J. Powell Thomas, the last Chairman of the HUAC, was jailed for corruption in Danbury Penitentiary – the very jail in which the Hollywood Ten had been incarcerated.

In arousing 'the Great Anti-Red Crusade' in the USA, Senator McCarthy had done great damage. The chance for rapprochement opened up by Stalin's death was lost. Faced with US voters' attitudes conditioned by the 'Red Menace', President Eisenhower had little choice but to reflect his voters' prejudices. Democracy is, after all, the will of the majority, however misguided, stupid or ignorant that majority might be.

At least America could find one crumb of comfort in the whole sorry saga of the McCarthy years. The smearing of dissent as pro-communist treason may have stained the USA's reputation, but in Stalin's Russia there was no dissent *at all*. Those who raised dissenting voices were jailed or shot. Even young ballet dancers who dared to talk to their girl friends about the real nature of Stalinism versus Lenin's socialism fell into the clutches of the NKVD-KGB. A young dancer called Susanna Pechuro was denounced by an unknown informer in the Bolshoi Ballet and jailed in 1951. She was lucky: three of the other ballerinas who had dared to discuss their political beliefs were executed by the Secret Police.

By 1955 the post-Stalin Cold War had settled down into a new permafrost. Both protagonists in the Cold War now possessed hydrogen bombs and credible means of delivering them. The balance of terror meant that not only could they obliterate each other – they could destroy the very globe on which humanity walked and lived. That master wordsmith Winston Churchill saw immediately the significance of this ultimate nuclear stand-off and its surprising consequences:

> It may be that that we shall by a process of sublime irony have reached a stage in this story where safety will be the sturdy child of terror, and survival the twin brother of annihilation.

There was now no advantage to be gained from a full frontal war, only death and destruction on a vast scale. So the opponents turned their attention elsewhere. Both were promoting proxy wars anywhere but in Europe, as well as backing their client states. Locked into a bitter war of words, east and west were jockeying for advantage on an ever-wider platform.

On to this stage now strode a stocky, ill-dressed figure. Russia's new leader was Nikita Khrushchev.

II

NEW LEADERS, NEW CHILLS

KHRUSHCHEV, THE PEASANT CZAR

The triumvirate that ran Russia after Stalin's death was based on the fear of ever again allowing too much power to be concentrated in one man's hands. So the surviving Soviet leaders on the Praesidium (from 1952 to 1966 the Politburo was known as the Praesidium) split up Stalin's powers and carefully spread them among themselves. Not because they believed in sharing power: it was just much safer. Beria's hasty execution at the hands of his colleagues confirmed that. The Praesidium intended to curb the over-powerful secret police and ensure that never again would the leadership fear the tyranny of a single dictator's whims. Beria's clumsy attempt at striking a secret deal with Yugoslavia behind his colleagues' backs was the excuse that sealed his fate. The Politburo suspected this was the prelude to a bid for absolute power and took no chances. Besides, Beria, with his secret files, network of informers and telephone taps, knew too much.

From now on collegiality ruled. No single individual among the Soviet leaders, and especially the head of the secret police, must ever again be allowed to make a unilateral bid to seize power and thus to decide who lived or died.

But Russians have ever admired a strong ruler. A firm hand in the Kremlin and on the knout had always been needed to run Russia's sprawling empire. The *boyars* of Czarist days had known this only too well. Most Russians expected little else from their leaders and indeed rather preferred things with a hard man at the centre. Whatever may have happened since the collapse of communism, President Putin's iron rule, dominating the management of Russia's far-flung affairs, has merely reinforced this historic truth.

So it proved in the years after Stalin's death. Malenkov's decision in 1954–5 to pump more consumer goods into the economy, and his 'amiable weakness' – as his colleagues later described it – in the face of what they saw as US provocation over the new hydrogen bomb, brought an angry reaction from his colleagues in the Party leadership. In a closed-session speech Malenkov urged that both sides in the Cold War must now accept the *status quo* of the balance of terror and find some new way forward through friendly co-existence. But the rest of the Communist Party hierarchy was not only not ready for such a change in policy, they actively opposed it. To them, it showed weakness. The Americans and their allies were still hellbent on crushing communism – you only had to read their newspapers. The Party were all for a hard line. Malenkov's conciliatory speech was never published by his colleagues: he was criticized openly by Molotov and Khrushchev, who denounced the idea that the hydrogen bomb and new world order meant 'the destruction of world civilization'. This new bomb changed nothing in Marxist theories of the class struggle with the imperialists. According to the Party, good communists should instead be 'mobilising world communism for the destruction of the *bourgeoisie*'. Malenkov was voted out of his post as Prime Minister. Harder men replaced him.

The new leader to emerge was Khrushchev, who had unwisely been appointed Party General Secretary by his colleagues. From this position at the centre of the Kremlin web, he soon pulled the Party and thus the reins of power into his own hands and equally soon dispensed with his cohort Bulganin. The former 'Chairman of the Council of Ministers' joined Malenkov, Molotov and any other dangerous rivals in political obscurity well away from Moscow. At least in one part of post-Stalinist Russia, things were better. Political defeat might still lead to humiliation, but by the mid-1950s the losers in the Kremlin's eternal game of musical chairs no longer had their brains blown out by a blank-faced KGB officer in a Lubyanka cellar.

Many people think of Khrushchev as some kind of badly dressed, ill-educated buffoon. A moment's thought brings the realization that clumsy buffoons are unlikely to rise to the top in any walk of life. The truth was that Khrushchev was a complex, highly intelligent individual whose personal story illustrates the history of Russia after the Revolution.

Born to a Ukrainian peasant family in Kalinovka, a village near Kursk, he was brought up a barefoot illiterate (the 1881 survey reveals that only 46 of Kalinovka's 922 adults could read and write). The family lived in a hut. His religious mother instilled in her offspring a sense of rectitude, ambition and an urge for self-improvement. To the end of his days Khrushchev revered the land, but took the Marxist-Bolshevik creed of 'the idiocy of rural life' to heart. Work in a coalmine and as a metal fitter took the boy out of the land but never the land out of the boy. This complex man never lost the dirt from under his fingernails.

Khrushchev was determined to better himself, and he learned to read in the evenings. Inevitably he was exposed to the waves of labour unrest and the left-wing political tracts that swept the country in the last days of Czarist Russia. Soon he aspired to the role of colliery foreman, and by 1916 was leading strikes in the Don Basin. In 1917 the Revolution changed everything. By 1918 he had joined the Communist Party, to be mobilized into the Red Army as one of the new political commissars attached to every battalion. Thereafter he rose steadily through the ranks of the Party, surviving the great purges of the 1930s and then acting as Stalin's ruthless plenipotentiary in the Ukraine during the Great Patriotic War, before rising to executive power on the Central Committee in Moscow and finally to the Politburo itself. By the time he came to power, Khruschev was an experienced, politically aware survivor.

Once he had established a firm power base, the new man in the Kremlin moved decisively for change. At home he eased the Party's iron control of the arts, increased pensions, and granted amnesty to thousands more political prisoners. 'Communism with a human face' even gave tea-parties in the Kremlin for children who had done well at school or merited awards.

Khrushchev's popularity at home was matched by his efforts abroad. He travelled widely, burying the hatchet with Mao (whose resentment against Stalin's greed over the Korean War had nearly caused a Sino–Soviet split) and even with the communist renegade Tito.

In Europe he concluded a deal that allowed Soviet troops to go home while still keeping Austria neutral and non-aligned, a diplomatic coup that won praise from his colleagues while at the same time saving foreign currency. But Khrushchev's real initiatives were made in the Third World. We know from his memoirs that he always regarded the Americans as the main

adversary of communism in general and the USSR in particular. While, in his view, the American power elite was divided
between realists and hardliners, which had to be reflected by
Russia's policies, he believed the real way for the communist
cause to advance was in what he called the 'zone of peace'.
This he defined as 'those peace-loving . . . states, which have
proclaimed non-participation in the power blocs as a principle
of their foreign policy . . .' In this zone America could, and
would, be confronted by Soviet strength. It was among these
non-aligned states that progress was to be made. In the post-
imperial era of anti-colonialism, the USSR made many new
friends in the developing world.

Khrushchev's coming to power also coincided with new
initiatives over Germany. By 1954 it was clear that the west's
aims were diametrically opposed to the Soviets'. America
(and Britain, with Churchill gone) wanted a strong Germany
as an ally. The USSR emphatically did not. Khrushchev went
to considerable lengths to keep Germany weak and divided.
The Soviets floated various proposals for security and cooperation under western noses, at one stage even suggesting
that the USSR join NATO! When that was ignored the
Kremlin tried to woo French public opinion by showing that
with the warmer international climate there was no threat
to Germany, so there was no need for Germany to be re-
armed.

Such an approach found sympathetic echoes for a time in
France, which – not unreasonably – viewed growing German
economic and political strength with considerable misgivings.
Memories of German aggression and occupation were still
fresh in 1954–5. France had even refused to ratify the idea of a
European Defence Community (EDC), something they themselves had originally mooted back in 1951. The EDC had been
a proposal for an integrated European Army Command to

discreetly capture and control any new German armed forces and keep the lid firmly on any German re-armament. Even this modest proposal had been vigorously rejected by the French Parliament. French resistance to the resurgence of German armed forces was eventually overcome by a round of British shuttle diplomacy based on Paris, a ban on any German nuclear weapons, and Germany's incorporation into NATO under strict US command. The new Germany guaranteed to toe the NATO-European line. In May 1955 the Allies handed over political power to President Adenauer. Occupation ended. A re-armed new West German state formally became a nation again, and joined the UN and NATO.

The Kremlin's response was swift. Russia, as ever, wanted secure borders against what it saw as a revitalized Germany. A united Europe and a strong, re-armed Germany, especially a Germany in the hated camp of NATO, represented a danger-ous threat to everything that the Kremlin had tried to prevent since 1945. Unnerved by obvious US technological and eco-nomic strength, plus bellicose talk from Washington, Moscow felt frightened and at risk from the western allies. The USSR moved to send its own signal of military and political soli-darity.

On 14 May 1955, the Warsaw Pact came into being in – confusingly – the Czechoslovakian capital Prague, formally binding the states of communist eastern Europe into an alliance to confront the enlarged NATO. The two rival camps glowered at each other over the Inner German Border (IGB). Churchill's and Stalin's separate visions of a unified, neutral Germany were gone forever. With the creation of the West German state came formalized polarization and the automatic continuation of the Cold War. The arms race, eternal vigi-lance, and constant anxiety would continue.

The Geneva summit of July 1955 between Eisenhower and

Khrushchev was primarily aimed at improving the atmosphere between Moscow and Washington in order to permit more wide-ranging talks at foreign minister level plus wider diplomatic exchanges. There was hopeful talk of 'the spirit of Geneva'. Sadly, the biggest breakthrough for the west seems only to have been the discovery of who was really in charge on the Soviet side. The grinning face of the overweight Khrushchev, with his peasant manners and peasant cunning, made it quite clear as Russia's new supreme leader waddled into the conference hall. 'At least we know who we are dealing with now,' sighed the US President. 'Well, I guess that's something.'

Nothing was really achieved at the 1955 summit. Even Eisenhower's dramatic offer of 'open skies' to allow each country to over-fly the other to inspect and verify nuclear weapons never got off the ground. It smacked to the Soviets of 'Yankee spying'. Despite the warm words, any idea that the Geneva Conference might have brought about a thaw in east-west relations was dissipated just two weeks after the delegates had packed up and gone home, when the Soviet Union detonated two massive hydrogen bombs in the frozen north. At any time such a signal would have been alarming. Coming when it did, it seemed to show western politicians and observers that the USSR now considered itself to be negotiating from a clear position of strength. For the hydrogen bombs had been dropped from bomber aircraft.

The message was clear. The Soviet Union's bombers could now hold continental US cities at risk from long-range nuclear jet bombers.

And Khrushchev's Red Air Force had a lot of bombers.

12

NORTHERN LIGHTS

SPYING ON THE USSR

The whole point of deterrence by the threat of force is that the threat must be believable. America's first atom bombs were certainly a potent threat to any post-war Stalinist aggression. But what made the atom bomb credible was its delivery system – the US Air Force. It was the ability of the US bombers to fly to Kiev, Moscow or Leningrad, to drop an atom bomb and – with any luck – make it back home, that constituted the nuclear deterrent of the 1940s and early 1950s. Everything depended on the strategic bomber as a credible delivery system. The doctrine of 'Massive Retaliation' by the USAF deterred any military adventures relying on conventional forces.

The Soviets were quite clear about this. Lacking any real strategic bombers themselves at the end of the war, they decided to steal them from their then allies. Four Boeing B-29 Superfortresses which landed off course in Siberia during the last months of the war found themselves unable to take off 'for technical reasons' and because officially the USSR wasn't at war with Japan. The protesting crews were, eventually, sent home. The captured B-29s were stripped down, measured, copied and built as the TU-4 by the Tupolev design bureau. Stalin's order was 'build an exact copy'. Code-named 'Bull' by the Allies the new Soviet bombers were dead ringers for the B-29. This was unsurprising as they effectively were B-29s, only *not* built under licence. The Soviet engineers even copied the imperial measurements of all the B-29's screws and fittings, rather than use their own metric ones. If Comrade Stalin ordered an exact copy, then that was what he got.

The US leapt a whole generation with their next bomber, the futuristic swept-wing B-47 Stratojet. The first squadrons of this six-jet high-altitude, high-speed bomber were in service in Strategic Air Command as early as 1949. Thanks to their looted access to the German scientific advances in aviation at the end of the war, the USAF now had a fleet of new bombers that were effectively invulnerable, flying too fast and too high for Soviet (or anyone else's) fighters to intercept.

The arrival of the Soviet A-bomb in 1949 changed the nuclear equation. Suddenly it became very important to know what bombers the Soviets had now that they had the bomb too. As conventional intelligence methods did not work in Stalin's closed Russia, the US resorted to top-secret intelligence collection flights directly over the USSR. Egged on by the fanatical USAF General Curtis Le May (who was effectively conducting his own private war on the Soviets' air defence system behind the White House's back) both Presidents Truman and Eisenhower quietly ignored international law and ordered these flights over foreign airspace because, above all else, they were concerned about the growing nuclear threat. The key question was, did the Soviets have the capability to deliver their bomb?

The only way to find out was to photograph their bomber bases. The problem was that 'ferret' flights off the Soviet Union, even in international airspace, had proved extremely hazardous in the past. The neutral Swedes had seen their over-nosy elint aircraft downed by determined Russian air defence fighters over the Baltic. America itself had lost intelligence aircraft over the Black Sea and the Soviet Far East as well as suffering the blatant interception and destruction of an NSA equipped PBY-42 Privateer over the Baltic in 1950. The British had lost an elint Lincoln when it strayed too near the Inner German Border in 1953. MiG jet fighters blew the old bomber out of the sky, and half of the doomed aircraft fell in East and half in West Germany. Collecting intelligence on the Soviets from aeroplanes was always a dangerous pastime. However, in the spring of 1952 the British showed that it was still possible. Three USAF RB-45 jet bombers, repainted in RAF colours and crewed by experienced Bomber Command Second World War crews, flew directly across the USSR at night, including a direct flight over Moscow. The results of this breathtaking incursion into Soviet airspace provided a wealth of electronic intelligence and infuriated the Soviets.

America looked on with interest at its ally's exploit. As both sides shared the information, the intelligence 'take' was of considerable use to the US intelligence community. The key seemed to be the right airframe. As the new high-flying American Stratojet flew higher and faster than any known Soviet fighter, it seemed to offer a new opportunity for photographing the USSR from the air. The result was that in the summer of 1952 General Curtis Le May, the gung-ho head of Strategic Air Command, ordered two specially equipped reconnaissance B-47s to be ready to take off. A few days later, after very heavy lobbying by the CIA and USAF, President Truman reluctantly approved an over-flight of the USSR. The first flight was launched from Fairbanks, Alaska. The RB-47 sailed over the Red Air Force bases at Stanovaya and Ambarchik without interference. Intercepting MiGs were sent up too late and were unable to reach the American jet, which was flying too high and too fast.

The spy mission was a complete success. Pin-sharp aerial photographs of Soviet air bases gave the intelligence analysts their first peek at some of the most secret installations behind the Iron Curtain. Not to be left out, the British returned to their dangerous pastime of flying over Soviet Russia. From August 1953 onwards, Bomber Command launched a series of daring photo-reconnaissance sorties using a modified version of their new Canberra fast-jet bomber. These still highly classified missions flew directly over Russia at 60,000 feet, even penetrating and photographing the Soviets' new top-secret rocket base at Kaputsin Y'ar in the Volga. Soviet air defences were unable to intercept the high flying reconnaissance flights. It was, however, illegal; and it did provoke Moscow to perfectly justifiable rage. A furious Kremlin fired off a volley of diplomatic protests and looked for ways to down these irritating intruders. Despite the dangers the Americans' cheeky spy flights continued. In the Far East, US Navy planes probed off the coast. Periodically a deep penetration flight flew overland. Soviet retaliation grew. Careless or unlucky American spy flights off the coast by conventional aerial reconnaissance occasionally ran into a hail of MiGs and were downed in 'accidents'. The Americans protested, the Soviets shrugged, and any surviving aircrews just disappeared, either into unmarked graves or, more sinisterly, into the Gulag after being interrogated by the KGB. No one knows just how many US airmen ended their days in a remote Soviet cell, their very existence denied forever. This deadly game of cat and mouse in the skies around the USSR's coastline always kept one part of the Cold War potentially incendiary.

For example, Captain Hal Austin was lucky to survive his B-47 flight in 1954. Although Austin's logbook makes no mention that he was secretly flying over hostile territory, the mission was in fact a deep (and therefore very dangerous) penetration into the USSR over the North Cape to look at the closed military bases in Murmansk. The USAF B-47 flew out of an RAF base in the UK and came in from the North Pole. With clear skies and in broad daylight, the B-47 photographed virtually every one of the Soviet airfields in the north. Secure in the knowledge that if they stayed above 40,000 feet they could not be shot down, the B-47 flew on straight and level, high in the stratosphere.

The first hint of trouble came when Austin noticed tracers flying past his wings. As he banked to look behind, a cannon shell exploded in the forward fuselage. To his horror, he saw MiGs on his tail. At that height there was little the American could do. The B-47 wasn't built for dog-fighting. His only option was to spray the sky behind him with the remotely operated tail cannon and swing the big aircraft from side to side to throw the MiGs' aim.

Fortunately the intercepting MiGs were at the absolute limit of their altitude and speed. Wallowing in the thin air they eventually fell behind, stalled and dropped down. A relieved Austin and his crew limped back to RAF Fairford to be met by a puzzled crew chief. The NCO inspected the damaged B-47 and asked what had made the hole in the fuselage. 'Bird strike, Chief,' said Austin. The NCO reached into the hole and pulled out bullet fragments. 'Some bird, Captain,' was the laconic reply.

The developed film from Austin's sortie was rushed to the Air Analysis Center in Washington, DC. Although these films have still (2006) not been declassified, there is evidence that the intelligence gained was very valuable. The President and the National Security Council were briefed. The Soviets clearly did have a significant bomber force. The question now was: *how big?* Despite Soviet protests the USAF redoubled its over-flights and the Russians redoubled their efforts to build more capable aeroplanes to counter American technical supremacy.

When the 1955 Geneva summit convened, therefore, it was hardly surprising that spying and over-flights figured high on the agenda. Eisenhower's most ambitious proposal was for an 'open skies' initiative. Each side in the Cold War would permit the other to over-fly and observe key installations in the interests of peace. This verification programme would be backed by an exchange of technical blueprints, as a confidence-building measure. The proposal was dismissed by a scornful Khrushchev. *'Nyet, nyet, nyet!'* he laughed in Eisenhower's face. 'You're just trying to see into our bedrooms.'

Part of the reason for this summary rejection may have been the unveiling at the various Moscow air shows of wave after wave of new Soviet strategic bombers such as the TU-95 'BEAR', capable of non-stop flight to the USA. To the shocked western attachés it seemed that dozens of TU-95s and the new MYA–4 BISON and TU-16 BADGERS jet bombers were roaring overhead. (In fact these were the only ten BISONS in existence, flying round and round, but the western observers didn't know that.) The USSR clearly now had a bomber that could threaten every part of the USA and, apparently, lots of them. The cold logic of deterrence dictated that America needed more and better bombers to match this new threat. But how many? It all depended on the Soviets. How many did *they* have? *Was there really a bomber gap?*

In response, Eisenhower temporarily doubled the rate of production of the new eight-engined B-52 Stratofortress to match any possible Soviet bomber superiority. Desperate efforts were made to rely on wind-floated 'weather balloons' over the USSR to photograph what was going on deep inside Soviet Russia (Operation Genetrix) with little result other than to infuriate the Kremlin. However, America's President had an ace up his sleeve. A new stratospheric 'glider' mounting a powerful jet engine was being developed at a secret 'skunk' works. The new Lockheed U-2 could fly at 70,000 feet and sail untouchably high above anywhere on earth. With its 3,000-mile range and superb new Polaroid cameras it was the perfect reconnaissance and intelligence tool. The US President handed control to the CIA and on 4 July 1955 the first mission set off to photograph the Moscow area. Shortly thereafter, a pilot called Marty Knutson made one of the early U-2's most important discoveries:

One of the flights I was on was across the Engels air-field. To my surprise and joy it was loaded with BISON bombers . . . this had to be the most important photograph ever taken by a recce pilot . . . it turned out that what I'd taken was not just a part of the USSR bombers fleet but a picture of the *entire* Russian bomber fleet . . . they were all on the same air-field at the same time . . . there was no bomber gap . . .

Marty Knutson's instant analysis was spot-on. The truth was that in 1958 there were over 1,700 atomic bombers available to the US Strategic Air Command against only 85 in the Red Air Force, a superiority of over twenty to one. It was the *Soviets* who had the bomber gap, if anyone. A relieved American President heaved a sigh of relief. Blocking his ears to the shrill protests of the aircraft manufacturers and their paid and unpaid lobbyists, he ordered a cutback on buying new bombers.

The truth was that Khrushchev had decided that bombers and ships were becoming obsolete. He came to the conclusion that missiles were the weapons of the future, especially after the awed reception worldwide of the first Sputnik earth-orbiting satellite in 1957. After this technological triumph, Russia's resources were to be turned over to the manufacture of missiles. Bombers could be shot down. Missiles could not, and the USSR was now demonstrably the world leader in missiles. In the open steppe of Central Asia a vast rocket base was to be built at Bakunur near Semipalatinsk. It would be staffed by the USSR's finest scientists and technicians and (in Khrushchev's vivid phrase) should be 'able to turn out missiles like sausages'.

The next gap, predictably, was going to be a 'missile gap'. But in 1956, both east and west had more important matters to worry about.

13

ICEPACK

HUNGARY AND SUEZ

The year 1956 was a crucial one in both the post-war world and the Cold War. Two key events altered the balance of power: the Suez Crisis and revolution in Hungary.

The Middle East had been predominantly a British sphere of control since the turn of the century. From India in the east to Libya in the west, Britain had shaped the region and influenced its politics. Despite the establishment of Israel and continuing Arab-Israeli hostility, the area seemed relatively stable. Even Britain's retreat from its bases along the Suez Canal had been accomplished without bloodshed. However, Egypt's new ruler, President Gamal Abdul Nasser, was looking to export his revolution and destabilize other local regimes in the name of revolutionary Arab politics everywhere, with himself as the standard bearer of the anti-colonialist struggle. Suez and the events of 1956 would certainly do that.

Communist theory laid down as gospel that the 'disintegration of the imperialist colonialist system' was assured. Khrushchev himself believed it was a Marxist duty to side with nations making a 'courageous struggle against imperialism'. His fellow Communist Chou En-lai agreed. In 1956 he correctly foresaw 'a major collision in the Middle East between the forces of Arab Nationalism and the Colonists and Reactionaries who oppose it . . . It is impossible for the Socialist Camp to adopt the role of a spectator.'

With this exhortation from their fellow Communists in Beijing ringing in their ears, Moscow had despatched the editor of *Pravda* to sound out the Egyptian leader. Alas, Nasser was no Communist, but he would as a good Arab Socialist welcome Soviet aid. And with aid went influence. Russian arms and weaponry poured into Egypt. This enhanced the USSR's standing and influence in the Middle East. But it also infuriated the United States. An ideological battle for aid was inevitable. Irritated, John Foster Dulles demanded that Nasser look to America for support, not the USSR. When Nasser refused, Dulles decided to teach the upstart Egyptian a lesson about power politics. He decide not to support Nasser's ambitious plan to flood the Upper Nile and build a massive dam at Aswan. If the Egyptian leader was so keen on Communists, went the thinking, then let him get his pesky dam built by them. America withdrew aid from Egypt. Suddenly Egypt was in deep money trouble. A revenue stream was needed and quickly. An alarmed but bellicose Nasser now ordered the Suez Canal and its assets to be nationalized. He needed the £35 million a year from its tolls. In future Egypt would take the revenue, not the 'British Imperialists'. The Arab world applauded this 'anti-colonialist' gesture wildly and crowds danced in the streets of Cairo. But the British were horrified at what looked to them like an illegal grab. Anthony Eden genuinely felt that Nasser might even become the new Hitler of the Middle East. Europe prepared to seize back their expropriated assets, by force if necessary. In secret talks with Israel and France it was agreed that all three would attack Egypt, Israel ostensibly to push Arab insurgents back from its border, and Britain and France to take back that which was rightfully theirs.

The Kremlin had followed this growing crisis in the Middle East abstractedly, because Moscow had problems of its own. The communist world was in turmoil. To a degree, Khrushchev had only himself to blame. On the last day of the Twentieth Congress of the Soviet Communist Party in February 1956, Khrushchev went to the podium and, in a speech that shocked his listeners, deliberately denounced Stalin. For six hours he listed the horrors, fear and brutalities of Stalin and his dictatorial rule. He called Stalin a 'pathological criminal', and confirmed that the purges and executions of the 1930s had involved trumped-up charges and enforced confessions. At a stroke, Khrushchev demolished the whole edifice of Stalinism. His Marxist audience and the whole communist world were astounded. Russia's new leader had actually admitted that under Stalin the Party had got it badly wrong.

But by doing so he loosened the bonds which had held eastern Europe in thrall since 1945. To ram the point home, two months later the Cominform was abolished, Molotov was despatched into the wilderness (literally) as ambassador to Mongolia, and the former 'pariah communist', Tito of Yugoslavia, was welcomed with open arms on a state visit to Moscow. The Stalinist status quo was unravelling. To stunned observers, it looked like the start of the break-up of monolithic communism. First in Poland and then in Hungary, the summer and the autumn of 1956 brought real trouble to the heart of the Soviet's eastern European empire. With Stalin and his policies debunked, the intelligentsia and workers of the workers' paradise moved to loosen the bonds of communist oppression.

In an echo of the East German disturbances of 1953, Polish workers took to the streets to protest against their working conditions. These industrial disputes soon spilled over into more general protests about the Party and the government. The Polish army was sent in to restore order. It did so with the usual communist severity. The People's Army gunned down 400 of the 'people' it was supposed to represent, killing at least 70 of them. Order was restored. Tanks once again patrolled an eastern European capital city. As ever it was the internal dynamics of the leaders of the Russian Communist Party and their need to control the satellites that dominated Kremlin policy in this growing crisis. Frantic debates about the balance between 'peaceful co-existence' and 'spreading the revolution' collapsed in the face of the troubles of eastern Europe. In the end Khrushchev and the ideologues prevailed. In the face of relentless encirclement, and challenged by John Foster Dulles – intent on 'rolling back Communism' – they saw where Soviet interests lay and who was to blame. In fact Khrushchev appears to have been convinced that the Polish and subsequent Hungarian troubles had been deliberately orchestrated by the US. Any threat which looked like destabilizing Soviet control over eastern Europe posed a direct challenge to Moscow's defensive *glacis* and must be suppressed as quickly as possible. That was one Stalinist policy that would not change.

The Kremlin swung into action. Bulganin and Marshal Zhukov hurried to Warsaw and tried to negotiate with the leader of the Polish Communist Party. The Red Army had not fought and died to liberate the Poles for them now to be free of Russia. To their mounting rage, the Russians discovered that the Polish Communists felt differently. They actually wanted their own appointee, Gomulka, as General Secretary of the

Party and not Moscow's nominee. The Kremlin swallowed hard and accepted this independent line, but insisted that Moscow's men should make up the reformist Gomulka's cabinet. The Poles refused. Moreover, they refused an 'invitation' to visit Moscow to discuss the affair. They had a shrewd suspicion what might happen in Moscow to satellite leaders who refused to accept the Kremlin's party line.

Furious, Khrushchev got on an aeroplane to berate his Polish allies. Unfortunately, in their haste the Kremlin failed to alert Polish air traffic control and Khrushchev's plane was intercepted by Polish fighters and very nearly shot down. In Warsaw the shaken Soviet leader threatened the Polish leaders, shaking his fist and shouting that he would unleash Soviet tanks if the Polish Communists didn't 'obey their orders' from Moscow. Gomulka faced the irate Russian down, insisting that although Poland was independent, it was still staunchly communist. Poles poured on to the streets and blockaded Soviet garrisons. Balked, a sulky Khrushchev ordered his divisions to stay in barracks. The alternative was a war with the Communist Party of Poland. In his turn, Gomulka pointed out that it was Khrushchev's own speech denouncing Stalin that had let the genie of independence out of the bottle. He stressed that he remained a good Communist and that Poland would stay in the Warsaw Pact. What more did the Russians want? It was a stand-off. Khrushchev flew back to Moscow. Gomulka stayed leader of communist Poland. And Poland stayed loyal to Moscow.

But the brushfire kindled by the exposure of Stalinist excesses had flared up elsewhere in communist Europe in the October of 1956. No sooner had Khrushchev returned to the Kremlin than Hungary erupted in violence. A hail of secret police gunfire met a student demonstration in Budapest in support of their Polish comrades. The infuriated students then teamed up with striking workers and assaulted the secret police. Party buildings were looted and wrecked. A statue of Stalin was dragged over for the cameras, amid loud applause.

The Hungarian government panicked. The Prime Minister asked for Soviet help. Khrushchev promptly ordered the Red Army garrison to seal off Budapest and restore order. It was a mistake. The rioting students met the Soviet tanks with a hail of stones and Molotov cocktails, and bitter fighting broke out in the narrow streets of Hungary's capital. The Soviets were driven back as order broke down. New revolutionary committees were formed. Impromptu elections were held to appoint new ministerial advisors. It all looked like a revolution.

But someone else's revolution was the very last thing the Bolsheviks' heirs in the Kremlin wanted. They turned their sights on to the Hungarian Communist Party and its new leader, Imre Nagy. Nagy assured Moscow of Hungary's continuing loyalty but begged to be allowed to set up his own Hungarian style of communism, embracing other political parties and with greater national autonomy. The Kremlin debated this new threat to Russian-style Communist Party control. After a stormy row in the Soviet leadership Khrushchev again reverted to type. Publicly the Kremlin cooed for peace. The Soviet tanks would be withdrawn; the new regime would be recognized. But behind the scenes a dozen Soviet divisions prepared to invade Hungary and snuff out any dissent against the iron rule of the Communists once and for all.

The Hungarian crisis was accelerated almost out of control by the Anglo-French and Israeli invasion of Egypt in October 1956. Both British and French claimed that they were intervening to 'save the canal'. A Middle East crisis of epic proportions erupted. No one at home or abroad was fooled by the 'impromptu' coincidence of Israel's timing either.

Clearly the whole affair had been plotted months before. And they were right: a secret deal to invade Egypt and regain mastery of the canal had been stitched together with the Israelis and the French at Sèvres weeks before. Large-scale amphibious invasions are, by definition, never improvised affairs. The result was that Nasser blocked the canal and called on neutral and friendly states for help. Thus America, only days from a presidential election, suddenly found itself confronting not one but two major international crises. The Russians were about to invade Hungary, and now, thanks to the British and their allies, the whole Arab and non-aligned world was up in arms against 'imperialism'.

From then on events moved swiftly. At Suez, British and French forces moved south to occupy the whole canal zone, any pretence of 'separating the Israeli and Egyptian forces and safeguarding the Suez Canal' was rightly seen as a blatant attempt to seize back the canal for the ex-colonial powers by force. The world was outraged. Khrushchev couldn't believe his luck at such hamfisted timing by the west.

In Hungary, events moved from bad to worse. On 1 November, Nagy unwisely told the Kremlin that Hungary would become a multi-party state and would leave the Warsaw Pact. There is considerable evidence that the US may even have secretly encouraged the new Hungarian leadership to take this provocative decision by giving false offers of support. This was the last straw for the Kremlin. All the old Stalinist reflexes reasserted themselves and on 4 November 1956 the Red Army's tanks rolled forward to crush the Hungarian freedom fighters. A bloody struggle ensued. But against the might of the USSR's tanks, civilians armed with rifles and bottles of petrol were never going to prevail. Within weeks it was all over, despite the ambiguous encouragement of the CIA's Radio Free Europe. No one came to the aid of the luckless Hungarians. The world was looking elsewhere. In Khrushchev's words, the Anglo-French invasion of the Suez Canal:

> provided a favourable moment [for the USSR] . . . there would
> be confusion and uproar in the West and the UN . . . but it
> would be much less at the moment when Britain, France and
> Israel were waging an aggressive war against Egypt.

Khrushchev was right. America, occupied with its presidential election, wanted nothing to do with this latest European imbroglio. There is some evidence that Washington may even have indicated secretly that the United States was prepared to turn a blind eye to any Soviet action against Hungary. Certainly the US diplomatic circuit went strangely quiet from 1 to 3 November 1956. Whatever the truth of it, the wretched Hungarians bore the full brunt of the Kremlin's wrath. The result was inevitable. Over 3,000 Hungarians were killed, 10,000 wounded and 12,000 taken prisoner. Of the captives, the Communists executed 450 for crimes against the state. Over 200,000 Hungarian refugees fled the country to find sanctuary in the west.

For the British and French at Suez, events took an equally disastrous turn. Their unilateral effort at regime change by invasion had failed. Roundly condemned and vilified in the UN, lacking support at home, and with the US threatening to collapse the pound sterling on the world's money markets, Britain's Prime Minister Anthony Eden caved in. To concentrate his mind, the diplomatic note from Bulganin of 5 November, in which the Soviet Union obliquely threatened to attack Britain and France with 'atomic rockets', may have helped. Headlines in the British press talked of nuclear war. Suddenly civil defence was a high priority again. Alarmed, the British public turned on their political masters. An even more alarmed and irritated President Eisenhower ordered US forces on to nuclear alert and further tightened the financial thumb-screws on Number 10 Downing Street and the sterling area to make the pound sterling unworkable as a strong exchange currency. On 6 November, sterling collapsed and so did Prime Minister Eden. He called for a ceasefire in the canal zone.

France was aghast at the British Prime Minister's cave-in to American pressure. The Elysée had placed French forces under UK command and now the British had betrayed them. More seriously, the USA had deliberately undermined a French enterprise. It was a humiliating betrayal and one that would have serious repercussions. Gallic pride took yet another knock. For Paris the message was now very clear: you cannot trust the Anglo-Saxons. Chancellor Adenauer of Germany saw the way ahead for France only too clearly. 'Don't worry: Europe will be your revenge,' he reassured the French premier the day after the debacle. Suez would cast a long shadow.

From the Kremlin's viewpoint autumn 1956 was a famous victory. The satellite states of eastern Europe were now firmly back under the jackboots and tank tracks of the Red Army, and, thanks to the British and French, no one had lifted a finger to stop them. Moreover, in the Arab and non-aligned world, the USSR was the hero of the hour, because it was widely – if erroneously – believed that it was the Kremlin's threat to stand up to the colonialists that had brought Britain and France to heel. The USSR was seen as the friend of non-aligned states everywhere, and the ex-colonialists as disgraced and weak bullies.

The outcome was a power vacuum in the Middle East, which the USSR moved swiftly to fill. Arms and aid flowed into Egypt. Washington, its internal democratic wranglings now safely out of the way for another four years, suddenly woke up. In January 1957 a re-elected Eisenhower told Congress that any 'vacuums' should be filled by the USA not by the USSR. 'Communist expansion, influence or aggression must be countered at every turn.'

This 'Eisenhower Doctrine' now placed the west and the Socialist bloc in direct competition well away from the Inner German Border. Egypt, Lebanon, Iraq, Syria and Jordan became new pawns in the game between east and west.

As well as the tensions of Europe, the Cold War would now encompass the volatile nationalisms of the Middle East.

14

MOSCOW HEAT

IKE AND KHRUSHCHEV

With hindsight – that ever-accurate guide – we can now see that after the events of Suez and Hungary in 1956, the Cold War accelerated and widened. International crisis seemed to follow international crisis, and always under the shadow of the bomb. Civil defence in the workplace, schools and home was accepted as a necessary response to the Cold War's dangerous new atomic threat. As ever, popular culture mirrored this bi-polar world, both sides mocking the other in light entertainment as well as the more overt and clumsy official political propaganda. For example, one popular Christmas show in the 1950s had a splendid little radio sketch that ended with the words (sung to the tune of 'I Saw Mommy Kissing Santa Claus':

> I saw uncle kissing Malenkov
> Underneath the Kremlin gate last night.
> And although I'm just his niece,

I rang up the Secret Police.
Now my uncle's in Siberia . . .

From the cartoons of the time, in both east and west, it is
possible to track the development of the global ideological
conflict and gain some sense of what it was like to live in a time
of permanent crisis and permanent threat. By the mid-1950s
the Cold War was accepted by both sides as part of everyday
life and a constant theme in international politics, as well as
everyday newspapers, culture and media of both sides. No one
summed up the spirit of the time better than Tom Lehrer, the
American singer and satirist, with his masterpiece of black
humour entitled 'And we will all go together when we go . . .'

The three years since Stalin's demise had not only frightened

A popular western view of the Cold War
(Reg Smythe, published in the *Daily Mirror*, 27 August 1958)

the public in east and west alike, they had frightened the Kremlin too. The pace of events, the rapid rate of reform, and the recent unrest among the satellites represented a threat to the Conservative element of the USSR's Party leadership. In 1957 his opponents on the Praesidium moved to depose Khrushchev while he was out of the country.

But the plotters miscalculated. On his return Khrushchev convened the Party's Central Committee, on the grounds that it was they who had appointed him Party leader, not the small elite of the Praesidium, and called on them to endorse his leadership. Only the Central Committee had the power to change the Party's Secretary. The plotters had failed to do their homework. The Central Committee backed Khrushchev and the plotters were left exposed as 'enemies of the Party', plotting behind everyone's back. Under Stalin this could only have had one end, but times had changed. A bullet in some tiled shower was not Khrushchev's way. Malenkov was despatched to run a power station in Kazakhstan and his supporters sent to equally lowly tasks in the outposts of the USSR's vast empire. Humiliated and dispersed, the plotters disappeared from view.

Khrushchev tightened his grip on power.

In 1958, the focus of the Cold War shifted to the Orient. On a fraternal visit to Beijing, an alarmed Khrushchev had discussed the global geo-strategic situation with Mao Tse-tung to be told by 'the Great Helmsman' that conditions were now ripe for a final nuclear showdown with the capitalist-imperialists. The Chinese leader had done a crude calculation and worked out that the combined populations of Russia and China made a nuclear war with the west winnable, as 'there would be more Communists left on their feet at the end of the fighting'. An appalled Khrushchev was, perhaps understandably, not as enthusiastic about Beijing's brutal calculations of attrition. Drawing the USA into a nuclear war did not appeal to anyone with a grain of sanity. Mao sulked and, despite strong Russian misgivings, on 23 August 1958 unilaterally ordered his forces to begin a bombardment of the offshore Nationalist islands of Quemoi and Matsui where (he claimed) Chiang Kai-shek's Nationalist forces were 'massing to invade mainland China'. By this means he hoped to draw the US into direct confrontation. Taiwan's secret service swung into action. A plan to kill Chou En-lai with a bomb on board an Indian passenger plane failed when the Communist Deputy Leader and Foreign Minister changed planes at the last moment.

Faced with a dangerous and escalating crisis, Eisenhower moved swiftly to defuse matters. Dulles was sent to Taiwan to 'knock some sense' into Chiang and his generals. All sides were reminded that there was effectively an armistice in place between Taiwan and Beijing. By the end of October Chiang Kai-shek publicly renounced the threat of force to return to mainland China. In return Mao Tse-tung magnanimously agreed to bombard the offshore islands only on the odd days of the month in future. It was a very Chinese 'compromise'.

The world heaved a sigh of relief.

With his political and diplomatic flanks now secured and his base in the Kremlin assured, Khrushchev could go on the diplomatic offensive. Stalin's heir looked to those issues which still needed to be tidied up. As early as November 1958 his eye lit on that assured lightning rod of Cold War conflict: Berlin.

Berlin was both a worry and a valuable tool to the Soviets. The airlift of 1948 had highlighted its vulnerability. It was also a hotbed of every kind of espionage. In 1954 the CIA and the British Secret Service had even built a daring 300-yard tunnel directly underneath East Berlin to tap the telephone cables and eavesdrop on the Russian and East German regimes. Fortunately for the Soviets, the whole plan had been betrayed to them by George Blake of SIS-MI6, a KGB agent. But it showed just how serious the Cold War had become. Berlin was always the front line. Its citizens were still effectively hostages, and its unique four-power status gave Russia a powerful control over Berlin and the Berliners.

Khrushchev recognized this advantage and the power it gave him. In simple peasant language he spelled it out: 'Berlin is the testicles of the West,' he famously said as assembled diplomats winced. 'Every time I want to make the West scream, I squeeze on Berlin.'

These advantages were, however, balanced by Berlin's open border between east and west. Almost 3 million East Germans had fled to the west since 1945: skilled workers, young academics (one entire *faculty* of Leipzig University had defected in a single day) and key scientists fled from the drab shortages and rationing of the communist east to the bright lights and opportunities of the west. It was hardly a good advertisement for the glories of socialism and it was draining off skilled labour. By the late 1950s the whole 1,500 kilometres of the Inner German Border had been closed off by the Eastern authorities to stop this crippling flow of talent. Mines, barbed wire, guards and watchtowers now kept the East German population safely enclosed within their Socialist Paradise. But in international Berlin, the city's underground ran freely between East and West under the post-war four-power agreements, an open door to the west.

Khrushchev and the Praesidium had good reason to be worried about Germany and Berlin by the late 1950s. The West German 'economic miracle' was well under way. The prosperous West German state was re-armed and now had nuclear missiles stationed on its territory. NATO was growing stronger and more credible by the year. Chancellor Adenauer was known to favour unification of Germany. Russia's nightmare of a strong, rich, well-armed, capitalist Germany on its western border looked like coming true all over again. The USSR had no doubt that it would need to deal with the German problem once and for all if it wanted to sleep secure. Berlin gave the Kremlin leverage. Berlin would be the issue that would force the west to talk.

Khrushchev's first shot in the Berlin crisis was potentially the most explosive. He called for a final peace treaty on the status of Germany. The treaty would recognize the *de facto* existence of the two Germanys. To grab Washington's and London's attention Khrushchev applied a little pressure on the west. They were to get out of Berlin within six months or Russia would sign a unilateral treaty with Germany that would recognize the DDR. Faced with such a blatant threat, the west reacted strongly. There was much talk of reinforcing the city and little talk of withdrawal. Military planners warned that any confrontation could go nuclear very quickly. Khrushchev's threat of a six-month deadline seemed to make war inevitable.

Quite why Khrushchev opted for the 'ultimatum' is unclear. He may have miscalculated; and he may have been influenced by his relationship with Beijing. The Chinese Communists had made it obvious that they found Khrushchev an unimpressive leader of world communism. A tough line over Berlin may have been a demonstration of Soviet firmness aimed as much at the global communist audience as at the west. Whatever the motivation, confronted by a resilient line from Washington and NATO, the six months' deadline over Berlin quietly died an unlamented diplomatic death. It did, however, frighten the west badly. As ever in the Cold War, a bad fright seemed to encourage a thaw.

One result of the scare was that his pressurizing the west over Berlin seems to have given Khrushchev greater confidence. From his Moscow office in 1959, things seemed to be going well for the USSR. The German border was more secure; the satellite states were suitably cowed; USSR influence in the Middle East was spreading; and the 1957 launch of Sputnik, the first-ever orbiting satellite, was a clear indication of the growing Soviet technological advances. The ever-industrious KGB could uncover no evidence of any planned surprise attack from the USA or NATO. From Khrushchev's perspective Soviet Russia was now clearly a co-equal superpower partner with America.

From this position of strength Khrushchev decided to bargain. In January 1959 he presented a bold new seven-year economic plan to the Twenty-first Soviet Communist Party Congress. The economy would shift some production from arms to consumer goods. There would be major cuts in Russian military manpower. Missiles would guarantee Soviet nuclear security in the future. Most important of all, the USSR would seek to build diplomatic bridges with the west. It really did look like a chance of a thaw in the Cold War.

Khrushchev followed up these new radical policies with some vigour. In the autumn of 1959, at Eisenhower's invitation, he became the first Soviet leader to visit the USA, where he presented a plan to the UN for 'complete and general disarmament over the next four years'. To everyone's surprise the portly and uncouth Russian in the baggy suit became a minor media star. Everywhere he went Americans turned out to see him. If Disneyland refused to welcome him (for reasons of 'security') then the rest of America did not.

The Soviet leader expressed astonishment at the high standard of living in America and was photographed wolfing down a hot-dog with obvious relish. America was flattered. New York likes to be liked. Eisenhower hosted his Russian guest at Camp David. Both sides talked freely and very frankly. In his turn, Russia's leader was flattered – the Ukrainian peasant was now an equal partner with 'Ike'. All sides felt that the process of melting a little of the Cold War's ice was under way. Eisenhower even hinted at possible flexibility over the 'German problem' in the final communiqué when he talked of 'East and West Germanys' and said, 'I don't know what sort of solution may prove finally acceptable.' Everything seemed on the table. All sides looked forward to a four-power summit to sort out the problems of Germany and the Cold War to be held at Paris in May 1960. As a new decade dawned, peaceful co-existence seemed a real possibility.

Although the Party faithful rose and applauded Khrushchev's diplomacy on his return to Moscow, not every good Communist was as delighted. A month later the Soviet leader flew to Beijing to be met by a wall of hostility.

The Chinese were upset on three main counts. First, they had little respect for the Russian leader as a Communist. They still regarded Stalin as a communist god and role model, and they objected to Khrushchev's revelations of his excesses. It rather showed up Chairman Mao's own iron terror and cult of personality, which by 1958–60 was in full flood. Secondly, they were resentful that Khrushchev had seen fit to visit the USA before coming to his communist friends in the People's Republic. The Chinese felt that this was a snub and that they had lost face. Last but not least, they were furious that Khrushchev was now refusing to pass on the secrets of the nuclear bomb to China as he had promised. On the ground this was emphasized by the withdrawal of Moscow's advisors to the PRC.

At tense meetings, they upbraided him for 'putting his personal relationship with the USA above Communist solidarity', and for 'going soft on imperialism'. Khrushchev left the tenth-anniversary celebrations of the Chinese Communist Party's 'liberation of the People's Republic' angry and uncomfortable, aware that the Sino–Soviet split was now a harsh fact of life. Even the capitalist Americans had treated him with more respect than his supposed communist 'comrades' in Beijing. But, without any doubt, it left the Soviet ruler with an uneasy feeling that he was expected, in future, to stand up to the 'Capitalist imperialists of the West' and their 'running dogs and colonialist lackeys', if he wanted to be seen as the leader of world communism.

One of the continuing themes of the Cold War was the need for strategic reassurance. In the nuclear stand-off, the 'threat' had to be known at all times. If ever one side got too far ahead of the other in the arms race there was always the danger that someone, somewhere, might try and seize the advantage conclusively. From post-Cold War revelations from the archives we now know that the 'frightened men in the Kremlin' really do seem to have feared a NATO nuclear first strike on Mother Russia. They appear to have needed constant reassurance from their army of spies in the west that some maverick USAF general was not about to unleash nuclear Armageddon about their ears. In all fairness, looking at some of the more extreme US political rhetoric from the right-wing and USAF generals of the day, it is easy to see why the Kremlin may have felt like a target.

In their turn, western leaders always feared an unstable leader or some Soviet drive to grab territory. The 'balance of terror' was a very real phenomenon. The only means to soothe political concerns of attack was very good and detailed information on the potential capabilities and intentions of the 'enemy'. That meant high quality, timely and accurate intelligence. The Cold War was, from beginning to end, an intelligence war.

Intelligence collection takes many forms. Nowadays satellites soar unseen high above the world. Sputnik's successors photograph objects the size of a golf ball, listen to radio and telephone transmissions, and hoover up every electronic emission from radars and weapons as they orbit unremarked. Back in 1960 the only way to see what the Russians were up to was to over-fly their territory. In their turn the USSR fitted secret cameras into their airliners flying over the west. Reports of Aeroflot flights wandering off track near sensitive military facilities were legion. For their part, the Americans used U-2 spy planes.

Within a year of the first U-2 flight the 'Dragon Lady' was flying over Soviet territory, its high-resolution cameras proving that there was no 'bomber gap' and, from Sputnik's launch in 1957 onwards, no 'missile gap' either. Although this jet-powered glider was one of the most difficult aircraft to fly (one pilot described it as like 'trying to ballet dance with a rhinoceros'), the US had a priceless advantage: at 70,000-plus feet the U-2 was out of range of all other planes or missiles.

Until 1 May 1960. On that date Francis Gary Powers, an ex-USAF pilot sheep-dipped as a 'civilian' CIA pilot, took off from Peshawar in Pakistan to fly across the Ural Mountains to Bodo in north Norway. His task was to photograph the secret Soviet rocket base at Bakunur. Eisenhower had serious misgivings about the over-flight. The President didn't want to jeopardize the upcoming Paris Summit by antagonizing the volatile Khrushchev, and 1 May was May Day, the traditional day of communist holiday and parades. Powers' over-flight therefore risked a double provocation. Leaned on by the CIA and intelligence agencies, the President reluctantly agreed to yet another breach of international law. But this time the over-flight went horribly wrong.

We now know that Khrushchev and all the Soviet hierarchy

had been humiliated and angered by the American U-2 over-flights. Not only were the imperialists observing all the USSR's greatest secrets, they were also demonstrating Soviet technical inferiority and impotence by soaring high over Soviet borders to cross Soviet territory. In particular, the Kremlin had been outraged by the 9 April 1960 over-flight. The U-2 had sailed over the nuclear test site at Semipalatinsk, the rocket centre of Sary Shagan, and then discovered the new missile secret complex at Bakunur (T'yura-Tam). Embarrassed, Chief of Soviet Air Defence General Biryuzov told his leader that he would personally fly a suicide mission to stop the U-2s – but they had no means of attacking these impudent incursions.

The U-2 was – and is – a very fragile aeroplane. At 70,000 feet its stalling speed is only 5mph lower than its cruising speed, and it will fall out of the sky. To make matters worse, its glider-like construction (lightweight alloy frames and thin outer skin) means that if it goes 10mph too *fast*, it can break up in the air. The U-2's pilot has to stay alert and watch the autopilot very carefully. On an eight-hour flight even the best pilot's concentration can waver.

To this day no one knows what really happened deep inside the USSR that day. Kelly Johnson, the U-2's inventor, had been toying with bamboo and balsa wood poles *outside* the air-frame to act as early radar absorbers. They may have affected the performance. Nobody knows. Powers claimed that his jet engine 'flamed out' and he was forced to descend below safety height. Many of his colleagues believed he 'dozed off at the wheel'. The Soviet PVO Strany (Air Defence) claim that one of their new SAM-2 anti-aircraft missiles brought him down. The truth is academic – the fact is that the U-2 came down over the USSR and the luckless Powers bailed out straight into the hands of the KGB rather than use the poison which the CIA had so helpfully provided. The whole affair was explosive.

Despite western claims that Khrushchev acted irrationally on learning of this latest provocation by the US, it appears that the Soviet leader played his cards with considerable finesse. There is significant evidence that Khrushchev actually wished for the Paris Summit to end without any treaty and was looking for an excuse to storm out. The USA had now provided a perfect pretext to withdraw and put the blame on the west. In May 1960 Khrushchev was facing mounting criticism from Kremlin hardliners, from the satellite Communist Parties and, inevitably, from China. The U-2 incident gave him the perfect chance to act tough. According to Troyanovsky, one of his close aides, Khrushchev told him as soon as he heard of the downed U-2 that it spelled the end of the Paris Summit and that he had prepared 'a kind of trap for the White House'. Khrushchev set out to make Eisenhower look both a fool and a liar and show the critical comrades in Beijing just how tough a good Communist should be.

With a U-2 and its pilot now in Soviet hands, Khrushchev played it long. First the Kremlin announced on 2 May that an American 'spy plane' had fallen deep in Russian territory, and allowed the US to think that it had been completely destroyed, along with its pilot. The US responded by getting NASA to report that one of their high-level meteorological flights had 'gone off course' and blandly asking for the pilot's body for the grieving family. Khrushchev then produced his killer punch. On 5 May he publicly unveiled the USSR's evidence of American spying and lying: the U-2's incriminating photographs; the wreckage of the aeroplane; the pilot's secret agent's 'suicide kit' and, worst of all, the pilot himself, very much alive and talking. The Americans' cover story was completely blown. The Americans were revealed as duplicitous liars whose reckless actions threatened world peace.

Eisenhower was stunned and publicly humiliated. Khrush-

chev demanded an immediate apology and a promise that
there would be no more over-flights of the Soviet Union.
Eisenhower refused. Khrushchev walked out. The great Paris
Summit was ended. To the delight of his critics and communist hardliners everywhere, Khrushchev had demonstrated
the steel behind the Soviet Union and had effectively been
forced by the Americans themselves to be seen to take a
tougher line with them in future. It changed the USSR's
foreign policy. The west could not be trusted, obviously:
therefore it was now *confrontation, not cooperation,* and the
Americans were to blame. Powers got ten years and went to a
Soviet prison after the usual well-rehearsed show trial – at one
point he fluffed his lines, and a helpful judge had to remind
him of just what it was he had confessed to. The Cold War
went back into the icebox.

Adding to the summit crisis of 1960 was a fear on the
American side that the US was now falling behind the USSR
technologically. The immense propaganda victory of Sputnik
and Soviet successes in space in the late 1950s had two effects,
apart from impressing the non-aligned onlookers. First, it
galvanized the embryonic American space programme. Secondly, it made American defence planners uncomfortably
aware that if the Russians really had such high quality missiles
to hand, might they not be the ideal way to unleash nuclear
weapons against the continental USA? The US had no such
long-range missiles – yet. Was a 'missile gap' developing?

The debate took on a sharper focus when the Soviet Defence
Minister, Marshal Malinovsky, boasted that his country now
had the weapons 'to strike at the "satellites" and the leader of
the Western Alliance, no matter what seas and oceans they
may hide behind'. Malinovsky may have had a point. The huge
SS6 rocket that had boosted the 184lbs of Sputnik into orbit
could easily throw a nuclear warhead 4,000 miles.

A kind of missile psychosis struck America in the late 1950s. When the news came out that the Russians had successfully tested an Inter Continental Ballistic Missile (ICBM) a mood something akin to mass panic began to infect the media and politicians alike. 'The United States has lost a battle greater than Pearl Harbor,' intoned Edward Teller, 'Father of the Atom Bomb', on national television. Asked what he thought a space flight to the Moon might discover, he said, 'Russians.'

American rocket failures didn't help. 'FLOPNIK' screamed the headlines as the US Vanguard system blew apart on its launch pad. A weary President Eisenhower was assaulted from every side by advice and demands for more tax dollars for more rocket research, more bombers, and a huge Civil Defense Program. Ike held his nerve. Turning down the Fall-Out Shelter plan he said firmly, '[in nuclear war] there is no defense . . . only retaliation.'

But in the last months of his presidency Eisenhower's determination to stand up to what he warned was a serious threat from the 'military industrial complex' was challenged as never before. Someone – probably a defence manufacturer or their agents – leaked a top-secret government report to the media. The Gauthier Report made alarming reading in 1959. What was intended as a limited study of civil defence had become a broad look at national security. The report warned in apocalyptic terms of US unpreparedness for nuclear war. In the words of one commentator, 'many who worked on the report were appalled, even frightened, at what they discovered to be the state of American military posture in comparison with that of the Soviet Union.'

The report contained grim warnings of American deficiencies. The USSR had '4,000 long-range bombers: fissionable material for 1,500 nuclear weapons: 250 deep ocean submarines: and were well ahead of the USA in development and production of the long-range ICBMs . . .'

The problem was that it was all wildly exaggerated. There was no 'missile gap'; the US was not at any increased risk at all, and the numbers of Soviet weapons were grossly inflated. None of this deflected the arms lobbyists and their friends in Washington who increased their shrill demands for more government tax dollars to offset the '1,000 Soviet missiles ready for 1961 . . .' The Pentagon was alleged to be 'shuddering at the gap in missile production'. Not for the first or the last time the USAF in particular appears to have struck some kind of Faustian pact with its arms suppliers, begging for more weapons to meet this increased threat from the communist east as a guarantee that Middle America's voters could sleep safe in their beds at night. The shareholders of the USA's military industrial complex were only too happy to oblige to satisfy their well-heeled customer's needs.

Eisenhower didn't believe a word of it and said so. He had intelligently seen that to devote all the internal resources of the state to protecting against some outside threat was completely ludicrous if the cost of the defence was more painful than the threat itself. The problem was that with the 1960 presidential election coming up, his Democrat rivals scented political advantage from Gauthier's catalogue of alleged woes. The media and the mob were deceived, and, being deceived, demanded more. The opposition demanded 'more rockets, more missiles'. Was Ike soft on communism? Even though he knew he had to stand down in January 1960, the outgoing President – against his better judgement – signed agreements for more missiles to show that the Republicans were just as tough on communism as their political rivals. It was not enough to appease his critics, and the Democrats' candidate for the presidency made much of 'American weakness'. But

Eisenhower did make one final attempt to restrain the self-interest of the nuclear and military procurement lobby. As he left office he warned of the power of greedy contractors anxious to get their fingers into the richly stocked till of American tax dollars. It was he who coined the phrase 'military industrial complex'. It may not have played well with the electors or the defence contractors who were busy setting up new offices along the Washington Beltway, but it was an important warning of a dangerous political force. Eisenhower pushed hard for a Test Ban Treaty on nuclear weapons as much to restrain excessive spending on defence as anything else.

Eisenhower left office an 'emotional, tragic figure' according to his Chief Scientific Advisor. Despite his best efforts to urge restraint, the nuclear arms race was growing and the 'armourers were thriving' only too well. Eisenhower's real achievement as Cold War warrior was to prevent foolish behaviour and to keep a sense of perspective. He had stood out as long as he could against the vociferous demands of the military and their well-paid lobbyists. 'Never has a general been hated as much as I am now in the Pentagon,' he commented wryly at the last. At least he had avoided the populist trap of following the baying of the mob and their agitators.

Those who followed 'Ike' would not be so scrupulous. But then, as it turned out, they faced bigger challenges.

15

HOT POINT

BERLIN

The new President of the United States was the young, dynamic John Fitzgerald Kennedy. Despite his election rhetoric, once ensconced at his desk in the Oval Office, the ex-officio leader of the Free World adopted a calm rational approach to national security. Like his drained predecessor, the 35th President was primarily interested in foreign affairs. Domestic policy bored them both, although Kennedy had to deal with the internal problems of civil rights and Ike had kept a tight rein on budgetary excesses. What both men shared was a healthy scepticism about the 'missile gap', despite Kennedy's campaign hyperbole. When Kennedy finally did come clean, admitting that there was no real missile gap (in 1960 the US had no fewer than 17,500 nuclear warheads in its inventory – a massive overkill) at a press conference a month after taking office, 'You couldn't hold them [the press]. They broke the damn door down to get to the telephones!'

Kennedy was keen to establish personal links with Khrush-chev. Unfortunately his good intentions were not helped by events closer to home. In 1959 a young Cuban lawyer called Fidel Castro had led his 'Revolutionary Socialist' fighters into Havana and seized power from the corrupt dictatorship of President Batista and his Mafia backers. Initially Castro's regime was more nationalist than communist. However, after a short visit by Russia's Foreign Minister Mikoyan in early 1960, Castro nationalized all US assets in Cuba and allied himself with the Kremlin. Over-emotional, as always, Khrush-chev appears to have seen some sort of socialist zeal in the ardent young revolutionary. Castro's henchman Che Guevara was even invited to stand with the other communist leaders atop Lenin's mausoleum for the November 1960 Red Square parade as a mark of communist solidarity. At the UN meeting that same month (at which he had waved his shoe over the microphone) an emotional Khrushchev embraced Castro as a 'fellow revolutionary'. Communist Russia and Cuba were allies.

For the US the presence of such an overt communist nation only ninety miles off Miami was a permanent affront. In the spring of 1960 Eisenhower secretly approved a CIA plan to topple Castro with a counter-revolution of Cuban *émigrés*. The CIA assured Eisenhower that the exiles' landing would be greeted by a spontaneous uprising against Castro's increas-ingly authoritarian regime.

Not for the first – or the last – time the CIA got it badly wrong. Although Kennedy inherited the plan for the Bay of Pigs invasion when he took over in January 1961, he removed all US servicemen and direct help. The Cubans would get US training and supplies; but they would actually have to fight it out on their own. The result was that on 17 April 1960 1,500 Cuban exiles trained by the US and the CIA and calling themselves 'Brigado 2056' stormed ashore at the Bay of Pigs. At the last minute a nervous JFK removed the invaders' US air cover. Without tactical air support or armour the Cuban exiles were doomed. Castro's tanks and aircraft moved to contain the bridgehead and seal it off. The unsupported invaders saw their headquarters ship erupt in a fireball under air attack, swiftly followed by most of their ammunition. The expected 'popular uprising' failed to materialize. Three days later it was all over. A hundred of the exiles were dead and several hundred wounded. The survivors were sent in chains to Havana. The Bay of Pigs was an embarrassing fiasco. The Kremlin and their new ally crowed at the imperialist-colonialists' bungling and defeat. The USA and its youthful new leader were humiliated.

This was the uneven playing field on which Kennedy met Khrushchev in Vienna in June 1961. After low-key – and not particularly successful – talks beforehand with Macmillan, Adenauer and de Gaulle, he set out to meet his chief adversary. It was a disaster. Kennedy's support for a scaling-down of any confrontation in Indochina and Laos and the Bay of Pigs fiasco was seen as evidence of weakness on the part of the new young President. Robert McNamara, Kennedy's Secretary of State for Defense, afterwards felt that Khrushchev thought he was facing a weak, inexperienced US leadership. Khrushchev seems to have felt so too: he began to bluster and bully Kennedy, using blunt and intemperate language. The tough little peasant was enjoying haranguing the rich boy from the decadent west. Even the interpreters winced. Kennedy came out 'shocked and upset', and Khrushchev gloated over his bullying of the youthful President. The meeting was a failure in every way.

There were three major outcomes of the Vienna meeting. The first was that Khrushchev, emboldened by what he saw as Kennedy's weakness, issued an ultimatum over Berlin demanding a peace treaty, recognition for the DDR, and a neutralized Berlin as an open 'free city'. If not, the Soviet leader threatened dire consequences, even openly using the word 'war' to the astonishment of the experienced Cold War warriors and diplomats listening to the exchanges. Second, the Americans – who had arrived in Vienna optimistically looking forward to a *thaw* in the Cold War – came away shocked instead, believing that they were confronted with a hostile and aggressive USSR that had more than ever to be contained. The last – and by far the most dangerous – result was that Vienna lit the fuse that would lead to the Cuban Missile Crisis, the most explosive confrontation of the Cold War, eighteen months later.

While Khrushchev went back to Moscow preening himself, chuckling over his success and 'riding the crest of history', Kennedy went back to Washington shaken and angry, and began to make contingency plans for a war. Both men had miscalculated. Khrushchev was bluffing over Berlin. Kennedy didn't know that. In his turn Khrushchev didn't know that his crude attempt to browbeat the young American leader had sent him off determined to stand up to any more threats from the USSR in future. Trouble was inevitable and its location was predictable: Berlin, the Cold War's constant catalyst for conflict.

The building of the Berlin Wall in August 1961 marked the beginning of the two-year crisis that many believe represented the ultimate symbol of the Cold War. An iron curtain literally descended across Berlin, the last open border between east and west. Soviet and American tanks, armed with live ammunition, bristled head to head at Checkpoint Charlie. The world held its breath, as an armed confrontation seemed a very real possibility. And the whole affair, we now know, was merely a stepping-stone in the rising tensions that would lead to the Cuban Missile Crisis of 1962.

The Berlin Crisis really began in 1958, when Khrushchev tried to end the city's post-war military occupation once and for all. The Soviet leader had good reason to be concerned at the time.

The East German state was struggling to survive, not helped by the brain-drain to the west. This haemorrhage of talent was making a bad situation worse. With 25 per cent of its industrial output being expropriated for the USSR, low wages, rationing, poor housing, and the bright lights of capitalism only too visible, it was hardly surprising that the East German leader Walter Ulbricht and the Communists of East Germany were begging their Russian overlords to 'do something'. As 1960 wore on it was clear that the Kremlin really had no choice. Economic and political realities gave the Soviet leadership little room for manoeuvre over East Germany and Berlin. The fact was that by the summer of 1960, East Germany was bleeding to death. In a curious omen of things still to come in the Soviet Union thirty years later, it looked as if the communist economy and regime really would collapse under internal economic pressures speeded along in the DDR's case by the flight of its citizens. According to Troyanovsky, Khrushchev's foreign policy advisor, 'If the Kremlin doesn't do something soon, Walter Ulbricht will soon be the last person left in East Germany . . .'

Ulbricht kept up the pressure throughout 1960 and early 1961. He begged Khrushchev and the Russians for emergency aid: $50 million in hard cash (which the Kremlin could ill afford; the USSR lost the equivalent of 540 million Deutschmarks/£60 million of hard currency in 1960/61), meat and butter, and even Russian workers as *Gastarbeiter* for seasonal labour. Khrushchev refused. 'Who won the war?' he allegedly snapped at the East German leader. 'Russian workers won't clean German toilets.'

However, there was another factor in Khrushchev's problem. Ulbricht was a communist hardliner, an old Stalinist. He had been shocked by Khrushchev's 'soft policy' towards the capitalists, highly suspicious of Soviet backsliding, as he saw it, and alarmed by the Red Army's reduced troop levels in East Germany. Ulbricht had also aligned himself firmly with Khrushchev's Chinese communist critics: Khrushchev had gone soft on capitalism. Ulbricht, however, had a predictably hardline solution to the Berlin problem: to seize West Berlin. He himself had prepared plans for an invasion of West Berlin – with the Red Army doing the fighting, naturally – and, ominously, was talking about rounding up and 'purging . . . a number of persons [in West Berlin] and organisations who are hostile to the GDR'. He even had arrest lists drawn up. As an alternative he would have to seal off East Berlin. The pressure on Khrushchev to act was tremendous.

But Khrushchev and his Kremlin advisors hesitated. Closing off East and West Berlin would be a major Cold War defeat for both the USSR and communism. Extending the fortified 1952 border between East and West Germany in order to close off the loophole of Berlin would make a nonsense of Khrushchev's own proposal a year earlier to make Berlin a free city. The political cost of acceding to Ulbricht's request would be a disaster for east-west relations. Any talk of a 'thaw' or peaceful co-existence would be laughed out of court.

In the end Khrushchev had no choice. Events, and what amounted to an ultimatum from the East German leader, forced his hand. In July 1961, Ulbricht informed the Soviet ambassador that if an open border remained, then 'collapse of the GDR will be inevitable', and that he, Ulbricht, 'would refuse all responsibility for what would then happen . . .' Faced with

such pressure – which may well have proved only too justified –
the Kremlin approved East Germany's plans to seal off East and
West Berlin, but insisted that any 'provocations to the west'
(such as blocking the air corridors) were called off. A secret
meeting of the leaders of the Warsaw Pact countries convened in
Moscow on 3 August to be told the grim news.

The Kremlin was now embarking on a policy of brinkmanship and confrontation with the west. Khrushchev was, in his
own words, 'walking towards the west with two nuclear
weapons under his arms'. To ram the point home, the KGB
began an intensive worldwide campaign of subversion and
disinformation. Even 'active measures' such as sabotage and
terrorism were authorized. Shelepin, Chief of the KGB, gave
the necessary orders. It looked like a return to the old days. It
was in fact a classic Cold War Kremlin campaign: nuclear
bluff, disinformation, mobilization of communist agents and
sympathisers in the west, and the threat of armed force.

Early on the morning of 13 August 1961, West Berliners
were shocked as thousands of East German soldiers and
labourers sealed off the border between East and West Berlin.
Western diplomatic protests were ignored. Fifty kilometres of
barbed wire sliced through the heart of the city. The elevated
railway (S-Bahn) and underground (U-Bahn) were blocked at
the new border. To ensure that there was no trouble from the
Allied powers, at Kremlin insistence the Communists laid their
barrier just *inside* East German territory. Within days a concrete wall had replaced the first barbed-wire barrier. Eventually the Berlin Wall would stretch for 110 kilometres (65
miles). The 4m/12-feet-high wall had over 300 watchtowers
and 50 bunkers, all manned by specially selected border guard
ZOPO (Border Police) units.

Although Ulbricht tried to justify the wall by claiming that it
was an 'anti-fascist barrier' and that 'West Berlin was a nest

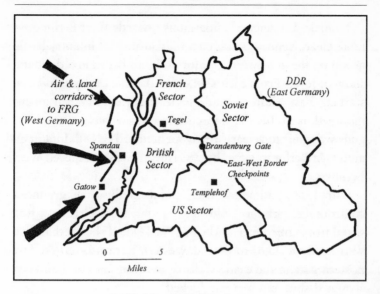

Berlin: the Cold War hot spot

of Imperialist spies' (both of which were true), the Berlin Wall was a propaganda disaster for communism. More importantly, it brought the Cold War to the boil. Although Khrushchev had refused the East Germans' request for an aerial and ground blockade, and Kennedy had accepted that US-NATO interests were confined only to defending incursions against the west, a confrontation seemed distinctly possible. Although Kennedy had, possibly as early as 24 July (when US intelligence agencies had warned of trouble brewing), decided that a wall across Berlin was not worth starting a third world war over, some show of western resolve was necessary. Accordingly, the President despatched General Lucius D. Clay, the hero of the Berlin airlift, as Special Ambassador to Berlin, accompanied by no less than the US Vice-President, a bemused Lyndon B. Johnson.

To make US defensive intentions towards West Berlin even
more clear, Kennedy ordered a fully armed US infantry battle
group up the *autobahn* corridor and into Berlin in a dramatic
show of force. From their shelters at the side of the *autobahn*,
startled East German and Soviet sentries watched open-
mouthed as 500 US armoured and other vehicles roared by,
guns swinging and clearly ready for action. The 18th Infantry's
arrival in Berlin was met by cheering crowds of relieved West
Berliners.

Both sides had made their point in this, the grimmest
confrontation of the Cold War so far. East Germany was
saved from collapse. The US and NATO had shown that they
were ready to fight to defend Western territory. But the last
postern gate in the castle walls of the Iron Curtain had been
slammed shut and securely locked.

The Berlin Crisis did not end with the building of the wall.
Both Kennedy and Khrushchev had been forced into a situation which, privately, both would have preferred to avoid.
Nevertheless, in public they had to be seen to be tough. We
now know that both leaders were trying to sort out some kind
of deal behind the scenes. The US Secretary of State, Dean
Rusk, met Russia's Foreign Minister Andrei Gromyko in
private to pass secret correspondence from Kennedy. Khrushchev replied via the GRU, even inviting Kennedy for talks in
Moscow. Although the President declined the Soviet leader's
offer, he did agree that they should continue to correspond
secretly. Despite these diplomatic moves to control the temperature, the crisis re-ignited on 21 October 1961 when the US
Defense Department admitted publicly that there was no
'missile gap'. In fact, the USA had strategic superiority. As
with so many things in life, timing is everything, especially in
the tinderbox conditions of the Cold War in the autumn of

1961. Khrushchev was in the middle of his Party Congress in Moscow extolling the triumphs of his reign and communism's golden future when the US press release appeared. This sudden boast of military superiority from Washington smacked of a deliberate threat to the Soviets and a badly timed one at that. To compound the error, the grumbling appendix of Berlin was far from healed and looked like flaring up again.

The East Germans had attempted to restrict Allied movement behind their new wall and to deny the Allies free access into East Berlin. This was a legal right enshrined in the Four Power Agreement at the end of the war. A nasty diplomatic stalemate ensued at the checkpoints into East Berlin; senior US officials refused to show their papers to East Germans as the US did not recognize East Germany, and were detained or turned back. Tensions rose. American tempers rose as well. The ever-observant KGB reported that General Clay, the US Commander in Berlin, had issued secret contingency orders to tear down the barbed-wire barricades and move into East Berlin to enforce the four-power right of access if necessary.

Khrushchev reacted swiftly. With communist eyes firmly on the Kremlin he had to be seen to stand up to this Yankee provocation or look foolish. Marshal Konev, a hardline Second World War commander, was despatched to Berlin to confront American force with force. Soviet battle tanks rumbled into view to confront the US armour massing at Checkpoint Charlie. At 100 yards' range, Soviet and American tanks stared down each other's gun barrels. World War Three was just a trigger-happy young conscript's nervous discharge away. The world's press – and the world itself – held their breath.

Kennedy backed down. He wrote secretly to Khrushchev offering not to push US access to East Berlin. The Kremlin ordered Konev to pull back from the wall and 'wait round the corner'. Twenty minutes later the US armour followed suit on their side of Checkpoint Charlie. The world breathed again. Allied diplomats could once more visit the Opera in East Berlin without officious East German demands for their papers. The Russians would oversee the process. The wall stayed up.

The wall itself was an ugly excrescence. A year after it went up the East Germans began a second fence 100 metres further in. This cleared area between the two barriers became known as the 'death zone', being gradually mined, wired and booby-trapped. By 1975, when construction was completed, the wall was topped with anti-climbing tubing, and backed by intruder-alert sensors, anti-vehicle ditches and a continuous line of floodlights. It cost East Germany 17 million Ostmarks and diverted millions of man-hours and scarce resources from an already enfeebled and incompetent economy. But it could be said that the wall saved the East German regime, even at the cost of east-west relations.

Naturally such an obstacle, as well as being an anti-communist propaganda gift for the west, became the focus of many escape attempts. Ulbricht may have 'imprisoned 17 million East Germans at a stroke', but an awful lot of them still wanted to get out. From the first impulsive flights – jumping the wire, clambering down from sealed buildings – East Germans became more resourceful. Two escapes were made by aerial ropeways; and a low-slung sports car roared past the noses of startled VOPOS and under a barrier at Checkpoint Charlie, to the delight of the press. And in October 1964, fifty-seven East Germans escaped through a 500-foot tunnel dug from the West Berlin side. One of the last escapes was a daring micro-light night flight to rescue the pilot's brother.

However, not all efforts to escape were successful. The Wall claimed 192 dead and over 200 wounded in unsuccessful attempts to flee the workers' paradise. One particular failed escape seared itself into the world's consciousness. On 17 August 1962, a young man called Peter Fechter was shot and wounded trying to escape. He lay for hours at the foot of the wall, bleeding and calling for help in full view of the horrified spectators on the western side. Some even tried to rescue him but were ordered back by East German border guards brandishing machine guns. Finally Fechter bled to death under the cameras of the assembled media who had gathered to watch the drama unfold. If it was intended to cow East Germany's captive population, it succeeded, but it became a rallying point for Free Berlin and a symbol of communist brutality. Peter Fechter was not forgotten, however, and German memories were long. Much later, after unification, the unified German prosecutors went looking for Peter Fechter's killers. In 1990, the charge was murder.

In the end the wall became more symbolic than Berlin. Its building, its policing and its purpose became synonymous with the Cold War. It became the recognizable concrete symbol of division between east and west. It was a highly visible embarrassment, not just to the DDR and the Kremlin, but to communism everywhere.

For thirty years Ulbricht's Berlin Wall would remain the icon of the Cold War.

16

WHEN ICEBERGS COLLIDE

THE CUBAN MISSILE CRISIS

If the Berlin crisis of 1961 was not bad enough, no other single event brought home the real dangers of the nuclear arms race and the Cold War to so many people as the Cuban Missile Crisis. It is no exaggeration to use that well-worn phrase 'the world held its breath' of October 1962. To those who lived through it, memories of preparing to go to nuclear shelters, watching nuclear weapons being readied for war and wondering if it really would happen, will stay forever vivid. Millions of lives all over the world teetered on the edge of a precipice. 'Brinkmanship', that equally well-used buzz-word of the US-USSR stand-off we call the Cold War, was the strategy deployed by both sides as they sent their nuclear weapons into the front line. Two men alone held the fate of the world in their hands.

The crisis had its origins in two fundamental factors: the need for Khrushchev to demonstrate his firmness to his fellow

Communists against the 'principal adversary'; and the relationship between the Soviet leader and President Kennedy. Against the backdrop of the Berlin crisis and amid inflammatory rhetoric on both sides, these two forces rolled, like historical boulders, down the slope towards the abyss of nuclear war.

Khrushchev's motives for promoting the crisis – and he did; of that there can be little doubt – were complex. For three years he had been sabre-rattling unsuccessfully over Berlin to try and achieve some solution to what the Kremlin saw as the problem of an ever more powerful West Germany. He was under pressure at home from the hardliners in the Politburo/Praesidium. The Sino–Soviet split had widened. Despite massive H-bomb tests that demonstrated the power of the USSR he was keenly aware of growing US technological superiority. Everywhere he looked, the Soviet Union was being encircled by the US or its NATO allies, from the Bering Straits to Berlin. Psychologically, Khrushchev was surrounded and ensnared, internally and externally. The volatile and impulsive Ukrainian appears to have decided that now he must act to show his strength. What better way to demonstrate both the USSR's power and his own commitment to revolutionary communism than by supporting Castro's socialist regime in Cuba? After all, he had the rockets. And the Cuban revolution looked at risk from US Marines, now massing in the Caribbean preparing for an invasion. The KGB warned of top-secret US plans to topple the Cuban regime.

Revolutionary sentiment, rivalry with the US, and a belief that the new US President was a shallow, weak and ineffectual adversary lured Nikita Khrushchev into his most dangerous gamble of all.

When Kennedy had emerged from his meetings with

Khrushchev at Vienna in 1961, battered and browbeaten, an observer commented wryly, 'at last he's met someone immune to his charm . . .' Now Khrushchev felt that he could take advantage of the boyish and inexperienced President. He had forced Kennedy into a humiliating climb-down over Berlin and had openly mocked the disastrous US-backed Bay of Pigs escapade in Cuba in 1961. Although the tragic circumstances of his death have given us a dewy-eyed memory of Kennedy, the hard fact remains that in 1962 Khrushchev regarded him as a lightweight, 'a rich, over-educated mummy's boy'. With Khrushchev ready to flex his nuclear muscles and a seemingly weak President to oppose him, the stage was set for an apocalyptic confrontation.

For Khrushchev had badly misjudged his opponent and had forgotten – if he ever knew – Kennedy's obsession with courage and the young naval officer's exploits in the Pacific.

Although some commentators try and link the Cuban missile crisis directly with Berlin, the evidence does not really support this theory. Whilst it is true that Berlin and the 1962 missile crisis were both part of Khrushchev's increasingly bold series of *aventyura* against the west, the real catalyst was not Berlin but the survival of the Cuban regime that drove the Soviet leader to challenge the US in its own back yard. Cuba was Khrushchev's choice alone and his adventurism and risk-taking would eventually lead to his downfall.

This curious blend of revolutionary commitment and nuclear over-confidence seems to have finally encouraged the Soviet leader's scheme to 'do something to help Cuba'. On holiday on the Black Sea in May, he realized that the US Jupiter missiles in Turkey could reach Moscow from the very border of the USSR. Suddenly the Soviet premier had an idea. What the USA could do, the USSR could do too. He could place missiles somewhere, as well. He decided, in the vivid Russian phrase, 'to put a hedgehog down Kennedy's pants'. He would place Soviet nuclear missiles just across the US border and see how they liked that. Strategically it made sense too: nuclear missiles close to continental USA were unstoppable and would discourage any attempts at a nuclear first strike by the notoriously hawkish US Air Force generals. On 24 May 1962 a reluctant Defence Council of the USSR signed the top-secret order for missiles to be sent 'to protect Cuba'.

Not all the Soviet hierarchy agreed with Khrushchev. The British Secret Service had a spy in the Soviet High Command. As early as July, Colonel Oleg Penkovsky, a GRU officer attached to the Soviet Scientific Cooperation Committee, was alerting his MI6 and CIA handlers to rumours of some new adventure from the Kremlin and reporting that senior officers were muttering:

> If Stalin were still alive he would do everything quietly, but this fool keeps blurting out his threats and intentions and is forcing our enemies to increase their military strength . . .

Even Khrushchev's closest foreign policy advisor warned that his master was now, 'out of control, gathering speed and rushing God knows where'. Misjudgement and over-enthusiasm had guided Khrushchev's eye when it lighted on Cuba as his next Cold War move.

We now know that the internal pressures on Khrushchev were even greater than is generally perceived. On 31 May he had cut back Soviet rations and pensions as part of an austerity drive and made a radio broadcast to the Soviet people. The comrades reacted strongly to this threat to their already dismal standard of living. A wave of strikes and protests swept the USSR. KGB informants reported widespread unrest and resentment, despite the Orwellian 'New-speak' claims that things were actually getting better. To the average Russian things were obviously getting worse. A particular grievance was Russian aid and food being given to the satellite states for a pittance. In Novocherkassk, in the heartland of the old Cossack country, workers even went so far as to throw out their local Communist Party bosses and set up their own committee. 'Khrushchev's body for gou-lasch!' read one rebel banner. Communist Party control in the region was threatened.

The Politburo did what it always did on such occasions: it sent in the Red Army to restore order. An obscure army general called Issa Pliyev established an open telephone line to the Kremlin and then, on Khrushchev's explicit order, told his troops to open fire. Twenty-three protestors were killed and ninety wounded. The usual wave of arrests rounded up 'anti-social elements' and 'agitators', to suffer the normal fate of would-be libertarians in a tyranny. Khrushchev personally congratulated Pliyev and rewarded him with an independent command in a semi-tropical posting. He sent the 'butcher of Novocherkassk' as Commander of the Soviet forces in Cuba to meet up with the sixty-five Morflot (Soviet Merchant Marine) ships now heading for the island. At least ten had nuclear-capable missiles in their holds.

The US had been keeping an eye on Cuba ever since the Bay of Pigs fiasco. It now seems clear that the CIA warned Kennedy of some Soviet adventure in Cuba, but Kennedy's Defense Committee decided that the Soviets were only despatching small patrol boats and old planes. Even Khrushchev wouldn't be so bold or so stupid as to provoke the USA by sending strategic weapons, let alone offensive nuclear missiles. In late August a US spy-flight spotted new construction near Havana, but analysts correctly identified the sites as SAM-2 anti-aircraft missile pads. The President assured Congress that there were no offensive missiles on Cuba.

During the night of 8 September SS-4 nuclear Medium Range Ballistic Missiles (MRBMs) began to be unloaded at Havana. It was planned that a total of forty SS-4 and SS-5 missiles would be deployed at nine dispersal launch sites. SAM-2 anti-aircraft missiles would protect the launchers along with the normal complement of rocket support troops. Construction continued unobserved and unreported. There now occurred one of those intriguing and apparently inexplicable gaps in the United States' usually watchful surveillance of potential sources of trouble. For over a month it seems no one bothered to keep an eye on events in Cuba: a curious and,

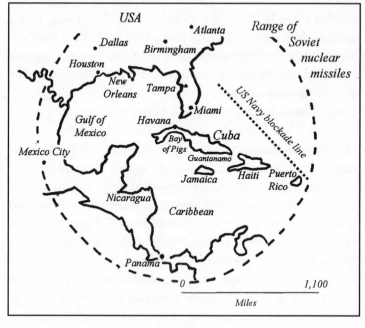

A tropical storm: the Cuban Missile Crisis, 1962

to some, suspicious omission. However, five weeks later American intelligence made an alarming discovery. On 14 October 1962 a U-2 intelligence collection flight brought back film of new concrete missile launch pads at San Cristobal.

The startled analysts at the National Photographic Interpretation Center couldn't believe their eyes. The Soviets were setting up a nuclear missile base on Cuba, with weapons pointed at America, right under their noses. They passed their intelligence up the chain to the Pentagon. Equally startled intelligence chiefs confirmed NPIC's worst fears. The NSA and CIA said that it all fitted with their intelligence as well. The White House sat on the explosive news all night to ensure that the President had been rested. News like this was going to spoil someone's day. On the morning of 16 October 1962 the President was informed that the USSR was deploying nuclear missiles 90 miles from the Florida coast. 'My God,' said a shocked Kennedy. 'Why, that's as bad as if we'd suddenly begun to put a major number of missiles into Turkey!' An aide reminded him, 'Well, if you remember, that's just what we did do, Mr President . . .'

The Cuban Missile Crisis had begun.

The fourteen days from 14 to 28 October 1962 had many effects and consequences. Two of the more important were the realization of just how close the world had come to nuclear disaster. The second was a conviction that such a crisis must never again be allowed to threaten global peace. In one frightening sense, the Cuban Missile Crisis was the peak, or hot spot, of the Cold War.

Although Castro had originally been reluctant to agree to Soviet nuclear weapons being based on Cuban soil, once he had accepted Khrushchev's idea he became an enthusiastic and active supporter. Because in fact the US *was* limbering up to invade Cuba in 1962. Despite endless denials, the volume of de-classified top-secret documentation now available shows only too clearly just how determined the US, and especially the Pentagon hawks, were to eliminate this irritating gadfly just off Florida. The debacle of the Bay of Pigs rankled as an embarrassing reminder of US failure. To take just one example of the extent of the planning to attack Cuba, the top-secret 'Operation Mongoose' group which met in September recommended to the President that the US needed to put its efforts into:

- Collection of more intelligence from every available source, including over-flights.
- An increased wave of sabotage on Cuba itself and against Cuban shipping in neutral ports.
- A careful policy of 'non-attributability' [*sic*] to avoid any blame being connected with the US administration.
- Getting rid of the Castro regime by any means possible.

In addition to the wave of 'piracy' off Cuba's coasts (attacks by diehard anti-Castro Cuban *émigrés*), it is clear that Castro and Khrushchev had every reason to fear some US-led intervention. The hawks in the Pentagon were undoubtedly readying themselves for action when the Soviet Union offered to 'protect the Cuban revolution from imperialist aggression'. The Americans' discovery that this now meant something much more dangerous than a handful of obsolescent IL-28 BEAGLE bombers and some fast patrol-boats accelerated the US response and raised the stakes beyond previous experience. One commentator even described the discovery of the Soviets' nuclear strategic missiles on Cuba as a shock comparable to Pearl Harbor. The Americans would have been even more shocked had they known that the Russians had also had tactical nuclear missiles hidden in caves on Cuba for months.

President Kennedy's first act was to convene a small 'war cabinet'. Known as 'ExComm', this group, which included his brother Robert Kennedy (the Attorney General), Secretary of Defense Robert McNamara, George Bundy (the National Security Advisor) and Secretary of State Dean Rusk, effectively managed the crisis over the next two weeks. At the time such crisis management was an innovation. Even more of an innovation to many of the participants was Kennedy's secret taping of the meetings. Few of those present at the time realized that their words and deeds would become one of the most studied pieces of decision-making in history. It was pure political theatre, with the grim realization that if they over-acted or fluffed their lines in this crisis, a nuclear war could result, with millions dead, including themselves and their families.

The 'shocked incredulity' (in Robert Kennedy's words) that the Soviets would have the cheek to risk such a venture, soon dissipated with the knowledge that, according to the Pentagon, the Soviet missiles would be active and ready for firing in just fourteen days. ExComm's options crystallized rapidly: do nothing (swiftly rejected); a blockade; invasion; a surgical air-strike (much favoured by the US Air Force hawks); direct talks with Castro; and diplomatic negotiations with Moscow.

In the end only two options were left open, apart from the obvious need to start talking to the Soviets: a blockade or combined air-strike and invasion. For nearly a week this sub-committee of the National Security Council debated their courses in great secrecy. All the options had serious draw-backs. An air-strike and invasion not only risked Soviet retaliation and another crisis elsewhere (like Berlin), it smacked of 'Pearl Harbor in reverse' and sat uneasily with American ideas of morality and surprise attacks. And, as the State Department pointed out, it would look to the UN and the rest of the world uncomfortably like the gun-boat imperialism of the British-French attack on Egypt at Suez six years before.

In the middle of all this frenzied debate behind the scenes, the President had a long-scheduled routine meeting with Andrei Gromyko. The meeting was diplomatically cordial, if guarded. Neither side raised the issue of the Soviet missiles, although Kennedy actually had copies of the secret aerial photographs in his desk drawer should he need to challenge the Russian. Eventually Gromyko accused the US of 'harassing a small country – Cuba'. In reply Kennedy assured the Foreign Minister that the US had no designs on Cuba but he had noted that the Soviets were encouraging a military build-up on the island. Gromyko countered by agreeing, but insisted that the Soviet arms shipments were purely defensive. No Soviet offensive weapons had been, or would be, sent to Cuba. Both men were lying in the finest traditions of international diplomatic relations. Kennedy kept his counsel, but the photographs proving Gromyko a liar must have been burning a hole in his desk drawer. But at least the US now had absolute proof of Soviet duplicity.

For his part, Gromyko went away delighted and reported to the Kremlin that the US appeared to have no inkling of their plans. 'A US military adventure against Cuba is impossible,' he reported. Khrushchev kept his counsel too, although secretly he must have been rubbing his hands with glee. His great secret plot to 'put a hedgehog down Kennedy's pants' and 'see just what he's made of' looked like coming off. In a week or so his Cuban missiles would be ready to use. Kennedy was facing mid-term elections in November. The Russian leader would soon be able to spring a political and diplomatic triumph that would seal his place in history as the undoubted leader of the communist world, and as the Russian who finally checkmated the Americans in their own back yard.

But Kennedy had now made up his mind: he was going to blockade Cuba. This course would give the Russians time to think things through. The problem was that a blockade is either illegal or an act of war. What if the Soviets ordered their Morflot merchant ships to try and run the US Navy blockade? Would the Navy have to use armed force to stop them? On 21 October the President finally authorized the action to impose a quarantine zone around Cuba, observing gloomily, '. . . there isn't any good solution . . . but this one seems the least objectionable . . .' Stunned Congressional leaders were briefed in private; the Soviet ambassador was called to the State Department; and on 22 October the President broke into prime-time television schedules to tell the American people the grim news.

Behind the scenes, an embarrassed Ambassador Dobrynin was being carpeted by Dean Rusk at the Sate Department. The Secretary of State handed Dobrynin a copy of Kennedy's public announcement and a personal letter – amounting to an ultimatum – to Khrushchev. The unfortunate Dobrynin, who appears to have known nothing about Khrushchev's secret deployment of nuclear missiles to Cuba, nearly collapsed with shock. Rusk thought that the Russian had 'aged ten years' before his eyes. By the time Dobrynin managed to signal Moscow, the Cuban Missile Crisis had exploded into the public arena and US nuclear forces had gone on to a war alert as a precaution. Khrushchev had been unmasked.

No one seems to have been more surprised than Khrushchev himself. Stopping only to authorize the Soviet Commander-in-Chief in Cuba to use tactical nuclear weapons if invaded by the Americans (but not the SS-4 MRBMs), the whole Soviet leadership seems to have been caught on the hop. Khrushchev had no clear plan of what to do next. 'This could end in a very big war . . .' he advised a startled Praesidium. This was a surprise, and an unwelcome one, to the Party comrades. Khrushchev had got them to agree to the whole Cuba adventure by assuring them that there was no risk. The Kremlin now tried to work out what to do next.

Having been caught out, Khrushchev immediately resorted to his favourite tactic: bluster. He alerted the Warsaw Pact countries, called Kennedy a warmonger and accused the US of piracy on the high seas. Such a violation of international law was 'a serious threat to peace . . .'. Moscow insisted that the Soviet intentions in Cuba were 'solely for defensive purposes'. Khrushchev warned of 'catastrophic consequences for world peace . . .' In fact, Khrushchev was as scared as anyone about the consequences of his reckless scheme now that it had been uncovered. Vasily Kuznetzov, his foreign policy advisor, observed dryly that 'Khrushchev shat his pants' with fright. Secret, and now-revealed, Russian sources make it quite clear that Khrushchev really didn't know what to do next.

Meanwhile, obeying Khrushchev's order, twenty-six Soviet merchant ships ploughed across the Atlantic towards Cuba. On 24 October a US picquet line of warships were on station, ready to bar their way. A confrontation was inevitable. Khrushchev sent a message that if the US stopped any Russian ships, then Soviet submarines would attack the US warships to protect their own shipping. 'If the US insists on war then we'll all meet in hell.' On the surface US anti-submarine Task Forces loaded their nuclear depth charges. The Soviets didn't know about those. The Russian submariners began to load nuclear-tipped torpedoes. The Americans didn't know about *those*. A Soviet *Zampolit*, or political officer, aboard a Soviet submarine actually wet himself and fainted with fright when the news came through and he saw his captain loading a nuclear torpedo and clearing for battle.

The first confrontation came on 25 October when a US

Navy destroyer ordered a Soviet tanker to heave to. But the *Bucharest* was only carrying oil and after inspection was allowed to proceed to Havana. Common sense and pragmatism had defused an increasingly tense situation. But on the bigger international stage, things had gone from bad to much worse. Khrushchev was now accusing the US of open aggression and had put his nuclear forces on alert. In response the USAF Strategic Air Command had gone to DEFCON 2, the US military's next-to-hostilities state of readiness for war, with 24-hour cab-ranks of nuclear armed B-52 bombers orbiting their fail-safe points over the polar ice-cap. American ICBM missile silos were prepared for firing. Nuclear submarines sailed to their war stations and made ready to launch their nuclear missiles. In Cuba the Soviet commander reported that his SS-4 missiles would be ready for launch within 24 hours. The US Marines prepared to invade Cuba once the order was given. The military on both sides loaded live ammunition, prepared for battle and headed for their war stations.

The low point, diplomatically, was also reached on 25 October. In a UN Security Council debate on the crisis, the Soviet delegate denied that the USSR had any missiles in Cuba and demanded evidence of the US's claims. In a dramatic *coup de théâtre*, the US delegate Adlai Stevenson revealed the top-secret aerial photographs of the SS-4 installations to the world's press. The Soviets had been caught lying, and in the world's most public forum. The embarrassed Soviet delegation were very taken aback. Caught out, they denied the American claims. The photographs were 'obvious forgeries'. No one present believed them. Diplomatically it looked as if all avenues were exhausted. It was against this uncompromising background that Kennedy and his ExComm now reviewed the first of two letters from Khrushchev.

The postman was a KGB officer masquerading as the Press

Counsellor at the Soviet Embassy in Washington. Aleksandyr Fomin called up John Scali, the ABC Diplomatic Correspondent and, over lunch, secretly offered a compromise deal between the US and the USSR. If America promised not to invade Cuba, then Moscow would withdraw its missiles: could Kennedy deal? An excited Scali passed the message to ExComm in the White House.

Behind the scenes the exchange of letters and messages between Washington and Moscow became frenzied. Khrushchev (who by now appears to have calmed down) had been authorized by the Praesidium to negotiate and seek a diplomatic solution. The Kremlin contemptuously brushed aside an encouraging suggestion by Castro that the Soviets consider a nuclear first strike. Peace, not a nuclear war, was Moscow's preferred outcome. Castro and Cuba were the problem now, not the solution. Both sides frantically sought a peaceful solution to stop the escalating spiral of a countdown to war.

Events conspired against the doves. A routinely scheduled Atlas missile test launch at Vandenburgh Air Force base alarmed the Soviets. Not unnaturally they took it as a deliberate warning. (Kennedy had not even been informed of this routine test.) An unauthorized high-altitude U-2 probe over Siberia had drawn swift retaliation from the nervous Russian air defences and the pilot had been lucky to escape and bring the aircraft home. Again the President had not been kept aware of the USAF's activities. 'There's always one . . .' the President sighed. The Soviets took it as a prelude to war.

The next day, 27 October, brought even worse news. A USAF U-2 had been shot down over Cuba by a Soviet SAM-2 and the pilot was dead. As their contingency plans ordered, the US military now prepared to strike back at a Cuba that had opened fire on them. As ExComm glumly contemplated the nuclear stand-off, with Cuba on the brink, a confrontation at sea off Havana all too probable, a U-2 shot down over Cuba and war seemingly inevitable, they received a *second* message from Khrushchev, much tougher than the first. The irony was that this harsher, more demanding message from the Russians had in fact been inspired by none other than the Kennedy brothers themselves.

Although the Kennedys later tried to hide the truth and even to rewrite history, we now know from Ambassador Dobrynin, Khrushchev and Theodore Sorenson, author of *Thirteen Days* (the White House version of events concerning Cuba), that it was an *American* climb down that finally broke the Cuban logjam. The fact is that the night before Khrushchev's second message was received, an agitated Robert Kennedy had met Ambassador Dobrynin in secret. Through the KGB archive we now have access to Ambassador Dobrynin's own top-secret telegram to the Kremlin, giving a version of that secret meeting between the President's brother and the Soviet ambassador. His account of the meeting is confirmed by both Khrushchev's memoirs and the 1989 'confession' of Sorenson at a special conference in Moscow attended by those involved on both sides.

Dobrynin's telegram gives an unchallenged version of events which conflicts sharply with 'JFK's Great Triumph'. According to Dobrynin, the younger Kennedy admitted that the shooting down of a USAF plane over Cuba had inflamed the situation and said that:

> because of the plane . . . there is now strong pressure on the President to give an order to respond if fired upon . . . we cannot stop these flights because they are the only way we can quickly get information about the state of the [Russian] missile bases in Cuba . . . There are many unreasonable heads among the [US] generals who are 'itching for a fight' . . .

Later in the lengthy telegram, Dobrynin was quite specific about how far, according to Kennedy, the US was prepared to go:

> If the Soviet government will halt work on the Cuban missile bases . . . in exchange the US government will repeal all measures relating to the quarantine [blockade of Cuba] and guarantees not to invade Cuba . . .

'What about Turkey?' Dobrynin asked Robert Kennedy in a key exchange that Sorenson later admitted he had deliberately omitted from *Thirteen Days*.

> If that is the only obstacle [Kennedy replied] . . . the President doesn't see any difficulties in resolving this issue . . . The greatest difficulty for the President is the public discussion of Turkey. The deployment of the missile bases in Turkey was done by a special decision of the NATO Council . . . to announce a unilateral decision to withdraw would . . . damage the entire structure of NATO and the US position as leader . . . However, if [the Presidents] can agree, then we can give the order to withdraw the missiles from Turkey in four or five months' time . . . but it must remain extremely confidential . . .

Dobrynin's telegram then makes the point that Robert Kennedy 'appears very upset . . . I've never seen him like this before.' Russia had long grumbled that the US had atomic missiles on the USSR's border – the Jupiters in Turkey. Robert Kennedy had quite explicitly offered to trade the US position in Turkey as a *quid pro quo* for the SS-4s being taken out of Cuba. The Americans wanted out of the crisis. Dobrynin cabled Moscow. The Kremlin accepted.

The problem was that neither the US military or ExComm

were aware of this dangerous secret backstairs bargaining by the President and his energetic young brother. When Khrushchev's second letter arrived, insisting 'that the Turkish missiles must be removed' as part of a deal, the military members of ExComm thought that Khrushchev was just playing tougher and was trying to turn up the heat. The generals and the hawks now believed that war was inevitable and argued that the US should strike first, if only to knock Cuba out of the equation once and for all. The Kennedy brothers wriggled and dodged uneasily in the tense discussion that followed. The President and his brother could hardly admit that it was *they* who had made the problem worse. They kept quiet. In the end Ex Comm (slightly to their own surprise, to judge from the transcripts), decided that the best course might be to pretend that they had not yet seen the 'second letter' and replied to Khrushchev's first, milder offer although the military hawks around Kennedy still advocated war. With some reason: the Soviets had fired at and shot down an unarmed plane over Cuba. They argued that they should now retaliate and at least 'take out' the dangerous SAMs, if only to guarantee continued air reconnaissance of the sites in those pre-satellite days. The SS-4s were now ready for action and would have to be bombed soon if they were going to be eliminated. They knew nothing of any backstairs deal by the Kennedy brothers. Time was running out.

It was Kennedy's reply to Khrushchev that broke the crisis. In it he promised to call off the US blockade if Russia removed its missiles from Cuba. However, and crucially, behind the scenes the US President and his brother secretly promised to remove the Jupiters from Turkey as well. That was the real deal. If it came out, however, the political fall-out with the American public and, perhaps more dangerously, with the hawkish military, would damage Kennedy's presidency be-

yond repair. It would look as if the Americans – not Khrushchev – were the ones who had 'blinked'. To cover their tracks,
therefore, and to save face should it ever come out, the
Kennedy brothers secretly primed the UN Secretary-General
U Thant with a cover story. They asked him to be ready to
claim that it was *he* who had suggested this scheme, should the
Soviets ever let the cat out of the bag to try and grab any
propaganda advantage from the real deal, which was a mutual
climb down. The White House could not be seen to have
backed off any more than could the Russians.

A delighted Khrushchev agreed to the deal and on 28
October ordered his ships to carry the offending missiles back
to the USSR. The missile sites would be dismantled and UN
inspectors would confirm that the Russians on Cuba had gone
home. The Soviets had backed down. The Americans crowed
in public. A grateful world agreed and heaved a collective sigh
of relief. Kennedy, the boy President, had stared down Khrushchev and saved the world.

Not everyone was fooled, however. Khrushchev pointed out
with some justice to his shaken colleagues on the Praesidium
that he had achieved *his* aim: a guarantee that the imperialist
Yankees would not now invade Cuba. *And* the Americans had
now promised to dismantle their missiles in Turkey (and, away
from the glare of publicity, the Jupiters in the UK and Italy as
well) as a bonus. It was a Soviet diplomatic and Cold War
triumph, boasted the Russian leader. His brilliant plan had
worked.

Many in the American military were unimpressed by Kennedy's 'great diplomatic triumph'. Insiders were far from
convinced that 'the other guy blinked.' 'We've been had . . .'
observed one laconic admiral. And he wasn't just referring to
the Russians.

Back in Moscow, the ever-paranoiac Praesidium of the

Communist Party of the Soviet Union eyed their impulsive and crude leader with increasing distaste. His lunatic – and completely unnecessary – scheme to embarrass the Americans had nearly killed them all.

At the time everyone was so glad to survive that they failed to examine Kennedy's 'statesman-like triumph' too closely. The real truth of the Cuban Missile Crisis of autumn 1962 was that – somehow – both sides had managed to prevent a disastrous nuclear exchange. The real victory was that both Washington and Moscow had achieved their goals without going to war.

Peace was the real winner.

The Cuban Missile crisis was to spawn another, grimmer, outcome a year later. Although no one knew it at the time, JFK's much-vaunted deal over Cuba had also signed his own death warrant.

As the crisis died down, the American right was waiting, political knives sharpened, for proof that the Russians had really all gone from Cuba. But Castro flatly refused to allow in the UN or any other inspectors, and many Russians stayed on. The problem festered. Throughout 1963 the political pressure for JFK to 'get tough on Cuba' grew more vocal and more critical. The Soviets were still 90 miles from Miami, and suspicions grew that Kennedy had failed to deliver his much-trumpeted victory over Khrushchev and the USSR. The Missile Crisis still hung over him as the political opposition and the Republican Party joined in. Kennedy began to worry that he might even be impeached for misleading Congress. With a presidential election due in 1964 the Kennedy brothers were in deep political trouble. They decided that they would have to fix the Cuban problem once and for all.

The astonishing result was that in the summer of 1963 the

White House put together a private top-secret plot for their own coup in Cuba. The plan was dangerous, illegal and unconstitutional, and was kept secret and totally separate from the CIA's 'official' efforts to topple Castro. On no account could America be seen to be involved in the Kennedys' own private scheme to solve the Cuban problem once and for all, because Khrushchev had openly threatened war should the US ever dare to intervene again in Cuba. This explosively sensitive *presidential* plot to assassinate Castro was called Plan Omega, or AMWORLD to the CIA. The President's brother, Attorney General Robert Kennedy, controlled the plan personally from the White House. The idea was that a lone Cuban gunman would kill Castro. Che Guevara, who had become increasingly disillusioned with Castro's authoritarian and Stalinist cult of personality, would then assume power. The Hero of the Revolution would then call for US 'assistance' to restore order. He had even been provided with a secret CIA radio. Not for nothing did the Cuban exiles involved call it 'the Judas Plan'.

Sadly for the Kennedys, their secret plot was leaked to the Mafia. The Mob had been well plugged in to matters Cuban for some time. They had been thrown out of their lucrative Cuban casinos in 1959 and 1960, along with all the other '*Yanqui* capitalists', and bore their own deep grudge against the new Cuban regime. *Mafiosi* had been natural recruits for a CIA looking for help and experience to operate undercover inside Cuba. The result was that the Mafia was already deeply involved in the CIA's plots to overthrow Castro and thus regain their lost criminal enterprises, when they became aware of some new deadly secret enterprise involving Cuba and the White House. Ironically the excessive secrecy failed to protect the Kennedys' new scheme. The problem was that some CIA officers were involved in *both* plans. No one really knew which was which. Eventually the Mafia dons in the deep South discovered the real truth through the ever-leaky Cuban exile leaders training on their turf. There were *two* plans to get Castro, and the Kennedys' illegal scheme was a ticking time-bomb should the truth ever come out.

The problem was that the Mafia bore an even bigger grudge against Bobby Kennedy than they did against Fidel Castro. The US Attorney General had been conducting a highly public campaign against organized crime over the head of his own FBI chief. Although J. Edgar Hoover had been fatally com-promised as a homosexual by the Mob and had been well bribed to keep Washington off the backs of the leading mobsters, he could not protect them from the Kennedys' vote-winning anti-Mafia crusade. The result was that Bobby Kennedy's public pursuit of the principal Mafia families would lead to a fatal outcome for his own brother.

Three Mafia bosses, Santos Trafficante of Chicago, Johnny Rosselli of Miami, and Carlo Marcello of New Orleans, finally moved against the Kennedy boys. Their own preparations to help the government and the CIA against Castro provided the perfect cover for another, more deadly, enterprise. The Mafia dons were already being hounded into court by the Attorney General, and had little to lose. They decided in their own words, 'to cut the dog's head off to stop the tail wagging'.

A year after the Cuban Missile Crisis three separate attempts were mounted to assassinate JFK. The first was in Chicago, the next in Tampa. Finally, on 22 November 1963, the President of the United States would have his brains blown out by a high-powered rifle bullet fired from a grassy knoll ahead of the presidential motorcade in Dallas. The gunman was probably a Frenchman, Paul Mertz, a Mafia hired gunman known to the French Secret Service as 'Soutre'.

In the desperate rush to cover up the Kennedys' secret plot, which could have led to a war with the USSR, the details soon became muddied. At the time, the frantic US investigators seem to have believed that the shooting was a *Cuban* hit, with Castro 'getting his retribution in first'. Had the Kennedys' plot to kill Castro and invade Cuba been uncovered? The real truth had to be covered up at all costs. The blame was placed squarely on a 'patsy' lured to the Dallas Book Depository by the Mafia. He was an underground intelligence agent of the Office of Naval Intelligence, and already deeply involved with the secret plots to bring down Castro. His name was Lee Harvey Oswald. Jack Ruby, the Mafia's paymaster to the Dallas police and sometime gun runner for the CIA, soon disposed of *him* on direct orders from the Mob. Ruby was himself later murdered in prison by a lethal injection. The White House's secret plot to stage a coup in Cuba died with JFK.

It was the Cold War that really did for John Fitzgerald Kennedy. In many ways it was the American President who was the real victim of the Cuban Missile Crisis.

17

TROPICAL INTERLUDE

VIETNAM

None of the ideological warriors thought for a second that the resolution of the Cuban Missile Crisis meant that the Cold War was over. Instead, the politicians and their advisors sought new ways to continue the fight. Nuclear weapons were definitely out, except as a weapon of last resort: all sides were agreed on that. US Defense Secretary McNamara believed after Cuba that nuclear weapons were pointless for 'war-fighting', and advised both JFK and Lyndon Johnson (who succeeded Kennedy as President following his assassination in 1963) that he should 'never initiate, under any circumstances, the use of nuclear weapons'.

Two courses now emerged for the immediate post-Cuba future. First, to try and put the dangerous genie of the atom bomb and its advocates back into its bottle; secondly, to avoid fighting the Cold War as a head-to-head confrontation between the superpowers, instead waging it far away, in the developing world.

Putting the nuclear genie back into the bottle was easier than it looked. While nuclear weapons could no more be 'disinvented' than the crossbow, firearms or the submarine torpedo (all of them weapons that destabilized the military *status quo* of their day), the various nuclear warheads could be controlled. What was needed was stability. So Kennedy and McNamara positively encouraged the Soviets' 'second strike' capability. Provided that any 'first strike' guaranteed a retaliatory or 'second strike' attack by the victim, both sides were safe, the theory went. Any attempt at a 'first strike' would only assure destruction by an enraged enemy. Therefore a first strike would, by definition, be suicidal. This lethal calculation became the basis of the Mutual Assured Destruction, or MAD strategy. 'Mad' it may have been, in the eyes of many critics, but it at least assured a kind of stability; and it was a damned sight safer than its predecessors, Massive Response, First Strike or Surprise Attack. Deterrence remained intact, now comfortably balanced on the nuclear triad of strategic bombers, ICBMs and the new submarine-launched ballistic missiles.

The whole point was mutual east-west stability. Anything that jeopardized 'assured destruction' was dangerous. So the US argued strongly *against* Anti-Ballistic Missile (ABM) defences around key points, on the grounds that such a plan would be very expensive, but also because such defensive weapons would make things *worse*, not better. Safety rested on deterrence, and particularly on the invisible nuclear Ballistic Missile (SSBM) submarines to deter any enemy stupid enough to launch an attack. Even the British agreed. Macmillan effectively sub-contracted Britain's nuclear deterrent to the US in 1964 at Bermuda when he begged Kennedy for the new Polaris missiles to replace Britain's own aborted nuclear projects. Ever-mindful of the need to spread the burden of nuclear responsibility among the NATO allies – and, cynics said, to ensure that Britain's deterrent force was never truly independent – JFK agreed. Kennedy's own follow-up proposal for a NATO fleet of merchant ships armed with nuclear missiles and mixed NATO crews, however, met with less success. The idea of putting medium-range missiles to sea under US captains, and locking NATO countries fully into defending themselves, was superficially attractive. However, the idea of a Multi-lateral Nuclear Force, or MLF, sank before even leaving harbour. In traditional NATO style, the allies dragged their feet. By 1965 the Americans had given up. Far away in Southeast Asia, they had more important things to worry about.

The second component of the post-Cuba struggle was in the developing world, using 'less defense-orientated regional links . . .' to quote the Kennedy White House jargon. This new shift of American emphasis stressed non-military intervention to contain communism. America now sought to influence smaller countries at risk from communist takeover by 'immunizing' them against the Red Menace. Diplomacy, aid, Medicaid, financial backing and military advisors would supplement regional military alliances such as SEATO or CENTO, neither of which had ever really worked. Thus for Latin America the US proposed the Alliance for Progress, a $20 billion programme of aid spread over ten years. The aim was to 'bring about stability . . . without leaving the transformation [of society] to be effected by Communists'. Quite simply, the US offered material inducements and lots of money to buy off other countries and to block communist revolutionaries.

America's overseas aid programmes were far-reaching. 'Argentina, Brazil, Colombia, Venezuela, India, the Philippines, Taiwan, Greece – even possibly Egypt, Pakistan, Iran and Iraq . . . [could achieve] self-sustaining growth . . .' wrote the

US State Department's chief strategic policy advisor as he urged new policies to Kennedy. The main architect of this new policy of 'butter *and* guns' was Walt Rostow, one of the National Security team, who saw that encouraging growth and stability in the developing world would reinforce America's overall aims as effectively as any aircraft carrier. In an un-balanced world, any means of re-aligning power in America's favour was worthy of consideration. Winning the Cold War now rested as much on Coca-Cola and the Peace Corps as on the new military advisors under training at the US Special Forces School.

The US's softer policy for containing communism was not all plain sailing. Khrushchev could not resist punctuating his calls for peaceful 'co-existence' with his usual crude bluster and declarations that 'we will bury you'. Perhaps most important of all was his call to encourage 'wars of national liberation'. The Soviet leader was more determined than ever to demonstrate his communist credentials. He was only too aware that his Kremlin colleagues were dissatisfied with the outcome of his Cuban adventure. Castro, having urged an all-out nuclear war, was now incandescent at what he saw as Khrushchev's betrayal. 'Bastard', 'son of a whore' and 'Rus-sian arsehole' were just some of the milder epithets hurled at Russia's 'new architect of global peace' by the furious Cuban. While Khrushchev could undoubtedly absorb criticism from that quarter without too much concern, Castro's threat to re-align Cuba with China in future was much more serious. Mao's People's Republic now regarded itself as divorced from Moscow. The Sino–Soviet split was a genuine rift. From 1967 onwards there were numerous border clashes in the Far East. In 1969 Soviet and Chinese troops actually fought at the Amur and Ussuri Rivers, with over 100 casualties. Communist solidarity was clearly a thing of the past.

Khrushchev was also under threat from two other quarters, from hawks and doves alike. His generals were leaking stories of their leader's 'weakness' over the Cuban Missile Crisis especially his order to place the offending missiles on the merchant ships' decks so that the US could see and count them. At the other end of the spectrum, many eastern European leaders were horrified at what they considered Khrushchev's foolhardy risk-taking. The Romanian ambassador even told Washington privately that his country completely disassociated itself from Khrushchev's 'mad adventurism' and wanted no part in any Soviet-led Warsaw Pact attack on the west. Premier Khrushchev and his policies were assailed from every side. He tried to conciliate allies and opponents alike and moderated his adversarial approach in every direction, except one: the unchanging banner of the Marxist Revolution. The Soviet leader genuinely believed that peaceful co-existence did not preclude the USSR giving assistance to communist insurgents engaged in 'their wars of national liberation' anywhere. In fact it was the Soviets' duty. He even saw Cuban rage against his own climb down as a reflection of the Russians' own revolutionary zeal in the far-off days of the 1920s. The old Bolshevik revolutionary urges still asserted themselves in Chairman Khrushchev.

So the Cold War with capitalism went on, but overseas. It was much safer.

Vietnam had been a running sore in Southeast Asia ever since the British liberated Hanoi in the late summer of 1945. The Vichy French regime's writ had not run ever since the Japanese captured Vietnam in 1941 and the Japanese surrender was treated with understandable jubilation by the liberated Vietnamese. So much so, that a harassed General Gracey and his 20th Indian Division were forced to re-arm the surrendered

Japanese soldiers and send them back on the streets as a *gendarmerie*, much to the surprise of the celebrating Vietnamese. The obedient Japanese officers and their well-armed soldiers soon re-asserted law and order. A Vietnamese patriot called Ho Chi Minh had led a highly successful guerrilla resistance movement against the Japanese between 1941 and 1945, called the Viet Minh. A committed Moscow-trained Communist, Ho now set up his own provisional Vietnamese government and declared Vietnam a free republic – free of French colonial authority, that is. Calm was restored until the French colonial authorities made a hasty arrival three weeks later. In September 1945 the British (having detained Ho Chi Minh briefly) politely withdrew, leaving the newly arrived French army to storm Ho Chi Minh's well-defended headquarters in downtown Hanoi and re-impose their colonial rule. Ho and his communist band fled back into the countryside to carry on their fight, this time against their colonial masters. The Vietnam War had begun.

The French tried to crack down hard on the elusive Viet Minh. Following the humiliations of wartime defeat and occupation in Europe they were anxious to retain their overseas empire, especially Indochina. But Ho's guerrillas had spent four years honing their guerrilla military skills against conventional forces and now faded back into the jungle and mountain to continue their own version of 'the war of the flea' which had kept the Japanese occupiers so busy. For the next eight years the cream of the French army fought what they called 'the dirty war' to try and re-assert their authority over Indochina, but without success. Ho's forces were armed with increasingly heavier weapons by their fellow Russian and Chinese Communists and grew in both power and daring. Ho called it the 'war of the elephant and the grasshopper'. By the early 1950s, the grasshopper was winning.

In 1954 it was all over. A major detachment of France's crack troops was cut off, and shelled to destruction in an isolated valley called Dien Bien Phu. After a two-month siege, the last French strongpoint was surrounded and over-run. Cut off, with heavy casualties, no food or ammunition, the surviving legionnaires surrendered to be marched off into a harsh captivity. A 'poor feudal nation had beaten a great colonial power,' General Giap, the Viet Minh's military commander, boasted. 'It meant a lot. Not just to us, but to people all over the world.' Colonial powers everywhere winced.

Washington, in particular, looked askance at the communist victory. America's involvement in Vietnam went back to 1950 when the presidential Griffin Mission had visited the region and recommended to President Truman that, as Indochina was 'strategically important to us', the US should help the French. America should begin to provide aid. A total of $23.5 million was fed into local regional governments in order to encourage greater political stability and to support nationalists against the Communists. Concern about the deteriorating situation and France's lack of success grew over the next four years. French requests for direct American military help in the region were refused, although there was growing unease about the communist Viet Minh's increasing strength and success. Southeast Asia was slowly becoming a major American concern. However, just one year after ending the Korean War and 'bringing the boys home', President Eisenhower was obviously reluctant to embroil United States troops in yet another military conflict in Southeast Asia. The danger for Ike and his State Department was that, should all Indochina go communist, then the whole of Southeast Asia might go communist too, 'like a row of dominoes'.

At the time that domino theory seemed logical. The British had their hands full with a communist insurgency in Malaya.

Cambodia, Thailand, Laos, and even India and Burma, might fall under the sway of 'world communism'. In their ideological struggle against monolithic world communism it seemed entirely logical that America had a definite strategic interest in Southeast Asia during the early Cold War. Ike even warned the incoming President Kennedy to keep an eye on the region, especially Laos, as Indochina was of 'vital US interest'.

The Geneva Peace Conference of 1954 had split Vietnam in two. Like Korea, the peacemakers opted for an arbitrary solution, slicing Vietnam in half along the 17th parallel of latitude, to form a communist North Vietnam, and an American-backed South Vietnam led by the anti-communist oligarch Ngo Dinh Diem. Buoyed up by generous American subsidies, Diem ruled like some old-style Oriental potentate. Elections were suppressed or ignored; dissenters were locked away or fled; and Diem's family creamed off the government posts and the lucrative American aid money. It was all splendidly corrupt. For the average Vietnamese peasant, Diem's South was little better than the oppressive communist North. Despite their equally authoritarian regimes, the two Vietnams withdrew into their two ideologically separate totalitarian selves.

By 1960 communist expansionism, added to a firm intention to reunite the country, encouraged the North to form the National Front for the Liberation of South Vietnam, or NLF, as an umbrella organization to overthrow the Diem regime in the South. By then Ho Chi Minh had already begun to carry his guerrilla war skills into the South. From 1957 to 1959 special units of the North Vietnamese army had secretly begun to infiltrate South Vietnam to build up a logistic base and to hew out the beginning of what would become known as the Ho Chi Minh trail. Hand-in-hand with this build-up went a systematic campaign of low-level terror and intimidation against the Diem regime's infrastructure. Between 1959 and 1961, the number of assassinations of South Vietnamese government officials, 'traitors' and even school teachers ('collaborators') soared from 1,200 to over 4,000 per year. Diem's unpopularity increased as the persecution of his – mostly Buddhist – opponents, reversal of the much-liked land reforms of the Viet Minh era, and general strong-arm tactics against dissenters raised discontent in South Vietnam to new levels. Eventually, in desperation, Diem called for help from his American backers.

Soon after his presidential inauguration, with its ringing promise to 'pay any price' and 'bear any burden', JFK had called for an assessment of the situation in Southeast Asia. His advisor was General Edward Lansdale, a Vietnam expert. Lansdale had been advisor to Diem as a colonel in 1954 and was a committed exponent of 'indirect' US military aid: deniable sabotage, special forces, 'hearts and minds' propaganda, and 'dirty tricks'. Kennedy read Lansdale's report, which urged him to use such methods to increase aid to Diem and the South.

Kennedy was impressed. 'This is the worst one we've got, isn't it?' he said to an aide, and immediately authorized greater American resources to South Vietnam. Another advisor, George Ball, protested, 'Don't do it, Mr. President. One day you'll need 300,000 troops.' Kennedy replied: 'George, you're crazier than Hell. That'll never happen.' The keen young President had committed the United States to propping up a corrupt totalitarian regime in the name of anti-communism.

Thanks to the enthusiasm of their new President, the long American nightmare of Vietnam had begun.

By 1963, Indochina was absorbing considerable presidential time. Under the influence of Secretary of Defense Robert

McNamara, Washington treated it as a 'management' problem. McNamara, sometime successful chairman of the Ford Motor Company, managed the Department of Defense and Vietnam just as he had managed corporate America. The large-scale investment of money, arms, supplies and advisors – properly managed by accountants and consultants – was going to 'win the war by '64'. Plans were even prepared to cut the number of US advisors to Diem's regime as part of a management wind-down once victory was clearly in sight.

Not everyone was convinced. The American officer corps was deeply suspicious of McNamara's 'cost efficient' management methods, muttering darkly as a small army of bright young consultants from the RAND and other corporations came to tell bemedalled combat veterans how best to fight their wars. Vietnam, the soldiers predicted, would prove to be far too complex a problem for business methods and managers, however talented. Others had similar doubts. A mission under Senator Mike Mansfield reported after a fact-finding tour in 1962 that the President should tread very carefully '. . . after all, it's their country not ours . . .' The problem, concluded Mansfield, was not with the Viet Cong but with Diem, the South Vietnamese leader. Mansfield recommended a major reappraisal of US policy to avoid any deeper involvement. He warned that deeper American involvement would 'not only be costly in terms of US lives and resources but it may also draw us inexorably into some variation of the position formerly occupied by the French . . .' Kennedy disagreed in public. But in private the President gave contingency orders to prepare for a complete US pullout in 1964 – after his re-election. Events, and assassins' bullets, would change all that.

Throughout the summer of 1963, support for Diem ebbed away. His high-handed manner, his family's greed and his harsh treatment of dissent caused mounting outrage. Diem

became ever more dictatorial. Buddhist monks burned themselves alive in protest, and the shocking pictures went round
the world. The American media told the truth about their
corrupt ally to the obvious discomfiture of Pennsylvania
Avenue and the State Department. South Vietnam's leader
was fast becoming a major embarrassment to the Americans.
In the end the White House decided on murder. We now have
clear proof that it was Kennedy himself who approved the fatal
order to do away with America's ally, directing the assassination of his 'friend' Diem. Although JFK later temporized, and
even suggested delaying the coup, he did it too late. The CIA
had already set the killing in motion.

Part of the problem seems to have been that Kennedy was a
Roman Catholic. Rightly or wrongly, many believed that his
links with the Church influenced many of his political judge-
ments. His father, Joe Kennedy, the old Mafia liquor supplier
of Prohibition days, certainly was. Cardinal Joseph Spellman
of New York, in particular, seems to have exerted unusual
influence over the Kennedy family and the White House
during JFK's presidency. The issue appears to have been that
part of the US's 'ally-problem' in South Vietnam now revolved
around religion, because Diem, like many of his South Vietnamese supporters, was also a Catholic. But the South Vietnamese *opposition* was mainly Buddhist. Catholic or not,
however, Diem was now a clear obstacle to US policy and
unacceptable to the majority of Buddhists in South Vietnam.
Diem had to go. The Catholic Kennedy wrestled with the life-
and-death responsibilities of superpower. A Jesuit would have
explained away the necessity of getting rid of Diem without
batting an eyelid, but Kennedy was no Jesuit. He agonized for
days before finally giving in to the CIA's and State Department's demands, and agreeing to the murder.

On 2 November 1963, Diem was assassinated along with

his brother, by his own officers in a palace coup. Washington was totally complicit. The CIA knew of the plot, encouraged it, and assisted the conspirators. Even that pillar of Yankee respectability, Ambassador Henry Cabot Lodge, admitted US guilt. But the US had at last removed one thorn in the side of their Indochina policy.

Once the coup was over, and Diem's bloodstained corpse had been unloaded from the back of an M113 APC, Henry Cabot Lodge signalled the President in Washington: 'The prospects now are for a shorter war . . .' Kennedy signalled back his approval to his ambassador in Saigon.

Three weeks later the President of the United States too fell victim to an assassin's bullet.

JFK's successor as President was his Vice-President Lyndon Baines Johnson. A large man, raised in the backwoods of Texas, LBJ was much more complex than his public 'simple country boy' manner indicated. Behind the scenes the backwoods boy was a consummate political wheeler-dealer, at the same time kind and generous, ruthless and untrustworthy. He had been helped to power by Mafia money and knew better than most how to make the corrupt side of Capitol Hill work. His skills as a wheeler-dealer in the corridors of Washington and his ability to use Federal tax dollars from the 'pork barrel' to further his political causes were legendary. The problem for LBJ was that he was not the man for the job. His very skills as a long-standing politician and as Senate majority leader – saying different things to different people, breaking his word when it was to his advantage, and just plain lying – made him unfit for presidential office. This large, surprisingly nervous, man now found himself caught between his political dream of a 'great society' domestically, and a foreign war of which he had disapproved. Politically he dare not cut and run from Vietnam, and it was too late to say that Kennedy should never have got them involved in the first place. The Vietnam War was a tar baby, covering all whom it touched with sticky marks, but which, if abandoned, would scream 'We surrendered!' to the American people, the media and the rest of the world. To make things worse, LBJ had to cope with riots during the hot southern summers at home as well as the simultaneous un-ravelling of his inherited war in Southeast Asia. Perhaps the greatest irony of all was that he had been the strongest opponent of the anti-Diem coup. The accidental President had inherited the results of a policy he detested. With great power go great problems. Such is politics.

The problem for America, by the time LBJ came to power, was actually a fundamental question of national geo-political policy. Did the USA have a coherent strategy during its war in Vietnam? For those unfortunate enough to have fought the war it often seems – as it did to them at the time – like an uncoordinated series of events. No discernible policy thread seems to be evident.

Nothing could be further from the truth.

American policy in Vietnam was *always* rational, at all times, and calibrated national strategic goals with both military force and events on the ground. The problem was that it was just plain wrong. LBJ's mistaken policies in Vietnam piled misunderstandings on to missed chances, miscalculation on to muddle on the ground. And over the whole sorry story lay the problem, not of North Vietnam, but of America's ally – the South. Because it was South Vietnam that was always the problem. At first it had to be encouraged as an anti-communist pawn; then it had to be backed up as an ally; and finally, Diem's successors had to be supported and controlled to prevent America's ally from going under. American policy in Vietnam failed in all three; either being too little too late, or being an inconstant and fickle friend. All along, South Vietnam's rotten, confused and corrupt regime was America's fundamental strategic weakness in Indochina. Against the single-minded nationalism and fanatical determination of Hanoi, South Vietnam lacked a cause.

By the time LBJ had established a firm grip on the presidency in 1965, he faced three clear policy options in Indochina. He could 'get the Hell out of Vietnam' and abandon America's allies, but that was unthinkable. He could go for a full military solution against North Vietnam. Or he could bring the North to the negotiating table by carefully graduated military blows, and force a binding solution on the two parties.

Johnson opted for a combination of his second and third options: to use military force and attack the North in order to coerce the Communists to the negotiating table. It was an entirely sensible and logical decision. Unfortunately, the strategy failed to take into account three crucial dangers: the softness of the American 'Home Front'; the weakness of the South Vietnamese; and, finally, the stubbornness of the North Vietnamese enemy. Despite these dangers and fundamental flaws, LBJ now sought to end his unwanted Asian war as quickly as possible. And the plan went ahead.

The problem both President and Pentagon faced was the old problem of rebel 'sanctuary'. Most of the anti-government activity in the South – but not all – was obviously coming in across the border from bases in the north. LBJ decided to go for the source of the trouble. In 1964 Washington decided to attack the Communist North Vietnamese Army (NVA) in the North in retaliation for its support for the Viet Cong attacks in the South. There was a danger in this strategy. The NVA – or the Chinese – might use the attacks on the North as an excuse to enter the fight openly against Saigon, just as they had in

North Korea thirteen years before. So the US had to tread carefully. It could not be seen to attack North Vietnam for no reason. Some kind of pretext was needed. LBJ and McNamara decided to find one.

As its reason for attacking the North, Washington found its pretext off the coast of North Vietnam.

The 'Gulf of Tonkin incident' of 1964 proved to be one of the turning points of the Vietnam War. Controversy surrounds the facts to this day.

The US Navy had for years been probing the electronic coastal defences of the USSR, North Korea and communist China. These sigint and elint missions, code-named 'De Soto' operations, involved sailing inshore to force the Cold War enemy to switch on their tracking and missile defence radars. Then the US collectors could pull away having recorded the valuable intelligence signatures of the radars, such as wavelengths or PRFs (pulse repetition frequencies.) On 2 August 1964 the USS *Maddox*, a destroyer equipped with a special NSA-CIA electronic intelligence suite, sailed into the Gulf of Tonkin to see if she could stir up a reaction as her radars swept the North Vietnamese littoral. She did.

As the *Maddox* cruised eight miles offshore, three North Vietnamese fast patrol boats (FPB) burst out from their three-mile limit and roared to the attack. The *Maddox* fled for the open sea, but the small FPBs were quicker. At 10,000 yards the *Maddox*'s captain, Herrick, ordered 'Open fire!' on his pursuers. In the ensuing *mêlée*, torpedoes and gunfire blazed in every direction. Two of the NV FPBs were seriously damaged and a third sunk. F-8 Crusaders flown in support from the carrier USS *Ticonderoga* completed the action by strafing the crippled patrol boats. That was, however, not the end of the *Maddox* affair. The political overtones were deafening. For the first time, US forces had deliberately and overtly engaged the North Vietnamese in battle. LBJ's stiff note to Hanoi, warning the Communists not to try it again 'or grave consequences would ensue', was the first formal recognition of the Northern regime by Washington. LBJ's call to advise Khrushchev that he had no wish to widen the conflict was the first-ever use of the new post-Cuba 'hot-line' to the Kremlin. Tonkin was a seminal event.

That *should* have been the end of the incident. Captain Herrick had pulled the *Maddox* back into deep waters and the US had collected its all-important electronic intelligence while teaching the North Vietnamese a sharp lesson. However, the senior commanders at sea and the politicians reckoned without the hawkish plans of the Pentagon. 'They'll get another sting . . .' Dean Rusk ominously warned a group of reporters back in Washington. The joint Chiefs of Staff and the Commander-in-Chief of the US Pacific fleet now ordered a second run inshore, this time accompanied by a back-up destroyer, the USS *Turner Joy*. The two American warships were also covering a secret South Vietnamese amphibious raid on North Korea. These pin-prick commando attacks on North Vietnamese coastal installations had got bolder during the summer of 1964. Operation 'Swift' of 3 August was 75 miles north of the 17th parallel, a long way behind the border and a very real provocation to the North Vietnamese, who appear to have been under the impression that although they could intervene in South Vietnam, any counter-attack on the North was somehow provocative.

As the US Navy ships closed the coast, the electronic ether became thick with North Vietnamese transmissions and warnings as the South Vietnamese commando raid was detected. Worried North Vietnamese commanders ashore ordered patrol boats to stop them. To make matters worse a storm blew up.

The Gulf of Tonkin is noted for sudden squalls. As darkness fell, the US warships' warning systems began to deteriorate as the thunderstorm swept around the ships, and wind and torrential rain lashed the delicate antennae. Rolling in heavy seas made electronic and sonar contacts erratic. Nervous lookouts reported possible threats in the blackness and watch-keepers opened fire at unseen targets as no fewer than twenty-two torpedoes were reported by sonar. Overhead, a flight of back-up Crusader jets patrolled fruitlessly in the gloom, unable to establish a clear contact with the invisible North Vietnamese patrol boats. *Maddox* reported herself as being under attack and sent an 'Enemy Contact' report.

As dawn broke, a tired and anxious Captain Herrick gradually came to the conclusion that his officers and crew had perhaps over-reacted. Bad weather, inexperienced young operators and degraded battle systems had conspired to bring about a false alarm; it was a phenomenon known in the First World War trenches as 'getting the wind up', as nervous sentries blasted away at non-existent targets. But far away in Washington, the political damage had been done. By the end of the day, LBJ's staff were briefing the UN and America's allies that 'a second deliberate attack had occurred against US forces on the high seas' and that US carrier-based jets had been ordered to retaliate against North Vietnam. President Johnson went on US national television to warn his fellow Americans that 'repeated acts of violence against the United States must be met with a positive reply. That reply is being given as I speak to you tonight.' Even as he was speaking, sixty-four US fighter jets were blasting North Vietnamese fast patrol boat bases and their support installations.

Two of those first jets failed to return. One of the pilots survived. As his burning jet fell apart around him, Lieutenant (jg) Alvarez of the USS *Constellation* ejected to become the first of the 600 US aircrew who would subsequently spend their war as prisoners in the infamous 'Hanoi Hilton', until their final repatriation eight years later. The US was now *de facto* at war. Its pilots had conducted an open act of war against North Vietnam in retaliation for attacks on the USS *Maddox* in the Gulf of Tonkin.

The problem was that the Maddox had *not* been attacked a second time.

The second Gulf of Tonkin attack never happened. Instead, a false alarm in the dark, and confused reporting of North Vietnamese radio traffic, had conspired with bureaucratic chicanery to give Washington its sought-after excuse to broaden the war and attack North Vietnam. Bi-partisan political support quickly rallied round LBJ's 'robust response' and, almost unanimously, his fellow patriots on Capitol Hill gave their President legal powers to 'take all necessary measures . . . to prevent further aggression' in Southeast Asia. Dissenting voices were over-ruled or ignored. It was political *carte blanche* for the US to take the war to North Vietnam and force them to the negotiating table. Unfortunately, it was all based on a deliberate falsification of the facts. Even LBJ admitted that he knew the real truth about the night's events in the Gulf of Tonkin: 'Hell, those dumb stupid sailors were just shootin' at flying fish,' he later confided to an aide. It mattered not. Thanks to political lies, bureaucratic trickery and a prepared contingency plan, the US military was now free to attack North Vietnam and to end the Vietnam War by military muscle.

Assured by being elected President in his own right in March 1965, LBJ now took up the military cudgel to beat North Vietnam into submission. The first American combat troops soon waded ashore at Da Nang. In all fairness, the US had been much provoked. For example, at Christmas 1964 the Viet

Cong planted a bomb in a US officers' hotel causing sixty casualties, and in February 1965 a daring raid on an advanced airfield and special forces camp at Pleiku destroyed ten US aircraft and killed or wounded over 100 Americans. LBJ's choice was clear: 'Do it right or get out.' 'Mac' Bundy, a presidential security advisor on a fact-finding mission in Vietnam, cabled the President direct, warning him that 'the great weakness in the US posture is a widespread belief that we do not have the will and force and patience and determination to take the necessary action and to stay the course . . .' As events were to prove a decade later, Bundy was 100 per cent correct.

LBJ ordered more air-strikes on North Vietnam and more ground troops to be despatched. The policy looked tough but missed a vital chance. Behind the scenes, Kosygin, Khrushchev's successor in the Kremlin, had been pressing the North Vietnamese to negotiate a deal with the South. Now faced by clear proof of 'imperialist aggression' against a small communist country, the Soviets – ever mindful of the critical comments of the increasingly scornful comrades in Beijing – had no choice but to provide plentiful military support for their beleaguered fellow communist North Vietnamese clients. Both sides had thrown away a chance of ending the undeclared war.

From 1965 onwards the Vietnam War developed its own momentum. LBJ's policy of 'minimum candor' hid the truth from the American people as the war escalated. Viet Cong attacks led to further American retaliation from the air, then commitment of ground forces, initially to protect US bases and then on 'seek and destroy' missions. Numbers grew from 60,0000 in 1964 to 215,000 by February 1966. Attempts at 'hearts and minds' counter-insurgency campaigns modelled on the British operations in Malaya fifteen years previously were clumsy and unsuccessful. Diem's successors and the

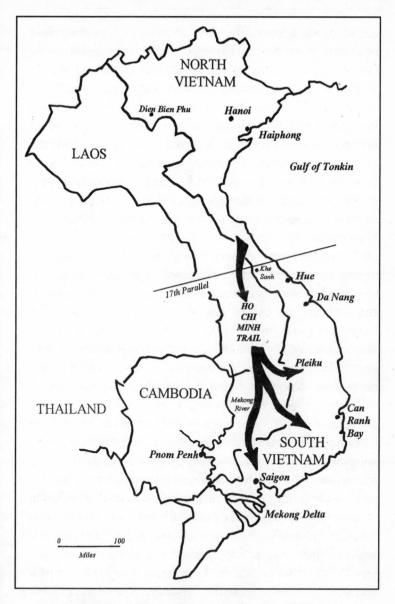

A Cold War defeat: Vietnam's long war, 1945–75

Saigon regime were rightly perceived as corrupt and remained unpopular in the South. There was little or no success to be found there. Like some inexorable military ratchet, air attacks were stepped up to destroy and blast the North Vietnamese into submission. The 1965 'Rolling Thunder' bombing campaign against the North lasted for three years. At no time did it force the North to negotiate, nor did it seriously impede the steady flow of manpower and supplies to the South.

Despite the lack of success, LBJ clung to his policy. Periodically he would halt the bombing and invite Hanoi to talks, using the US ambassador in Moscow as the go-between in these diplomatic moves. The stubborn North Vietnamese refused to cooperate, even on one occasion returning the President's personal letter unopened, and denouncing the bombing halt as 'a well-known trick'. The bombing intensified. LBJ had no one to talk to and could only fight on. American support to the South swelled and American operations intensified. By mid-1967, a million tons of US supplies were arriving in South Vietnam every month. Slowly but inexorably, US firepower and numbers began to take effect.

By the end of 1967, contrary to popular belief, the United States had effectively beaten the North Vietnamese. Massive sweep-and-destroy missions, like Operation 'Cedar Falls' in the summer of 1967, had broken the Communists' stranglehold on the South, even if they failed to stop them filtering back in dribs and drabs. The NVA forward command HQ was forced to flee back across the Cambodian and Laotian frontiers and their logistic supply chain was disrupted and dispersed. Only twenty of the 242 provinces of South Vietnam were still officially designated as 'insecure'. By autumn of 1967 defeat stared Hanoi in the face as the Politburo admitted that they had no real military options left. As 1968 opened with half a million US servicemen in South Vietnam and victory in sight, LBJ's policy of bludgeoning North Vietnam to the negotiating table by military force seemed to have worked.

Then came Tet.

The Tet Offensive of January 1968 was planned by the communist government in Hanoi in the belief that unless they made one last effort they would have failed in their long campaign to conquer the South. They made one desperate last-ditch attempt to bring about a speedy communist victory. The final plan was complex and based on the Viet Minh's experience with the French. A diversionary attack on an American airbase at Khe Sanh on the northern border was intended to draw US attention to a new Dien Bien Phu, like a matador's cape draws a bull. Then, while the US was bogged down in a conventional siege, and with all eyes on beleaguered Khe Sanh, the Viet Cong and their NVA allies would launch a massive insurgent offensive throughout the whole of South Vietnam to raise the 'toiling revolutionary masses' and incite a countrywide rising of the 'workers and peasants' against their 'hated oppressors'. Victory would ensue. Marx said so. The Revolution would triumph.

It was all a ghastly failure. None of the Communists' plans worked. The 'oppressed masses' in the South failed to rise. Indeed, in many cases the South Vietnamese 'oppressed masses' actually fought off the Communists from the North with considerable ferocity or turned them in to the authorities. Despite having been taken completely by surprise, the Americans in Vietnam reacted swiftly too. Infiltrators into the US Embassy's compound were cornered and gunned down like rats in full view of astonished TV crews. In savage fighting throughout the southern cities the communist invaders were trapped by well-led US and South Vietnamese forces and killed off where they stood. Hue, the only city to fall to the Communists, was surrounded and re-captured after a fierce battle by US Marines, these events being captured by the rolling cameras and news reporters like the outstanding war photographer Don McCullin. With 30,000 dead and their plans in ruins, Hanoi's Communists admitted defeat. Tet had failed completely.

Then the American media won it for them – or so embittered Vietnam veterans often claim.

The idea that the US media lost the Vietnam War is understandable. The fact is that it did not. The media – for most of the early part of the war – simply reflected the national mood and supported both the administration in Washington and the prejudices of most Americans. It was the *American public* that really lost the war. The mendacities of the Pentagon and their President, the lack of governmental candour, proliferating stories in local newspapers of friends' sons not making it home, and rising taxes, all began to gnaw away at American public support for the war. Vietnam seemed a long way away, its war never-ending and costly in young lives and money, and appearing to be going nowhere. A widening credibility gap opened up between the people and their government's claims. Protest against the war increased. The sight of young Americans burning their draft cards became as common a sight in the late 1960s and early 1970s as the emerging feminist movement burning their brassières in public. Rebellion was everywhere in the air. Vietnam offered a powerful rallying standard for protest against the establishment.

Many of those eligible for military service, including at least one future President, dodged the draft by going to Canada, enlisting in the home-based National Guard or fleeing overseas to study, an option much favoured by rich, educated families.

The burden fell increasingly on the poor and particularly the blacks. America became even more divided and resentful. A growing refusal to be drafted into the army, and the perception that America was just not winning, all raised public doubts. The widely respected magazines *Life* and *Time* ran articles questioning the purpose of the war. Popular songs like 'The Times They Are a-Changin'' and 'Where Have All the Flowers Gone?' mocked the administration, singing wistfully of peace and dead soldiers.

America itself exploded in protest: 1968 was a watershed year of revolutions and unrest. Black protest was aflame in the Deep South as the Civil Rights movement piled savage riots on to anti-war protest. Inflation was spiralling. Despite LBJ having enacted more liberal and progressive economic and social reforms than any President since Roosevelt, to many Americans his 'Great Society' was just another politician's empty boast and his Vietnam War its very symbol. The truth was that the media, for good or ill, merely reflected the American viewers' and readers' prejudices.

Tet, with its pictures of devastation, *looked* like a US defeat. The camera may have lied, but America had had enough.

Faced with growing protests at home and the shocking images from Tet, Washington weakened. LBJ was assailed on every side. The People's Republic of China secretly moved 50,000 'volunteers' into North Vietnam, and behind the scenes warned LBJ that any attempt to move against North Vietnam 'risked another Korea'. LBJ kept this firmly from the American people and the world. The China of 1968 was not the China of 1951: Mao had exploded his first atom bomb in 1964, launched a ballistic missile in 1966 and detonated his own hydrogen bomb in 1967. China was a force to be taken very seriously, even by the United States, in 1968. The result was that America's room to manoeuvre was constrained both at home and in Southeast Asia.

The shock of Tet coincided with yet another American debacle. The loss of the intelligence collection ship (AGER) USS *Pueblo* off the coast of North Korea in January 1968 was yet another blow to American prestige and pride. The *Pueblo* had been spying on communist radio traffic when she was intercepted by North Korean warships and boarded. There was no US backup, no air cover. The virtually unarmed auxiliary was captured along with a complete haul of the latest American naval sigint technology, and ignominiously towed into Wonsan. Scores of classified documents were seized and the eighty-three crewmen captured, interrogated and beaten, even the wounded. The captain and his officers were forced to sign 'confessions'. The Americans protested about this 'piracy on the high seas' but short of starting another Korean War there was little that the US President could do. One war in Southeast Asia was enough. Privately, the enraged Johnson discussed 'using a nuke' on North Korea, but cooler heads prevailed. The *Pueblo* eventually became a museum exhibit of 'Yankee perfidy' and spying in Wonsan harbour, where it remains to this day. Only when the Americans admitted that they had been spying on North Korea were the surviving crewmen released a year later.

Relations with North Korea, already glacial, became if possible even colder.

LBJ (who by now had had quite enough of the burdens of office) announced that he would not run in any future election, and began talks with the North Vietnamese. They were adamant: the US must stop the bombing and Hanoi would – perhaps – discuss a settlement. But domestic unrest, mounting taxes and endless casualties, all fuelled an increasing climate of war-weariness, and undermined Washington's increasingly desperate policy makers. Many Americans began to believe that it had been a mistake to commit US combat troops to Vietnam in the first place. What was it for? Public opinion was clear: 'Either win – or bring the boys back.' LBJ was trapped.

Hanoi was well aware of the US public mood and played on it. Abortive preliminary peace talks using President Brezhnev and the British Prime Minister Harold Wilson as intermediaries had previously foundered on the semantic rocks of words like 'could' and 'should' as both sides niggled away at the issue of who, in a pre-condition for talks, should – or would – cease their offensives first. America's friends and opponents in the Cold War struggled equally to broker a solution for Washington, because both the UK and the USSR had clear Cold War interests in Vietnam.

The Kremlin still officially backed the communist regime in North Vietnam, if only to prevent the Chinese from increasing their influence in the region. The Sino–Soviet split was nearing an ugly climax in 1968 as Mao's Cultural Revolution destabilized communism everywhere. In their turn, the Chinese had never accepted Moscow's version of world communism since Khrushchev had exposed Stalin's totalitarian excesses in 1956. The Russian leader's subsequent climb down over Cuba and his flat refusal to share nuclear secrets with Beijing had widened the communist powers' rift still further. China now saw the People's Republic as communism's standard bearer in the fight against imperialism, in direct competition with Moscow. Khrushchev and his successors could not permit China's version of communism to prevail, but still had to co-exist with the west, and particularly with the United States.

The Kremlin solved this thorny dialectical conundrum by leaning on Hanoi, promising even more aid from the USSR to help the fight against the American imperialists, but only if the

North Vietnamese would open negotiations with the US. Hanoi refused. They would accept Russian aid; but whilst the Americans were bombing the North, they could not possibly negotiate with Washington. Anyway, they were winning and throwing the imperialists into the sea. The Russians argued in vain. Eventually they stormed out, calling the North Vietnamese 'a bunch of stubborn bastards' in an ironic echo of American negotiators' own frustrations at dealing with Hanoi. The British, for their part, were also resisting increasingly strident pleas from their principal ally to come and help. LBJ begged Prime Minister Wilson to send just one single British battalion to Vietnam to demonstrate solidarity. Mindful of British public opinion and the ugly anti-American and anti-Vietnam riots in London, Wilson wisely refused. He had a socialist Labour government, most of whose members were instinctively anti-American, to keep onside. As a further complication, all sides were also keenly aware that Soviet and British merchant ships were moored in Haiphong harbour and were potential targets should the US ever decide to attack North Vietnam's vital supply port. US war planes bombing Soviet merchant ships in a communist port would really have set the Cold War cat among the pigeons. In the midst of all this muddle sat the stubborn North Vietnamese with their simple strategy: 'fight *and* talk'.

American public opinion was swinging against the war, giving the North an invaluable new ally in their battle with Washington. With the leaking of the supposedly secret 'Pentagon Papers', revelations of White House duplicity over Vietnam going back for decades exploded into the headlines. Americans were outraged and confused. Their boys were still dying out there. Was the war in Vietnam, let alone a moral anti-communist Cold War crusade, really worth it? Presidential advisors were now openly advocating exit strategies. From

Hanoi it looked as if, as long as the North Vietnamese held out, victory would fall into their hands like a ripe plum. But they reckoned without the new President, Richard Nixon, elected in 1968. Nixon was quite clear that he wanted to cut US forces in Vietnam but he had to be seen to do it as part of a handover to the South Vietnamese, not as a humiliating climb down to Hanoi. 'Vietnamization' of the war and an orderly withdrawal of US forces was the way ahead for Washington. Peace talks in Paris groped for a solution that would enable the White House to clamber out of the Vietnamese swamp. But Hanoi's intransigence didn't help.

Hanoi's position was weaker than it realized. Mao Tse-tung's Red China was now a considerable factor in the Cold War equation. Neither the USA or the USSR wanted any more trouble with China than Mao was already providing. Having finally acquired nuclear weapons in 1964, Mao had launched his Cultural Revolution and given millions of copies of his Little Red Book to friend and foe alike. 1968, a year of widespread unrest, saw demonstrators in Europe and America waving the Little Red Book as they marched down the boulevards in a glorious carnival of anarchy, bawling, 'Ho! Ho! Ho Chi Minh!' and frightening governments everywhere. Suddenly Chinese communism was an irritant to everybody. Not surprisingly, Presidents Brezhnev and Nixon sought common cause against this unstable new threat from the east. The first stirrings of *détente* began to emerge between the Kremlin and Washington and it was China, as much as anything, that was pushing Moscow into talking to Washington.

By 1970, however, China's Cultural Revolution was running out of steam as Beijing's central government re-asserted control over the wilder regional and Party excesses fomented by the Great Helmsman of the East and brought his armies of Red Book-waving Red Guards back into line. The People's

Republic let it be known that the Party was back in charge, and that China wanted to re-establish normal relations with the international community as soon as possible. In the midst of this changing re-alignment Washington decided to play one communist giant off against the other as a new Cold War strategy. Nixon decided to 'play the China card'. In 1971 Henry Kissinger flew to Beijing for friendly talks with the Chinese government. China's quarter-century of isolation was over. North Vietnam was, however, the principal stumbling block. If only North Vietnam could be made to see sense, argued Kissinger, US-Chinese relations would blossom. The US President himself was prepared to fly to Beijing. But someone had to put the bite on Hanoi and get the stubborn North Vietnamese to talk.

The American strategy worked perfectly. The Kremlin was more than anxious to prevent the formation of any US-Chinese communist axis, and even willing to talk about limiting nuclear weapons as a means of seducing Washington back into the old Cold War. Beijing was equally keen for recognition and respectability from Washington. Washington played the shy bride between these Red suitors for her favours. The problem was, said Kissinger, that North Vietnam's stubbornness was now an embarrassment to everybody except the ideologues in Hanoi. Gradually all sides became aware that Vietnam with all its problems was dispensable. China needed the 'ping-pong diplomacy' and links with the west to grow. The USSR needed to stop any anti-Soviet alliance between America and China at all costs. Nixon's United States needed an Arms Limitation Treaty with the Soviet Union, and to get out of Vietnam. These were all linked. The problem of Vietnam needed to be got rid of.

If only these complex diplomatic moves fell into place – what Henry Kissinger called 'the biggest diplomatic coup of all time' – then North Vietnam would be reduced to a mere nuisance for the big three. 'A settlement in Vietnam is the key to the whole thing,' Kissinger told the Kremlin. Hanoi, its sanctuaries in Laos and Cambodia now under direct attack, increasingly isolated and increasingly vulnerable as its fellow Communists, paymasters and allies baled out, made one last desperate power-play. In spring 1972 the NVA launched an all-out invasion of the South to try and steal a quick victory. Like Tet, the April 1972 NVA assault was a total failure. The now well-armed and well-trained South Vietnamese army fought the NVA's invading tanks to a standstill. Nixon threw the full might of the USAF into the battle again. 'Operation Linebacker' targeted Haiphong harbour for the first time and combat supplies dried up as the bombing took effect as never before. The giant B-52 bombers blasted the shocked North Vietnamese to the negotiating table. Once again the US was poised for final victory over a broken North Vietnam. Hanoi's backers looked the other way. Hanoi called for talks to end the pain.

This time it was South Vietnam that stopped a negotiated peace. President Thieu, who had known nothing of Washington's secret negotiations with China and the North Vietnamese, refused to cooperate. He demanded many more concessions and guarantees from the North before he would agree to anything. He certainly didn't trust Hanoi. By now desperate, Nixon and Kissinger decided to 'really turn the screw' and force Hanoi to make major and highly visible concessions to reassure Saigon. The war spilled over into Cambodia and Laos as the Americans went for the NVA's supply bases across international borders. The final bombing offensive of the war, called 'Linebacker 2', finally unleashed the unrestrained might of the USAF's B-52s over North Vietnam. More bombs were unloaded in 1972 than in the whole of the Second World War. Hanoi and Haiphong were hammered into ruin. Key bridges, railways and power stations were struck. North Vietnam really did look as if it was going back to the Stone Age. Once again the US had demonstrated that if it had to, it could always win the war by sheer military force.

Under this bludgeoning Hanoi gave in. On 23 January 1973 a peace deal was finally signed in Paris. The US would pull out, North Vietnam would withdraw from the South – but still maintain a 'legitimate interest' in South Vietnam's affairs (which meant that the Viet Cong stayed in place) – and the US POWs would be freed. Even this deal was only agreed under duress. At the last minute President Thieu, rightly suspecting that the Paris Treaty was primarily a device to get the US President off the hook and throw South Vietnam to the wolves, refused to sign. Only when Nixon and Kissinger threatened to sign a separate pact with North Vietnam and leave South Vietnam in the cold, did Thieu grudgingly sign. On 27 January 1973 the US flew its last combat mission over North Vietnam. The POWs began to trickle back home and US combat troops began their final pullout from the South. By March 1973, the last US soldier had gone. Kissinger won the Nobel Peace Prize, to the astonishment of many.

At its peak the Vietnam War had seen no fewer than half a million US troops on the ground. The war had cost America 58,100 dead and nearly 300,000 wounded. Its taxpayers had paid out over $150 billion at 1970s prices, or nearly $500 billion in 2006 values. Over 3,400 aircraft had been lost. Even the powerful US economy had been seriously damaged by the burden of such a war. In August 1971, with the US national debt spiralling out of control, Nixon had been forced to take America off what was effectively the gold standard, thus signalling the end of the post-war Bretton Woods economic agreement. Vietnam, increased oil prices, and grieving parents across the United States, would leave an indelible legacy on American life for years to come. Nixon called it 'Peace with Honor', but it was seen as a humiliating defeat for American diplomacy, American arms and, above all, for American pride. Even Nixon, the President who had 'brought the boys home', was finally humiliated totally. Brought down by the unravelling scandal of Watergate and the continuing controversies about the US's true role in Vietnam revealed by the leaked 'Pentagon Papers', he was forced from office in 1974, one jump ahead of impeachment or worse. Kissinger, his *éminence grise* and architect of many of the murkier aspects of the war in Southeast Asia, somehow managed to avoid his master's fate.

The greatest tragedy was that it was all a terrible waste. Within two years, South Vietnam was lost. In a climate of corruption, unemployment, total war-weariness and without US military aid, South Vietnam fell apart as, on 29 April 1975, North Vietnamese tanks finally stormed Saigon. There were chaotic scenes as the last US officials fled, their loyal Vietnamese allies still clinging desperately to the skids of over-loaded US helicopters. Many fell to their doom, a fitting metaphor for Saigon's long and sorry involvement with Washington. Vietnam became one unified communist state. Saigon was re-named Ho Chi Minh City.

From Washington, and from Moscow too, it looked as though America had suffered the biggest defeat of the Cold War.

18

THE CHILLS OF AUTUMN

PROBLEMS IN THE USSR

Moscow had its own preoccupations during the Vietnam era.

As America became increasingly absorbed with its Asian problems, so Europe began to stir. France's rejection of NATO, growing German economic and political power, and strengthening links between eastern and western Europe, all combined to foster a climate of reconciliation and greater friendliness there. America, as a protector, became increasingly distant. The Cold War now seemed manageable. Chancellor Willi Brandt's *Ostpolitik* between East and West Germany led to a gradual convergence of interests. Economic, cultural and social links multiplied. All over Europe, new hope stirred beneath the ice-cap of the post-1945 Cold War. By the early 1970s there was a definite breath of spring in the air.

Ironically this change of mood had to some extent blown across from America and was a by-product of the Vietnam War. The stiff-necked America of the 1950s had changed. By

1967 a complete counter-culture had grown up to challenge the accepted social *mores* of respectable middle America. Whereas in 1966 'My Country – Right or Wrong' had been the slogan of choice for many Americans as a bumper sticker, by 1968 it had turned into 'Hell, no – we won't go!' as thousands of unwilling conscripts for the US Army burned their draft cards. 'Make Love, Not War' was the rallying cry. Sex, drugs and rock 'n' roll became the lodestars of a youth now more prosperous, educated and free than ever before. In both America and Europe, societies became polarized between protest and the establishment, young and old, change and stability; and Vietnam became the battle standard of a protest movement that marched to Top Ten pop songs.

Such capitalist shenanigans had little effect on the tightly closed and controlled societies of the east. The Kremlin and the all-seeing Party kept a firm grip. But the mood of the clash between youthful idealism and old conservatism permeated everything in the late 1960s, from Mao's Cultural Revolution in China to hippy love-ins in California. Worldwide, a wave of riot and revolution stirred young people to challenge their leaders. Change was in the air. Inevitably, the Soviet empire too became infected with the virus of liberalism and the urge for change.

The pressures on 'the old men in the Kremlin' had in fact begun to build even as the 1960s dawned. The Cold War was an expensive road to follow and Moscow could ill-afford it. Communism's planned social economics meant a command economy, with the Party bureaucrats controlling the means of production, distribution and capital investment as good Marxists should. As with all bureaucracies, costs were high, as government money (not for nothing had Lenin's thugs invaded and robbed the Petrograd banks as their first step) was spent on an army of civil servants and planners. This clumsy, inflexible and wasteful economic system sat atop a massive military-industrial complex that rivalled anything in the west. The revolving door of cushy jobs between generals and arms manufacturers didn't exist in the USSR. Thanks to the Party it didn't need to. In the Soviet Union the military needs of the Cold War were all part of one single massive military enterprise, paid for by the state, and working for the all-powerful Party and the final triumph of Socialist endeavour. In such a system 'the people' didn't get a look in, whatever the blessed Marx had decreed. Without votes, without money and without rights, the communist worker ants of the east toiled for the Party: and the Party, the generals and the bureaucrats toiled for themselves.

The effect was inevitable. Starved of investment, with wretchedly poor productivity – 'The Party pretends to pay us for our labour,' said one underground slogan, 'so we pretend to work' – and unable to provide or distribute even the most basic consumer necessities, the sluggish economies of the east began to bend and break under the demands of the arms race. The Cold War was making the USSR and its people poorer by the day. In Seattle, ordinary Americans working for Boeing got richer; 'Heroes of Soviet Labour' in Novosibirsk had to queue for bread.

This economic pressure – which would one day break the Soviet Union – was made worse by the pressures of modernization. The industrial revolution had come too late in Russia. Stalin's Five Year Plans, and the subsequent Great Patriotic War with its trail of destruction, had both slowed and distorted Russian economic progress. Urbanization now dragged millions off the land into grim overcrowded cities to live in hopeless pre-fabricated grey tower blocks. The irony that what Engels had observed in the proliferating slums of Manchester in the 1840s was now being visited upon the

Marxist workers' paradise was not lost on either perceptive western commentators or cynical Communists. The difference, however, lay in the results of their labours. Whereas the new urban poor of nineteenth-century Britain had made their capitalist bosses rich and benefited society as a whole, in the one-party communist state all 'profit' went to the Party, to be diverted to satisfy the insatiable demands of Russia's great national industries: the space race, missiles, tanks and guns. The truth was that the new Russia couldn't even feed itself. To survive, the Soviet Union – once, thanks to the Ukraine, the breadbasket of the east – now had to import grain because its Soviet-style collective farms couldn't feed its population. The Soviet economy was polarizing, into its own version of the scientific-military complex on the one hand, and a run-down industrial and agrarian sector on the other. For the privileged workers in the former, the state provided only the best: for the rest, the sullen ill-educated peons of the communist economy, life offered little more than unremitting labour, constant shortages and a hopeless future. To his credit, Khrushchev tried to address this contradiction. Unfortunately, his attempts at 'regionalization' met with open resistance from the Party bureaucracy, suspicious of change and resentful of any loss of central power to the regions. The Party connived to obstruct sensible, but hasty, reforms. 'Decentralization' was anathema to the Communists' planned economy. Production fell, tractor parts sat in far-off railway sidings, and meat and milk became rare items for most. More than anything else, distribution was the problem, one that the Soviet system and its Party managers never really solved. Khrushchev recognized that he had alienated the Party machine, but without the steel grip of Stalin's secret police there was little he could do. Increasingly he ignored the Party and tried to rule by decree, but even dictatorship has its limits. The dead hand of the

Party's vast bureaucracy stifled and distorted his attempts at agricultural reform. Even the new Science Academies' research projects became ever more 'centrally directed' and stultified by new orders from Moscow, and the state's infant consumer industries were further starved of investment, materials and labour.

In the end it was this economic failure that finally did for Khrushchev. Many of his rivals on the Praesidium/Politburo still 'yearned for the old days', in the words of one dissident poet, and the old guard of the Party hated his reforms. His limited attempts at economic and political liberalization had inspired great resentment among the conservative Stalinist faction and, as ever, a small loosening of the state's oppressive bonds was used by reformers and critics as a licence for excess. To the ideologues of the Kremlin this was too much. The *avant garde* in art might even lead to some unthinkable change in society or politics. Corrupting western influences like the Beatles and consumerism were seen as undermining the fabric of Lenin's socialist paradise. The innate conservatism of the Party's ruling clique closed ranks against reform, whether social or economic. Khrushchev was viewed not just as a would-be reformer – 'changer' in fact best describes the precise criticism against him – of all that the old guard in the Kremlin held dear, but as a *failed* changer at that. In particular, the failure of agricultural reform had been especially damaging as it had led to social unrest. Cuba and Khrushchev's external Cold War 'adventures' were seen merely as the last straw in a long catalogue of dangerous and destabilizing policies.

In October 1964, while Khrushchev was at his holiday home at Pitsunda on the Black Sea, the Praesidium/Politburo finally voted their erratic Chairman out of office. Former KGB chief Shelepin masterminded this cabinet coup, along with Khrushchev's chosen second-in-command Leonid Brezhnev who, on

12 October 1964, telephoned Khrushchev from the Kremlin, urgently summoning him to Moscow for a special Praesidium meeting the following day. Khrushchev suspected a plot but flew to Moscow to be assailed by a well-planned political ambush. The Politburo accused him of high-handed behaviour, a cult of personality and 'being rude to his colleagues'. In vain did the Kremlin leader try to defend himself. He was shouted down by his own appointees and *protégés*. 'It's time to send Comrade Khrushchev into retirement,' one said ominously. Another accused him of 'setting himself up as opposition to the Praesidium'. Surrounded by men who had once been his friends, a crushed Khrushchev hardly spoke in his own defence. He accepted the criticisms and, weeping openly, offered to retire and leave, a broken man. Just to be sure, the conspirators convened a Party Plenum of the Central Committee to elect a new leader. Suslov, the Party's hatchet-faced principal ideologue, explained why Khrushchev had to go, to well-rehearsed shouts of 'Criminal!', 'Exclude him from the Party!', and 'Hand the traitor over to the courts!' from the floor. Fortunately for the shattered Khrushchev, 'sitting with his head in his hands', the senior Praesidium members resisted such Stalinist suggestions, but the point was clear. By the end of the day Khrushchev had 'retired'. The Party despatched the shoe-banging Ukrainian peasant to virtual house arrest in his country home. Premier Khrushchev overnight became 'Pensioner Khrushchev'. One of the big personalities of the Cold War had disappeared into obscurity.

The Party's new leader and the new Kremlin ruler – voted in by his colleagues as First Secretary – was Leonid Brezhnev, with Andrei Kosygin as his number two. A firm hand, coupled with stability at home, became the watchwords for Moscow. Adventurism was out.

Brezhnev's hard line against liberal reform re-united the Politburo. Using the Party machine as the guiding force of Soviet affairs, the old guard re-imposed strict Marxist-Leninist doctrine on the country. The Army and the KGB were encouraged to re-assert their strength in national life, wars of 'national liberation' in Angola and Ethiopia received full Soviet backing and were presented as communist initiatives, while the Mir space station demonstrated Soviet power to all. From the conservatives' point of view, Brezhnev 'sorted the USSR out' on good Marxist-Leninist lines.

But this concentration on domestic affairs loosened the Kremlin's hold on its satellites. The failures and stupidities of the Marxist command economy were not solely a Russian phenomenon. Eastern Europe's old Stalinist-style leaders may well have approved of Moscow's new theoretical orthodoxy. But the real world does not run on ideological theories, however clever. Incompetent and corrupt communist management was not just confined to the Soviet Union. Comecon's restrictions made foreign trade either impossible or expensive outside the communist trading area. By a massive irony, many eastern European states could only keep going by importing western technology and bank loans to bolster their ailing economies. Thanks to West Germany's policy of *Ostpolitik*, western money came to lubricate communism's wheels of trade; but with western trade came western influences.

The satellites started looking for their own answers to eastern Europe's economic ills. Each country tackled its command economy problems of falling productivity, food shortages and economic stagnation differently. *Détente* with the west encouraged ideas of radical reform and new solutions. All over eastern Europe, dissenting voices began to call for reform of what was quite obviously an ailing economic system. In Poland, Gomulka took the traditional communist line with any demands for change: brutal repression. The army moved in to put down striking workers. The Kremlin looked on with approval and backed their client leader with secret police and armed forces. The forces of reform in Poland faded into obscurity or into the Gulag. But shoving problems under the mattress is never a long-term solution, as the Polish Communists would one day find out.

Czechoslovakia was different. The Czech Communist Party was rejecting oppressive measures as early as 1966. This pragmatic line was reinforced by the 'market socialism' reforms of Antonin Novotny. Central controls were regionalized, a limited profit motive introduced, and Party censorship relaxed. This was heresy from the communist ideologues' point of view. Unsurprisingly, however, the economy began to pick up. But even these liberating measures were not enough for the growing coalition of reformers, students, workers' leaders and Czech Party reformers seeking major change. When Alexander Dubçek was voted in as Party leader in early 1968, he unleashed a tidal wave of reform based on the Czechoslovak Communist Party itself.

In all fairness to Dubçek he was first and foremost a committed Communist. His problem was that he was intelligent and objective enough to see past the rhetoric of Marxist-Leninist dogma to the practicalities of real life. By April 1968 Czechoslovakia's new leader had pushed through an unprecedented wave of reforms. He proposed the 'widest possible democratization of the entire socio-political system'. Dubçek's aim was nothing less than to make the Communist Party more responsive to the popular will. He wanted to *reform communism*. This was dynamite. 'Democracy' means something entirely different to a follower of Marx and Lenin than to a western voter. Only the Party could express the people's will democratically in a Marxist-Leninist state because, by definition, the Party was the highest expression of the people's will. To make the Party the vanguard of change was therefore a highly dangerous course in the communist system. The old guard looked on, suspicious. Like all reformers, Dubček had to steer a careful middle course between the forces of revolution and the forces of reaction. But in talking about 'democracy' he was challenging the Party's monopoly of power. It was a dangerous game, whatever the economic benefits.

By the spring of 1968, it was clear that the Czech Party had lost control of events. The playwright Vacláv Havel was openly calling for genuine opposition parties and *real* democracy. The activists of the Party became a leading voice demanding reformist measures to change the system. Moscow and, crucially, the other satellite Parties began to be seriously concerned about what was to become known as the 'Prague Spring'. The whole fabric of the Kremlin's eastern European *glacis* of tightly controlled satellite states appeared to be threatened. Czechoslovakia's economic reforms challenged, root and branch, the principle of one-party communist control; Dubček's independent line ultimately threatened the Kremlin itself and the Warsaw Pact (there were no occupying Red Army troops in Czechoslovakia). For Czechoslovakia was no Poland; its geography represented a corridor pointing straight through the heart of the Warsaw Pact's defences aimed at the Russian border.

The prospect of Czech independence alarmed the other satellites. How could the Czech Party be tolerating dissent, opposition even? Dubček's 'weakness' was a mortal danger to good Communists everywhere, and particularly to his fellow eastern European communist leaders, sitting uneasily on relatively sophisticated populations who, unlike the wretched Russians, had known better days. The wails of dismay from the other satellite Communist Parties grew shriller. We now know from the Kremlin's secret archives that one of the most worrying aspects of the 'Dubçek problem' was the flow of information inside the communist bloc. Many Czechs were corresponding with friends and colleagues throughout the satellite states and even with Russians. A 'secret' telegram in August 1968 to the Soviet Communist Party's Moscow Secretariat from the Moldavian Party's Second Secretary Kishinev reflects the growing alarm among the comrades and makes the Kremlin's dilemma clear:

In connection with the events in the CSSR . . . certain individuals have shown that they do not understand the essence of events . . . in Czechoslovakia and some express support . . . toward the so called 'liberalization'

Rather grimly, it adds:

Individual work is being undertaken with these people . . . some Soviet citizens who have relatives or friends in the CSSR are receiving letters with articles from Czech newspapers and magazines . . . the Director of Public Relations [in Czechoslovakia] sent to Moscow a letter appealing to Soviet citizens, which attempts to convince the Soviet people that the policy conducted by [the Czech leaders] is correct . . .

Pressure grew on Moscow to bring Dubçek and these dangerous Czech heretics into line. Hardline old Communists inside Czechoslovakia secretly begged the Kremlin to intervene and stamp out Prague's dangerous heresy. When Brezhnev telephoned Dubçek on 15 August, exhorting him to 'see sense', it was – in the Kremlin's eyes – a final appeal to reason from his communist friends. Did he not realize that events in

Prague could threaten them all? Dubçek failed to take the hint.

On the night of 25 August 1968 the Warsaw Pact invaded Czechoslovakia.

Soviet tanks moved along the main roads and sealed Prague. Russian paratroopers landed in a *coup de main* to seize Prague airport. Within three days, the Prague Spring was no more and the Kremlin had brutally re-asserted the Communist Party's primacy in eastern Europe. The Czechs did not fight their invaders. Hungary in 1956 had been a clear lesson in Soviet military brutality. Instead, the Czechs surrounded the invaders' tanks and asked them politely why they had invaded a fellow communist ally? Bewildered Russian tank drivers muttered 'orders', and looked puzzled when they were told that they were in Czechoslovakia. They had never been briefed. Officious Red officers and the KGB looked for 'counter-revolutionaries' to arrest and found none. The Czechs' passive resistance baffled the invaders and was well publicized, thanks to television. The image was one of Kalashnikovs versus flowers. Eventually Dubçek and his fellow reformers were effectively kidnapped by the KGB and dragged to Moscow to recant their sins, and to be told to toe the Kremlin's Party line, or else. There was no room for reform in Brezhnev's Soviet empire. Pluralism was forbidden. The Marxist-Leninist orthodoxy of the one-party state remained sacred, frozen for all time.

Back in Prague a new hardline regime of anti-reform Communists took control. They failed to govern. After all, it had been the Czech Communist Party itself that had led the reforms. For a short time, the hardliners even had to turn back to the crushed Dubçek to lead their country back to stability. The chastened First Secretary of the Czechoslovak Communist

Party did as he was told before finally being voted out of office and out of the Party in 1969. The Kremlin had re-asserted its authority. The Prague Spring was no more.

Although the events in Czechoslovakia in 1968 were as traumatic and shocking as any other Soviet exercise of naked force in their East European empire, they differed markedly from previous uprisings. First, the leaders were not mysteriously hurled from upper-storey windows or executed for crimes against the state; Dubçek merely disappeared to run a power station in the country. Second, the west very obviously did nothing. No one threatened Moscow. No nuclear weapons were brought to readiness. In 1968 western European capitals were dealing with their own mini-revolutions as protestors shouted, 'Hey, hey, LBJ! How many kids did you kill today?' The *événements* of 1968 even forced a panicked President de Gaulle to flee to Germany to beg the army to intervene and help put down a student rebellion in Paris. In Chicago, Mayor Daley's well-armed police force clubbed defenceless demonstrators outside the Democratic national convention. The Civil Rights movement tore the southern States – and Washington – apart. As far as the west was concerned, the Communists' difficulties were their own affair. America and the west had their own problems. If the Kremlin wanted to crack down on their own dissenters, that was none of anyone's business. Eastern Europe was Brezhnev's and the Kremlin's sphere of influence. The principle of co-existence and *détente* was that neither side interfered in the other's back yard.

This Brezhnev Doctrine clearly demonstrated that the Kremlin believed it had the right to impose its own version of communist orthodoxy in its own sphere of influence. America, still reeling from its own internal problems, seemed to agree.

Mutual co-existence with the competition was now enshrined as policy. It ensured stability, if nothing else.

The Cold War would continue, but – from now on – according to strict rules.

19

MICROWAVING THE PROBLEM?

DÉTENTE

From the Soviet point of view, *détente* and co-existence as a Cold War strategy made absolute sense. As the Russian economy struggled to keep up with the west throughout the 1960s, the gradual deterioration of relations with Beijing and the Kremlin's own problems had made matters worse militarily as well as politically. It had been difficult enough for the USSR to maintain what was effectively a heavily garrisoned empire in eastern Europe. Now, as Sino–Soviet tensions mounted, it became increasingly important to build up Soviet defences along the Chinese border as well. Not for nothing had the idea of the 'Yellow Peril' been originally a Czarist-Russian concept. This threat from two fronts encouraged rapprochement with the west. Whatever the threat from Washington, it didn't begin to compare with the erratic lunacies of Mao Tsetung, who was busy building up his Chinese forces along the Ussuri River to over a million men, and digging underground nuclear shelters all over China as the Cultural Revolution raged unchecked.

The Ussuri River clashes of March 1969 were extremely serious and did not rate as much attention in the west as they should have done. The whole affair nearly brought Mao's China and the USSR to nuclear war. Border problems in the Far East had plagued the two countries for centuries. In the middle of the nineteenth century Russia, taking advantage of a weak China, had annexed the area north of the Amur River and built Vladivostok as its Far Eastern naval base. The Chinese resented this land grab – as they saw it – and it was always a contentious issue. Events came to a head in the late 1960s, encouraged by the excesses of Mao's Cultural Revolution.

Mao had raised the issue of their common border and the disputed territories with Khrushchev during the latter's visit to Beijing in 1962. The Chinese leader received little satisfaction. In the aftermath of the Cuban crisis Khrushchev had responded to Chinese criticism of his 'weakness with imperialists' and leadership of world communism by mocking China's own willingness to tolerate 'fragments of imperialism' like Macao and Hong Kong. The Chinese were astounded. They denounced the equally unfair nineteenth-century land grabs by Czarist Russia and pointedly asked if the Kremlin really did want to open the whole question of unequal historic treaties? The Kremlin ignored this obvious provocation in the struggle for the soul of global communism, but the matter festered and incidents along the disputed frontier increased. Attempts to negotiate a settlement failed, as the Chinese seemed to have an almost 'pathological fixation', in the words of one observer, on insisting on a Russian admission of guilt concerning the old Czarist treaties. The Russians refused and pressed instead for more practical discussions about land. The Chinese, ever conscious of 'face' and equally conscious that time was on their side, refused to budge and demanded an apology for the actions of the past. On the ground, tensions rose.

The events along the Sino–Soviet border in the late 1960s remain a mystery to most westerners. It was, however, a very serious Cold War crisis and could easily have led to a nuclear exchange. The number of incidents and border clashes increased between 1964 and 1969. The Chinese claimed that the Soviets intruded into the disputed Damansky area sixteen times in the year before the Ussuri clash. They also claimed that the Soviets were guilty of 'harassing Chinese fishing boats, robbing Chinese, turning high pressure hoses onto Chinese fishing boats, firing and wounding Chinese border guards and violating Chinese airspace with 4,189 over-flights'. Real or imagined, it was an impressive catalogue of grievances.

The USSR eventually decided that some show of force was necessary. Moscow increased its military garrison in the Soviet Far East from eight to twenty-four divisions, and in 1968 signed a mutual defence pact with Mongolia. This dangerous combination of an increasingly confrontational regional force balance, the great communist ideological power struggle, harassment of Chinese along the border, and Soviet programmes to indoctrinate the local population, finally came to a head on the night of 2 March 1969. About 300 People's Liberation Army soldiers crossed the frozen Ussuri River on the ice and set up a camp on Damansky Island. Next morning the Red Army border guards were puzzled to see about thirty Chinese soldiers advancing through the fog towards them in line abreast and apparently unarmed. An official Red Army photographer stood up to record the scene. At about 15 yards' range the Chinese suddenly stood aside, revealing a second line of PLA soldiers who opened up with submachine guns. As the hapless Red Army soldiers and their photographer were cut down the Chinese opened a machine gun and mortar barrage from the flank of the Soviet backup force sent to reinforce the post under attack. The Chinese charged home and nineteen Soviet soldiers were killed. The wounded Soviet lieutenant in command managed to direct a counter-attack and after three hours of battle, some of it hand to hand, about sixty Chinese survivors withdrew, leaving the ice littered with bloodstained bodies. It had been a brutal confrontation. Protests flew from both sides and the Soviets moved menacingly to reinforce in strength.

In classic Russian style, the Kremlin now dealt with Beijing by hints and rumbles that a nuclear strike against China might be needed to stop any more dangerous adventurism along the Bamboo Curtain. SS-9 ICBMs were rolled up to the border and the Soviet Far Eastern Group of Forces increased to no fewer than thirty-five fully manned combat divisions to make the point to the Chinese. Reinforcing aircraft and wartime headquarters staff flew into the Soviet Far East. The military intimidation worked. Beijing decided to negotiate about the disputed Ussuri River border.

In circumstances like these the Kremlin needed some kind of deal with America, if only to allow it to face the growing challenge from its fellow Communists on the USSR's Siberian border. A policy of limiting the number of nuclear weapons to parity with the west therefore made eminent sense. It would save the USSR money and guarantee stability with its principal adversary. Moreover, as Nixon's 'China card' policy made some sort of deal between Washington and Beijing look possible, the Kremlin became increasingly anxious to block off this dangerous avenue by offering Washington a better security and diplomatic deal with Moscow instead. The awful possibility of an alliance between the United States and communist China made Russian blood run cold. In this climate some kind of rapprochement and arms control treaty with Washington made complete economic, military and diplomatic sense to the Politburo. The result was that, under Brezhnev, suddenly the superpowers were talking to each other. The last thing land-locked Russia needed was a war – even a Cold War – on two fronts simultaneously. Better America and NATO under some kind of control than uncharted problems with an unpredictable and critical China any day.

The success of German Chancellor Willy Brandt's *Ostpolitik* had transformed the Cold War scene. As a former mayor of Berlin, Brandt knew only too well that both the Germanys, capitalist and socialist, had to co-exist, and he more than anyone knew how to talk to his East German counterparts. He therefore sought to build bridges to the east. The unremitting hostility over Berlin, for example, had been replaced by a genuine deal over the disrupted city by which the Soviets agreed to the Allied presence and the Allies effectively recognized East Berlin – the old Soviet Occupied Zone – as part of East Germany, the DDR. Further West German agreements, with East Germany, Poland, Yugoslavia, Romania and even the USSR, opened new doors to the east and softened the edges of previously sharp diplomatic relations. Brandt's policies worked.

In this he was greatly assisted – although he never realized until it was too late – by the presence of Günther Guillaume, an MfS spy, as his personal assistant. Guillaume, probably the best-placed Moscow agent ever to penetrate the West German government, passed every top-level NATO secret he could on to the DDR's spymaster Markus Wolf and his KGB masters. (Ironically, Guillaume's top-level disclosures may have contributed to the lessening of east-west tension – the Communists were furious when their ace spy was finally unmasked in 1974 and Chancellor Brandt forced to resign in disgrace.) But things were definitely thawing by the early 1970s. Although the underlying military confrontation between east and west continued, particularly in Europe, the climate of the Cold War undoubtedly warmed, thanks to Brandt and the *Ostpolitik* he inspired. Certainly it warmed enough to consider the practicalities of limiting expensive armaments and recognizing the realities of Germany's borders.

This atmosphere was encouraged by changed thinking in the Kremlin. Between 1969 and 1972, the Soviet leadership felt they had at last achieved full superpower status and strategic parity with the United States. With the confidence that comes from a perception of equal status, comes the inevitable decision: to go for superiority or maintain the *status quo*? Could the Soviet Union afford to compete for superiority and raise the Cold War stakes? The nuclear arms race was not only dangerous, but very expensive. Any attempt to outstrip the USA with costly new strategic toys would further weaken an already sick economy. However, the alternative – to hold off strategically and concentrate on major domestic reform of the Soviet system and the economy – was unthinkable. The lessons of Czechoslovakia in 1968 had seen to that. With fundamental economic reform went social and political change. For the Party leaders in Moscow, that possibility had to be resisted at all costs. For Brezhnev and his team, change was the one thing they strove to avoid. The political and social *status quo* suited them nicely.

Thus it was that, at the Twenty-fourth Party Congress in early 1972, Brezhnev announced his Peace Programme, opening the way to progress at the Strategic Arms Limitation Talks (SALT) in Vienna. These Mutual and Balanced Force Reduction (MBFR) talks led, in turn, to a conference of Security and Confidence (CSCE) and eventually to the all-important Helsinki Agreement of 1975, which was effectively an outline framework of draft treaties to control the Cold War. This rolling programme of *détente* contained one other element vital for the Soviet Union. The relaxation of tension not only made war less likely, it also eased the burden on the ailing Soviet and east European economies. For the Kremlin's Cold War policy, *détente* had everything: security, stability and savings.

The SALT agreement of May 1972 between Nixon and Brezhnev was therefore a hugely significant development. It went much further that the 1963 Partial Test Ban (PTB) Treaty, which had merely outlawed atmospheric testing. SALT 1 not only capped the number of ICBM and nuclear weapons on both sides, it also started the process of delivering the practical benefits of *détente*. In international affairs goodwill is all very well: much better to have solemn and binding agreements limiting arms. From their side American policy makers reflected the anxieties of their Soviet counterparts. McNamara himself had concluded as early as 1965/66 that the US should stop wasting tax dollars on more and more nuclear weapons and cap its armoury. His argument, coming from the very heart of the US military-industrial complex, is both interesting and persuasive. McNamara reasoned as follows:

- The US had more than enough nuclear weapons to be a credible deterrent against any first strike.
- Without a cap on nuclear weapons the US was getting the worst of both worlds. It was paying for a full 'first-strike posture' but actually only guaranteeing a minimum deterrence capability.
- America could get the same deterrent effect for less money, provided the Soviets did so too.
- By building more and more weapons, all the US was doing was to encourage the USSR to match them and build more

nuclear weapons too. That policy was, therefore, self-defeating *and* expensive.
• Limit nuclear weapons, and everyone benefits.

The key to McNamara's thinking was: just how many weapons did America need to achieve its political aim of nuclear
deterrence? Being the numbers man he was, the former chairman
of the Ford Motor Company got his army of accountants and
analysts at the Pentagon to work it out. By the time his analysts
finally sat down, the US nuclear inventory had risen to no less
than 32,000 warheads and over 7,000 tactical (depth charges,
battlefield short-range missiles, air defence missiles) nuclear
weapons. This was, by any standards, more than enough. The
numbers men and the RAND Corporation came up with a figure
of 500 strategic bombers, 1,000 well-dispersed ICBMs, and 41
submarines carrying Polaris SLBMs. This 'Triad', argued McNamara, should be quite enough to meet any Soviet attempt at a first
pre-emptive nuclear strike by guaranteeing a devastating US
second – or retaliatory – strike response that would easily kill
over a quarter of the Russian population and virtually obliterate
its war-making potential. That was all that was needed to ensure
Mutual Assured Destruction. The grisly calculation made sense.
The key was mutual stability.

Not everyone agreed. The US Joint Chiefs of Staff argued
strongly for more spending when it emerged that the Soviets
were developing an Anti-Ballistic Missile (ABM) defensive
system. This could seriously degrade any incoming US coun-
ter-strike and destabilize the whole nuclear equation – if it
worked. In vain McNamara argued that the key was not to
build a new American ABM system; that would only ratchet
the arms race up another notch. Much better – and cheaper –
to negotiate an agreement with the Soviets and convince them
not to deploy an ABM defence.

The strategic struggle continued until Henry Kissinger inherited the problem. Kissinger had thought long and hard about nuclear weapons and was one of the fathers of 'nuclear theology'. His solution was simple: negotiate a reciprocal deal that separated the offensive from the defensive systems. Deal with them one at a time; that made life easier for both sides. If the Americans promised not to build an ABM system, provided that the Soviets did the same thing everyone would be happy and both sides would save cash. The world would be no more dangerous than it was before. Then they could move on to talk about offensive weapons.

Moscow agreed with relief. The supposed Soviet ABM system turned out not to work and would have been hideously expensive for the Soviets' next Five Year Plan. In 1972, the ABM Treaty was signed, to the relief of everyone, except – inevitably – the US hawks in the Pentagon and the Soviets' ideological paranoids. Under the treaty's terms, each side was limited to one ABM system to protect their national capital, and a second system around one designated ICBM site. As no one had an effective ABM system anyway, it was, to a degree, irrelevant; but what the 1972 ABM Treaty really did was provide a forum and a bi-lateral mechanism for the two Cold War protagonists to discuss their fears.

The two Presidents had signed a document which effectively confirmed the basic principles by which the two sides would conduct their future relations. A 'common determination that in the nuclear age there is no alternative to conducting . . . mutual relations on the basis of peaceful co-existence' underpinned the agreement. They also concluded that the importance of preventing the development of situations 'capable of causing a dangerous exacerbation of their relations' was vital to both their interests, and that both sides had a special responsibility to do 'everything in their power to avoid inflaming international tensions'. The 1972 Treaties were an impressive clutch of ambitious agreements and reflected the clear desire of both sides to prevent the Cold War boiling over again. Kissinger's plan to build a new international system as a framework for future American-Soviet relations looked a much safer alternative to the confrontational 1950s and 1960s. The future looked hopeful and much more stable.

It was all a far cry from the Cuban Missile Crisis of a decade before.

Reactions to this hugely significant attempt to chart a path out of the bog of military confrontation that was the Cold War were wholly predictable. The media and the public heaved a sigh of relief. Dialogue had begun at last and links between east and west could now converge and maybe – one day – even become normal. The arms manufacturers and the hawks were outraged and poured out dire predictions of disaster as a result of this craven sell-out by the politicians to the ever-deceitful Reds. General Alexander Haig, Kissinger's military advisor, called the agreements 'a day of lasting shame', and big defence contractors had to downsize their future business plans. It mattered not. On his return from Moscow, President Nixon reassured a packed Congress that the USA 'would continue to be the strongest power on earth'. And in Moscow, the Defence Chiefs assured the Supreme Soviet that the USSR retained more than adequate defences to 'defend the state interests of our Motherland'. The big difference now was that defence spending had been capped and a framework to manage future tensions was in place. At the 1973 summit in Washington, Nixon and Brezhnev signed another agreement, 'On the Prevention of Nuclear War'.

This new framework for international relations and the prevention of nuclear war was soon tested. The basic rivalry of the Cold War fuelled other tensions besides the terror of the nuclear arms race. By 1973, the Middle East – yet again – became the focus of Great Power rivalry.

Britain's 1917 undertaking to provide a national homeland for the Jews had long been a source of trouble in the region. As the Zionist movement bought and fought its way into Palestine in the 1920s and 1930s, Jewish immigrants began to displace the indigenous Arabs. The inevitable conflict grew into a minor guerrilla war and Britain struggled to police the area during the 1930s as part of its League of Nations Mandate. The Second World War brought matters to a head. The Holocaust encouraged Jewish death camp survivors to flee to Palestine in the late 1940s, flooding the countryside with thousands of desperate illegal immigrants and further displacing the local Arab population.

The competition for land and resources between the encroaching Jewish immigrants of this new Exodus and the local inhabitants finally exploded into open warfare. In 1948, the exhausted British quit, to leave Jew and Arab to fight it out between themselves. Since then, the new state of Israel had fought off invading Arabs three times: in 1948; in the ill-fated Suez crisis of 1956 (see page 138); and in the Israelis' deadly pre-emptive strike of 1967. This last had expanded Israel's borders as it held on to the gains of conquest as terms for some future peace treaty with the Arabs. However, Israel's enemies still refused to recognize its existence, so Israel clung on to vast tracts of Arab land. The consequence was that even more Palestinian Arabs now lived under Israeli control, and Arab hostility, if anything, increased as a result of Israel's search for national security. By 1973, the Middle Eastern situation had become explosive. Israel was viewed by the Arab world as a new Outremer. The Palestinian refugees, huddled in their filthy camps, felt a burning sense of injustice. Israel felt encircled and embattled.

The Soviet Union had been taking a deep interest in the region since the Suez debacle. From 1956 onwards Gamal Nasser had sought, and been given, aid from a Kremlin only too anxious to twist the old colonial imperialists' tail. Being Soviet Russia, that aid consisted mainly of that which the USSR did best: exported arms and armaments. As the Cold War powers jockeyed for advantage in the quicksands of the Middle East, the USSR felt that, as with Cuba, the revolutionary tide of 'wars of national liberation' was flowing their way. After 1967, the increasingly revolutionary regimes in Iraq, Libya, Sudan and Syria auto-matically looked to communist Russia for aid and assistance. Washington was stymied. Increasingly in thrall to a powerful Jewish domestic lobby at home, successive US presidents found that their freedom of manœuvre over any Middle East policies affecting Israel became progressively more boxed in. Every would-be President needed at least some of the Jewish lobby's votes to be elected. The ever more powerful Israel Public Affairs Committee and its supporters in Washington made any Jewish electoral support conditional upon unrestricted US support for Israel, the 'only democracy in the Middle East'. Having such a powerful backer as the USA both distorted Israeli policy and polarized Middle Eastern politics, as well as effectively giving the Jewish voters of the US control of US foreign policy in the region.

The death of the revolutionary firebrand Nasser in 1965 had brought Anwar Sadat to power. Egypt's new ruler found himself at the mercy of Soviet support, every bit as much as the Israelis in their turn depended on US backing. The Cold War had re-invented itself as a proxy conflict in the Middle East between the forces of 'reaction and imperialism' on the one hand, and the historic tide of 'national liberation' on the other. The first challenge real loomed for *détente*.

By 1973 Sadat was under extreme pressure at home. He had

thrown out his Russian advisors and was embarked upon a strategy designed to demonstrate Arab – and his own – prowess to the world. On Yom Kippur, the Jewish Day of Atonement, in October 1973, the combined forces of Syria and Egypt sprang a coordinated surprise attack on Israel. There was no warning. Israel's much-vaunted intelligence failed them and the outnumbered Israeli forces were hammered and driven back. In the north only a tiny handful of tanks on the Golan Heights denied a frontal onslaught by 600 Syrian tanks and barred the road to Jerusalem. Along the Suez Canal, the Israelis suffered a humiliating defeat as new Soviet missiles blew their tanks and aircraft apart. By 8 October Sadat had achieved his aim: a decisive Arab victory and proof to the world that the all-conquering Israelis were far from invincible against Muslim arms. Operation Bad'r was a stunning military success. More importantly for Sadat, it reinforced and cemented his position as Egypt's all-powerful leader and the figurehead of the Arab world. The UN called for a ceasefire.

Unfortunately for the Arab cause, Sadat then over-reached himself.

In response to their Syrian's ally's mounting desperation for some kind of diversion, and ignoring the UN call for an end to hostilities, the Egyptians now launched themselves out of their well-defended sanctuaries along the Suez Canal to attack the Israelis in Sinai. It was a serious mistake. Away from the anti-aircraft missile umbrella and running short of anti-tank missiles, it was the turn of the Egyptians to be hammered. The well-practised, well-armed and highly trained IDF ripped a whole brigade of the Egyptians' Soviet-built tanks apart as they emerged from their defensive positions. A call from Israel for American aid, and especially new defensive missiles, was followed by a flood ($2.2 billion) of airlifted US weapon supplies to match the torrent of Soviet arms pouring into

Syria. The results were totally predictable. Inspired Israeli generalship sliced through the over-extended Egyptians and poured across the Suez Canal to cut off the whole Egyptian 3rd Army deep in the southern Sinai. Israeli tanks rampaged far behind them on the west bank of the Suez Canal, heading for Ismailia and even threatening Cairo.

Disaster now loomed for both Egypt and Syria, as on the northern front Israeli tanks had advanced to within 22 miles of Damascus. The Soviets threatened unilateral intervention with airborne divisions unless the Israelis obeyed the UN's call for an immediate ceasefire. In response, the US military went to 'DEFCON 3', the highest state of armed readiness since Cuba, and issued a nuclear alert. Suddenly the Arab-Israeli crisis had become a full-blooded Cold War crisis and, potentially, a nuclear one. Both Washington and Moscow moved rapidly to defuse the growing danger. Both sides now enforced cease-fires on their exhausted clients. Neither Tel Aviv nor Cairo was worth a nuclear war involving Moscow and Washington. *Détente* might have been compromised, but it had managed the explosive Yom Kippur crisis of autumn 1973 and pre-vented it from turning into a major superpower confrontation. However, the verdict of history, supported by Brezhnev him-self, is that without the mechanisms of *détente* and the diplo-matic bridges built by the 1972 summits, the 1973 Yom Kippur situation could have turned out much uglier. *Détente* had been tested and it had worked.

Détente however did not extend to the whole of the Cold War. Far from the Inner German Border and the cockpit of the Middle East the underground conflict between east and west still raged, little changed from the early clashes between Britain's Secret Service and the embryonic Cheka. By the 1970s, however, it had grown into a global intelligence war between the CIA and the KGB. In virtually every country a bitter underground struggle for influence and power raged between the two standard bearers of capitalism and communism. Not for nothing did many people believe that it was the secret services of a country that best summed up its true values. From the CIA and KGB secret archives we now know that two of the most serious struggles were in Chile – the only country ever to have genuinely voted in a Marxist government by democratic ballot – and India, the world's biggest democracy. Their experiences speak for many in the Cold War. In Chile the high-living Allende made an unlikely Marxist, with a taste for fine wines, designer suits, a collection of fast cars and expensive ladies. 'So he's a little like Brezhnev, then . . .' one British intelligence officer commented dryly. The KGB had had their eye on this champagne socialist for a long time. Even so, Allende's election to power in 1970 shook the United States administration. Nixon and Kissinger were stunned and the embarrassed CIA briefing officer in the White House had to admit that they 'hadn't seen it coming . . .' A furious President Nixon ordered an all-out effort by the State Department and the CIA to 'save Chile'. However, part of the problem was that Chile's economic difficulties had led to genuine disenchantment with previous regimes. Allende's personal charm and obvious high living had reassured the Chilean middle class that he was trustworthy and that their savings were safe. The CIA's hasty two-track plan was to stop the Chilean Congress confirming Allende in office and, should that not work, to arrange a military coup. Both plans failed. The Chilean Congress confirmed their new President and there was no military coup. The CIA gave up in disgust. Langley could only sit and watch events unfold.

The Kremlin was delighted with this new Castro in South America, and despatched a high-ranking intelligence officer to 'help the Socialist cause' and to maintain close links with the

Chilean leader. To the watchful and increasingly frustrated CIA, Svyatoslav Kuznetsov looked very much like an agent-running case officer, and they were right. The KGB were going to run Allende – and then the USSR could run Chile. Fat bribes of hundreds of thousands of dollars were paid to Chile's new President for him to use in his work of 'strengthening political ties' with sympathetic groups such as trade unions, party leaders, military commanders and politicians. He was given a personal gift of $30,000 to 'solidify the trusted relations between our two countries'. Allende and Kuznetzov became close personal friends and the KGB residency in Santiago an open outpost of Moscow's influence.

The CIA became increasingly alarmed as an ever more irate Nixon secretly ordered them to destabilize Chile, and 'make its economy scream'. Despite this presidential exhortation the CIA enjoyed little success on the ground in the face of ever greater Soviet influence. At this point, in 1972, the Kremlin despatched a new ambassador to Chile. Aleksandr Basov set out to make a name for himself with the Politburo and tried to wrest control of Moscow's finest 'agent of influence' away from Kuznetzov and the KGB. An epic bureaucratic power struggle now ensued between the Russians, while the CIA worked hard on its own counter programme of bribery, to little avail. They offered millions of dollars to Chilean generals. They paid off journalists and friendly newspapers. America also tried to exploit a month-long truckers' strike to under-mine the authority of Allende's Government of Popular Unity (UP) and wreck the economy of a country that depended on the traffic along 3,000 miles of coast road to survive. None of these US ploys worked although, slowly, without any help from an increasingly baffled CIA, Allende's administration and the Chilean economy began to unravel of their own accord. Within a year his Marxist economics transformed a positive trade balance of $700 million into a deficit of $300 million as the Communists squandered government revenues on a bizarre programme of expropriating everything 'for the people', with predictable results. By mid-1973, with 90 per cent of the Chilean economy nationalized and 40,000 angry housewives banging empty pots in the streets of Santiago to denounce food rationing, Allende's days were clearly numbered. The small but important Chilean middle class turned firmly against the 'democratic socialist experiment'. Fresh elections confirmed the deposing of Chile's Marxism by democracy. In March 1973 the UP lost its majority in the Congress and Allende was isolated.

Both the CIA and KGB now redoubled their efforts to control Chile; ironically, both – for entirely different reasons – advocated a coup. The CIA wanted the army to seize power, and the KGB was urging a full-blooded communist revolution. Where the CIA failed, however, the increasingly concerned Chilean armed forces, after much soul searching, finally delivered for them. The last straw appears to have been Allende's attempt to politicize the deeply traditional Chilean armed forces along good Marxist lines.

This was too much for the conservative and essentially constitutionalist military. Their exasperated leaders now struck. Despite warnings from his KGB friends of an impending coup attempt, Allende ignored them and on 11 September 1973 the Chiefs of Staff, led by the Navy, reluctantly launched their military coup to 'save Chile'. The Communist Party was unable to 'mobilize the masses' to stop the advancing tanks and Allende finally blew his brains out in the presidential palace (with an assault rifle presented by his friend and fellow Marxist Fidel Castro) as Air Force jets roared overhead.

The Army member of the new junta was an obscure general called August Pinochet. Although he and the other service leaders had seized power on the understanding that it would be handed back to the Congress after elections, Pinochet now moved to consolidate his own position. Within six months he declared himself sole leader and turned democratic Chile into a typical South American military dictatorship. In Santiago's football stadium thousands of left-wing activists and Communists were rounded up to join the ranks of *los desaparecidos* – 'the disappeared' – never to be seen again. The White House breathed again. A shamefaced CIA had to admit that, for once, a Third World country didn't need American help to mount a coup: they could manage it perfectly well for themselves.

The CIA's and KGB's war in India, on the other hand, was more a struggle for influence. The principal target in the 1970s was the government of Indira Gandhi. In a country where bribery and corruption were a way of life the opportunities to buy influence were obvious. Not for nothing had one departing British Indian civil servant said, 'The biggest contribution the British Raj ever made to India was to convince railway booking clerks that the tickets they sold were not to make extra money for themselves but actually to be sold at face value.'

In such a climate the rival superpowers intelligence services' bribery war assumed epic proportions and went right to the top. The Treasurer of the Congress Party of India, a slippery, greedy piece of work called L. Mishra, was the main conduit of funds from the KGB to the Indian power elite. Suitcases of hard cash flowed into the Gandhi household. One aggrieved KGB officer actually complained that the greedy Gandhis 'even kept the suitcases'. A well-funded Congress Party and an equally well-heeled Mrs Gandhi now signed suitable treaties of 'peace friendship' and 'cooperation friendship' with the USSR, while the local CIA station ground its collective teeth. Literally thousands of articles were placed in Indian newspapers by KGB agents of influence. They ranged from lies about the Aids virus being an escaped bug from an American biological warfare programme that had gone wrong, to internal political pressure on Indira Gandhi to declare a state of emergency and rule by decree because of the 'grave situation in the country'. Truly, a well-planted journalist can be a weapon as deadly as any explosive device or a spy at the heart of government.

Ties between India and the Soviet Union grew ever closer as the 1970s wore on. Both America and Britain became increasingly uneasy about developments in the subcontinent as the state of emergency and press censorship began to bite. Would India turn towards Moscow and the communist path? Not everything went quite as the Soviets planned, however. India is a vast country and the Gandhi dynasty almost as large and equally uncontrollable. Indira's son Sanjay Gandhi was made an offer by a kind and friendly CIA man based in Delhi. On the day after her return from a triumphant state visit to Moscow, a furious Indian Prime Minister was reading press interviews given by her son praising the benefits of the free market, capitalism and democracy, and implicitly criticizing the Soviet Union. After a suitable handbagging the wretched Sanjay was forced to issue a retraction, which of course only drew more attention to his original statement and infuriated both the KGB and, more alarmingly, his formidable mother. By the time new elections were eventually held in 1977 the gloves were off both KGB and CIA in this underground struggle. All sides prepared for a dirty election campaign of Hogarthian corruption. Nine of the candidates were actually full-time undercover KGB agents; twenty-one others were on the payroll of the Delhi KGB Residency.

The CIA threw its weight behind the Hindu opposition of Moraji Desai and in a desperate struggle his anti-communist Janata opposition got 40 per cent of the popular vote, to

Gandhi's Congress Party's 35 per cent. Moscow's woman fell from power and the polite conventions of *détente* were – at least in public – still firmly in place.

The early 1970s were the high point of *détente*. The USSR even offered to repay a hoary old wartime Lend-Lease bill of £700 million and the US made huge stocks of grain available to the Kremlin at advantageous prices. In 1973 Mutual and Balanced Force Reduction talks opened in Vienna between east and west. It seemed that a real thaw was in the air. However, not all was sweetness and light. Although the US was obsessed with Watergate, the external problems of what to do about the Soviet Union still dominated American national policy on many levels, domestic as well as international. Suspicions still lingered on both sides. When a tearful Richard Nixon was forced out of the White House on 8 August 1974, there were many in the Kremlin who saw this domestic political cataclysm as an anti-*détente* conspiracy designed to remove a President who had actually dared to do business with Moscow. Even the experienced Soviet ambassador in Washington could not believe that an incumbent President could be forced from the highest political office 'over stealing a few silly papers'. In Moscow some analysts even claimed that the whole thing was really a secret 'Jewish-military conspiracy' to oust the architect of *détente* and wreck the SALT agreements in order to re-instate hawkish anti-Soviet Cold War policies and benefit the American arms industry.

The new American President rapidly disabused them. Gerald Ford flew to the Soviet Union for an urgent conference with the Russian leadership. There he reassured Moscow that he intended to continue his hapless predecessor's *détente* policies. Some kind of meeting of minds took place at Vladivostok in November 1974. Ford and Brezhnev hit it off and a surprised Henry Kissinger found that his new boss had brought home the bare bones of a draft Strategic Arms Limitation Treaty. He had also opened the door for new proposals to balance US and USSR nuclear strategic weapons, including the new 'Multiple Independently-Targetable Re-Entry Vehicle' (MIRV) warheads, whose development had threatened to undermine the whole balance of the SALT 1 nuclear arms control treaty. *Détente* rolled on despite such hiccups as America's refusal to agree to a joint US-USSR alignment against communist China and, on the Soviet side, the bitterness arising from the US Senate's demand that the Soviet Union let Russian Jews emigrate to Israel without hindrance if the USSR wanted to gain special trading advantages. An outraged Kremlin refused. Superpowers did not interfere in each other's internal affairs. Back in the US the Jewish lobby cried foul, and the Trade Agreement died.

Despite these setbacks, the Cold War was officially declared ended in Helsinki in 1975. As he signed, Brezhnev himself spelled it out: 'The leaders of the bourgeois world have come to realize that the Cold War has outlived itself and that there is now a need for a new sensitive and realistic policy.' As the final act of the Conference on Security and Co-operation in Europe of 1975, the superpowers, plus thirty-three European nations, finally agreed what was effectively a post-1945 Peace Treaty. Agreement was reached on post-war borders, and the division of eastern and western Europe seemed to have become *de jure* as well as *de facto*. It looked like *détente*'s finest hour.

It was not to last.

The seeds of the slide from *détente* to discord lay not just in the continuing struggle between capitalist America and communist Russia, but in their treaty obligations. The Helsinki final act consisted of three separate 'baskets' of agreements. The first was a final resolution on European territorial boundaries which was universally hailed as an important step forward and the end of an era. It led, naturally, to the second basket, a closer exchange of trade and cultural links between east and west. Both sides were happy thus far.

It was the third basket that caused the real trouble. For Helsinki's 'Basket 3' was about humanitarian issues and human rights. While many Americans disapproved strongly of the Helsinki settlement splitting Europe in two, they went along with it. But to the autocrats of the Communist Parties who held down the populations of eastern Europe, the idea of 'human rights' was potentially very dangerous indeed. Human rights were the very thing that they had spent their careers suppressing. Human rights challenged the primacy of the Party.

Brezhnev and the Politburo dealt with the problem by choosing to ignore the provisions of Basket 3. 'We'll decide what we do inside our own house,' said Brezhnev to the Politburo, urging his colleagues to sign the final document. But to both the people of eastern Europe and the readers of western newspapers, freedom and human rights were very important indeed. To the Kremlin's surprise, some folk took Basket 3 very seriously. Some of them even had the temerity to insist that their communist overlords actually *did* what they had signed up to do.

Even a Treaty of Friendship contained the potential to reignite the Cold War.

20

FROSTBITTEN CRUSADER

THE CARTER YEARS

Although the Helsinki final acts were effectively a Cold War peace treaty that accepted the division of Europe they bore the seeds of new trouble to come. Part of the problem was that 'Helsinki' was not a treaty in the formal sense of the word; rather it was a series of solemn promises of goodwill. Covenants without swords to back them up are usually the first to be broken or overlooked. Thus it was with the Helsinki agreements.

The 1976 Treaties became not the cornerstone of a bright new future marking the end of the Cold War but a new source of disputation, broken promises and recrimination between the Cold War rivals and their allies. Helsinki had been – perhaps deliberately – also full of ambiguities. So Russian dissidents, and the Czech Charter 77 Group set up by individuals to monitor compliance and human rights, were dealt with ruthlessly in the communist bloc following standard

Soviet procedures to deal with such impudent challenges to state authority. Protests from the west were met by bland indifference, citing Helsinki's pledge of non-interference in the domestic workings of the signatories. It looked as if the Soviets were going to ignore Basket 3.

Critics of the US line were not slow in pointing this out or in drawing attention to the fact that the Soviets did remarkably well out of the Nixon/Ford/Kissinger/Brezhnev deals. The heart of the problem was that there was no real link between the three baskets' success and general compliance. US irritation increased further as Moscow meddled in the Middle East, Marxist Ethiopia and Angola, while middle America confronted the realities of a disgraced President, quadrupled oil prices (after the 1973 Arab-Israeli war), the humiliating retreat from Vietnam, and an increasingly restive Senate. To most Americans it looked as if a more confident, stable and assertive Soviet Union was winning the Cold War, certainly the struggle for global influence. Many in the west were beginning to feel that 'peaceful co-existence' was not quite what they had expected and certainly not the end of the Cold War.

Part of the problem lay in the two superpowers' goals. To the USA, 'peace' meant a single world order in which a dominant, well-armed and secure continental US could dominate the globe commercially. To do this it needed to ensure that values such as self-determination, free trade and unfettered access to raw materials were paramount.

The USSR had a very different post-war agenda. Having seen its economy and cities wrecked and its people slaughtered in the Second World War, what the Soviet Union wanted above all was a stable country, a protective screen of allies (willing or not) to protect its borders, and no foreign interference. Any challenge to the regime or the Party represented a mortal threat. Stability and order were the watchwords.

American ideas of 'one world, open and free' were met with incomprehension and alarm. What Russia wanted was security and stability, and freedom to go its own Marxist-Leninist way. This fundamental clash could be seen in eastern Europe: to Russia it was a security *glacis* against future troubles, to America a serious infringement of self-determination and a closed barrier to trade markets. This failure by each side to recognize the other's needs gnawed away at the Helsinki agreements, just as it had gnawed away at the heart of the Cold War dispute since 1917 and onwards. The two systems' requirements were irreconcilable. So the whole issue of 'human rights' *à la* Helsinki became just another stage on which the actors could spout well-rehearsed lines emphasizing their differences.

The human rights issue between east and west was always going to be an unbridgeable chasm. There was never any universal understanding of what was meant by 'human rights' at Helsinki, any more than at the UN today. The Helsinki Basket 3 was really a pious, non-binding statement of hope by the west and a shrugged-off irrelevance to the east, signed to keep the west happy and ensure that the Kremlin got agreement to Baskets 1 and 2. The result was that America's new President Jimmy Carter inherited a basket of trouble when he was elected at the end of 1976.

The Carter administration was famously inexperienced. One Republican wag even said that 'Jimmy Carter had to make Cyrus Vance Secretary of State because he was the only one of the bastards who had a passport!' US domestic hostility to the USSR was already well entrenched and growing by the time he came to power. But it was now querulous and uncertain. The era of disillusionment after Vietnam had questioned some core US values and made many Americans doubt themselves, their cause, and their freedom to colonize the

world with American products and values. They called on
their new President to redress the balance. America has never
shrunk from trying to protect its own cultural, ideological and
moral superiority over others or from spreading it abroad.
President Carter saw himself in an almost evangelical role,
accepting that America was facing a crisis of confidence,
'sapping worldwide faith in our own policy and our way of
life'. Carter took it upon himself to project a confident new
image of liberal idealism. It might have played well among the
sophisticates of Washington DC and among the moral majority, but ideas of liberalism, freedom and the rights of man
worried the Russians and nibbled away at *détente*. Naïve,
idealistic Democrat presidents had always caused the Kremlin
far more trouble than hard-nosed, pragmatic Republicans.

Although his 1978 success at Camp David brought a kind of
peace between Egypt and Israel, Carter was running into
serious problems with the Kremlin. However, even this initiative had a serious downside from the Kremlin's point of
view in that it effectively now excluded them from one of the
major sources of influence in the Arab world. Cairo has always
been a linchpin of Arab opinion and for decades Moscow had
courted Egypt with mixed results. Now the US diplomatic
success in this long-running problem left twenty years of
Russian diplomacy out in the cold. Time, effort and energy
had been wasted. Moscow's attitudes towards Washington
cooled. Things got worse.

The Carter administration believed that human rights mattered and kept sending exhortations of hope and mouthing
moral pieties to the various Helsinki Watch Committees
springing up in eastern Europe. An alarmed Moscow reacted
with well-rehearsed vigour to these unwanted challenges to its
internal authority. Dissidents were monitored and harassed in

the usual way. Leaders were arrested and jailed and Anatoly Sharansky, a prominent scientist and critic of the regime, was accused of working for the CIA and sent to a labour camp. Particularly virulent critics were labelled insane and locked up in psychiatric hospitals to be chemically lobotomized. None of this endeared the USSR to human rights watchers – or voters – in the west. *Détente* was fading, leaving a sour taste and a morning-after feeling that the party hadn't been that good. Where were the real benefits? By 1979 relations cooled.

The process of fracturing *détente* was accelerated by the Soviets' unilateral destabilizing of the military status quo. From 1978 on, as part of a programme of replacing obsolescent nuclear missiles with more up-to-date weapons, the USSR began to deploy its new SS-20 missiles. The SS-20 was a solid-fuel, technically advanced rocket that could reach any part of Europe or the Middle East. Moreover, it was mobile, being transported on a giant truck, and could be hidden in a way that the earlier liquid-fuelled SS-4 and SS-5 missiles could not. This new mobile nuclear theatre-level missile seriously altered the military balance on the ground in Europe and set alarm bells ringing in European capitals and NATO headquarters. Why, in the middle of a period of supposed peace and goodwill, had the Soviets suddenly deployed a new Intermediate Range Ballistic Missile (IRBM) that made a nuclear first strike possible against military targets throughout Europe? And, if the Soviets ever did try such a theatre-level onslaught, would Washington's new President really come to Europe's aid and risk trading Boston for Berlin, or Miami for Mons, in a strategic nuclear exchange? Europeans doubted it and felt, once again, exposed to the Red Menace. The Kremlin had uncoupled deterrence and with it the US from Europe. *Détente* withered and died as concerned European leaders began to press their US protectors for tangible guarantees of nuclear support.

Carter's Washington kept the problem at arm's length. An SS-20 IRBM may have been strategic to the Germans and the Dutch, but it was only a theatre-level weapon to the Pentagon. It couldn't reach continental USA. So the new round of arms limitation talks (SALT 2) failed to include the SS-20s on their agenda. An increasingly agitated German Chancellor pressed Washington to act and restore confidence in NATO's security. Washington's response was to suggest that if Europe was scared of the SS-20s then the answer was for Europe to pay more for its own defence and invest in some conventional weapons.

This was an alarming and an expensive option. Despite their cost, nuclear weapons are in fact relatively cheap for their effects. 'Nothing gives more bang for the buck than a nuke,' as the old NATO saying goes. Conventional weapons systems like missiles, warships, tanks and aircraft quite literally cost a fortune. For example, the overall costs of the British Rapier surface-to-air anti-aircraft missile pro-gramme were at one time estimated to be more than the whole British nuclear programme. Moreover, very large numbers of conventional weapons are needed for credible defence. Relying on conventional weapons was an expensive and very unwelcome suggestion indeed to the European capitals. What NATO wanted were some nuclear assurances to restore *deterrence* in Europe. There were, after all, over 20,000 Soviet tanks in eastern Europe. How was that level of threat supposed to be countered?

Carter realized that the only way to restore stability was by parity, so in 1977/78 in a new harder line he ordered the development of Cruise Missiles (pilotless jet-powered flying bombs) to counter the SS-20 threat and restore a status quo. This combination of a moral idealism that the Soviets saw as interference in their domestic affairs, communist support for wars of national liberation overseas, and finally the deployment of new nuclear missiles, was lethal to the balance of *détente*. The NATO response, especially the decision to site the US's version of the SS-20, the Pershing, and their new nuclear cruise missiles across Europe nailed down the coffin lid. The idealist, Jimmy Carter, may have restored nuclear parity in Europe: but by the end of the 1970s between them he and Brezhnev had ratcheted their rivalry up another notch in the arms race.

The Cold War was back with a vengeance.

If *détente* means a relaxation of tension designed to restrain harmful competition, then by 1980 it was effectively dead, except for academics and commentators writing their learned theses and articles. The explicit and well-documented breaches of human rights in the east were only the outward symbols of a renewed suspicion and jockeying for power as the superpowers once again acknowledged their military and ideological differences in their national interest. With the fading of *détente* went the realization that war – nuclear war – had never really gone away. Confusing signals between the two sides muddied the water. Dialogue began to break down and with it what little trust existed.

The US itself was not blameless in this renewal of mutual distrust. The message sent out from the White House during the Carter years was confusing to friend and foe alike. Carter's Southern Baptist *Weltanschauung*, or view of the world, sat particularly uneasily with the Kremlin. Cynical, pragmatic politicians they could deal with – they recognized those traits in their colleagues – it was the moral, high-minded ones who made erratic and incomprehensible decisions that worried the men sitting round the Kremlin table more than anything else.

For example, Carter's cancellation of the Enhanced Radiation Weapon (ERW) programme pleased them. These American low-blast, high-radiation 'mini-nuclears' had been specifically designed to counter the 20,000 Soviet main battle tanks lurking in eastern Europe. A concentrated KGB campaign of denunciation against this dangerous threat to Soviet conventional superiority was remarkably successful. Fellow travellers in the west lapped up the notion that the ERW destroyed people but not property, and must therefore be a 'capitalist' bomb. The liberal establishment and media set up their usual outcry. Bowing to pressure, Carter eventually cancelled the programme, only to reap the fury of the military – who this time really did need the weapons to balance the huge numbers of Soviet tanks – of the manufacturers, who saw lost profits, and, perhaps most important of all, of America's allies. West Germany in particular was angry at Carter's unilateral change of tack. Chancellor Schmidt had only reluctantly agreed to station these potentially unpopular weapons on German soil as a result of *American* pleading. Now it looked as if the White House didn't know what it wanted and he was left to take the political flak.

Carter's cancellation of an effective but politically unpopular programme may have been driven by a desire to get his new SALT 2 agreements finalized with the Soviets, who were genuinely concerned at the US's own latest strategic missile developments. A new generation of mobile ICBMs called the 'MX Series' looked like tipping the delicate balance of nuclear stability in America's favour. The MX made Mutual Assured Destruction a little less mutual. Kissinger's secret offer to provide US intelligence to the Chinese in their latest spat with Moscow – a secret of which the KGB was well aware – also worried the Russians. The nightmare of a US-China alliance kept Kremlin leaders awake at nights. China's invasion of

Vietnam in 1979 to 'teach the Vietnamese a lesson' seemed to reinforce their fears. Vietnam was a Russian ally and Beijing had warned President Carter what it had in mind. But Carter had done nothing. He had failed to alert Moscow of Beijing's plans, let alone warn the Chinese off. What was the White House up to? Were Beijing and Washington conspiring behind Moscow's back? The knee-jerk suspicion of the USSR's communist rulers re-asserted itself. Foreign Minister Gromyko issued a grave warning, and Premier Brezhnev called for a summit with President Carter. The international scene grew ever more confusing.

America, for its part, was worried by what looked like a positive blizzard of Soviet successes elsewhere. 'What's mine is mine, and what's yours is negotiable' still seemed to characterize Soviet Cold War thinking in the 1970s. Angola, Namibia, Ethiopia, Yemen and Eritrea all fell into the Marxist sphere of influence. A whole brigade of Cuban 'volunteers' were openly fighting for the pro-communist rebels in Angola after the 1975 uprising. A territorial battle between US-backed Somalis and Marxist Ethiopia erupted in 1977 when the Somali 'rebels' invaded Ogaden. The Horn of Africa became another Cold War source of conflict by proxy. Soviet warships actually shelled Eritrean rebel positions in support of Ethiopia's Moscow-backed communist troops. This 'Arc of Crisis', where communism openly sought to seize power, seemed one-sided and destabilizing to Washington. Worse than that: Soviet advances seemed successful.

The result of all these developments was that as the 1970s drew to a close, the *détente* relationship between the Cold War rivals was fast cooling. Even the signing of the SALT 2 treaty between Carter and Brezhnev in 1979 failed to bring about any real sense of renewed harmony. The treaty had been discussed since 1974 and, against the discord of international events, seemed almost irrelevant to many. Two other developments brought the new sense of Cold War tension to near breaking point for the Carter administration at the close of the 1970s, and in a particularly volatile region for both the USA and the USSR: south-west Asia.

Iran had always been a vital area of interest for both east and west. The British had bought a controlling interest in the Persian oil fields in the early years of the century and had exercised influence in the region ever since. The Soviets had been noticeably reluctant to leave Iran and its tempting riches of black gold after their occupation in 1945 and had required strong encouragement to do so. Iran had always had the potential to become a catalyst for conflict. The west tried to keep it under control.

The Shah of Iran had been an American client since 1953 when a joint MI6-SIS and CIA coup had ousted his predecessor Mussadeq and ensured that Reza Shah Pahlavi sat securely on the Peacock Throne. Since 1952, Iran had replaced the UK as 'policeman' of the vital Persian Gulf oil routes and Iran's influence at OPEC was crucial to western interests. The tripling of the world oil price in the aftermath of the 1973 Yom Kippur War had placed billions of petrodollars, and with them much power, in the hands of the oil producing states. It was clear to all that western economies needed oil to survive, a lot of oil. Staying friends with a major oil producer made eminent sense to the Cold War policy makers in Washington.

Successive presidents ensured that the Shah and his regime got every support. American business liked Iran too. From 1972 to 1976, Iran had bought over $10 billion worth of advanced weapons from US arms manufacturers many of which, like the advanced F-14 fighters, were too complicated for the Iranians to work themselves. According to the US State Department, Washington supplied 'everything but the atomic bomb'. In a throwback to an earlier era, Iran's regime was to be supported, not undermined, by America because it was both firmly anti-communist and well placed geographically.

Iran was also nicely situated as a listening post enabling the NSA's listening stations to reach deep into Soviet south-west Asia. From this fortunate strategic position it could also be guaranteed to supply uninterrupted oil to the US and, in the cynical phrase of one US newspaper, 'was more than adequately repressive of its own people'. SAVAK, the Shah's secret police, was as efficient as the Gestapo and routinely 'cooked' political prisoners on electric griddles to encourage swift confessions from those unwise enough are to criticize the Shah. Many of his subjects were prepared to do just that. Over 100,000 Iranians were in jail for their political beliefs by the end of 1977. The civil courts had been abolished, and Amnesty International described the Shah's methods as 'beyond belief'. Despite this minor humanitarian hiccup, to maintain their loyal ally in power the US kept 25,000 'advisors' in Iran, from the CIA to the Exxon Corporation. The ever-helpful Shah even went so far as to secretly provide a complete brigade of elite Iranian Guards to the British in Oman to help smoke out the final rebels from an especially troublesome complex of caves in Dhofar. Whatever the drawbacks, the Shah's Iran seemed a reliable regional ally during the Cold War, despite the excesses of its over-enthusiastic secret police. The highly moral President Carter even called it 'an island of stability'.

The Iranian people did not agree. Gradually opposition to the Shah and his repressive regime grew. Opposition began to crystallize around one particular group of victims, the Islamic clergy and the Mosque. To the imams of Shi'ite Islam, the Shah's espousal of western values, western aid and western ideas represented a threat to the values of God, as revealed by the Prophet in the Holy Koran. In his turn the Shah considered the Mosque and its turbulent priests as nothing but a source of trouble, with their endless calls for a return to the semi-medieval ideas of traditional Shi'ite Islam. He threw many into prison, dismissing them contemptuously as 'black crows'. Others fled into exile to avoid the long arm of SAVAK. The Mosque was affronted. The Shah could get away with much, but not with denying God himself. He was anathematized as a blasphemer. The grim medieval figure of the exiled Ayatollah Khomeini glowered from a thousand posters while cassette tapes of his speeches calling for God's Revolution were passed from hand to hand in the market place as the opposition went underground and into the Mosque to denounce Iran's ruler and his Godless ways. The Iranian revolutionaries began to use Islam as their rallying call for change. Insidiously, impercept-ibly, removal of the Shah's regime became synonymous with its replacement by the Party of God, led by the clergy, the Mosque and the forbidding rage of Khomeini himself. The Holy Men of God would remove the dictator and re-instate the *Umma*, or Kingdom of God, for the good of all. Even, astonishingly, the Tudeh (the Iranian Communist Party) even-tually backed Khomeini's revolution, on the grounds that once they had got rid of the pro-western Shah the Party could take over. They were to be proved sorely mistaken.

The Shah was not without his own problems. Oil revenues had begun to dry up and wages and the standard of living were squeezed for most Iranians. The disparity between the rich sophisticates of Tehran and the huddled masses of the majority of the Iranian people began to be more extreme. Revolution was in the air. In December 1978, a million protestors flooded the streets of Tehran demanding reform, the Shah's removal and Khomeini's return. Strikes paralysed the capital and the all-important oil industry. Riots and unrest flared. The secret police finally lost their nerve, followed closely by the conscripts in the Air Force and Army.

In January 1979 the Shah abdicated and fled, finally betrayed by his own *protégés* and favourites in the armed forces.

The grim figure of Khomeini was now despatched from Paris on an Air France plane to spread the contagion of revolutionary fundamentalism – 'a little like Lenin being sent to Russia in 1917', in the words of one concerned intelligence officer – to do his worst. The rapturous crowds of relatively sophisticated Iranians who greeted their Islamic Messiah at Tehran airport in January 1979 could have had little notion that within six months their idol would have transformed Iran into a semi-medieval theocracy ruled by a tyranny as savage as anything the Shah had ever dreamed up. America, and everything it stood for, from Coca-Cola to the CIA, was promptly anathematized as the Great Satan, women were forced back into the veil, homosexuals were executed, strict Shariah law was imposed on everybody and clerical powers made legally supreme. Iran's new constitution made Khomeini Supreme Religious Guide for life, as the vengeful old man laid about him with a will. Thousands were executed, from the Shah's officers to drunken rent boys. The Mosque reigned supreme, its secret religious police as intrusive as SAVAK had ever been.

None of this would have mattered by itself. One more rotten and corrupt regime falling would not have distressed Washington too much. Normally, some anti-communist deal could have been struck with a new government. After all, oil spoke the language of black gold.

But Khomeini's Iran struck two swift blows that changed everything: he declared America the deadly enemy of all Islam; and he eventually encouraged his supporters to storm the US Embassy in Tehran and 'arrest' all the diplomats and spies. The hapless diplomats and CIA men were humiliated and held as hostages by the mullahs and their supporters. The incident would have wide-spreading effects. The storming of the US Embassy was never just a local, regional difficulty; Iran's new militancy and truculence would have an impact on the wider Cold War too. Khomenei had destabilized the whole region and unleashed the spectre of Islamic fundamentalism directed against the enemies of God, in east and west alike. For the Soviet Union it lit a fuse that would end in Chechnya and Afghanistan. For the USA and Israel it began the glorification of the cult of religious martyrdom in the name of Allah, Hisbollah and suicide bombers.

By the end of 1979, a seemingly impotent US President was suddenly facing an international crisis of the gravest proportions. It was to bring Jimmy Carter down.

Psychologically, the events at the Tehran Embassy in November 1979, and the subsequent disastrous US rescue attempt Operation Eagle Claw, which ended among burned-out aeroplanes in the Iranian desert and bitter recriminations between the various armed services in Washington, were yet another humiliating disaster for America. But at least the US had one sympathetic, if unlikely, friend among the international community: the Kremlin. For the USSR had been as appalled as the rest of the region when Khomeini's fanatics overthrew the Shah. Russia shared a common border with Iran in south-west Asia and had millions of Muslim citizens. A resurgence of religious zeal in the region was a decidedly unwelcome development for Brezhnev and his communist colleagues. Moscow was wrestling with its own little problem on its southern border too. We know now from access to the Kremlin's secret files that the upsurge of Islamic Shi'ite fundamentalism both inside and outside Russia's borders was a matter of major concern to Moscow. Russian eyes, once again, turned south. Afghanistan had long been a cockpit of colonial rivalry. There the British and the Czar's agents had conducted their own vicious little undercover struggle for mastery throughout much of the nineteenth century. With well-practised ease, the Afghan tribesmen had long seen them off from their mountain fast-nesses. Not for nothing did the old Hindu prayer say: '*Oh, Lord Shiva, save me from the tiger's claw, the cobra's fang and the vengeance of the Afghan.*'

With the invaders gone, the Afghans settled back into their normal regime of clan feuds, vendetta and growing dope.

Marxism changed all that. Gradually family and tribal feuds became ideological fights too as a proto-communist Afghan Party strove for political mastery, supported inevitably by Moscow. A primitive coup by the Communists in 1978 even tempted America's CIA to dabble in the muddy pond of Afghan internal affairs. Unfortunately for the would-be Afghan Red Comrades, in 1978 their timing could not have been worse. Everywhere Islam was on the march. A pro-Soviet government in Kabul was not only meddling and unwelcome to the Muslim tribesmen of Afghanistan, it was semi-communist and therefore atheist and heretical. Tribal factions attacked the new govern-ment. The new regime begged Moscow for help, especially arms and soldiers. However, in the year that Khomeini had incited a mass riot to try and seize the Grand Mosque in Mecca during the Hadj, and when Islam was threatening to destabilize the Muslim populations of the whole region, the last thing the Soviet Union wanted was its own Vietnam in Afghanistan. Moscow sent aid but no troops while the Politburo stalled for time.

It was American Cold War policy as much as anything that unleashed the Armies of God or *Mujahidin* in Afghanistan against the new government, the same zealots who would one day fall upon the west. The CIA was only too well aware of the Kremlin's difficulties in Afghanistan and now sought to twist Moscow's tail to make things worse for them. Despite Carter's high-minded rupture of relations for human rights abuses with President Zia ul-Haq's Pakistan, the CIA now began its own secret aid programme to support the Islamic Afghan rebels via Pakistan's Intelligence Service, shipping US weapons to the Mujahidin and ensuring that the anti-communists in Afghanistan were well supplied with arms and money. One day the United States would rue letting this particular genie out of the bottle, but in 1979 it made sense for America to encourage Islamic fanatics to kill Afghan Communists and so help the Cold War along. The Afghan rebels were both delighted and very successful. Soviet advisors were murdered. The pro-communist regime of President Taraki became increasingly beleaguered and fought back with reprisals against its own people, now stigmatized as 'Islamic' enemies. Kabul's calls for help from Moscow grew more urgent.

Matters came to a head in autumn 1979. Taraki, Moscow's man, was suffocated in his bed by three of his chief rival's thugs and the more western-leaning Amin seized power in Kabul. Not for long: over Christmas 1979, Soviet Spetsnaz (Special Forces) troops landed unannounced at Kabul airport and, in a daring *coup de main,* stormed the presidential palace to kill Amin and install yet another pro-Moscow regime, this time headed by Babrak Karmal. Simultaneously, three divisions of Soviet armoured troops poured into Afghanistan from the north to occupy the country and consolidate Moscow's *putsch.* They were met by scattered resistance from the surprised Islamic warriors of the Mujahidin. The USSR had moved in. The Afghan War had begun. Thanks to the Shah, militant Islam was on the march. The USSR would be first to feel its lash.

In retrospect, we can see that the Soviet Union's last war was a disaster from the start. The fatal decision appears to have been reached following a Politburo meeting on 12 December 1979 (where a drunken Brezhnev left the meeting to be chaired by

Mikhail Suslov, the cadaverous guardian of communist ideology) and was confirmed at an un-minuted meeting held in Brezhnev's office on Christmas Eve 1979. We do, however, now know the main factors behind the Kremlin's policy decision. They sum up much of the USSR's Cold War thinking:

- The Brezhnev Doctrine. Intervention in another country was necessary to prop up a pro-communist regime in the USSR's sphere of influence.
- The need to frustrate US/western policy ambitions around Russia's borders and prevent the west gaining any advantage or encircling the USSR.
- Moscow's historic expansionist drive south to get towards warm weather ports.
- A fear of external contamination of the Muslims of the USSR by the forces of fundamental Islam.

Two other factors also influenced the secret Politburo meeting: Brezhnev's near-senility and his dreamy attempts to recreate his Czech operation of 1968 in Afghanistan; and Defence Minister Ustinov's confident assurance (in the teeth of a quite explicit General Staff assessment to the contrary) that the military operation would be a short sharp drive on the capital, followed by a triumphant 'mission accomplished'. We know that Ustinov made no contingency plans for continued guerrilla war or insurgency in Afghanistan after the Soviets' invasion to effect regime change and subsequent occupation. The meeting was swayed by this misplaced and quite wrong military counsel from the Politburo's senior military advisor.

At first the Soviet's coup seemed only too successful. NATO's startled intelligence officers were hastily recalled from Christmas leave; nearly 5,000 Soviet civil servants and 'advisors' took over the running of the Kabul bureaucracy; Russian military police 'regulators' were soon controlling Kabul's traffic as if nothing had happened; and a pro-Soviet regime was firmly in place by the New Year. On 8 January 1980, the Spetsnaz units went back home to Russia to be greeted with flowers and medals. The Soviet 40th Army was left to garrison a pacified communist Afghanistan on Moscow's behalf. The USSR appeared to have taken ground in the confrontation we call the Cold War.

From Washington, still watching an increasingly muddled President Carter pleading impotently with an intransigent and hostile Ayatollah and struggling to get American hostages released from a Tehran jail, all was gloom.

President Carter's response was a direct return to Cold War rhetoric. In January 1980, he addressed the US Congress, spelling out America's vital high ground in the region, in the light of the Iranian and Afghan shocks:

> Let our position be absolutely clear: an attempt by any outside force to gain control of the Persian Gulf will be regarded as an assault on the vital interests of the United States of America and such an assault will be repelled by any means necessary, including military force . . .

This stark warning from Washington could not have been clearer and was aimed directly at the USSR. Soviet successes in the Horn of Africa and Soviet influence in Syria, Iraq and now Afghanistan, all looked suspiciously like a major regional strategic power play by the Soviet Union. Carter, whatever other high-minded ideas he may have held, was quite clear that unrestricted access to the oil supplies of the Persian Gulf was a vital national interest for the USA, and he wanted others to know it too. Oil was – and still is – a fighting matter for the USA. Its economy depended on it. Without regular and cost-effective supplies of oil the US – and the whole of western civilization – would be in deep trouble, economically, politically and socially. To make matters even clearer, therefore, after two terms of high-minded muddle and strategic drift, at last the American President took a clear stand, ordering a strategic review that eventually emerged in July 1980 as Presidential Directive 59. This effectively rejected *détente,* called for a Rapid Reaction Force (RRF) to be able to ensure a swift military response to crises, and announced the decision to deploy Ground Launched Cruise Missiles (GLCM) in Europe. To rub salt into the Soviet Union's economic wounds, Carter even called for China to be given Most Favoured Nation trading status.

The ailing Brezhnev took the hint. He could read the Cold War runes as well as any other powerbroker and, truth to tell, the Kremlin was not really looking for trouble in the early 1980s. The Soviet leadership had quite enough on its plate already, although western intelligence was slow to spot the signs in the closed society of Soviet Russia at the time. The Kremlin's over-confident assumptions of strategic parity with the USA dating back to the early 1970s had turned out to be seriously mistaken. The Soviet economy was sinking ever deeper into some kind of Marxist mire, over-regulated, over-controlled and just plain inefficient. The cost of a new arms race didn't help. Worst of all, the Soviet successes of the previous decade turned out to be running sores. Russia's Third World 'allies' such as Ethiopia, Angola or Cuba contributed little to the USSR and demanded much. The satellites of eastern Europe were slowly growing ever more restive and expensive.

The American boycott of the 1980 Moscow Olympic Games was merely a symbol of a deeper malaise as the 'Second Cold War' bit home in the early 1980s. The gerontocracy of the ageing Politburo sought in vain for some kind of solution to Moscow's growing problems. Marx – for once – seemed to have little to offer. The arrival of a new American President only compounded the Kremlin's growing problems. Ronald Reagan's accession to power in 1980 crystallized America's strategic and psychological change of heart.

Because Ronald Reagan wanted to win the Cold War once and for all.

21

THE ICE MAN COMETH

RONALD REAGAN'S GREAT PLAN

Reagan's arrival as President was met with dismay in more than one quarter.

The Great Communicator, like his predecessor, came to the White House with virtually no experience of foreign policy. Moreover, to many Europeans, the former Governor of California was judged as being merely another hick actor, and a right-winger implicated in the McCarthy era into the bargain. He was promptly stigmatized by the left as 'ill equipped for the great responsibility he bears . . . bellicose, ignorant and with a simplistic view of the world, pieced together from journals of right-wing opinion and Hollywood B-movies'. This contemptuous dismissal of the leader of the Free World by one of London's *bien-pensants* indicated a failure to grasp that, like his British counterpart Margaret Thatcher, Ronnie Reagan was an experienced conviction politician.

Above all, Reagan and his backers were convinced that

America had grown weak and had allowed the USSR far too free a run against US interests. He sought to redress the balance, and, unlike Jimmy Carter, he had a plan. He also had two other advantages: a strong team in the White House, and genuine pride in America and American achievements, something not seen since the debacle of Vietnam. Reagan genuinely believed in America and he wanted the American people to rediscover their pride in America too. He set out to take a firm line with the Kremlin from the start. He and his Secretaries of State, the experienced but over-ambitious Al Haig and then the steadier hand of George Schulz, master-minded an American foreign policy designed to make the world sit up and take notice.

Although by the end of his term Jimmy Carter had effectively abandoned *détente*, as his final tougher line with the Kremlin eventually demonstrated, his earlier see-sawing between hawk and dove had done much damage. Clear policy guidelines are important to friend and foe alike. Ronald Reagan changed all that. In one of his first speeches, he announced that 'détente is a one way street the Soviet Union has used to pursue its own ends.'

No one could misunderstand the Reagan administration. Carter's final legacy of a new strategic doctrine, PD-59, had stressed America's strength and willingness to fight if necessary. The new President built on this foundation and authorized a $30 billion re-armament programme. To match the USSR's massive build-up of arms, NATO was encouraged to re-arm too by some surprisingly blunt arm-twisting. Above all, new nuclear weapons were to be deployed specifically to hold the Soviet Union's massive conventional armies in Europe at risk. A ripple of concern went through the Kremlin. Reagan's policies were militarily hardline; but, more worryingly for the Kremlin, they were going to be expensive to match.

Despite his B-movie actor image, Reagan and his advisors had had a very clear strategy about how to handle the Cold War from the start. His security policy had been moulded by a right-wing think tank, the Committee for the Present Danger, whose views could be best summarized as: 'Carry a big stick, but be prepared to talk. And let's try and win the Cold War, because we *can*!' To back this tougher, simpler policy, the US embarked on an internal publicity campaign designed to reassure the US voter that their new President would stand tall against any aggression by the USSR and to reaffirm America's self-confidence. Reagan presented his message in simple but clear terms, even inviting a Florida congregation to 'pray for the salvation of those who live in totalitarian darkness'. He called Soviet Russia 'the Evil Empire', and said that communism was 'just another sad, bizarre chapter in human history, whose last pages are even now being written'. This 'stand up and be counted campaign' was not just directed at domestic audiences. The Kremlin listened to this new Cold War rhetoric too, but with growing alarm, and counterattacked. Reagan was fiercely denounced as a warmonger in robust and traditional Cold War invective.

Once again the KGB was ordered to mobilize their usual band of fellow travellers for the 'invisible front', and its army of left-wing activists in the west began to chant a new mantra: 'Reagan Means War!' The President was characterized as a 'stupid cowboy' and a political simpleton in the liberal press in both Europe and America, much to the delight of political cartoonists. Gromyko revealed just how concerned the USSR was when he called the American government '[a bunch of] compulsive gamblers and adventurists who . . . are ready to plunge mankind into a nuclear catastrophe for the sake of their ambitions'. Significantly, he made these remarks in Bonn. The Great Publicity War of the early 1980s was specifically aimed

" RED UNDER THE BED? SORRY, I DIDN'T NOTICE ! "

Britain finally wakes up to the reality of communist infiltration
(Stanley Franklin, published in the *Sun*, 11 November 1982)

at a NATO, and specifically a European, audience. If
the Kremlin could convince Paris and Bonn that Reagan's
America was an out-of-control maverick, then Europeans
might be decoupled from an increasingly hardline Washington.

In some cases the Kremlin's line fell on fertile soil. President
Giscard d'Estaing, ever ready for France to be seen as a global
power independent of the Anglo-Saxons and NATO, talked bilaterally to Moscow, although without much result. More
seriously for NATO's unity, Chancellor Schmidt of Germany
grumbled that 'we won't let 10 years of détente and defence
policy be destroyed.' But, as ever in a growing crisis, the
European sheep tended to huddle for security under the American umbrella. Germany, above all, needed NATO and the USA.

The US made its weight felt and its views known quickly

elsewhere, and not just to Moscow. First, Reagan decided to clear up America's back yard. In the final years of the 1970s it had seemed as if everywhere in Latin America was about to go communist in one form or another. Nicaragua and El Salvador had drifted away from the US camp and the Nicaraguan Sandinistas had even achieved minor cult status as anti-American icons among impressionable youth and left-wing activists in the west. The FSNL and their Cuban advisors soon felt the full weight of US power. The Sandinista Marxist insurgents in Nicaragua were suddenly confronted by Reagan-armed and better-trained government troops, with US military advisors deployed in support and new weapons to hand. The message was clear: America was prepared to walk tall. After an initial hesitation, the US threw its full weight behind Britain's storming of the Falkland Islands after Argentina's invasion in 1982. In the Middle East, the US and CIA aided and abetted Israel's invasion of southern Lebanon where the PLO and now the Shi'a fanatics of Hisbollah were widening their guerrilla war against Israel. Under Reagan, American global muscle was back in business.

An alarmed Kremlin talked of new international tensions.

Events conspired to heighten tension even further. In Poland the first-ever visit of a Polish Pope aroused huge and long dormant feelings of national pride. The Catholic Church was a bigger influence in most Poles' lives than the Communist Party. An independent trade union called Solidarnosc (Solidarity) sprang up in the Gdansk shipyards, demanding reforms and an end to the fat cats of the Party and was only suppressed by the imposition of martial law backed by the Army's bayonets. The Polish Solidarnosc crisis was far more serious than was ever revealed at the time. Behind the scenes, NATO secretly went on full intelligence alert at this new threat of war as Soviet tanks and high-category assault divisions massed across the Polish border in Belorussia, poised to invade and crush Lech

Walesa's challenge to the Communist Party's monopoly of power. Major Soviet military headquarters deployed with sealed orders, and large-scale exercises replicating the 1968 move into Czechoslovakia were practised in the Western Military Districts. The Soviet General Staff team that had master-minded and controlled the Czech invasion a decade before was brought to alert status and began opening communications with its deployed divisions. Washington and London worried that NATO might be facing a new 1968. In the event, the Polish leader Jaruzelski and the Polish Communist Party suppressed the incipient rebellion themselves without the Red Army's assistance, but the Gdansk shipyard workers and their counterparts elsewhere in eastern Europe would one day have a part to play in the overthrow of communism.

As the first years of the decade unfolded some kind of hysterical panic appears to have seized the Kremlin leadership. The reason for the panic was that, according to French analysts who called the 1981–5 period the 'Second Cold War', the confrontation between the superpowers had by 1981 slipped from *détente* back to the old confrontational reflexes of Berlin and Cuba. Veteran Cold War warriors like George Kennan agreed, remarking that the crisis of 1981–83 had 'a well known feel . . . the unfailing characteristics of a march towards war . . .' The reasons for this rising tide of war fever are obscure. But by 1983 the war of words between the two superpowers had risen once again to a crescendo, with Reagan talking of the 'Evil Empire' and Andropov comparing Reagan to Hitler. In this climate of fear and suspicion, rational political reactions were increasingly unlikely.

The Kremlin was also secretly aware that, according to their new (1981) computer-assisted assessment of what the Soviets called 'the correlation of forces', the USSR was 'losing the Cold War'. Marxist analysis of history and ingrained political convictions made such forward-looking assessments 'scientific', and therefore historically inexorable. This tended to make such a prediction more troublesome to the dogmatic communist mind than any similar prognosis put forward by the CIA or the British JIC, which would be treated on its merits and not as some 'scientifically revealed truth' about the 'historic forces' as revealed by Marx. (In the west, such predictions by futurologists tended to be treated at best as interesting discussion topics; more often, they were dismissed as expensive mumbo-jumbo from overpaid defence consultants.) To this gloomy forecast of the future of the USSR was added the knowledge that the west was now beginning to overturn many of the Soviet gains of the 1970s. Such places as Afghanistan, Angola and Nicaragua seemed to be falling back into the clutches of the CIA or American influence generally. Moreover, the Politburo was grappling with the unpleasant realization that all these Marxist regimes were costing the Soviet Union a great deal of money. Cuba was draining Soviet funds, and the Nicaraguan rebels were being increasingly squeezed by American-backed government forces and demanding more aid. To the Politburo the world picture in the early 1980s looked both dangerous and, even worse, expensive.

So when Brezhnev and Andropov had taken to the podium at a closed gathering of senior KGB and intelligence officials in May 1981 to issue a warning of impending American threats it set the tone for a growing confrontation. The Kremlin went further and ordered a full-scale defensive intelligence collection effort called Operation RYAN (*Raketo Yadernoye Napadie* – Nuclear Rocket Missile Attack) to monitor any indications and warnings of war. RYAN dominated KGB collection priorities all through 1982, and by 1983 was feeding messages of gloom into the centre. Part of the problem with this kind of political hypothesis-led approach to intelligence problems is that, unsurprisingly, they tend to find the answers to support the original hypothesis. Objectivity goes out of the window under the pressure of political masters demanding intelligence to fit the facts as they see them, and not as they are. Intelligence officers are only human, as Prime Minister Tony Blair and his spin doctor Alastair Campbell's duplicities over the 2003 invasion of Iraq proved. Even western intelligence officers know how to guard their jobs and pensions when politicians demand answers that are just not true. It is therefore no surprise that the obedient Soviet intelligence officers found much evidence to support their political masters' ideas. As a result the Kremlin's threat perception of a surprise attack grew by the day. Quite why Andropov became the first Russian leader since Stalin actually to believe that the USA was about to launch a surprise attack on the USSR remains a mystery. Neither Ambassador Dobrynin, Oleg Gordievsky or Oleg Shvets, Head of the KGB Residency in Washington at the time, can throw any light on the matter. A simple explanation might be that Andropov had formerly been Head of the KGB. A certain *déformation professionelle* is to be expected and becomes almost inevitable with long-time intelligence officers whose view of life sometimes become warped out of all touch with reality. For many, paranoia becomes their normal approach to life.

There is another theory, however. When the Reagan administration came to power, one of their carefully designed offensives against the USSR was a deliberate – and still highly secret – campaign of psychological operations designed to jangle Soviet nerves. Premiers Andropov and Chernenko both seem to have shared these fears, and their nerves were as easily jangled as any KGB analyst's. The US Psyops campaign of the early 1980s was a success, but had some unintended consequences. Few people know of this secret campaign, whose details have still never been fully revealed, to destabilize and worry the Soviet leadership. The programme was intended not to demonstrate American intentions but to keep the Russians guessing as to what might come next. Thus bombers would swoop over the North Pole and turn away when alarmed Soviet Air Defence radars were just about to switch from 'detection' to 'target illumination' mode. The US Navy also stepped up its activities as part of the Psyops campaign, beginning with a massive ninety-ship NATO Fleet exercise off the Soviet Red Banner Fleet's headquarters in Murmansk in the autumn of 1981. During the next twelve months US carrier jets practised aggressive air-to-air interceptions of Soviet maritime patrol aircraft and demonstrated that they could evade Soviet warning radar by popping up in unexpected places. US and British nuclear submarines made increasingly daring – and frequently undetected – incursions into Soviet undersea submarine 'bastions' to jangle Soviet nerves.

What worried the Russians at the time – and has only become apparent since the end of the Cold War – was the increasing number of NATO, and especially US, incursions into what the Soviets felt were their defended air and sea space *without being spotted*. To an increasingly worried Kremlin, the USSR's defences appeared to be full of holes. What this meant for deterrence and the nuclear balance was anyone's guess, but of one thing we can be sure: for the Soviet leadership the Cold War was suddenly beginning to look very unbalanced and therefore very dangerous.

1982 dawned with the Cold War raging anew and a positive blizzard of recriminations between east and west. The CIA embarked on a vigorous funding campaign to destabilize the satellites of eastern Europe. The KGB encouraged their own equally vigorous campaign in the western media, aimed at the Peace Movement and doing all that the Kremlin could to prevent the deployment of the so-called Intermediate Range Nuclear Forces (INF), Pershing and Tomahawk Cruise missiles to their bases in Europe. Somehow the Soviet's own SS-20 nuclear missiles were overlooked in many of the vociferous western newspaper denunciations of Reagan's 'crude warmongering'. Women marched on Greenham Common, the first Cruise missile site in the UK, and set up camp, virtually imprisoning the base. The European press polarized sharply between left and right as denunciations flew between 'warmongers' and 'peace-niks'. A new Cold War arms race was accelerating and the propaganda campaign grew shriller on both sides.

America's President and his advisors had been watching events carefully throughout the early years of his presidency. From the very beginning Reagan had been prepared to ne-gotiate with Brezhnev, but this time the American President intended the talking to be done from a position of clear US strength, with none of Carter's vacillating inconsistency. That way Washington knew it would get the Kremlin's full atten-tion. After the old man's death in 1982, Reagan tried again with Brezhnev's equally geriatric successor, Yuri Andropov. In 1983 Reagan wrote personally to Andropov, suggesting to the new leader that the best way forward was for 'private and candid' personal communication between them both. Then events intervened to stop all that. The Korean Airliner incident of 1983 stopped any attempt at dialogue and raised interna-tional tension to new levels. The shooting-down of a defence-less civilian airliner over a Soviet closed military zone in the Far East by a Soviet air defence interceptor was never going to endear the old men in the Kremlin to the free world's press, whatever the circumstances.

The KAL 007 incident shocked the world. The Soviet Union predictably denounced the flight as an American spying attempt (as if Aeroflot never spied on behalf of Soviet intelligence), while the rest of the world saw the death of 269 innocent passengers as a ghastly blunder, caused by incompetent Soviet air defence controllers and trigger-happy Soviet pilots. Denunciations flew. An indignant Washington played tapes of the conversations between the Soviet ground controller and the Sukhoi 15 interceptor to the press. The pilot's cold-blooded, matter-of-fact report that 'The target is destroyed' sent a chill down even the most experienced Cold War spines. Either the Kremlin was deliberately sabre-rattling, or the USSR's military was out of control.

However, we now know that all was not quite as it seemed. KAL flight 007 had refuelled with an abnormally large fuel load for its scheduled flight plan. It was several hundred miles off course, but reporting back to air traffic control as if on its normal flight path. The pilot of the intercepting fighter jet had completed all agreed international procedures before finally opening fire. He had called the airliner on the open international hailing frequency before 'buzzing' it with his landing lights fully on, and had even fired a burst of highly coloured tracer across the Korean plane's nose. Despite all these warnings, the Jumbo jet ploughed on and Captain Chun and his crew and 269 passengers paid the final price as the aircraft plunged into the sea in Soviet restricted airspace.

Many questions remain unanswered about KAL flight 007. However, its effect on international relations in 1983 was disastrous, stoking up Cold War tensions yet again, but now to a new peak. The US banned Aeroflot airliners from landing in the US and the third – and final – crisis of the long Cold War came slowly to the boil, with growing suspicion and animosity on both sides.

Moscow was as alarmed as the White House at this unwelcome new direction in events. Gromyko warned that 'the
world situation is now slipping towards a very dangerous
precipice . . .' and the Kremlin discussed civil defence and
made discreet preparations for war. The Kremlin appears, by
1983, to have been badly rattled by the new tough Reagan line
and the accelerating pace of events. From MI6-SIS files we now
know that the Soviet leadership genuinely believed that the
USA was actively preparing for war, even a nuclear first strike.
The head of the East German Secret Intelligence Service,
Markus Wolf, was tasked by the KGB to recruit a high-level
spy inside NATO HQ in Brussels. Reiner Rupp (Agent 'To-
paz'), was specifically tasked with finding a copy of the top-
secret NATO plan to attack the USSR. The bewildered Rupp's
report that no such plan existed, and certainly not in the
NATO duty officer's Cosmic Top Secret war safe, was met
with disbelief by the KGB, the GRU and the Kremlin. Such a
plan *must* exist, insisted the Russians. Rupp was even given a
special communications device to turn on the moment NATO
took the decision to strike using its aggressive master plan to
destroy the USSR. His assertion that really there was no such
plan in NATO threw the Politburo and their KGB advisors
into incomprehension and confusion. Of course there was a
plan. There had to be. Once again the Kremlin leadership had
made the fatal error of judging others by their own perverse
and paranoiac standards. How on earth could NATO *not* be
planning a first strike?

A bewildered Politburo was becoming increasingly jumpy
and uncertain. A later and now-declassified top-secret US
Special National Intelligence Estimate (SNIE) of 1984 assessed
that the US actions of the early 1980s had been deemed
provocative by the USSR and were in fact contributing to
the increased levels of Cold War tension. Markus Wolf con-

firmed this after the end of the Cold War, revealing that the KGB was obsessed by the dangers of a nuclear missile attack. He reveals that the Kremlin was 'in a panic' by 1982–3 and was insisting that all his East German MfS agents should be now redirected to looking out for any warning of a nuclear strike and war.

Anti-Soviet sentiment in the west following the KAL 007 incident was matched by a genuinely held view in Russia that America was re-arming and looking for some kind of provocation for war. The combination of major NATO exercises, the deployment of Cruise and Pershing missiles, and a worldwide US military alert following the killing of 220 US Marines in 1983, convinced the Kremlin that America really was preparing for a war, and that it was now only a matter of time. To make things worse, having walked out of the Arms Limitation Talks in Geneva, the Soviets were further hampered. They had cut off dialogue with the west. In late 1983, Soviet fears of an attack by the west grew in direct relationship to the Kremlin's growing fear of a US first nuclear strike.

This then was the climate in which the routine NATO exercise 'Able Archer' was launched in the autumn of 1983. Able Archer was a regular command post exercise that ran NATO's Allied Forces Europe's numerous headquarters through a war scenario, leading from some imaginary minor crisis right up to a practice request from the Supreme Allied Commander in Mons to NATO's Military Committee in Brussels, calling for a notional nuclear release, as he 'could no longer contain the military situation in Europe . . .' This kind of routine exercise, regularly rehearsed by both sides during the Cold War, together with its patterns of radio traffic, was well known to the numerous intelligence officers and agents of the Warsaw Pact busy spying throughout Europe.

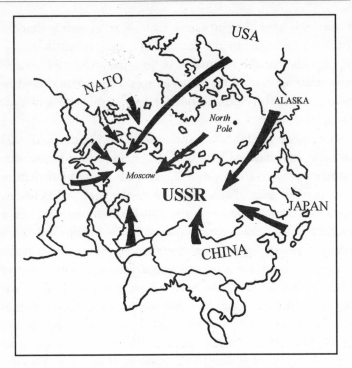

The view from Red Square, 1983:
a Kremlin perspective of Cold War threats

This time, however, according to Oleg Gordievsky, the Kremlin seems to have panicked. A flash signal from Moscow
Centre alerted all KGB residencies worldwide to go to 'intelligence of war alert' status. The increased American activity,
the loss of KAL 007 with 269 lives, Andropov's 1981–2
apocalyptic warnings to the senior members of the Communist
Party, and the Kremlin's own perception of vulnerability,
suddenly all combined to create a crisis out of thin air. Even
Ambassador Dobrynin, that unfailingly acute observer of the
true state of the Cold War, admitted that 'both sides went a
little crazy'.

According to Gordievsky, on the night of 8/9 November 1983 the Kremlin issued a Flash Top Secret 'warning of war' signal, claiming that US forces in Europe had gone on alert and that some units were being mobilized. This was just plain wrong, but in human affairs erroneous beliefs, however sincerely held, often encourage greater error. The Warsaw Pact was immediately ordered to war-readiness. The Soviet High Command ordered a military alert in eastern Europe. Ammunition was out-loaded at airfields, tanks brought to battle-readiness, and leave cancelled. The Group of Soviet Forces Germany prepared to move to its dispersal stations. The Kremlin talked about civil defence, that sure Cold War sign that things were getting really serious.

Allied intelligence swiftly picked up this change in posture and alarmed NATO intelligence officers reported that 'the Soviets are up to something.' *Both* sides now feared a pre-emptive attack, the Russians from newly deployed Pershing and Cruise missiles, the NATO allies from a massive conventional invasion of Germany by 20,000 Russian tanks. British agents deep inside the Kremlin and the Soviet High Command warned that the Kremlin really did believe that a nuclear war could be imminent. The American National Security Agency and British GCHQ signals intelligence intercepts confirmed KGB's Colonel Oleg Gordievsky's explosive 'humint' revelation. The Russians really were very jumpy indeed and believed that NATO was about to attack them, and, in Stalin's words, 'wring their necks like chickens'.

The US and NATO leadership were astounded. The idea that the NATO Alliance was contemplating a nuclear first strike against Moscow would have been laughable, had it not been so deadly serious. Most alarming of all, the fact that the Kremlin could actually believe such a thing to be possible was a sinister insight into just how dangerous the

Cold War had become, and how ignorant the Kremlin leaders really were. The experienced old diplomat Anatoly Dobrynin – still Soviet ambassador in Washington – was recruited one more time to help lower the temperature and carry messages back.

Reassuring messages were sent and Exercise Able Archer wound down and stopped. But it had been a frightening demonstration of just how quickly the nuclear pile at the core of the Cold War could go critical and become dangerous. Very few people in the west are aware of just how close the world came to war in the autumn of 1983: seasoned Cold War observers believed that the crisis was every bit as dangerous and explosive as the Cuban Missile Crisis two decades earlier. After Able Archer a belligerent Andropov raised the stakes by refusing to talk to the US President, informing Reagan that the US deployment of Cruise missiles had 'destroyed the very basis on which it was possible to seek an agreement' before retreating back into the fastnesses of the Kremlin and the Politburo. Cruise missiles and a downed Korean airliner meant that 1983 ended on a very sour note indeed.

Behind it all, the pressures on the Soviet Union were building on every front. Afghanistan was fast becoming a major insurgency and a running sore, eating up Russian men, machines and money. The Soviet economy could no longer cope with the demands of a renewed strategic arms race, a major war on its southern border and feeding its own people. The classic issue of 'guns or butter' looked like providing neither in satisfactory quantities. As 1984 dawned, the USSR and the communist system began to creak. Andropov obligingly died shortly afterwards, the second member of the Kremlin's supreme leadership to go to Marxist Nirvana within three years. Doubtless gritting his teeth, Reagan tried dialogue with the Soviets once again, this time inviting the Soviet's latest leader,

Konstantin Chernenko, to a summit at the Los Angeles 1984 Olympic Games. 'Carrot and stick' was the strategy, and the US had some major carrots to offer to encourage the USSR to be more cooperative. As early as 1981, Reagan had offered to lift the US grain embargo 'in order to assist us in our joint obligation and to find a lasting peace'. The Soviet economy desperately needed grain. However, nothing, it seemed, could overcome the mistrust and suspicion between east and west, particularly on the Soviet side.

President Reagan and Britain's Prime Minister Thatcher now realized that the time had come to make concerted efforts to connect with the collective leadership in Moscow, if only to reassure them. Reagan made conciliatory speeches; Thatcher asked for a meeting with the Kremlin's emerging new junior leadership. It was obvious to all that the ailing Chernenko was not long for this world, let alone premiership of the Soviet Union. Satirical television pro- grammes in the west openly mocked Moscow's geriatric leaders, showing the Soviets pulling a succession of old men in wheelchairs out of a Kremlin deep freeze to answer Reagan's letters.

The result of the Able Archer crisis was that by early 1984 both east and west realized that things risked getting out of hand. A Cold War crisis always risked becoming a nuclear crisis. That was unacceptable. Each side now looked for new channels to keep a dialogue going and sought ways of keeping the lid on the kettle of what was looking like an increasingly dangerous renewed Cold War confrontation. Behind the scenes, Foreign Minister Gromyko and US Secretary of State Schulz met in Stockholm for a long and 'serious' private chat. Tensions eased and both sides relaxed.

1984 ended with one of the more significant meetings of the Cold War. To the Kremlinologists of Whitehall's Foreign and

Commonwealth Office and the analysts of the British Defence
Intelligence Staff, the identity of the most likely successor to
Chernenko seemed fairly predictable. The Soviet leader was
now so old and frail that he routinely handed over chairman-
ship of the Politburo's meetings to his Head of the Secretariat:
Mikhail Gorbachev. Despite the usual doubters and dissenting
voices, Washington agreed with Whitehall's assessment of the
USSR's 'coming man', and in December 1984 the 54-year-old
Gorbachev and his glamorous wife Raisa came to London on
an official visit, representing the Kremlin leadership. The visit
was a great success, on all sides. The media liked the photogenic and cheerful Gorbachevs, so different from the usual
Soviet visitors, miserable old men in ill-fitting suits. 'I like Mr
Gorbachev,' opined a smiling Mrs Thatcher, adding in a
hugely significant judgement, 'We can do business
together . . .'

Her snap opinion to a press query on the steps of Number
10 Downing Street was more important than Mrs Thatcher
realized.

For within three months Chernenko was dead, the third
Kremlin leader to die in three years, and the fresh and
relatively young Mikhail Gorbachev had been unanimously
elected Chairman of the Politburo and the Soviet Union's new
leader.

22

HUNTING A POLAR BEAR

THE SECRET ATTACK ON THE USSR

All this time, Reagan's master plan to win the Cold War was ticking. For on coming to power Reagan and his advisors had begun a strategic security policy that went far beyond the simplicities of the 'carrot and stick' to induce change in the USSR. The Reagan administration and the Committee for the Present Danger had agreed a deadly new tactic in the Cold War. They planned to bankrupt the communist USSR once and for all.

Some commentators have even described the Reagan administration's new policy towards Russia as 'a deliberate attempt to murder the Soviet Union'. These policies were codified in Reagan's National Security Directives, especially NSDD 32 of 1981, which effectively declared a secret economic and diplomatic war on the USSR. The key was the cutting-off of western technology to the Kremlin. Bill Casey, the new Director of the CIA, and his advisors calculated that without access to western industrial advances it would only be a matter of time before the Communists' economy would begin to shrivel. Their analysts had identified that the Soviets' command economy needed unrestricted access to western advances. Without that access, the Soviet economy would collapse. Like all good strategies, it was really very simple. For example, the USSR desperately needed British oil technologies developed for North Sea oil rigs to exploit the oil fields of the Barents Sea. Without the new drill head technology and specialist drill bits the Russian oil industry could not bore deep enough to get access to newly discovered gas and oil reserves. All this would hit the Kremlin and the Soviet Union where it would hurt most: in the pocket.

To neutralize the Soviets' continuing build-up of tanks, submarines and missiles, Reagan also agreed five key policy goals for national security, all of crucial Cold War significance:

- To keep the Soviets at the negotiating table.
- Nuclear Arms Limitation and Verifiable Reductions.
- Modernization of US forces.
- Economic pressure on the Soviet Union.
- To make the US safer by developing anti-missile Strategic Defense Initiative (SDI).

The last was explosive – as Reagan and his advisors knew full well it would be – because at a stroke it challenged the basic assumption of Mutual Assured Destruction. If one side in the Cold War suddenly acquired a successful and effective defence against incoming strategic missiles then – theoretically at least – it could defeat a nuclear attack, retaliate, and survive a nuclear war. SDI was completely destabilizing. It threatened the whole basis of Cold War nuclear strategy and the nuclear balance of power.

But SDI carried a much more insidious threat to the Soviet Union than some future ability to defend against incoming ICBMs. The SDI programme was based on high technology and cutting edge systems, many as yet undeveloped and unproven. To put it into space would be hideously expensive. Vast sums would be required for research and development over many years, with little guarantee of success. 'Star Wars' (as SDI quickly became known) destabilized the whole security equation of the Cold War and challenged the USSR both militarily and economically. It was a mortal threat to the Communists' entire system.

SDI was the most important, and controversial, weapons development since the first successful test of the atom bomb forty years before. Yet eight years and $25 billion later the full programme was quietly dropped, destined to become just another high-tech feasibility study. Why? Because it had served its purpose. The Strategic Defence Initiative was essentially a political, not a military, weapon intended to provide leverage for the US's efforts in the Cold War. The leverage, however, was not even political or military; SDI was intended as a deadly economic missile aimed at the heart of the most vulnerable target of all – the Kremlin's budget. SDI was intended to break the enfeebled economy of the Soviet Union once and for all.

American strategic thinkers had for some time been musing on the whole philosophy of the arms race, never mind its crippling expense. They, like many other thinking defence analysts, had realized that it was now technology that was the real battle winner. The so-called Zuckerman Philosophy was seen as an unfortunate truth. In 1980, Solly Zuckermann, Chief Scientific Advisor to Britain's Ministry of Defence, had written:

It is the technician, not the commander in the field, who is at the heart of the arms race, who starts the process of formulating a military . . . need. The men in the nuclear weapons laboratories of both sides have succeeded in creating a world with an irrational foundation, on which a new set of political realities has to be built. They have become the alchemists of our time, casting spells that embrace us all . . .

He added that the military chiefs 'usually serve only as the channel through which the men in the laboratories transmit their views'.

Zuckerman's vivid phrases – though wounding to the military's *amour propre* – do nonetheless represent a significant truth. Very often in the wonderful world of weapons, new strategies only emerge because scientists have discovered something new or invented a new toy. So it was with SDI. Advances in computers, X-ray lasers, microelectronics and advanced optical sensors opened exciting new possibilities for satellites. Radar tracking became ever more precise. The busy and curious scientists in American laboratories had also discovered by 1976 that particle beam weapons were technically possible, especially in the vacuum of space. By 1977 *Science Magazine* in America was quite openly publishing articles like 'Particle Beams as Anti-Ballistic Missile Weapons?' and *Scientific American* was talking openly of 'laser weapons' and 'high-power infra-red free electron lasers'.

It was all exciting stuff to the men in white coats. The realization that these scientific breakthroughs could be collectively harnessed to knock out incoming ICBMs from space electrified the ambitions of the USAF's senior commanders (one of whom was now grandly entitled C-in-C Space Command), and sent a tingle of anticipation through the ever-greedy wallets of US high-tech defence manufacturers. What cause could be more noble than defending America and Americans against the deadly menace of 'Red Rockets'? Especially when such an R and D effort opened the tantalizing prospect of literally billions of tax dollars. The 'Iron Triangle' of the Pentagon, of congressmen grabbing a slice of the defence budget for their 'folks back home', and the defence industry ever on the hunt for lucrative contracts, reached out to grab this arms contract of a lifetime.

Science had found them a new weapon, and a very expensive one. The academics who had made or linked the SDI discoveries were, like their predecessors on the Manhattan Project years before, far from innocent seekers after truth operating in some vacuum of moral neutrality. If the Cold War has taught us anything, it is that the scientists who invent the weapons bear as heavy a moral responsibility for the conduct of war as any politician or soldier. The first Presidential SDI Advisory Committee included no fewer than five university professors, as well as the usual suspects from the Mitre Corporation, RAND and Burroughs. Edward Teller, the Father of the Atom Bomb and subsequently of Lawrence Livermore Laboratories, also attended. SDI was a growth market for everybody with a stake in 'Defense'. At a projected total cost (in 1983 values) of over $500 billion, it had to be.

When, therefore, on 23 March 1983 President Reagan made his famous SDI speech signalling his authorization of a programme to overturn the whole basis of US Cold War strategy, he knew that he would be talking to a sympathetic and hopeful audience. Coming just two weeks after his famous 'Empire of Evil' speech, it seemed to hold out a new hope for a more secure future. Reagan painted a vision of a bright, nuclear-free world. He was 'changing the course of human history', and asked, 'Is it not better to save lives rather than avenge them?' His ringing peroration, 'Is it not worth every investment necessary to free the world from the threat of nuclear war?' went down a storm with the media, with the voters back home and, of course, with US defence contractors. The TRW Defense Corporation rep said, 'We're standing on the first rung of a development that will dominate the industry for the next 25 years.'

SDI provoked a furious reaction in the Kremlin. Andropov, despite the entreaties of his advisors not to over-react, fired off an angry broadside, accusing Reagan of deliberately lying about Soviet military strength in a fraudulent attempt to justify SDI. Space-based defence, said Andropov,

> . . . would open the floodgates of a runaway race of all types of strategic arms, both offensive and defensive. Such is the real significance of, let us say, the 'seamy side' of Washington's defensive conception . . . The Soviet Union will not be caught defenceless by such a threat . . . Engaging in this is not just irresponsible, it is insane . . . Washington's actions are putting the entire world in jeopardy. . . .

The announcement of Star Wars was also greeted with some shock by both Reagan's own cabinet and, more significantly, from the US administration's own Office of Management and Budget. The inevitable and well-orchestrated wails of dissent arose from the communist world's usual clutch of anti-American 'useful idiots' throughout Europe; this time, however, they were joined by more serious and influential voices. Many European defence commentators, even Margaret Thatcher herself, were worried by the strategic implications of a system that could render continental USA invulnerable to a nuclear strike, whilst leaving Europe still open to Soviet attack. SDI made many Europeans deeply uncomfortable for a wide range of reasons; of those, a nagging doubt about future security guarantees over a naked Europe by a well-defended USA was the most important.

Reagan dealt with these worries with his customary breezy aplomb. Having (in his own words) been given 'a good hand-bagging' by the Iron Lady on one of her visits to Washington, he offered the technology of space-based nuclear defences, once – and when – it had been developed, to the allies. Then they could invest in their own defence systems. Above all, however, Reagan offered SDI *to the Soviets*.

This was a masterstroke. It meant that Reagan still kept the economic threat at Moscow's throat while bilaterally offering to 'help their national security' by sharing the technology with them. This neatly circumvented the ABM Treaty of 1972, while at the same time keeping the US programme on track as a 'major contribution to global peace and security'. Knowing full well that the ever-suspicious Kremlin would feel duty-bound to keep up in this new arms race, the White House only had to wait for the cost of such a programme to rip the heart out of communist Russia's already enfeebled economy. From Andropov's angry denunciation of SDI the US could see that the Kremlin was not only panicked by Reagan's policy, but would try to disrupt it by any means possible. The CIA began to accumulate growing evidence that the KGB dirty tricks brigade had been mobilized to stop Star Wars by any means possible. A mysterious rash of terrorist murders hit Europe. Scientists associated with the SDI programme or working on specialist SDI contracts suddenly became targets for organizations like the Red Army Faction in West Germany and the Red Brigades in Italy. The KGB's fingerprints were all over this sudden upsurge in 'terrorism'. Allied to the hysterical press campaign by many on the European left, it confirmed that the SDI initiative had touched a very raw nerve indeed.

It also confirmed the CIA Economic Directorate's increasingly confident assessment that the Soviet economy was the Politburo's main source of anxiety and that the Russians were becoming more and more worried about US technological prowess. Marshal Nikolai Ogarkov, Deputy Defence Minister and Chief of Staff, admitted as much in an interview with an American journalist:

> We cannot equal the quality of US arms for a generation or two. Modern military power is based on technology, and technology is based on computers . . . In the US little children have computers to play with. Here we don't even have computers in every office in the Defence Ministry. And, for reasons you know well, we cannot make computers widely available in our society . . .

And then in a perceptive forecast that went to the heart of Soviet Russia's problems he added:

> We will never catch up with you in modern weapons until we have an economic revolution . . . And the question is, can we have an economic revolution without a political revolution?

If the Cold War was a game of poker, Ronnie Reagan had just raised the stakes dramatically and was staring his opponent down. To the Kremlin, however, Reagan's upbeat offer of everlasting peace – perhaps – only conveyed one message.

America had changed the Cold War rules. And it was going to cost . . .

The truth was that the Cold War and its arms race had by the early 1980s cost the USSR dear.

In relative terms, the Soviet economy could ill-afford the arms race and maintaining a bloated defence-oriented manufacturing base, and certainly much less so than the USA, the biggest economy in the world. The idiocies of Marxist command economics made things even worse. At one time, GOSPLAN, the Soviet Union's central economic authority, was trying to control the manufacture, distribution and 'sale' of over 4,000,000 separate items, from nuclear missile parts to nappy pins – the reader only has to guess which of these had priority in order to appreciate the long-suffering Russian housewife's problem. Foreign adventures in support of international communism, the massive nuclear programme and the Space Race had further weakened Russia's ailing economy.

The Space Race was a prime example of how both sides had been sucked into a pointless and expensive competition by the Cold War. The 1945 capture of German V2s and their rocket scientists had stimulated both the USSR and the USA to find new ways of delivering weapons and to advertise their technical prowess in the international tensions following the Second World War. Space exploration and its accompanying satellite technology could help the Cold War both militarily and in terms of prestige.

The Soviets were first off the blocks with the launch of Sputnik in 1957. The 80kg satellite overhead astounded the world and raised the USSR's reputation for technical expertise to new levels. The political, economic and military implications were not lost on the US. Lyndon Johnson summed up the American view of the contest: 'In the eyes of the world, first in space means first – period. Second in space is second in everything.'

The American scientists rolled up their sleeves and went to work. Despite some discouraging failures (see 'FLOPNIK', page 161), rockets and satellites became an American obsession, well funded and well supported by the government's tax dollars. By 1958 the American communications satellite

SCORE enabled President Eisenhower to broadcast a Christmas message to the whole world. In 1960 the Soviets sent two dogs into space. Both survived, unlike the unfortunate Laika which had perished in orbit in Sputnik 2 in 1957. On 12 April 1961 Yuri Gagarin became the first cosmonaut, orbiting the earth to return successfully to a hero's welcome and a short life of alcoholic celebrity. Achievement in space became a touchstone of prowess and the symbol of Cold War superiority. For a while the Cold War was virtually defined by the Space Race. For most of the 1960s it was the USSR that was ahead, notching up some notable firsts with space walks, orbiting the Moon, landing a Moon probe and beginning the technology that would lead to a space station. America concentrated instead on being the first to land on the Moon and threw everything behind Project Apollo. US thinking was best summed up by President Kennedy who told NASA's Director James Webb that:

> Everything we do should really be tied into getting on to the Moon ahead of the Russians . . . Otherwise we shouldn't be spending that kind of money because I'm not interested in space . . . The only justification [for the cost of the programme] is because we hope to beat the USSR and to demonstrate that instead of being behind them by a couple of years we have passed them . . .

American public opinion was entranced. Schools changed their curriculum to turn out more scientists and engineers. The high spot for the US and millions round the world came in July 1969 when Apollo 11 landed on the Moon. Neil Armstrong stepped on to the lunar surface with the simple phrase: 'That's one small step for man but a giant leap for mankind.'

But behind the public face of the Space Race a more deadly military confrontation was going on in the background. Both sides had been planning reconnaissance satellites long before Sputnik 1 was launched. The Soviet Vostok was a photoimaging satellite, and America's Discoverer 13 sent back packets of photographs from space in August 1960. The military implications were obvious as both the USSR and the USA invested heavily in military space technology. The public Space Race slowed after the triumph of the Moon landing, and finally petered out in 1975 when the American Apollo and Soviet Soyuz space modules docked in orbit in a very public demonstration of *détente*.

The cost of the Space Race was ruinous, but particularly for the USSR which could ill afford expensive technological adventures. One estimate puts the cost of the US space programme at $25 billion (in 1970 prices); and that is just up to the Moon landing in 1969. The difference was that America could afford it. The Soviets could not. Although their official figures are highly suspect, one source, General Moiseyev, the Armed Forces Chief of Staff, admitted that in 1989 over 6.9 billion roubles ($4 billion) had been allocated for that year's budget alone. The Soviet Union never could afford the Space Race.

The truth was that the Cold War had for over thirty years bled the USSR dry, from the Aswan Dam in 1955 to Afghanistan in 1985, and beyond. Military economic aid, covert operations, trade subsidies, interventions abroad and aid to the satellites had cost the long-suffering Soviet people a fortune (an estimated $40 billion in 1980 alone). Like the British seventy-five years before, the Soviet Union had discovered that an empire that actually costs money is a liability, not an asset. The result was that the communist-run economy of the USSR had atrophied almost to stasis. The USSR's growth rate had slumped from 5.5 per cent in the post-reconstruction of the 1950s to an estimated 1.5 per cent – at most – by 1985. By the time Mikhail Gorbachev came to power, communist Russia was in fact a second-rate, half-developed state, but armed with a superpower's armoury. As one commentator wittily described it: 'The USSR is really only Upper Volta with rockets.'

Mikhail Gorbachev was only too well aware of the Soviet Union's economic problems when he took over as leader on 12 March 1985. The previous December he had made a keynote speech at a Communist Party Conference. Although its ostensible theme was Marxist-Leninist ideology, Gorbachev had used it as a rallying call for reform, accompanied by a grim warning of the consequences of Russia doing nothing. He called for 'profound transformations of the economy and . . . a higher standard of living for the Soviet people'.

This kind of 'motherhood and apple pie' political hot air was little different from the usual blether spouted by aspiring politicians from party conventions in Boston USA, or British party conferences in Blackpool or Brighton. What made Gorbachev's colleagues, and Kremlin watchers, sit up and take notice was his prescription for action. This was more – much more – than routine Kremlin hot air. Chernenko's Number Two called for nothing less than a complete *restructuring*, or *perestroika*, of the Party, and 'a new openness or transparency' – *glasnost*.

This was explosive stuff. Not all of it was Gorbachev's own. His right-hand man was an economist called Aleksandr Yakovlev, who had been ambassador to Canada, understood the west, and had a clear view of where the Communist Party was headed should it fail to make some big changes. He questioned the very basic tenets of the Soviet system and warned that unless the economic base of the USSR was reformed then the leading role of the Party itself would be in danger. His views were not universally popular but by 1985 even the most reactionary die-hard old ideologues of Soviet Communist Party purity could see that major change was needed if the USSR was to survive. Gorbachev's confirmation as leader at the hastily convened Party Plenum was met with genuine applause as, at last, a new generation of more youthful reformers were voted into power by the Party faithful. In his acceptance speech, Gorbachev talked of the need for the USSR to move forward, with *glasnost* and *perestroika* as the principles of change. Significantly he then turned to foreign policy and went straight to the heart of the Cold War problem: 'We want to stop . . . the arms race, and consequently propose to freeze nuclear arsenals and cease any further deployment of missiles.'

Within days, Vice-President George Bush Sr and Secretary of State Schulz were in Moscow attending the late Premier Chernenko's funeral. They met Gorbachev and had face-to-face exchanges with the new leader. Back in Washington they reported to President Reagan and, like Margaret Thatcher, confirmed that Gorbachev was someone with whom they could 'do business'. Gorbachev, they told a delighted Reagan, was 'different'. Truman would have been astounded. Thirty years before he had called his Russian opponents, 'pig-headed', 'stupid', 'stubborn' and 'liars'. A British Chancellor of the Exchequer, Hugh Dalton, had come away from Moscow at the start of the Cold War dismissing the Soviets as 'puppies not yet house-trained', and Dean Acheson had sorrowfully advised his President that the men in the Kremlin could not be trusted – 'You just cannot sit down with them.' For nearly fifty years, the behaviour of Soviet leaders and their officials had in fact contributed greatly to the maintenance and the course of the Cold War, and had often prevented any accommodation between east and west.

Now, at last, Mikhail Gorbachev had broken the mould.

In many ways Gorbachev was a typical Soviet communist *apparatchik*. Born to a peasant family in a village near Stavropol in the north Caucasus in 1931, he was only ten when the Wehrmacht over-ran the region during the Great Patriotic War. After the liberation, he worked on the land and in 1952 was awarded the Red Banner of Labour for his work as a combine operator. Son of a committed family of Bolsheviks, he inevitably gravitated towards the Party, becoming a full member in the same year whilst reading law at Moscow University. Following his graduation he went – equally inevitably – to work for the Party, firstly as a Komsomol (Young Communist) official and then as First Secretary of the Stavropol Youth Area. His skill at handling people, his knowledge of the real problems of the Soviet system in the agricultural regions and good Party contacts, saw him elected to the Central Committee in 1971. At the age of forty he was a fully paid-up member of the Nomenklatura or Party élite. The early death of the Central Committee's Agricultural Committee Chairman was fortuitous – for Gorbachev, if not the luckless chairman Fyodor Kulakov – as the young activist from the Caucasus was suddenly catapulted into a highly exposed appointment in a key area. Agricultural failures were dragging the USSR down. The new boy could sort them out.

By 1980 Gorbachev was elected to the full Politburo. Still only forty-nine, he was the vanguard of the young reformers. Everyone, from Brezhnev down, knew that change was both necessary and unavoidable. The only question was just how this should be accomplished. Gorbachev looked like the perfect choice to be handed the poisoned cup of reform. It was a decision that would have momentous consequences.

The usual political infighting followed, but none could deny that Gorbachev discharged his duties as Second Secretary of the Party's Secretariat with considerable efficiency and, important for any politician on the make, without making too many enemies. His name became a byword for anti-corruption and anti-alcohol campaigns, which Andropov had pushed hard in his last year. The dying Andropov had been well aware of the need for reform and as an ex-KGB chief knew how to achieve it: by strict control. Gorbachev had cooperated enthusiastically in these crack-downs and made a name for himself as 'Mister Clean'. Indeed, Gorbachev's very success and positive image inspired jealousy among his envious colleagues and we now know that his 'election' following Chernenko's death in March 1983 was partly rigged by the pro-Gorbachev faction.

The Politburo had no rules about what constituted a quorum. Three key members were absent when the remaining seven convened their hastily arranged meeting to bring Gorbachev to power on 11 March 1983. The pattern continued: the so-called 'Plenum' session of the Central Committee which convened the next day (only the Central Committee could elect a Secretary under the Party's rules) turns out, on close examination, to have been equally flawed. Over 200 Central Committee members did not attend as they 'could not be summoned in time' and the meeting was hurried through 'as quickly as possible'.

With supreme power now concentrated in his hands, Gorbachev did some surprising things. Instead of becoming President of the USSR as 'First Secretary' of the Party (as his predecessors had done), he deftly removed the veteran Foreign Minister Andrei Gromyko from his long-established base in the Foreign Ministry by publicly inviting him to become President of the USSR. Gromyko could hardly refuse such an honour after a long career serving the Party. But this astute move now left foreign policy firmly in Gorbachev's reforming grip, as it removed one of the old guard conservatives and allowed Gorbachev to replace him with his own nominee for Foreign Minister, the Georgian Eduard Shevardnadze, a close personal friend and fellow reformer. Boris Yeltsin and Alexander Yakovlev completed Gorbachev's 'kitchen cabinet', which swiftly turned its attention to reforming the Soviet Union.

The big headache was, as always, the constipated Soviet command economy and its constant inability to, quite literally, deliver the goods. Gorbachev, accompanied by the photogenic Raisa, went out to meet the people. For the Party hierarchy to leave the Kremlin and go on 'walkabouts' was unheard of in post-war Russia. (In the case of Andropov and Chernenko, they could hardly have walked half a dozen steps in the Kremlin without a nurse and a portable oxygen supply.) Astonished Muscovites, and then ordinary people throughout the USSR, flocked to see the extraordinary phenomenon of a Soviet national leader who was actually asking them what *they* thought. 'We can't go on like this!' was the cry in every region. 'You're quite right!' Gorbachev shouted back, shushing the embarrassed attempts of the local Party officials to silence such unheard-of candour. 'We need *perestroika.*'

From Siberia to Smolensk the message was clear: the Russian people had had enough, and were looking to their dynamic young leader for radical changes. Change could not come quickly enough. Gorbachev ordered reform to be accelerated by a third catchword to add to *perestroika* and *glasnost*: *uskoreniye*, or 'speeding up change'.

The process of change in Soviet Russia became inexorable.

23

THE ICEBOUND REFORMER

MIKHAIL GORBACHEV

Many people, particularly in the west, regard Gorbachev as the great reformer, and they are right. However, the truth is that Gorbachev, the ultimate *apparatchik*, didn't want a new system. What the new First Secretary of the Communist Party of the Union of Soviet Socialist Republics really wanted was to make the old communist system work better.

Like Dubçek, who strove to reform Czechoslovakia in 1968, Gorbachev was always a committed Communist to his fingertips, and a man who really wanted to reform the Party, not to invent something new. And, like the hapless Dubçek and many other reformers before him, Gorbachev found that once the cat of reform had been allowed out of the bag, it showed a marked reluctance to go back in. In fact, it raced off down the garden at a brisk pace with its owner following hurriedly behind. Gorbachev and the Politburo discovered that change was indeed accelerating, but not in the way *they* wanted. Like

a man on a mountainside being carried down by scree once it
starts to move under him, Gorbachev and his team of reforming Communists could only look on as sixty years of Marxist-
Leninism started to slide away under their very feet, carrying
them downhill with it.

In order to reform, the Communist Party itself had to
become the principal agent of change; but if the Party was
also the principal source of *opposition to change,* then reform
became impossible. A dreadful truth began to emerge from the
fog of rhetoric about reform: it was the Communist Party itself
that was the obstacle to change inside the Soviet Union.
Turkeys do not vote for Christmas. The *nomenklatura* and
apparatchiki of Russia's Communist Party were equally unwilling to give up their privileged and safe way of life.

The principal opponents of change were, not surprisingly,
the Soviet military. The Soviet generals, just like their US
counterparts, grumbled at major reductions in their defence
budget. They were not accustomed to such radical new con-
cepts as defence cuts. They cited the growing threat from US
and NATO re-armament and the worrying potential of Star
Wars. They warned of America's continued hostile intent. In
1986 a triumphant Viktor Chebrikov told Gorbachev that his
KGB had once again uncovered incontrovertible evidence of
American skulduggery. A Russian aviation expert called Adolf
Tolkachev had been unmasked by the CIA traitor Aldrich
Ames, had confessed to spying for the US since the 1970s, and
was shot. On being told that 2 million roubles had been found
in Tolkachev's apartment, Gorbachev murmured, 'The Yankees have been generous.' In circumstances like this the hard-
nosed members of the Soviet hierarchy insisted that the Soviet
economy must keep up its previous pattern of defence spending. The Head of the KGB agreed with them. In vain: Gorbachev and his advisors knew that not only had the Soviet

economy been crippled by the distortions of the defence budget in the past, but there was now just not the money available to match US spending. Cuts were unavoidable. The days of the Politburo not querying the defence estimates and not daring to ask what was included in a line item of 100 billion roubles for 'Classified Party Projects' were over for good. Did the marshals have any better ideas? Gorbachev and Shevardnadze pointed out that defence spending was already consuming up to 40 per cent of the USSR's gross domestic product and that people were clamouring for changes and major reform. The Party's – let alone the military's – very existence was at risk if the Politburo failed to meet the people's expectations. The generals backed down.

Western commentators, and especially the White House, had been following these developments with interest. In 1984 the veteran ambassador Anatoly Dobrynin had been called back to Moscow to head up the Foreign Ministry's International Department. This was a significant move, because Dobrynin had been ambassador to Washington for over twenty years and, arguably, understood the US position and White House thinking better than any other living Russian.

The time for serious dialogue about the Cold War had come.

The first summit between Reagan and Gorbachev was held in Geneva in November 1985. It started in typical Cold War fashion, with each side accusing the other across the table of trying to win the Cold War or of not keeping their word. Reagan accused the Soviet Union of human rights abuses and of deploying vast numbers of unnecessary weapons, from SS-20s to tanks. Gorbachev retorted in his turn that the US military-industrial complex was really running the country in the interests of big business, and that the US was backing and arming regional conflicts around the world. At lunch Gorbachev apparently told his aides that Reagan was a 'cave-man' and 'a political dinosaur'.

However, after lunch something curious happened. In the middle of a bitter exchange about SDI – a project which he flatly refused to cancel – Reagan suggested that he and Gorbachev take a walk and 'get some fresh air'. When they came back the two leaders retired to cosy armchairs in front of a log fire and continued to talk man to man, away from their advisors. The astonished interpreters gradually became aware that the two men were beginning to laugh and joke: they were getting on; they had almost become friends.

Next day, the arguments continued, but the tone had changed. Soviet-US relations were being conducted as a 'civilized dialogue', in Shevardnadze's words. Reagan absolutely refused to budge on Star Wars, but offered Gorbachev access to the technology instead. A disbelieving Gorbachev refused the offer. Even so, progress was being made. Both sides agreed that talks about limiting nuclear arms should continue, the aim being to cut nuclear arsenals by 50 per cent. They both concurred that a nuclear war was unthinkable and 'cannot be won'. But most importantly, the two men, by now easy in each other's company, agreed to meet again. Geneva 1985 was the birthplace of the process that was, eventually, to end the Cold War.

At the time, however, this was not so apparent.

Back in the Kremlin, Geneva seemed to spell nothing but trouble for the worried Politburo. For the communist old guard, it looked – correctly – as if the Americans were trying to corner them. One gloomy analysis by a Kremlin advisor concluded that the communist system of the USSR was now under pressure on at least eight fronts:

- A more aggressive Reagan-armed America.
- A plot to keep the oil price low to damage the Soviet economy's biggest provider of foreign currency.
- Anti-Party propaganda using short-wave broadcasts to the Soviet people.
- Aid to Solidarity in Poland.
- Weapons to the Afghan Mujahidin.
- An open challenge to the Communist Party's moral legitimacy.
- Encouragement of independent freedom movements around the world.
- Star Wars/SDI.

The Politburo added, for good measure, their other two great worries: an economy in crisis, and the Russian people's genuine feeling that they had had enough.

The Soviet citizen of 1980 was a different animal from the peasant farmer or heavy industrial worker of the immediate aftermath of 1945. Soviet isolation from the rest of the world was breaking down as the communications revolution of the 1980s showed just what the long-suffering Russians had been missing. Desirable consumer goods were almost non-existent in the Soviet Union, which was still foolishly subsidizing its satellites by swapping valuable oil, and other expensive raw materials that could be raising foreign currency, for poor-quality Hungarian shoes or shoddy cheap Bulgarian shirts. Russia's increasingly urbanized population was demanding butter, razor blades, refrigerators, cars, T-shirts, pop records, Pepsi-Cola and Levi's. This time, repression was not an option. The Politburo hastened to clear the decks internationally to deal with their growing domestic troubles.

The result was that within two months of Geneva, Gorbachev was offering to eliminate *all* nuclear weapons by the year

2000. Gorbachev's great 'Offensive for Peace' was given a standing ovation by the assembled comrades at the Twenty-seventh Party Congress in February 1986. The new thinking in Moscow was slowly beginning to knock down the communist barricades.

At this critical juncture Reagan's Washington played hardball. In early 1986, George Schulz warned the State Department's key personnel that they were now approaching the critical moment of ending the Cold War. It 'might be a long haul . . . [but] our intention is to put relations with the Soviet Union on a stable and constructive basis for the long term'. The Reagan team scented victory. If they were to follow a policy of engagement with the USSR, then they would do it from a position of advantage. Gorbachev was under pressure from both within and without. He was running out of time and money, and dared not risk alienating his domestic constituencies or the Politburo.

Increasing the pressure, the White House denounced the Peace Offensive as a trick and a propaganda ploy. Even if the Soviets did pull back all their nuclear weapons, what about their 20,000 main battle tanks still poised in eastern Europe? The European allies heartily agreed with this apparently robust line from Washington. It was, they argued, the presence and threat of massive Soviet conventional forces in Europe that had made them sufficiently nervous to allow nuclear weapons on their soil in the first place. The Red Army was still massed where it had stopped in 1945: why? Never mind the nukes, what about the tanks? The Cold War had started because of too many Soviet tanks in Europe.

At Geneva the Arms Limitation Talks made slow progress. As 1986 wore on, pressure piled on pressure for an embattled Kremlin. American warships sailed provocatively near the Russian Black Sea coast, seemingly inviting trouble. Moscow sent a stiff note denouncing such blatant intelligence-gathering provocations. Washington replied haughtily about exercising 'freedom on the high seas'. Relations cooled further as the Libyans opened up on America's 6th Fleet, pushed inshore in the Mediterranean, and were smartly rebuffed with a punitive demonstration of American air power as US planes took off from the UK and hammered targets in Tripoli and Benghazi. Libya's leader, the erratic and highly vocal Colonel Gaddafi, narrowly escaped being a victim of the American bombs. In Afghanistan the new US-supplied Stinger missiles were knocking Soviet helicopters out of the sky at an unacceptable rate. To add insult to injury, Reagan approved another $300 million military aid to the Mujahidin, to 'drive the Communists out of Afghanistan'. Gorbachev's idea of a follow-up summit in June 1986 began to fade as evidence of American intransigence and hostility seemingly closed off all avenues of contact.

The Stinger missiles coincided with an even more alarming development for the Kremlin. If the Mujahidin in Afghanistan were bad news, with their sudden ability to hack Soviet helicopters out of the air, then the eruption of Muslim violence *inside* the borders of the USSR came as a terrible shock. In late 1986 the Mujahidin began a series of effective strikes within Russia's borders. Specialist attack teams began infiltrating Soviet Central Asia to attack Red Air Force bases, checkpoints and power stations. It looked as if the Islamic guerrilla war in Afghanistan was spreading into the Soviet Union itself. Faced with this ominous new development – still unknown to many Western observers – the Kremlin took fright. Afghanistan was bad enough. But an Islamic insurrection in Tadjikhistan would be uncontainable.

To add to Gorbachev's catalogue of woes, the nuclear disaster at Chernobyl in the Ukraine in 1986 turned out to be far worse than it had initially seemed. Only the suicidal bravery and dedication of the Army and fire service had saved western Russia from the worst nuclear catastrophe in history. The wind blew a plume of radioactive dust 3,000 miles across Europe, stretching from Poland to Scotland, an only too public demonstration of the Soviet Union's failings. Outraged farmers in northern England had to pour their milk away and slaughter their sheep, and newspapers' scientific correspondents across Europe wrote busily about the dangers of Strontium 90 to children, forgetting that the British at Windscale and the Americans at Three Mile Island had experienced something very similar themselves in the past. Even journalists photographing the wrecked nuclear plant from a distance became victims of the intense radioactivity.

The Kremlin's feeble attempts to deny the accident were shown to be blatant lies by the photographic evidence of US spy satellites high overhead, obligingly released to the world's press. Soviet efforts to play down the scale of the disaster only further exposed the secretiveness and weakness of the Soviet Union: it was corrupt, inefficient and incompetent, and Chernobyl was almost the final straw.

Chernobyl exposed the USSR's bankruptcy in every sense.

The disaster stands as an illustration of all that was wrong with the Soviet communist system. It explains to a great extent the real reasons why the Soviet Union failed to 'win' the Cold War. Chernobyl revealed moral, economic, industrial and political failings on a grand scale and advertised the USSR's ingrained weaknesses as a horrified world watched the disaster unfolding on TV. The Soviet government lied and dissembled, denying it had happened, even when US and NATO satellites overhead could clearly see the extent of the devastation. Industrially, it was apparent that the reactor at Chernobyl was of a poor and obsolete design. Worse, it was of particularly weak construction, built using sub-standard materials and shoddy workmanship. Evidence of bribes and corruption during building slowly emerged from western intelligence reports. There was not even a proper containment vessel for the reactor in case it blew. As the enormity of the disaster emerged, intelligence revealed that it had even been caused by Soviet incompetence. A group of local scientists had been conducting an unofficial experiment to see what would happen if they disconnected the nuclear core's emergency cooling system. They found out the hard way: 31 were blown to smithereens and nearly 500 ended up in hospital.

Some of the many questions that have been debated since the end of the Cold War have been: *Who won? And why?* Did the Reagan administration's brutal strategy of economic and military gamesmanship bring the USSR to its knees? Or did the Soviet system merely implode, without any outside help, under the weight of its own internal contradictions? The truth is even subtler than either of these simplistic answers, and combines elements of both as well as several other key factors. But on one point all can agree: the collapse of communism in the 1980s and 1990s was indissolubly bound up with, and hastened by, the Soviet economy. The Soviet Union's own composition and outlook was as much a contributor to the end of the Cold War as any Cruise missile or 'Dreamworks' vision of a space-based missile defence system dreamed up in Silicon Valley and the Pentagon.

The Marxist command economy was the Soviets' Achilles' heel all along. The cracks in the foundations of Soviet communism had become apparent during the post-Stalin years. The old tyrant's legacy of absolute totalitarianism, accompanied by control of every single aspect of Soviet life and backed by state control of the economy, enforced by a brutal and all-seeing internal secret police, was the baseline for post-war Russia. The man in Moscow controlled everything though the

Party and for the Party, including what passed for business and commerce inside the USSR. There was no profit motive, no incentive, and the government owned virtually everything. From wages to raw materials, from the distribution chains to the very shops themselves, the man in Moscow decided what was to happen. The problem was that in a country that stretches across eleven time zones, what looks good on a civil servant's planning chart in some far-off government ministry is often economic madness on the ground.

Stalin's economic successors faced the dilemma of all reformers. They could not guarantee to limit 'reform' to suit their own agenda. People and events press impatiently on the reforming politician in every land. For the Kremlin leadership, the question was always how to balance the problems of Stalin's system in a vast and relatively backward country, while retaining the Party's absolute monopoly on power and control. Khrushchev had tried to reform the system and the Party had brought him down. His bold attempts to revitalize agriculture and break up the huge 'monopoly ministries' in Moscow had long since foundered. Despite opposition and obstruction from the Party, the corruption and overmanning of the centre had merely become displaced to the regions. The problem was that Khrushchev dared not attack the central problem of the Soviet system – the Party's total control of everything in the sacred names of Marx and Lenin.

Khrushchev's more conservative successor put reform on the back burner. The Party heaved a collective sigh of relief when Brezhnev cracked down on the notions of change. For the older members of the *nomenklatura*, Brezhnev's era ushered in an era of stability and a chance to enjoy the fruits of their labours after the terrors and insecurities of Stalin and the dangerous adventures of Khrushchev. Everyone knew that the system was corrupt and inefficient, but it worked.

Not for everyone. Russians became very cynical about their leaders and the Party's system during the 1960s. Brezhnev's collection of luxury automobiles became a particular joke. As ever, the man in the street could vent his feelings (*sotto voce*, naturally: the KGB's men might be standing at the bar too) in black humour. One joke current in the Brezhnev era was the story of the naked lunatic running through Red Square shouting, 'Brezhnev's a bloody fool! Our leaders are idiots!' At his trial he was found guilty and sentenced to ten years in a state psychiatric prison: five years for breach of the peace, and five years for revealing state secrets.

Although Brezhnev and Kosygin tinkered with reform, they were at all times hampered by conservatism, reaction and the sacred economic texts of Marx. These decreed that in the socialist workers' paradise everyone would have a job. Therefore a commitment to full employment was axiomatic under communism. This ideological stranglehold ran directly counter to any ideas of industrial or market efficiency. Marx and Lenin had in fact decreed a bloated, job-sharing work force. As a result, there was not only no sense of Darwinian competition in the market place: there was no market place at all. It was, more than anything else, 'the perception of dismal economic performance that drove Gorbachev's reform programme', in the analysis of one distinguished Kremlin watcher. This gradual economic decline manifested itself in numerous ways. Computers are one very clear example. In 1987 there were over 25 million personal computers in the USA; in Soviet Russia there were only 208,000. Anyone who wanted a PC not only had to register it with the authorities (at one time even photocopiers were seen as dangerous invitations to the illegal distribution of state secrets, and controlled accordingly) but probably had to acquire one through the black market, or 'second economy'.

It was this second economy that helped to end the Cold War

by accelerating the breakdown of the Soviet system, with all the political and social change that followed. The black market fulfilled the role of the real market, supplying scarce or unobtainable goods. Everyone used it, from artisans to academics. But, by the stern rules of the Communist Party, black market private enterprise was highly illegal, except for a small list of privately grown vegetables and the like. Everything was theoretically held in common for the benefit of all by the all-powerful Party representing the state. Property and profit were not for the individual. This political article of collective faith encouraged a climate of corruption (or *blat*) across communist society. It failed, like so many of Marx's nostrums – and indeed, like the man himself – to recognize or understand the reality of human affairs. In the east, it meant that the factory official over-ordered raw materials and sold the excess for his own pocket to buy things for his house. It meant that being a trade union official ensured that you could get free holidays in the union's resort hotels along the Black Sea, or even 'sell' such agreeable holidays to your friends either for cash or for favours in kind. It meant that a government job equalled an opportunity to sell off or barter government property and hope that no one ever noticed.

The problem was, quite simply, the overpowering impact of the all-powerful state. It was the state that was a source – indeed the only source – of material goods to be plundered by everyone. It was the state that supplied commodities that the individual could sell at a mark-up – provided he wasn't caught – from railway tickets to rifles, from candy bars to car parts. Thus, for example, Soviet conscripts in Afghanistan actually sold their new AK-47 rifles to Afghan villagers in exchange for dope, claiming 'I've lost my rifle, sir' to their officers. In Britain a similar offender would have been thrown in the slammer for three months, or ignominiously discharged following a court martial. But among the ill-disciplined and corrupt Soviet conscripts in Afghanistan, no such sanction was available. Soviet Army corruption was in fact arming their enemies to shoot at them. It was an unexpected – and ironic – reversal of Marx's portentous maxim: 'The capitalist will sell you the rope with which you may hang him.'

By the time Gorbachev came to power, the extent of this corruption or *blat* was simply breathtaking. Although official figures are impossible to obtain, by 1980 virtually everything was for sale in the Soviet economy. Petrol was siphoned off from state garages; high quality goods went under the counter. Mid-level bureaucrats colluded with local *mafiyas* to even sell off jobs. The going rate for that of Chief of Police in Azerbaijan was apparently 50,000 roubles. Senior Party officials dined on fine food, drove expensive cars and lived in villas or even palaces. In Romania, Nicolae Ceausescu's extravagant lifestyle was only emulating those of his masters in Moscow. By 1980 virtually *everyone* in Soviet Russia was on the take. The most petty theft of state property could be excused with the jibe: 'Of course we steal from the Party; after all, don't they steal everything from *us*?'

This was the economy that Gorbachev inherited. It was an economic structure that had gone well past stagnation and was into terminal decline and fragmentation. Even food was sometimes in short supply; fruit, milk, meat and even vodka would often be unobtainable at state stores, but around the corner, a man might be selling stolen 'state goods' out of a suitcase. The reforms of *perestroika* now only made things worse. A little relaxation of controls revealed the law of unintended consequences. Customers and consumers could now buy un-rationed goods. This they did – but to hoard or resell them at a profit. Things ran out and attempts by the Party to ration staple items were met by fury from the regional suppliers, seeing their newly liberated income streams drying up. At one point the local agricultural *oblast*s refused to send milk to Moscow, and Georgia forbade the export of its citrus fruits until the Central Committee sent more industrial raw materials down to the Caucasus. By 1986 the Soviet Union's internal economy had not just collapsed: Russia's regions were involved in an internal trade war. Marx had somehow never mentioned this, and Stalin's heavy hand of enforcement was now long buried.

The final straw was inflation. Just about the only big convertible commodity that the USSR had was oil, and the drop in oil prices in the early 1980s had hit the Russian economy particularly hard. With national oil revenues falling, the government was running out of money to fund a vastly over-inflated state sector. The Kremlin then did what many governments do when short of cash: they use their monopoly of printing money to print more notes in the hope that something better will turn up. The results were inevitable. By the end of the 1980s, galloping inflation had torn up the command economy's control of prices to keep them artificially low. *Perestroika* did not help. It had removed several key economic controls: state enterprises could now set their own prices. Wage increases ate into budgets. Moscow's growing budget deficits were met by rocketing money supply as the state printing presses worked overtime to churn out billions of new rouble notes. Disasters such as Chernobyl and, later, the 1988 Armenian earthquake, soaked up the state budget in emergency relief. And, all the time, the running sore of the Afghan war drained blood and treasure from the USSR. By mid-1986 Gorbachev and the Kremlin were in desperate trouble and had reached the point of no return.

Reagan's deliberate policy of applying pressure on the Kremlin leadership at every turn added to their woes. Despite his encouraging speech to the Party Congress in 1986 Gorbachev knew that he was running out of time and money. The falling price of oil was ripping the guts out of the Soviet economy. The CIA reported that the combination of a falling dollar (oil was paid for in dollars), low energy prices and declining production was hitting the Kremlin hard. Gorbachev's push for a technological revolution to sustain the USSR's position needed massive investment and it was just not forthcoming. By the middle of 1986 the Soviet Union's economy had effectively depreciated against the rest of the world by a staggering 75 per cent. That made *imports* – and the USSR needed to buy high-tech imports like computers and expensive machine tools for its economy to grow – over three times more expensive. To make matters worse, the Soviets' profit margins on arms exports were already low, so that revenue crashed too. Gorbachev and his colleagues could not afford this kind of financial pressure.

The final straw for the Soviet economy was a secret meeting of international bankers in New York in 1986, chaired by CIA Chief Bill Casey. An ex-banker himself, over dinner Casey told the Wall Street money men the truth: Russia was broke. He showed the financiers the top-secret CIA analyses of the plummeting Soviet economy. The bankers looked at each other, worried. The secret official US figures confirmed the alarming reports they had been getting from their own analysts. The message was clear. If they extended any more credit to the Kremlin, the chances were that they would never see their money. The international bankers took the hint. The Soviet Union was a poor financial risk. There would be no more credit for the Kremlin. Reagan's Cold War noose was tightening.

Economically, by the mid-1980s, Soviet Russia was a basket case. Marx's theories of a centrally planned socialist economy just didn't work: and certainly not in an ideological Cold War.

24

THE MELTING OF THE PACK ICE

THE SOVIET RETREAT

This was the catastrophic economic background to Gorbachev's increasingly desperate efforts to end the Cold War and get the Americans and their allies off his back. He needed to redirect scarce resources from a sterile military confrontation to the much more pressing needs of domestic reform and *perestroika*. Reagan and the White House watched and waited as Gorbachev sweated. Eventually Gorbachev cracked. Armed with a negotiating position ratified by the Politburo, he agreed to a summit in Iceland in October 1986.

The Reykjavik summit was the turning point in the ending of the Cold War. If Geneva had seen the turn of the tide, then Reykjavik was the beginning of the end. Both Reagan and Gorbachev arrived with careful briefs from their advisors. Gorbachev, from the start, proposed arms reductions. Reagan joined in with a counter-proposal and then, in a breathless two days of exchange and counter-exchange, the two men raised the stakes to an extraordinary level. By the end of the day Reagan and Gorbachev had agreed to remove *all* their SS-20s, Cruise and Pershing missiles from Europe and to *eliminate all nuclear weapons within a decade*. It was a breathtaking opportunity. One final question remained: SDI. Gorbachev insisted that the programme must cease and 'go back in the laboratory, where it belongs'. Reagan refused. The meeting collapsed.

Reykjavik was not a failure, however. The two men had got on extremely well: they trusted each other. (Gorbachev allegedly asked Reagan, about UFOs, 'Are they yours?' 'Hell, no,' replied the President. 'We thought they might be yours!') Both men realized that they had come within a whisker of the most dramatic arms control deal in history. The fact that a treaty wasn't signed at Reykjavik didn't matter: the summit had opened the door for a tantalizing glimpse of real change and a chance to end the Cold War forever. One delegate compared it with the great wartime conferences between Stalin, Roosevelt and Churchill.

Joy was not unalloyed, however. European leaders were shaken by the American President's willingness to sign away their nuclear security umbrella without so much as 'by your leave'. Gorbachev bitterly denounced US intransigence in a speech designed for domestic consumption and that of the satellites, castigating the US for lacking any will 'to maintain an atmosphere for the normal continuation of dialogue'. Washington retaliated with an equally routine denunciation of Soviet human rights abuses. This was normal Cold War knockabout dialogue. Behind the scenes both sides manoeuvred for advantage knowing that a new deal was inevitable. Gorbachev had said that 'Reykjavik marked a turning point in world history.' In early 1987, he called for an end to the Cold War and unleashed his full programme of *perestroi-*

ka. He tongue-lashed his complacent Party elite, and talked of 'a crisis in Soviet society'. They listened glumly and applauded. They knew that Gorbachev was right and that there really was no alternative. To NATO and the USA he offered – unilaterally and without any trade-off – to eliminate all the USSR's intermediate-range nuclear forces. He called for a 'nuclear-free world' and urged that 'we should waste no more time on trying to outplay each other.' Gorbachev was by now quite obviously a man in a hurry.

He was speeded on his way by one of those events which seem to rub salt into a nation's wounds. Yet again an event intervened that seemed to encapsulate all Russia's woes. The flight into the USSR by a young West German called Mathias Rust in May 1987 heaped further coals of humiliation on the Kremlin's head. His unarmed civilian Cessna had flown across Soviet airspace for nearly 1,500 miles undetected before landing before the cameras of an amused world's press in the middle of Red Square. NATO and Europe roared with laughter. The Head of the Soviet Air Defence was sacked, with his tail between his legs. Soviet Russia was becoming a joke.

The speed of events in 1987 took the cautious bureaucrats in Washington by surprise. There had been rumblings after the Reykjavik summit about what one appalled State Department advisor had called Reagan's 'imperial style' in rejecting his advisors' careful briefing notes and going head-to-head with Gorbachev. 'Who does he think he is?' asked one sulky aide after the summit. 'He's the President, son,' Secretary of State Schulz is alleged to have replied. 'That's what got him elected twice.'

Reagan met Gorbachev's offer by challenging the Russian leader to go to Berlin and look at the wall. 'If you [really] seek peace, Mr Gorbachev . . . tear down this wall.' The US rejected the Soviet Union's calls to abandon SDI and stonewalled at the

INF talks to await Gorbachev's next move. Eventually Gorbachev and his Politburo agreed to another summit, this time in Washington in December 1987 – and significantly without any pre-conditions on SDI.

The Washington Summit saw the signing of the Intermediate Nuclear Forces (INF) Treaty. It was historic because it removed, at a stroke, a whole class of destabilizing intermediate-range (i.e., non-strategic) nuclear weapons. The controversial SS-20s, Pershing and Cruise missiles would now go and be cut up under the watchful eyes of verification inspectors from both sides. The Gorbachevs went on 'walkabouts' in Manhattan to meet adoring crowds of Americans, delighted at this new, likeable Soviet leader. (In fact, he was more popular than the US President. The Cold War enemy leader polled a 65 per cent approval rating with the American public, in contrast to the 58 per cent who approved of Ronnie Reagan, now deeply mired in the Arms-to-Iran/Contra scandal.) Gorbachev even received the supreme accolade of appearing on *Time* Magazine's cover as Man of the Year.

With the Washington visit the Cold War logjam was broken. In spring 1988, at a ceremony witnessed by George Schulz, the USSR agreed to withdraw from Afghanistan over the next ten months; Gorbachev heaved a sigh of relief. Afghanistan had cost the Red Army more than 20,000 dead and 70,000 wounded over the previous decade. The long nightmare of the 'USSR's Vietnam' was finally over, even if its legacy of Islamic terrorism was now firmly rooted as the source of another, more widespread conflict in years to come.

The summits continued. Reagan returned the compliment by visiting his Cold War adversary's capital during the summer of 1988. He, too, went on a walkabout, this time accompanying the Gorbachevs in Red Square. In a well-publicized – and probably rehearsed – exchange, a reporter shouted, 'Do you still think you're in an evil empire, Mr Reagan?' to which the President replied, 'No, I was talking about another time and another era.'

Gorbachev, increasingly desperate, pressed new offers on the President, suggesting that both sides pull out 500,000 men, and even offered unilaterally to pull 10,000 tanks out of Europe. He accompanied what looked like an almost desperate gesture by proposing a declaration to renounce war as a means of ending disputes. This pacific move was too much for increasingly alarmed American officials. The US delegation panicked, advising Reagan not to listen to these siren calls, as such proposals 'would seriously undercut Washington's defence budget'. There were a lot of American jobs locked into a vibrant defence sector of the economy. It seemed that the Soviets' accusations – that it was the US arms industry that really ran the country – were true.

The 'Iron Triangle' of the American military-industrial complex's steel claws even reached out into Red Square.

Gorbachev's offers of unilateral zero-option cuts in nuclear missiles at the White House summit of December 1988 had the smack of desperation. The truth was that his whole reform programme was now threatening to get out of control. Gorbachev was trying to rid the Soviet Union of the drain of continued external confrontation in order to address his energies to what he saw as the real problems of Russia, which were essentially domestic. But by stripping away the Cold War threat, with it went the need for massive military forces. The consequence would be that Russia would no longer be a superpower. Not everyone agreed with such a downsizing of the USSR's status. The Soviet Union had its own military-industrial complex, every bit as entrenched as the USA's.

Not everyone around the Kremlin table agreed with Gorbachev's methods or indeed his push for reform. In particular Gromyko and Ogarkov, the Chief of the General Staff, had fought openly in the Politburo to resist Gorbachev's ideas. What was good enough for Lenin was good enough for them. Gorbachev sidelined both of them. 'More guns is better' may have worked for the old USSR, but by 1985–88 it was financially and technically no longer feasible. The Soviet Union was falling behind in the arms race. It had been falling behind long before Reagan announced his Star Wars initiative. SDI merely highlighted the problem.

As ever, the diligent KGB sought to fill the gap for its masters. French intelligence has uncovered proof that, by the mid-1980s, the KGB had refined a list of over 3,000 intelligence collection priorities, mostly technical, and ranging from phased radar arrays to fibreglass air tanks for submarines; from computers to control systems. One CIA estimate reckoned that the theft of F-14 and F-18 aircraft drawings alone saved the USSR 'some five years of development time.' The intelligence successes, however, highlighted the ever-present problem gnawing away at the foundations of communist Russia. The Soviets had to steal western secrets because the Soviet economy could no longer deliver, technically or industrially. The nation that had launched the first Sputnik into space was now reduced to stealing others' secrets merely to survive. In a war, even a cold one, espionage is no substitute for real technical innovation. The new Head of the Soviet Institute of Economics and International Relations had even admitted glumly in 1984 that the Soviet Union had become 'gravely deficient' in comparison with the 'scale and might' of the USA, western Europe and Japan.

The economy, loss of technical superiority and increasing domestic pressures made the USSR's position untenable. However much they wriggled, by the end of 1988, the Politburo was effectively trapped both within and without. The USSR could no longer afford to compete in the Arms Race. Any doubts on that issue had finally foundered on the challenge of SDI, hideously expensive and threatening to destabilize all the Soviet Union's efforts in Cold War competition. Unless Gorbachev and his Party hierarchy changed course, the USSR could not survive without total economic collapse. The old days of relying on military might were gone for good.

Gorbachev did have some genuine allies in his internal battles in the Kremlin. Former ambassador Dobrynin was particularly scathing in his coded criticism of the old guard and their old policies. In particular he challenged three basic Soviet Cold War assumptions. Firstly, he asserted that military power had cost the Soviet Union a fortune, but had made the nation *less*, not more, secure. Secondly, he suggested that Soviet diplomacy would be better directed to seeking constructive dialogue with the west, rather than furthering wasteful and provocative adventures in the Third World. And lastly, Dobrynin attacked the KGB's rigid handling of the human rights issue as clumsy and obstructive of the USSR's overall policy goals, because it had alienated western public opinion. This was explosive stuff, and bitterly resented by the Kremlin's old guard. Men like Chebrikov, the KGB chief, argued strongly, even as late as 1987, that continued military spending was still the best policy for national security. Gorbachev and his allies retorted by pointing out that the military should do more with what they had, rather than continually demanding more money and resources from the Party and the people, who were strapped for cash.

Gradually the battle lines became more clearly drawn. On the one hand was the old guard of the Politburo and the Party, disagreeing bitterly with the reformers' agenda, but unable to offer any solutions of their own to the nation's intractable problems. On the other hand were the reformers, seeing a clear link between the USSR's domestic woes and the nation's external security policy. With his sullen opponents bereft of new solutions and mute, Gorbachev seized the initiative. In 1988, the new magazine *Kommunist* carried an important article on USSR security assumptions. It was, in effect, a call for a complete change of the Kremlin's Cold War policy. The three foreign affairs specialists who wrote the piece were plainly advocating Gorbachev's wishes. The authors rejected the idea that the west was out to attack Russia. 'It is difficult to imagine for what goals western forces might invade . . . socialist states.' There was 'no evidence of any desire' by the west to go to war. In fact, they argued, the soft life and prosperity of 'bourgeois capitalism' were a positive disincentive to war. Finally they warned that a 'paradoxical situation' was developing: the risk of deliberate nuclear aggression was declining, but the threat of accidental nuclear war was on the increase. The unstated solution was plain. It was that the Arms Race and the Cold War were linked, and that they were in fact the real threat to Russia's security. Soviet policy should stop trying to intimidate the west by force of arms. What was needed for a peaceful world was less military muscle and a lot more diplomatic reassurance.

The Kremlin wanted out of the Cold War.

Reagan had sensed this all along in his dealings with Gorbachev.

In his own way, Reagan was every bit as much of a man in a hurry as his Soviet counterpart. Despite his hard line over SDI and his genuine belief that only an overwhelming demonstration of US power and political resolve would force the Russians to negotiate, Reagan was personally sympathetic to Gorbachev's plight and did all he could to move the US forward to meet the Russians. In the words of one of his staff: 'There will be many people who can't stand the notion that the credit . . . will go to the man who spoke of the "evil empire", but to my mind it is an inescapable conclusion that Ronald Reagan made the difference.' Reagan tried to give as much help as he could to Gorbachev in his internal struggles to end the Cold War. His place in history will be assured on that point alone.

Whatever criticisms of him the Soviet – and western – press may have expressed, for the professional diplomats and senior military men who watched Ronnie Reagan in action there was no doubt whatsoever. The ageing B-movie actor turned politician had done more than any of his predecessors to engineer a successful outcome to the ruinous confrontation with the Soviet Union that we know as the Cold War. At President Reagan's final NATO meeting some hard-bitten and experienced diplomats openly wept and the allied leaders queued up to shake his hand. Sir Michael Alexander, Britain's Permanent Representative to NATO, was in no doubt that they were seeing the passing of an era, and of 'a great president' and 'a great politician'.

Reagan's replacement as President in January 1989 was George Bush. Bush (Senior) was a Washington man to his fingertips (he had been Director of the CIA) and was an altogether different animal from the flamboyant former movie star and Governor of California.

Unlike Reagan, Bush's administration was careful and deeply suspicious of the changes in the USSR. A senior aide cautioned the new President that Gorbachev was 'only an aberration' in the Soviet system and would not survive. He warned that Gorbachev's changes in the Soviet system were really designed to give the USSR *peredyshka*, or breathing space, to restructure the Soviet power base in order to sally out for fresh Cold War battles to come.

Bush tended to agree with this view. The former CIA chief was cautious by nature, and, in his own words, lacked 'the vision thing' of his predecessor. The new President preferred to sit back and await developments, content to let 'history and events' do the work and solve the problem. Key advisors like James Baker disagreed and urged their leader to act and take advantage of the greatest opportunity of all – an end to confrontation with the USSR. But Bush refused. All this talk by Gorbachev, he grumbled, about 'freedom of choice' and 'freeing of international relations from ideology' was all very well, but 'What happens if Gorbachev loses? And things go to hell in a handcart over there? . . . We've got to make it clear that we are not trying to take advantage of the Russians' troubles.' His policy was best expressed by his Deputy Secretary of State, Lawrence Eagleburger, who in September 1989 said:

> For all its risks and uncertainties, the Cold War was characterized by a remarkably stable and predictable set of relationships between the great powers . . . Already we are hearing . . . that we need to take measures to ensure the success of the Gorbachev reforms . . . [we should keep] the security consensus which has served the West so well over the past forty years until the process of reform in the East has truly become irreversible.

Eagleburger's wistful plea for the good old certainties of the Cold War, however, perpetuated one serious error and hid one unpalatable fact. The error was that the west had not been 'served so well' by the Cold War at all. Any fool could see that the Cold War had been expensive, dangerous and frightening.

For whom then was Eagleburger speaking? Only the US military-industrial complex and their beneficiaries and friends had been 'served so well' out of the old certainties of military confrontation. Secondly, Eagleburger's nostalgic views of the 'good old Cold War' did, however, reveal the unpalatable fact that many Kremlin watchers, intelligence officers and commentators in the west, had made very nice careers out of being Soviet experts. For them the safe call was: 'It can't be happening: it can't be true!' The loss of the Soviets as the great enemy meant a devaluation of their hard-won expertise and, even worse, the loss of their whole *raison d'être*. No Soviet Union meant no communist enemy. No communist enemy meant no Cold War. No Cold War meant the disappearance of jobs, careers and pensions. Legions of Cold War intelligence officers and Soviet experts hastened to explain to their political masters in the west that these events in Russia might be just a cunning ploy.

After all, went the argument, were not the Soviets the masters of *maskirovka* – deception? Worst of all, the experts forecast in doom-laden terms, what if Gorbachev were to be deposed and a group of hardline old Communists seized power to govern in an alliance with the growing Russian nationalists (the so-called 'Red-Brown' option), but still armed with the USSR's rocket arsenal? 'Greater danger than ever now looms' was the message. It could all be a cunning trick by the wily Reds. In Germany Chancellor Kohl warned that Gorbachev, with his reforms, was really nothing more than 'a modern Communist leader who understands public relations . . . But Goebbels, one of those responsible for the crimes of the Hitler era, was an expert in public relations, too.' A warning couched in language like this from the leader of West Germany, the nation at the very heart of the Cold War, carried particular weight and could not be ignored. The irony was that cries of danger grew shriller as the real Cold War threat actually subsided. Better to do nothing, and keep NATO's guard up, the pundits urged their political masters, who swiftly obliged. Better the *status quo* than change. The Kremlin conservatives were not the only ones to oppose Gorbachev's reforms.

Once again however, doing nothing as a political option was washed aside by the tide of events. During 1988 Gorbachev had talked of freedom and began unilaterally to remove nearly half a million Russian soldiers from eastern Europe. Poland was already unstable, as Solidarnosc stubbornly refused to buckle under the Party's increasingly inefficient attempts to suppress the biggest Polish mass movement ever. East Germans also felt increasingly trapped and resentful of the stultifying regime of the Ministry of State Security, the hated MfS. The pressures for freedom from Soviet rule had been growing like a backed-up flood in the satellites ever since the Berlin airlift in 1948. The cracks in the dam had appeared in eastern Europe in 1956 and 1968. Now Gorbachev had removed the controls. In 1989 the dam burst.

Once again Germany was at the root of the problem.

The German Question had dominated the Soviet Union since the end of the war in 1945. It can be argued that it had dominated Russia since the rise of Adolf Hitler's Nazi Party and even before that, all the way back to the Revolution and the Treaty of Brest-Litovsk which ended Russia's involvement in the First World War. Soviet attempts to keep Germany down after the Second World War had ended in a divided Germany, split between the capitalist West and the communist East. While this arrangement may have been acceptable to the Kremlin and, secretly, to many European capitals that had suffered under Germany's martial ambitions in the recent past, it was unacceptable to many Germans. Willy Brandt's *Ostpo-*

litik had softened many of the sharper Cold War tensions in the 1970s; but the Berlin Wall still stood, a concrete excrescence across a divided nation.

By 1986 Chancellor Kohl had revived *Ostpolitik* and breathed new life into the initiative. He took up Gorbachev's line of a Common European Home, and put out tentative feelers to explore the possibilities of a relaxation of tension and an acceptance of German re-integration at the level of humanitarian matters, especially the reuniting of divided families. Kohl's CDU were deeply worried by the idea of a thaw in east-west relations. Like Washington, they suspected some Soviet trickery. Kohl's coalition partners, the FDP Free Democrats, were openly critical of such a conservative and timid approach by their Chancellor. Hans-Dietrich Genscher, the FDP Foreign Minister, warned of throwing away the golden opportunity proffered by the Kremlin:

> Are [Gorbachev's proposals] really only words to lull the West? Is this new foreign policy of Gorbachev's merely a policy presented in a new . . . more flexible way . . . but ultimately pursuing the old goals of expanding Soviet . . . hegemony over the whole continent?

Genscher answered his own rhetoric by pouring scorn on the west's timid reception of Gorbachev's revolutionary moves:

> It would be a mistake of historic dimensions for the West to let this chance slip away just because it cannot rid itself of a way of thinking which when it looks at the Soviet Union can always and only suppose the worst possible case . . .

Genscher then effectively called on his international audience to end the Cold War:

The proper, urgently necessary policy for the West seems to me today instead to take Gorbachev and his 'new politics' at their word, with all consequences.

Genscher's trail-blazing call was a step too far for Bonn, Washington and NATO in 1987. But by 1989 it was clear not only that Genscher was reflecting the reality of the view from the far side of the Iron Curtain, but that there was no Kremlin trick. The Red Army really was withdrawing from the east. For Germany, an extraordinary opportunity to bring the two halves of the divided country closer together was being offered on a plate. Kohl visited Moscow. Trade deals worth 3 billion Deutschmarks greased the wheels of diplomacy, as did the offer of a new, efficient (and safe) German nuclear reactor. West Germany and Soviet Russia were becoming friends, even setting out their 'guidelines for the course of European politics in the next decades'. Honecker in East Germany encouraged temporary visits to the east while making little change in the DDR.

This careful pussyfooting towards change was, however, taking place against a background in which the old certainties of Kremlin control of eastern Europe were fast disappearing. Gorbachev had signalled his policy on the satellites as early as 1986, warning the assembled COMECON leaders (whom, according to several observers, he did not like) that if they wanted to survive a changing world then they should restructure their regimes.

No one could expect the Soviet Union to keep them in power ... Every [Socialist] Party is independent ... its responsibility to its people in its own country, and the right to decide questions of that country's development, are unconditional principles for us.

The ruling gerontocrats of eastern Europe didn't like the sound of that. For them the iron fist of the Red Army was their ultimate method of staying in power. Gorbachev had effectively removed their guarantees and told them to get on with it themselves. Gorbachev, and his Kremlin colleagues, could no longer afford the satellites. Khrushchev had admitted as much twenty years previously when he had cited the massive savings that resulted from the Red Army's withdrawal from Austria. Now, finally, forty years after the Soviets' victory over Nazi Germany, it was time to bring the boys home. The communist leaders of eastern Europe were on their own.

Events moved quickly. All over the Soviets' East European security *glacis* the first stirrings of dissent soon appeared. The Hungarian Parliament voted for a Bill legislating the freedom of assembly. The effect was to permit the formation of new parties. 'Pluralism' would in future challenge the Communist Party's total monopoly of power.

In February the Polish leader Jaruzelski met the leaders of Solidarity for round table talks. It was an open acknowledgement that, despite the crackdown of 1981, Lech Walesa's trade union was still a thorn in the Polish Party's side. With the Catholic Church openly criticizing the system as well, Jaruzelski's meeting was both a recognition and an attempt to try and outflank Solidarity. By offering to create a communist-led Popular Front coalition, the Polish Communists thought they could easily win an election. Then they could sideline or ditch the 'extremists' who ran Solidarity; that at least was the hope. It was a dangerous mistake.

Suddenly the old Communists of eastern Europe were feeling very isolated indeed. Everywhere change was in the air. In Hungary the border fence with Austria was cut down to allow free passage to the west. Riots in Prague were suppressed and Vacláv Havel arrested, but unrest continued. Gorbachev's 'freedom of choice' was being taken literally across eastern Europe. The Baltic states were in turmoil, pressing for the removal of Soviet garrisons and control. 1989 was a year of momentous change.

Washington was slow to react to all these events. One critic at the time described George Bush and America as 'sleepwalking through history'. The leaden-footed Bush administration struggled to keep up with events, never mind influence them. The Kremlin denounced Washington's timidity and slowness – 'Even time has its limitations' – as the Soviet Union turned in on itself. The Speaker of the Hungarian Parliament best summed it up: 'Gorbachev and all of them were so fully occupied with internal affairs that events were slipping out of control.'

Gorbachev's principal preoccupation was the first free elections to be held in the USSR since 1914. The Kremlin had rigged the list, reserving a third of all seats for the Communist Party. Although most of these Party *apparatchiks* were genuinely elected by the voters, a significant minority (20 per cent) was rejected by the simple expedient of crossing out the unopposed Communist Party candidate's name. Moscow's popular mayor, Boris Yeltsin, was returned with over 5 million votes. Ominously for the old guard, Yeltsin was a vociferous critic of the un-restructured Party and a notable reformer. The new Congress met in triumph and elected Gorbachev their President. Soviet reform was now legitimized.

Elsewhere in the communist bloc, Gorbachev's reforming zeal was met with a more explosive reaction. When the Soviet leader visited Beijing to patch up the old quarrels with China, he was greeted by over a million young Chinese demonstrators, many camped in Tiananmen Square, calling for reform in China too, and chanting 'Gorby! Gorby!' The young enthusiasts of the Chinese Movement for Democracy were kept well

away from the distinguished visitor, who departed well satis-
fied with mutual force reductions in Siberia and Mongolia and
new Sino–Soviet bilateral trade deals.

Once the Great Russian Reformer had been safely seen off
on his Aeroflot jetliner, a vengeful Chinese Communist Party
moved in on its embarrassing protestors to show them what
they really thought about reform. Beijing declared martial law.
Next day, a grim line of tanks advanced across Tiananmen
Square, gunning down several hundred of the activists. It was a
massacre. Worse, it was a public massacre. The bloody scenes
of communist repression went round the globe, live on CNN
TV. It showed a horrified world that, in the People's Republic
of China at least, the old communist methods were still the
preferred methods. The Party was still the only source of
government. Stalin's ways and Mao's ways were still the best
ways for communist China. The Bamboo Curtain stayed
firmly up. Gorbachev and the Kremlin said nothing as the
rest of the world denounced Beijing's brutality.

Events in Tiananmen Square had an unexpected side effect,
however. The universal revulsion at the spectacle of army
tanks gunning down unarmed protestors finally closed the
door on any ideas the old communist leaders of eastern Europe
may have had of trying to use the army to control their own
protestors. The worldwide media's reach made gunning down
your own people in public virtually impossible if you wanted
to stay in charge. Eastern Europe was not distant China.

Amid this whirlwind of events, President Bush visited Europe. First on his itinerary were Poland and Hungary, where he
was welcomed by large cheering crowds chanting 'Democracy!' Suddenly the cautious, lacklustre Bush was fired up. Out
of the blue, years of careful Washington bureaucracy and
doom-laden briefing were washed away. This was no time
for pessimism. At the Paris celebrations for the 200th anni-

versary of the French Revolution, the President rounded on his aides, ordering them to fix a one-to-one summit with Gorbachev 'as quickly as possible'. At last, he had a clear insight into what was going on. 'Change is so fast, future change is so unpredictable that I don't want to pass in the night with this guy,' he told a startled Brett Scowcroft. 'Just fix it – now!'

The next day the President wrote to Gorbachev personally. The two most powerful men agreed to meet at sea just off Malta to avoid a media circus, in early December. There would be no agenda. This was just as well, for although neither man knew it at the time, by then the Cold War would be virtually over.

25

THAW

THE SOVIET UNION UNRAVELS

The last half of 1989 blew the structure of the Cold War away. Like some political hurricane, gigantic changes tore across eastern Europe and the Soviet Union, uprooting political leaders, institutions and established ideas everywhere. Poland's June 1989 elections in particular were a disaster for the Communist Party. Thirty-three of the thirty-five communist leaders in the lower house were voted out, their names blacked out by angry voters. Solidarity won ninety-nine of the one hundred seats in the upper house. The Polish Party leader Rakowski phoned Gorbachev in the Kremlin to ask for instructions. Gorbachev told him to go ahead with a coalition government, provided that it 'doesn't attack the Communist Party or the achievements of Socialism'. The Red Army was no longer an option for Poland's communist leaders.

Gorbachev's distracted telephone call about the future of Poland and the Russian leader's suggestion that it was now 'time to yield power', lit a fuse under the old communist leaders of the satellites. The truth was that by autumn of 1989, Gorbachev had become a prisoner of his own reforms. *Perestroika* and the restructuring of the USSR had brought a wave of protests, particularly about inflation, and even strikes. But for Gorbachev to crack down hard on dissent would wreck his whole policy of openness and reform. The satellites were now at last seen as the expensive luxuries they had always been (Poland alone owed Moscow \$40 billion). The trouble-some partners of the Communist Party of the Soviet Union must sort out their own destinies from now on. Gorbachev's priorities lay inside Moscow and across eleven time zones of his own, not in supporting unreconstructed old east European Communists.

With the realization that the Russian jackboot had lifted, events moved rapidly. Any attempt to control the situation in the satellites was now at the mercy of East Germany's captive population, and they wanted out. A trickle of *Ostpolitik*-encouraged visitors to the west in 1987 had become a flood by 1988. When the Hungarian and Czech parties began their own process of reform in 1989, the outflow from East Germany became a landslide. Once the border fence between Hungary and Austria had been torn down, there was nothing to stop East Germans travelling – quite legally – to Czecho-slovakia and Hungary to escape the prison of their 'socialist paradise'. Once there they could escape to Austria and the west; and escape they did, in huge numbers. East Germany's ageing and ailing communist leadership was baffled as the effective depopulation of East Germany's skilled workforce accelerated in 1988/89. Even when Honecker, the DDR com-munist leader, finally did address the problem it was too late and the DDR's problem was fast becoming a crisis. By late 1989 East Germans were not just fleeing; they were protesting and demonstrating against their Communist Party leaders in large numbers. The East German government was unable to grasp, let alone control, the situation, and found itself split: some demanding reform and negotiations with the disaffected crowds, others insisting on the old tough methods. The Czech border was sealed off once more. Through the whole unravelling crisis there seems to have been a blank incomprehension on the part of the old communist dinosaurs about what was really happening. The old and sick Honecker failed to grasp the point. There would – there *could* – be no change unless it included the 'leading role of the Communist Party', declared the East Berlin Politburo. Thousands of demonstrators were rounded up in the usual communist way and hundreds jailed. But it was too late. Everyone, from the 70,000 protestors in Leipzig to the Kremlin, could see that it was the Communist Party itself and its methods that were the problem. Marx and Lenin had been wrong. Like men marooned on a rock while the tide of history rushes in, the East Berlin Politburo could only watch in amazement and apprehension as all about them changed. In Hungary, the Communist Party officially abandoned Lenin and all his works to vote for democracy and capitalism. Poland was now effectively a non-communist coalition. Unrest was spreading in Czechoslovakia and the Baltic States, too. Even – unthinkably – some of the republics that went to make up the Soviet Union were flexing their muscles for independence. Georgia and Azerbaijan were calling for more autonomy while the Central Committee in Moscow debated the problem of a new wave of ethnic unrest sweeping the USSR's regions. Moscow had its own problems. The increasingly worried leadership of East Berlin realized that, for once, they were really on their own.

Gorbachev's visit to East Germany to mark its fortieth anniversary was the final straw. Honecker, who had been in power for nearly two decades, ran one of the toughest and most feared communist regimes of all the satellites. Thanks to the agents of the MfS and its superlative puppetmaster of spies, Markus Wolf, Honecker had kept an iron grip on the DDR and an all-seeing eye on the west. Now he looked to Moscow and his fellow communists for an equally tough line and full support to suppress the unrest. Gorbachev shrugged and suggested East Germany try a little *perestroika*, before addressing a public rally to tell them to reform their own system and that East German policy was decided 'not in Moscow but in Berlin'. An outraged Honecker stared angrily at the crowd and his Soviet colleague. What price communist solidarity now?

The crowd loved it, chanting 'Gorby! Gorby!' It was a moment of great historical irony for communism and the Cold War. For here, in communist East Germany, a *Russian* leader was being hailed by Germans, and against the East German Communist Party, as the figurehead of a new revolution. Stalin would have been turning in his grave. Gorbachev left, appalled at the clumsy old reactionaries of the East German Communist Party. As a parting shot, he warned the Red Army garrisons in East Germany to stay in their barracks and on no account to get involved in the chaos on the streets.

It was a wise move. Next day Honecker ordered the DDR Interior Ministry troops and police to fire on a demonstration in Leipzig. They refused. The Red Army sat tight as East Germany descended into what was effectively a political whirlpool, out of control. Honecker and half the Politburo were 'retired' by their alarmed colleagues. Egon Krenz took over and tried to hold the communist ring, promising reforms and claiming to be 'the German Gorbachev'. However, he said, 'the Party must lead the people'; on that Krenz would not budge. It was too late – a wave of protests and demonstrations swept the DDR. Protestors and even Party members mocked the Berlin leadership. More and more East Germans fled to Austria. 'Small steps' reforms *à la* Krenz were too little, and came too late.

Events came to a head on 9 November, when Krenz and the Politburo announced 'as a concession' that from the next day any DDR citizen with a valid visa could visit the west. Huge crowds built up at the crossing points at the wall in Berlin as dusk fell, just staring at the wall and holding vigils. Gradually, as the numbers grew, the mood changed. Why wait for tomorrow? The border guards and Volkspolizei were hugely outnumbered. One estimate claims that 300,000 increasingly vocal East Berliners were pushing at the checkpoints, demanding to be let through *now*. Panicky officers called HQ for instructions: HQ called the Politburo: the Politburo dithered. The Red Army refused to help. Calls to the Kremlin went unanswered: Moscow was unavailable, in every sense. A Tiananmen Square massacre of Germans by Germans on live television would have provoked a cataclysm of rage around the world. While the DDR's leaders agonized, the decision was taken for them. The guards at the wall opened the gates and started to let the East Berliners through one at a time. A trickle became a flood and suddenly East Germans were pouring into the bright lights of West Berlin and the glare of the media. Their West German counterparts came out to greet them. Jubilant young men climbed on the wall and attacked it with hammers and chisels while the crowd cheered. The VOPOs faded away into the night. Flag-waving crowds swarmed like ants; suddenly the wall had been stormed by People Power. The hated symbol of the Cold War was to be chipped away in the weeks ahead to make a million souvenirs. As joyful Germans embraced and sang '*Deutschland, Deutschland Über Alles*', the Kremlin just looked on. Observers in Moscow, Paris and London shifted uneasily. A reunited Germany was now only a matter of time.

These momentous events effectively passed Washington by. Although Secretary of State James Baker and Eduard Shevardnadze had formed a close and workmanlike relationship, their attempts to steady the pace of the international agenda and control change have now, with hindsight, all the appearance of some stately diplomatic quadrille. The White House did little better in 1989, appearing like a startled spectator as Shevardnadze placed Cold War concession after concession on the table. The USSR would sign up for Strategic Arms Talks (START) without any pre-conditions on SDI. The massive Ballistic Missile Early Warning Radar at Krasnoyarsk would be dismantled to meet American demands. Soviet withdrawals from eastern Europe were confirmed. Chemical weapon stockpiles would be phased out. And all without demands for corresponding changes by the US. Eventually the penny dropped for a dazed Baker. This was no trick; the Soviets really *did* want out of the Cold War. Gorbachev was on the level, and had been throughout.

President Bush was slower to react and watched the events in Berlin unfold on television in a state of bewildered disbelief. Richard Gephardt's soundbite on his President's reaction went to the heart of the White House's pedestrian approach to the momentous events of 1989: 'As the walls of the modern Jericho come tumbling down, we have a President who is inadequate to the moment . . .'

It was a fair judgement. President Bush couldn't believe his eyes. Nor could many other well-briefed observers. But America's President did spot one link immediately. If East Germany really was dispensible to Moscow, then the Russian Communists must really be serious about a Cold War deal.

And George Bush had a major summit booked with Gorbachev in a month's time . . .

*   *   *

By the time Bush and Gorbachev met in the Grand Harbour at Valletta in the first week of December 1989, the Force 9 gale lashing the Maltese harbour was matched by the gale that had swept eastern Europe. Once the Berlin Wall had collapsed, the rest of the Cold War dominoes went over one by one. The Bulgarian and Czechoslovakian communist governments were both toppled by People Power. The Bulgarian Communist Party would cling on for another year trying to reform communism from within; but communism now seemed incapable of reform. A million Czechs evicted the Party from its self-appointed leading political role and Vacláv Havel's Velvet Revolution installed a coalition government with a dazed and disbelieving Alexander Dubçek as speaker of a new democratic assembly. The events of 1968 seemed an age away.

Only Germany remained a problem. Despite Egon Krenz's reforming efforts, he was quickly ousted after the events of 9/10 November by Hans Modrow, the Dresden Party boss, and rapid changes were set in motion. The Stasi, the hated symbol of the old DDR regime, was disbanded, old Stalinist ideas denounced, and both political and economic controls relaxed. Everyone seemed delighted. But Chancellor Kohl of West Germany spoiled the party. On 28 November he spoke to his fellow Germans in the Federal Parliament. There he had publicly acknowledged the reality of the great Cold War problem: German unification.

The idea of a reunited and strong Germany worried the rest of Europe, and with some reason. A single German state, set in the middle of Europe, with nearly 100 million people and potentially the biggest economy on the continent, was not something that could be simply overlooked or ignored. Of all those uneasily watching the events of 9/10 November 1989, none were more worried than the Russians. The prevention of a powerful and unified Germany on their western frontier was really what the Cold War had been about all along – it was the very last thing the Kremlin wanted to see. For their different reasons, London and Paris sympathized. Gorbachev moved swiftly to dampen the FRG's new-found enthusiasm for German re-unification. That was something that would have to wait until Russia was ready.

Everything else – except the sea – at the Malta summit went smoothly. When the talking started aboard the rolling cruise liner *Maxim Gorky*, it was immediately apparent that the original idea of the two leaders just getting to know each other would be overtaken by events. Bush had, at last, caught up with the galloping pace of change. Now he came determined to help Gorbachev in any way he could and to encourage the wave of reforms sweeping the USSR. Even the reports of growing alarm and opposition to the changes in Russia actually helped Bush to help Gorbachev. Things were unstable enough already, without the Great Reformer being replaced by some hatchet-faced old guard Communists, standing on Lenin's tomb surrounded by grim marshals in big hats, all determined to turn the clock back to Stalin's Good Old Days.

The American President unveiled a series of economic initiatives designed to help the Soviet Union (and thus Gorbachev), including a bilateral trade treaty, membership of the GATT, and an offer of Most Favoured Nation trading links. This was heady stuff. Bush then turned to things military. For their next summit, in June 1990, he endorsed a full Conventional Forces in Europe Treaty (CFE) to reduce non-nuclear arms, with intrusive MBFR verification inspections on both sides, an urgent agreement on START to limit nuclear weapons, and the destruction of chemical weapon stocks.

Gorbachev agreed. He welcomed the proposals, inviting inspectors from the west into the Soviet Union and happily confirmed the total withdrawal of the Red Army from Europe – 'They didn't like us anyway,' he quipped. The only issue that divided the two men was the vexed question of intervention in the Third World. Gorbachev admitted that Castro's dabbling in Nicaragua was unhelpful, but, he added ruefully, 'Castro's his own man.'

As the storm raged around the ship, the 'seasick summit' continued, with the two men wrangling about their respective overseas adventures. The Soviets told Bush not to be so self-righteous; the US was intervening too wherever it suited its interests. Gorbachev even asked if the old Brezhnev Doctrine of intervening in a superpower's area of influence was now to be called the new Bush Doctrine? Bush pulled a face. On that slightly sour note the two men parted, promising to meet up the next day.

It was the day that would see the end of the Cold War. Gorbachev led off by explaining that what Moscow really wanted was America as a partner, 'not as an enemy . . . things have changed.' Looking Bush straight in the eye, he said, 'We need a strong America,' and 'You need to be in Europe.' The American delegation looked at each other in wonder as the leader of the Soviet Union leant towards his American counterpart: 'The Soviet Union will never start a new war against the United States . . . we should cooperate . . .'

By lunchtime it was all over. No treaties were signed but an unprecedented joint US-USSR press conference was thrown together for the media on board the *Maxim Gorky*, where the world's media heard Gorbachev say, 'We are at the start of our long road to a long-lasting peace,' and Bush confirm, 'Today we stand at the threshold of a brand new era of US-Soviet relations.'

The dazed reporters rushed off to file their sensational stories.

After forty-four years of open confrontation, from Yalta in 1945 to Malta in 1989, the Cold War was finally over.

26

SPRING AT LAST?

THE COLLAPSE OF COMMUNISM

The end of the long Cold War between the Soviet Union and the west did not, despite the historian Francis Fukuyama's famously optimistic comment, mean 'the end of history'. On the contrary, for Gorbachev, having got the Americans off Russia's back once and for all, the effective end of the Cold War signalled the start of something much more fundamental for the USSR. Even as the Soviet leader flew back from Malta in December 1989, his own country was beginning to unravel from within.

To add to the Soviet Union's perennial problems with the economy, Gorbachev now faced two new challenges to the Kremlin. The first was the rising tide of nationalism in the regions and the Union's constituent republics. The second, more sinister, was the growing power of the opposition to his regime and his 'dangerous reforms'. This came from a wide coalition of interest groups, including the Churches, liberal reformers and even historians keen to reveal the truth about the Communist Party's excesses of the past. At the other end of the spectrum were the hardliners who resisted Gorbachev's vision. This group included old guard members of the Party and the military, resentful at the loss of their influence and worried about losing their Party jobs and privileges.

Gorbachev's first stop was Lithuania, the southernmost of the Baltic republics. The infamous secret clauses of the Ribbentrop-Molotov pact of August 1939 had acknowledged that these independent states fell within the USSR's sphere of influence and Hitler had stood back and watched as Stalin gobbled them up in 1939–40. The Balts had never accepted their status as captive republics of the USSR. While Gorbachev had been dealing with the Americans, the Communist Party of Lithuania had actually voted for independence from Moscow. Gorbachev was trapped. His reforms meant that he could not reach for the Stalinist solution and send the tanks in to coerce a fellow Communist Party, however much his colleagues may have wanted to. This was reform. The KGB and the military recommended the tough solution. Soviet Special Forces prepared for action. Politburo colleagues warned that any failure of will on Moscow's part over the Baltic states could signal the break-up of the Soviet Union. Gorbachev temporized.

Lithuania's demands for independence increased. Russia must go, bag and baggage, said the reformers in Vilnius and Riga. Even the very icons of communist Russia were replaced by the old nationalist symbols of the Baltic states: their own language, laws, holidays and flags. Gorbachev groped for a negotiated compromise; and as he did so, 2,000 miles to the south, on the Iranian border, Azerbaijan exploded. The mainly Muslim population came out in open rebellion against their Russian overlords. This time Gorbachev

and the Kremlin did not hesitate. Azerbaijan had a lot of oil
and gas and was a long way from the prying eyes of the media.
The Red Army was sent in: tanks and infantrymen gunned
down hundreds of demonstrators in Baku, while KGB snatch-
squads lifted the ringleaders in best Stalinist style. Hardly had
the Kremlin restored an uneasy calm in the south of its stricken
empire, than riots and demonstrations broke out in Moscow,
with thousands on the streets calling for democracy and for the
Party to disband and hand over power to the people 'like the
East Europeans'. East Europe was the *one* thing Gorbachev
did not want to hear about at this point. The reformed East
German government had accepted Chancellor Kohl's proposals and was calling for a new reunited Germany; the very last
thing Soviet Russia wanted and which, in order to prevent, it
could be argued, it had sustained the long Cold War.

Events were running out of control. The cat of reform was
not just out of the bag. It had multiplied with a vengeance and
Gorbachev and his Politburo colleagues were discovering the
hard way that it is virtually impossible to herd cats. Demands
for more – and sometimes less – reform were being made from
all sides. In desperation, Gorbachev cracked, agreeing to
multi-party elections throughout the Soviet Union, a new
programme of economic reforms and, most astonishingly of
all, an end to the Communist Party's monopoly of power and
the acceptance of a multi-party state. The tide of history was
bearing its sons away and Gorbachev and the Supreme Soviet
frantically tried to keep control of an out-of-control torrent of
changes. After a bitter debate in the Kremlin between the
reformers, who felt that change was not going fast enough, and
the old Communists, who felt that the whole edifice of the
Soviet state was crashing about their ears, Gorbachev was
given presidential powers. February 1990 was a momentous
month for the USSR.

Events then accelerated even further out of control. An astonished world looked on as the Soviet Union caved in on itself. Sanctions and the usual KGB dirty tricks against the Baltic states were both self-defeating and ineffective. Inflation took off and prices exploded. In Moscow the popular – and populist – mayor, Boris Yeltsin, resigned from the Party and stood as a Russian nationalist to become Speaker of the Parliament of the Russian Republic. Mass movements like the Democratic Union and the Democratic Party of Russia surged out of the universities and cafés on to the streets. The DPR called for 'a market economy based on private property and a Constituent Assembly which would make a clean break with the Communist past'. The elections in Russia signalled the beginning of the end.

By 1 June 1990, the Soviet Union was facing the moment of truth. Russia, the dominant republic in the Union and master of the rest, effectively declared its independence from the USSR. The combination of old Communists, nationalists and military that made up the opposition to Gorbachev were aghast. To make matters worse, Gorbachev was virtually forced to accept the *fait accompli* of a united Germany as part of the EU and, most explosive of all, as a member of NATO. Everywhere he looked, in that hot summer of 1990, Mikhail Gorbachev was assailed by crises, political enemies and seemingly insurmountable problems. He had to stop the individual republics that made up the Soviet Union from going their own way; he had to fend off his increasingly vociferous critics on the Supreme Soviet; he had, in effect, to sell off the Soviet economy to put state enterprises into new managers' hands and create a market economy, and he had to deal with unrest on the streets and calls for more reform. The final straw for Gorbachev seems to have been his enforced condemnation of Saddam Hussein's invasion of Kuwait in the autumn of 1990. Trapped by the need to keep NATO, the Americans and the CFE treaty 'onside', Gorbachev had little option but to support the US-UN line over the rape of Kuwait. But Iraq had been a staunch Soviet ally over the years and Baghdad paid good hard cash for its plentiful purchases of Soviet weaponry. Under intense criticism from the Party and pressure from the military, Gorbachev finally decided to crack down hard. But now it was too late for a return to the old communist prescriptions.

On 1 January 1991 Gorbachev and the Party ordered Soviet forces to occupy key buildings and seize back Lithuania and Latvia for the Soviet Union. The KGB and secret police moved in, with the army. The world's television showed scenes of people power, and Soviet tanks gunning down civilians in Vilnius. Suddenly the Cold War was back. President Bush cancelled a planned summit. Boris Yeltsin – now a 'Socialist, not a Communist' – refused to cooperate with the Supreme Soviet: he was the lawful ruler of the Russian Republic, 'not some non-elected Communist Party official'. From Siberia to the Ukraine, miners went on strike calling for better wages, better food and, in the Donets Basin, Ukrainian independence.

Gorbachev was isolated and embattled. He even managed to alienate the reformist wing of the Communist Party by putting over 40,000 troops on to the streets of Moscow as a show of force against his own people when they had the temerity to march in protest against rising prices and call for more reform. Promises of American aid dissolved.

By the summer of 1991 it was obvious that some major cataclysm was inescapable. Yeltsin's Russia was ordering CPSU officials to pay rent or quit their offices. Red Army troops were pouring back from their old bases in east Europe. Comecon and the Warsaw Pact had been disbanded, the GNP fell 10 per cent in the first six months, and inflation was running at 12 per cent every month. Small savers saw their money confiscated as 50- and 100-rouble notes were with-drawn. The Soviet Union was broke, disorganized and on the verge of disintegration. Nemesis was fast approaching.

On 19 August 1991 Gorbachev, on holiday at the Black Sea resort of Foros, suddenly found that his telephone didn't work. Shortly afterwards, a delegation from Moscow arrived demanding that Gorbachev sign a statement resigning 'on grounds of ill health', and declaring a National State of Emergency. Gorbachev refused. He also refused to stand down as President. His presidential guards stood firm and un-slung their rifles. The conspirators had two choices: to try and shoot Gorbachev and seize power; or to continue with their constitutional fiction of a legitimate handover of power. Stalin would have known what to do. But Gorbachev's reforms had, at least, paid off. Shooting Gorbachev would almost certainly have led to civil war in the Soviet Union. The conspirators backed off, consigning Gorbachev to house arrest, and rushed back to Moscow to go on television and proclaim that, as the President was 'gravely ill', they were now in charge.

Their declaration of a State of Emergency was greeted with genuine outrage by Muscovites. Opposition to the putsch began to mobilize; Yeltsin appealed to the 'People of Russia' and denounced the plotters' Emergency Committee as illegal and unconstitutional. There was a call for a general strike and large crowds barricaded themselves outside the Parliament Building or 'White House'. Army units arrived, unsure of what to do. In his finest hour, Yeltsin – who was no friend of Gorbachev's – clambered on to the back of an armoured vehicle and called on the crowd to resist the illegal and unconstitutional forces of the Communist plotters and restore the legitimate rule of law. The KGB's crack Alpha unit waited to go in to storm the building and crush the anti-coup protesters. Gunfire broke out, and Russian died at the hand of Russian. It was the decisive moment.

But the plotters' nerve failed them. They had not only failed to strike their Caesar down; they had failed to sway the mob as well. By a massive irony, the only person who seemed to give them tacit and ambiguous support was the ever-cautious US President, George Bush, worried that the Moscow coup might succeed and plunge him back into the Cold War with a new bunch of the old communist hardliners. He went on American television to agonize in public and suggest that it was all very difficult, although Gorbachev was 'an historic figure'. In an astonishing remark he called the attempted coup 'extra-constitutional', whatever that meant, and called for 'prudence'. America's President hummed and hawed in public while old-time Communists tried to re-establish a new version of their Marxist-Leninist Soviet Union. It was definitely not the White House's finest hour.

Back in Moscow the plotters bungled things. They went on television and gave an unconvincing press conference. Meanwhile, on the streets, the coup was collapsing all around them. Small-scale fighting had already broken out. The army and police could no longer be relied upon and the world's TV and press had sided with Yeltsin and his supporters' heroic stand for constitutional government. The now-desperate conspirators flew back to the Black Sea and demanded to see Gorbachev. He refused and, critically, the presidential guards stood firm around their leader, who had been monitoring the whole affair on the BBC's ubiquitous World Service. Eventually the telephones were reconnected and the President of the USSR was able to phone his capital. The first man he spoke to was Boris Yeltsin, who sent a *Russian* – not Soviet or Party – delegation to fly the Soviet President back to Moscow.

But Yeltsin was now the master, not Gorbachev. Next day,

both men appeared before the Russian Parliament. Gorbachev talked of 'the Party' and was jeered for his pains on live television while the global television audience looked on. Baffled at the response, he looked up as Yeltsin thrust a piece of paper into his hand and shouted at him, insisting he read it – aloud and for the record. An astonished Gorbachev then read out the minutes of a secret Communist Party meeting held behind his back on 18 August. Of the twenty communist ministers present, eighteen had either voted for a secret coup or had failed to oppose it. They were all his personal appointees. The secret minutes were clear proof to all the world and to all the citizens of the USSR. It was the Soviets' own Communist Party that was alone responsible for the unrest and bloodshed of the past week: no one else. Gorbachev's public humiliation was complete. The Communists' position in Russia was revealed for all to see as treasonable, illegal, and weakened beyond redemption. It was the Marxist plotters of the CPSU who were the class traitors now. The Party was over.

On 24 August, Mikhail Sergeyevich Gorbachev resigned as General Secretary of the discredited CPSU and, as a final act, ordered that all its property be handed back to the lawfully elected government. Communist Party cells were banned in the armed forces and KGB. The Party's 'organs' were disbanded or suspended: *Pravda*, Komsomol and even the Party's head-quarters. The Soviet Communist Party ceased to exist. The Soviet Union became a Confederation of Independent States.

By the end of the year it was clear that it really was all over. Near Brest-Litovsk, on 8 December 1991, the Soviet Union was formally dissolved. President Bush went on television to recognize the new Confederation of Independent States and to praise Gorbachev, while claiming that America had 'won the Cold War'. Gorbachev called it 'our common victory', and with some justification: he had been the one who had made the bold decisions and risked his neck in the process, not George Bush.

At midnight on 31 December 1991, the Red Flag over the Kremlin gave way to the national tricolour – red, blue and white – of Russia.

Lenin and the Bolsheviks' long Cold War with the *bourgeoisie* had, at last, been consigned to the dustbin of history.

27

CONCLUSION

Looking back at the Cold War, the reasons for the increased tension between east and west at the end of the Second World War are reasonably clear. Europeans were frightened by Soviet expansion into the vacuum of land and power left in eastern Europe. In their turn, the Soviets were alarmed by the Americans' monopoly of the atomic bomb and, later, what they saw as their country's encirclement by the US and its allies. These two key factors inevitably polarized relations between the two wartime allies against Nazi Germany from May 1945 onwards. Human factors, such as the poisonous and distrustful relations between the leaders of the Grand Alliance in the last years of Hitler's war, did not help.

But the Cold War did not start in 1945, despite the general belief that it did: it had started a long time before and was based quite unequivocally on ideology, not just on the threatened clash of arms. Lenin had said so in 1917, when he declared open season on the *bourgeoisie* worldwide. George Kennan and Churchill had recognized that reality long before 1939, let alone 1945. The struggle had been waged by the secret services of the two sides ever since the Bolshevik revolution, and was as clear a demonstration of Clausewitz's dictum – 'War is merely the continuation of policy by other means' – as we have ever seen. This unremitting ideological Cold War never stopped, even at the height of the Second World War. The ever-suspicious Stalin saw to that. Above all, it was the ideological dimension that gave the Cold War its particular intensity.

To this implacable background of confrontation and the events of post-war Europe, the world gradually provided a gigantic stage for the epic struggle between east and west. The only thing that seems to have reined in the protagonists and their allies was the terrifying reality of nuclear war. The evidence of the two primitive nuclear devices dropped on Japan was a compelling demonstration of the power of the atom bomb and a stark warning of the consequences of nuclear war. Even Japan, a proud nation with a fanatical cultural aversion to surrender, had capitulated in the face of such terrifying weapons.

The lesson was clear. The atom and hydrogen bomb had made war, in the traditional understanding of conflict between states, impossible because now a full-blown war would be suicidal. No one wanted to become a crispy martyr for capitalism and democracy, any more than rational thinkers thought that the triumph of the socialist Marxist-Leninist cause could best be accomplished by annihilating the globe on which mankind lived. It did not make sense. It is one of the ironies of history that it was the balance of terror itself that provided a hitherto undreamed-of containment vessel for all-out conflict and seems to have prevented Armageddon. Deterrence worked.

The result was that the Cold War became a new kind of *limited* war, with restraint on both sides in a manner that harked back to the limited wars of the eighteenth century. It was a war that, for very sound reasons, eschewed the all-out clash of the citizen in arms that has been our inheritance from the Napoleonic era. Warfare *à l'outrance* was – and is – still possible. It is just that with nuclear weapons it would be pointless, as it would be self-defeating. A fight to the death makes no sense if it kills both parties. Much more important is to know whether your equally well-armed opponent is secretly planning some deadly surprise. Collecting intelligence became the most important battlefield. The Cold War was at all times primarily an Intelligence War and as such was fought under strict rules of engagement.

Both sides in the confrontation therefore exercised considerable restraint and tried to compete in other ways: the Space Race and arming proxy combatants in the Third World being but two examples. These restraints on open battle did not, however, emerge without great danger along the way: the international crises of the Cold War were always extremely dangerous. The dangers of a false alarm or an over-reaction by military forces relying on technology and human beings for warning of war were always present.

Thus the U-2 over-flights, false alarms caused by radar or communications breakdown, power failures, even faulty computer chips and accidental satellite explosions, all added to the inevitable dangers of political confrontations like Suez, Hungary, Berlin, Cuba, Czechoslovakia, Able Archer and the all-too-frequent brushes between the well-armed military forces of the two sides above and below. The Cold War might have been contained, but it was still at all times deadly dangerous. It is little short of a miracle that a 'Dr Strangelove' situation never developed in real life. Stanley Kubrick's masterly black comedy sometimes came perilously close to the truth.

Much of the credit for stopping the Cold War turning hot belongs to those much-derided people, the diplomats. The input of men behind the scenes, like Ambassador Dobrynin, Sir Michael Alexander and James Baker, transformed Cold War crises into manageable problems. The better western diplomats realized that if they could only keep their nerve and hold together, the USSR could not survive, because of its inbuilt weakness of rigid dogma and economic inflexibility. At the time, of course, it often did not seem that way to the protagonists, mired in the day-to-day clash of cultures and ideology. But serious thinkers always admitted that the Cold War was an expensive drain on the resources of the combatants. An economic time-bomb was all the while ticking underneath the two sides. Whichever could last out longest through economic strength would come out on top.

In the end it was the collapse of the USSR's economy that finally forced Gorbachev to admit defeat – but only at the price of a ruined USSR and a waste of its treasure for nearly fifty years. He realized that the Cold War was quite simply not worth the effort. Gorbachev stands as an almost heroic figure, who did more to end the Cold War than any other individual, although perhaps not in the way he had envisaged.

He and Reagan are the real heroes of the clash, along with the other titans of the Cold War stage, the larger-than-life leaders who stamped their personality for good or ill on the course of events: Stalin, Truman, Eisenhower, Khrushchev, Kennedy, Kissinger and Bush. But above all it was Gorbachev and Reagan who wrote their names indelibly in the history books as they struggled to deal with their inheritance of a global conflict of Homeric proportions. It is no exaggeration to say that Gorbachev's own tragic saga is a story worthy of Shakespeare's pen.

The Cold War did also achieve some historic results. The peaceful transition of Germany into a single prosperous and pacific unified state was no mean achievement and had looked impossible in the decades of confrontation between east and west. Communism was finally discredited as a serious or effective mechanism to run the affairs of nations, much to the chagrin of those who had devoted their lives to the service of their lost cause, but the idol always had feet of clay. Only Castro's Cuba and North Vietnam remained at the start of the twenty-first century as beacons of hope to the socialist faithful as even Mao's China graduated to become effectively a capitalist nation, albeit under one-party control. NATO emerged as a powerful and unified alliance with an ability to police turbulent states that the United Nations has never quite managed since Korea half a century ago. Yet again NATO demonstrated the sad truth that covenants without swords are no true covenants. The peaceful existence of NATO's resolve and its potent weaponry did as much to enforce a final peace as any peace camp or CND march during the Cold War.

The legacy of the Cold War lives with us to this day. Old international suspicions die hard. Nation still spies upon nation and the great game of diplomacy, competition for scarce resources and political advantage, continues as it has throughout recorded time. Humanity will ever seek its catalysts for conflict. But the ideological edge between east and west and between communism and capitalism is gone forever. The shadow of the bomb and the crazy sanity of nuclear deterrence still hangs over all our heads, but no longer with an inbuilt *casus belli* of ideology to spur it on. The end of the Cold War has brought a surprising peace.

But, in the words of the haiku: 'When the glaciers melt and

retreat, old weeds bloom afresh.' The most deadly problem of the Cold War was always *ideology* armed with power. That danger has not gone away. On the contrary, we may one day look back on the simplicities of the old Cold War with nostalgia as a straightforward and controlled era of bilateral stability. Because, now that the great ice-cap of Cold War confrontation has melted, new 'dangerous snakes', in the words of an ex-CIA chief, of 'fanaticism armed with power', have emerged. These new ideological fanatics seek their own weapons of mass destruction with all the fervour of any Cold War general. The problem is that, alarmingly, they may not be so reluctant to use them. Therein lies the danger. Because the Cold War was always rational. Deterrence worked.

But for the irrational, however, seeking a martyr's death, the Mutual Assured Destruction of the nuclear bomb is no deterrent. Deterrence cannot work with those who crave death. On the contrary, the lure of a nuclear holocaust may even prove to be the fanatics' ultimate goal, in the name of their own, older, ideology.

The next confrontation is unlikely to be as cool or as controlled as the long Cold War.

GLOSSARY

Russian Secret Police and Intelligence Service (the names of what is effectively the same organization change confusingly over the period):

Okhrana   Czarist Secret Police pre-1917
Cheka   Soviet Secret Service 1917–22
OGPU   Soviet Secret Service 1923–34
NKVD   Soviet Secret Service 1934–46 (NKGB 1941)
MGB   Soviet Secret Service 1946–54
KGB   Soviet Secret Service 1954–91
GRU   Russian/Soviet Military Intelligence and Security Staff

For clarity, the Soviet Secret Service is described by the familiar term KGB as well (thus NKVD/KGB); and Britain's Secret Intelligence Service (SIS, often referred to, incorrectly, as MI6) is similarly indicated as SIS/MI6.

Able Archer   NATO Annual Command Post Exercise (Cpx)
AGER   US Navy auxiliary intelligence gathering ship
ARCOS   Soviet trading organization (1920s)
B-52   USAF heavy jet bomber, 1958 to present day
BAOR   British Army of the Rhine
BfV   Modern German security service
Bletchley Park   Location of UK sigint service (WW2)
BND   Modern German intelligence service
BRIXMIS   British Military Mission to Soviet Forces Germany
Bull, Bear, Bison, Beagle   Soviet bombers (NATO code-names)
C3   Command, Control and Communications
C4I   Command, Control, Communications and Intelligence
CDU   German Christian Democrat Party
CENTO   Central Treaty Organization
CFE   Conventional Forces in Europe
Cheka   Soviet Secret Service 1917–22
CIA   Central Intelligence Agency (US intelligence service)
CINCLANT   Commander-in-Chief US – NATO Atlantic Fleet
CIR   Critical intelligence requirements
Comecon   Soviet bloc economic and trading group
Comint   Communications intelligence
CPGB   Communist Party of Great Britain
CPSU   Communist Party of the Soviet Union
Elint   Electronic intelligence
Enigma   German WW2 encoding machine
FBI   US Federal Bureau of Investigation
FCO   UK Foreign and Commonwealth Office
FDP   German Free Democratic Party
FSNL   Socialist Front for the Liberation of Nicaragua
GATT   General Agreement on Tariff and Trade
GOSPLAN   Soviet Central Economic Planning Ministry
GRU   Russian/Soviet military intelligence and security staff
Humint   Human intelligence – agents, debriefings, POW
  interrogation
ICBM   Inter-Continental Ballistic Missile
INF   Intermediate Nuclear Forces
INO   Soviet Foreign Ministry Intelligence Department
IRBM   Intermediate Range Ballistic Missile
J2   Joint Military Staff Intelligence and Security Branch
JIC   UK Joint Intelligence Committee
KAL   Korean Airlines
KMT   Kuomintang (Chinese *Nationalist* Army)

KT Kiloton (equivalent to 1,000 tons of conventional explosive)
Langley CIA headquarters
MAD Mutually Assured Destruction
MBFR Mutual and Balanced Force Reductions
MfS Ministry of State Security (East German)
MGB Soviet secret service 1946
MI5 UK domestic security service
MI6 UK intelligence service (*see* SIS)
MI Military Intelligence
MiG Soviet Aviation Design Bureau
MOD Ministry of Defence
MT Megaton (equivalent to 1 million tons of conventional explosive)
MVD Soviet secret service 1953
NATO North Atlantic Treaty Organization
NGO Non-Governmental Organization
NKGB Soviet secret service 1943
NKVD Soviet secret service 1934
NSA National Security Agency (US sigint service)
NV North Vietnamese
NVA North Vietnamese Army
Okhrana Czarist secret police
OGPU Soviet secret service 1923–34
OSA Official Secrets Act
OSS Office of Special Services (US, WW2)
PI Photographic Interpretation
PLA Chinese People's Liberation Army
PLO Palestine Liberation Organization
PRC People's Republic of China
Psyops Psychological Operations
RAF Royal Air Force *or* Red Army Faction (German terrorists)
RAND Research and Development Corporation
RB-47 USAF reconnaissance jet, 1949–60
RCMP Royal Canadian Mounted Police
RYAN Raketo Yadernoye Napadie (code name of 1980 Soviet Intelligence Collection Plan)
SALT Strategic Arms Limitation Talks
SAM Soviet Surface to Air Missiles
SAS British Army Special Air Services Regiment
SAVAK Shah of Iran's secret police
SDI US Strategic Defense Initiative ('Star Wars')
SEATO South East Asia Treaty Organization

SHAPE   Supreme Headquarters Allied Powers Europe
Sigint   Signals intelligence: intercept, analysis, code breaking
SIOP   Single Integrated Operational Plan
SIS   Secret Intelligence Service (*see* MI6)
SLBM   Submarine Launched Ballistic Missile
SNIE   Special National Intelligence Estimate (US)
SOE   Special Operations Executive (UK, WW2)
Sputnik   Popular name for first orbiting satellite (Soviet)
SS   Schützstaffel (Himmler's Nazi Party army)
START   Strategic Arms Reduction Talks
Stasi   East German (DDR) state intelligence and security service
Stinger   US hand-held anti-aircraft missile
Techint   Technical intelligence (equipment, electronics, weapons)
Triad   Three forces of nuclear deterrence: ICBMs, bombers,
   submarines
TRW   Major US defence contractor
U-2   Lockheed Very High Altitude Reconnaissance Plane
UKAEA   UK Atomic Energy Authority
UNDP   United Nations Development Programme
UNHCR   UN High Commission for Refugees
USAF   United States Air Force
USSR   Union of Soviet Socialist Republics
V1 German flying bomb (WW2)
VC   Viet Cong
Venona   Code-name for intercepted, encrypted Soviet espionage
   traffic (WW2)
VOPOs   Volkspolizei, East German police
WMD   Weapons of mass destruction

APPENDIX:
HOW THE COLD
WAR WAS FOUGHT

Wars are fought.

However, not every conflict entails pitched battles. The clash of ideas can often be every bit as brutal as the clash of arms, albeit without the bloodshed. Thus it was in the Cold War, which was at source essentially a struggle between two opposed ideologies.

In one of the great ironies of history, the terrifying power of the atom bomb discouraged any actual fighting between the principals in this titanic duel. Although their seconds often fought out their masters' wars in vicious little proxy duels, the main protagonists were at all times very careful never to let their disputes escalate to the all-out nuclear exchange that would have been disastrous for them both. Both the White House and the Kremlin were keenly aware of the old fencing term, the '*coup des deux vierges*'. Killing each other is but a hollow triumph for rational men who wish to survive to enjoy their victory.

It was the atom bomb that made victory well-nigh impossible, because it made taking a chance too risky to contemplate. In a startling paradox the nuclear bomb was a weapon that brought no destruction: the threat of war actually enforced peace. No one summed it up better than the American general Omar Bradley: 'The only way to win an atomic war is to make damn' sure one never starts.'

The ideological intelligence struggle between east and west with its associated dirty tricks and deniable special operations started as early as the first days of the Bolshevik revolution, and continued throughout the Second World War until the very end of the Cold War. However, the period of open conflict can be dated fairly precisely from the end of the 1945 war, when the two remaining global powers suddenly confronted each other across the ruins of Hitler's Thousand Year Reich. Despite the alarms of those early post-war years, it was the threat of American nuclear monopoly that balanced the looming presence of a massive Red Army, now deep inside Europe.

By the end of the European war the Soviets' conventional forces were vast. The Red Army that moved on Berlin in May 1945 in the final assault on Hitler's capital consisted of 120 divisions, 2.5 million men, 40,0000 artillery pieces and 6,000 battle tanks. Over 7,500 war planes supported this huge enterprise. Three years of brutal combat on the eastern front had produced an invading army that was plunged deeper into Europe than ever did the Mongol horde of Genghis Khan. In the east, on the Siberian front, the Soviets' Manchurian army fielded another 1.5 million men, 3,500 tanks and 5,000 planes. The Red Army – conventional forces or not – was simply huge. This experienced, ruthless fighting machine now stood poised to carry the USSR's cause anywhere in Europe or Asia. Only the threat of American nuclear power kept Stalin's legions from venturing even deeper into a wasted, conquered continent.

This was the Cold War balance that would for fifty years endure on land, sea and in the air. For the first few years the threat of the US bomb kept the USSR's huge conventional forces in check – and, once the Soviets had got their own nuclear weapon, both sides faced a deadly stalemate. Everyone was agreed though, at all times: it was the nuclear option that had changed – and controlled – the nature of war.

Nuclear Forces

The earliest nuclear weapons were just crude atom bombs and even the US only had a few. The Trinity test in the Nevada desert on 16 July 1945, and the two atom bombs dropped on Hiroshima and Nagasaki, exhausted the US arsenal. These were all relatively small devices by our present-day standards. Nonetheless their power was still frightening.

If 1,000 tons of high explosive (1KT) – which could blow the entire centre of most cities to rubble – was alarming, then the Hiroshima and Nagasaki bombs (at 15KT and 21KT respectively) were, quite literally, devastating. These early weapons also revealed that the atom bomb's effects were not just a simple big bang like the thousands of tons of TNT in which it was measured. Science had found something new. Thermonuclear and atomic weapons have very different consequences.

First there is the flash, 'brighter than a thousand suns' in the words of the thousands whose retinas were burned by the first explosions. For a split second the explosive ball of fire is as hot as the sun. From this instantaneous release of energy and the ensuing detonation comes a searing thermal pulse that vaporizes everything near the point of impact. It then roars out to set wooden buildings and trees on fire miles from the explosion, and brand the silhouettes of vanished bodies on to concrete as eerie mementoes of what was once a human being. An associated electromagnetic pulse (EMP) of radio energy accompanies this intense heat across the electronic spectrum that fries computer chips and transistors and sets electric wiring on fire. This EMP is far reaching: in one American test in the Pacific the EMP blew fuses on the street lights on Hawaii, over a thousand miles away. These massive electronic disturbances also ionize the upper atmosphere for hours, playing havoc with radios and radar transmissions.

The most dramatic effect of a nuclear weapon, however, is the blast, radiating from the Ground Zero of the fireball. This blast wave travels very fast indeed, much faster than many conventional explosives. As the ground ripples like an earthquake, a fiery wind scorches out at hurricane force, blowing over buildings and trees, buckling steel structures and flattening anything in its path. One side effect of the blast wave is that once it has blown out and dissipated, the vacuum it has left is filled by another gale of hurricane intensity, roaring back *into* the scene of the explosion to demolish buildings already weakened by the outward shock wave. Petrol stations erupt spontaneously into fireballs: cars and trucks are blown like leaves.

The most deadly effect of nuclear weapons is the unseen hazard of radiation, which blasts out as an invisible pulse of atomic rays. Most deadly are the neutrons and gamma particles, which can penetrate planes and ships and even armoured tanks in an instant. Worse, they can penetrate skin and bone, disrupting the body's normal processes. Bone marrow is especially vulnerable to radiation, breaking down and inducing leukaemia, cancers and the loss of key blood cells.

This Initial Nuclear Radiation (INR) also contaminates every-thing it hits, from the ground itself to the dust in the air, by irradiating the atomic particles to make all matter radioactive for months and even years afterwards. After the explosion, the drifting radioactive fallout of the explosion is carried away by the wind to create a downwind plume of radiation that can travel for thousands of miles. The Chernobyl disaster affected sheep as far away as Northern Ireland.

Radioactivity is measured in 'rads' or Roentgens. It can either be induced or absorbed in flesh and bone. A one-megaton (1MT) device will pump out sufficient instant radio-activity to kill anyone unlucky enough to be exposed within a one-and-a-half-mile radius within the next month or so. Vom-iting, diarrhoea, wasting and death invariably follow as the body breaks down. If the fire and the blast from the bomb don't get you, radiation sickness will. For months after Hir-oshima the suffering went on, as badly burned and injured survivors succumbed to radiation sickness, as their ability to generate white blood corpuscles collapsed and their hair and teeth fell out.

The area covered by just one atomic weapon can be im-mense. A single one-megaton airburst (where the fireball does not reach the ground) will cause burns on exposed skin *over ten miles away*. These flash burns increase exponentially the closer you are to the burst. At up to two miles from the burst most matter – especially fat and soft tissue – just vaporizes or spontaneously combusts. Combined with the blast waves which will knock down almost every structure within a radius of three miles and blot out all radio waves for at least 24 hours, the effects are catastrophic. A major nuclear attack on a city like London or New York would see over a million killed instantly, with several million survivors homeless, injured or dying, and a firestorm raging in the rubble. There would be no rescue services. One 1980 estimate of the effects of an all-out nuclear exchange between the United States and the USSR put a figure of over 30 million dead, plus an average of 45 million other people worldwide suffering from the long-term effects of nuclear radiation. Nuclear war is unimaginable.

Delivering the Bomb

Even such a massive weapon requires a delivery system.

The US were first off the mark with the USAF's fleet of B-29 Superfortress bombers at the end of the war. The B-29 – the only aircraft ever to drop a nuclear bomb in war – could fly a ten-ton bombload over 4,000 miles, and fly at 400 mph above 30,000 feet. With 800 of these formidable bombers in service in 1945 the USAF was in a strong position to deliver a bomb deep into the heart of the Soviet Union and hold Stalin's expansionist ambitions in check. The Soviets copied the design (see page 130) and when the USSR exploded its own atomic device in 1949 the nuclear equation changed for ever. American nuclear superiority was no longer unchallenged. The nuclear arms race was on with a vengeance.

Both the USA and the USSR had captured large numbers of German V1 flying bombs and V2 (A4) rockets in 1945. More importantly, they had also captured a number of the key scientists who had headed the German missile programmes in the last days of the war. Both sides promptly set them to work on new missile programmes in a frantic search to develop an unstoppable strategic system to deliver the atomic bomb. The flying bomb solution was the easiest but it suffered from too short a range. However, by putting crude flying bombs on to submarines the US Navy could take their primitive Regulus missiles (1954) to sea and field the first *maritime* strategic system by launching close inshore and on the surface. The US Air Force's own Snark (1957) flying bombs inspired little confidence, taking over eleven hours to (theoretically) reach their targets. A bomber or an ICBM was always going to be a more reliable bet. The way ahead for nuclear weapons lay with missile or rocket delivery systems.

The result was that even as the bomber fleets and their strategy of 'massive retaliation' held sway in the 1950s, rocket research went on apace. The German V2s became the proto-type of a series of rocket developments that led to the Amer-ican Thor and Jupiter programmes (1958–65), clumsy liquid-fuelled rockets with a range of about 1,500 miles. The Soviets, lacking the large bomber fleets of the USAF, concentrated on missile and rocket development from the start. By 1957 their massive 300-tonne SS-6 series of rockets were launching Sputnik and threatening a new generation of long-range ICBMs capable of throwing a heavy thermonuclear warhead a very long way.

America responded with the Atlas (1960) series of rockets, with a range of up to 7,000 miles, as the missile race was joined. Warheads got bigger, then smaller as the missiles themselves became more accurate. The more stable and manageable solid fuel rocket motors replaced liquid fuel, and concrete silos were exchanged for exposed surface launch sites. By the end of the Cold War the USA was relying on over 500 Minuteman solid fuel missiles in hardened silos, deploy-ing three separate warheads, each over twenty times the size of the Hiroshima bomb, and capable of hitting a 200-yard square 9,000 miles away. The Soviets' Strategic Rocket Forces were based around a force of 300 SS-25 solid fuel Sickle ICBMs based on a large transporter erector launcher (TEL), and able to deliver a single 500KT warhead over 6,000 miles.

All these new nuclear weapons spawned a completely new industry – thinking about just how to use them. Nuclear strategy was far too important to be left to the military – or to the politicians either. A whole generation of serious academic thinkers applied themselves to the arcane disciplines of 'nuclear theology'. Just how, and in what circumstances, could – or should – these lethal weapons ever be employed? Would politicians order nuclear release? What about the other side? A kind of lethal chess game of logic and counter-logic explored the deadly quadrille of nuclear threat, counter-threat and response. Out of this process of analysis and wargaming, clear strategies emerged. From the brutally simple Massive Response of the early Cold War to the nuanced sophistications of Graduated Response and the US's Single Integrated Operational Plan (SIOP), which strove to provide the answer for any problem along the nuclear calculus, nuclear strategy became the driving force of national security policy. To many, such thinking about a nuclear holocaust was literally incredible and immoral. How could anyone think and plan for the unthinkable? To others, who saw the world as it was and not how they wished it to be, keeping the nuclear see-saw balanced was a bedrock fact of life. Cynic and realist alike, however, had to acknowledge that the existence of the bomb and the likelihood of Mutual Assured Destruction had exercised a powerful brake on politicians and their adventures over the previous fifty years.

The War at Sea

The 'Triad' of Mutual Assured Destruction insisted that the nuclear arsenals of the superpowers could never be trusted to any single weapon or arm of service. From 1960 onwards,

ICBMs and fleets of strategic bombers were complemented by a new strategic nuclear weapon. At sea the rival navies had developed their own inter-continental strategic systems based on *submarine* launched missiles. The US were first off the mark with their Polaris programme (1961), launched from below the water by a new fleet of nuclear-powered submarines carrying sixteen ICBMs and able to hit a target over 1,500 miles away with a 500KT warhead. These Sub-Surface Ballistic Nuclear (SSBN) submarines changed the nature of warfare, making a surprise attack almost impossible to detect and challenging all previous notions of nuclear strategy and stability. Britain and the USSR quickly developed their own equivalent systems, and by the end of the Cold War all members of the UN Security Council had their own submarine-based nuclear deterrents at sea.

Inevitably such a potent threat inspired a counter. New, fast hunter-killer nuclear submarines were specifically intended to seek out and neutralize enemy SSBNs in the event of war. In the dark silent depths of the world's oceans a deadly game of hide and seek went on as rival submarines tried to locate and track each other. Whoever had the noisiest boat would be the victim in case of war.

On the surface, aircraft carriers and anti-submarine groups practised tracking enemy submarines, ready with nuclear depth charges and torpedoes to enforce their will should the need ever arise. The Cold War at sea, far removed from the prying eyes of newspapers and television, became as deadly as it ever was on land or in the air. Under the icy waters of the Arctic Ocean 13,000-ton submarines played chicken with each other and, over the Mediterranean, aircraft-mounted dummy attacks on the other side's warships to see if the enemy would switch on their radars.

Cruise Missiles

In its final years the US moved to a new and even deadlier nuclear weapon based on the V1: the Cruise missile. These small, precision-guided, pilotless missiles were, however, a long way removed from Hitler's crude flying bombs of the late 1940s. The new Harpoons and Tomahawks could be launched out of torpedo tubes from submarines below the surface, or released from aircraft or warships hundreds of miles away from their targets. Using miniaturized computers and terrain-following radar, the new Cruise missiles could fly unchallenged hugging the ground at very low level to their destination without detection to place a mini-nuclear – or any other – warhead precisely on target. The advent of these precise delivery systems helped make the emerging strategy of 'graduated response' believable.

Technology Rules

Finally, the Reagan Star Wars or SDI programme alerted the world to the next generation of nuclear weapons: orbiting bombardment systems, based on satellites and forever hanging over any potential aggressor. Nuclear war from space was technology's and the scientific community's final contribution to the progress of civilization in the final years of the Cold War. 'Chicken Lickin' eventually found that the sky really could fall on his head.

Naturally the progress of nuclear weapons was matched by developments in conventional weapons as each side jockeyed for advantage. Nuclear bombers needed to be intercepted; ICBMs had to be stopped if possible. New fighter jets and

Surface to Air anti-aircraft missiles (SAMs) were developed at horrific cost by both sides in the endless pursuit for technical superiority. By the mid-1950s the USAF was fielding their new series of Century fighters, the F100, F104 and F105 leading eventually to the ubiquitous F4 Phantom. In their turn the Soviets fielded ever more advanced jets. The MiG 15, which gave the Allies such a nasty shock in Korea, eventually evolved into a new generation of fighter jets, from the slippery MiG 21 dogfighter to the huge MiG 25 strategic interceptor, able to fly at 70,000 feet and, by burning its engines to the limit, at over 2,200 miles per hour (three times the speed of sound).

The insatiable need for intelligence on the opposition during the Cold War also meant that the reconnaissance aeroplane became as indispensable and as important as any armed warplane. The British discovered that their superlative new jet bomber, the Canberra (1949), could fly faster and higher than any fighter and slowly adapted it to carry cameras. At over 63,000 feet and well above the vapour-trail line, the almost invisible Canberras gave British intelligence a decided edge. America looked on with interest, eventually buying and making their own version, the B-57. To their astonishment they discovered that, suitably modified, their own reconnaissance variant, the RB-57 (1958), could easily float up to 70,000 feet, making the development of the high-flying and top-secret U-2 almost unnecessary. Other aerial reconnaissance platforms included modified versions of the popular Boeing 707 (the RC-135) and a wide variety of other airliners and transports able to carry cameras and radar equipment for great distances and stay in the air for a long time. To service this fleet of ever more sophisticated fighters, bombers and reconnaissance aircraft, large numbers of airborne tankers were required to act as a 'force multiplier' and keep the airpower airborne. The best known tankers were the

KC135 and the British Handley Page Victor. (The British sent no fewer than fourteen Victor tankers deep into the South Atlantic as 'flying gas stations' to support *one single* Vulcan bomber in a daring raid on Stanley airport after the Argentinian invasion of the Falkland Islands in 1982.)

Cold War developments in the air were matched at sea by the rise of the US Navy's carrier battle groups, memorably described by *Paris Match* as 'America's Battle Star Galacticas'. A single carrier group could project US power anywhere on the globe. Behind its screen of destroyers, radar picquets and anti-aircraft cruisers, a 100,000-ton nuclear-powered aircraft carrier like the USS *Eisenhower* could, by 1990, collect electronic intelligence, control airspace and launch her carrier air-wing of nuclear bombers, Harpoon or Tomahawk Cruise missiles, to enforce military power on land or sea. Below the surface US nuclear-powered hunter-killer submarines prowled in their endless search for the Red Banner fleet's nuclear boats, and any other surface ship. Not for nothing did Cold War submariners cockily divide all other vessels into two categories: 'submarines' and 'targets'.

This relentless drive for faster, bigger, deadlier weapons inevitably inspired large numbers of technical innovations. We naturally tend to think of western, and particularly American, technology as leading the field in this area. However, the Soviets came up with their own technical surprises too, from the launch of Sputnik to the MiG 25 Foxbat. One of these priceless Soviet fighters was landed in Japan 'by mistake' in mysterious circumstances by a 'lost' Lieutenant Belenko in 1976. Examining American scientists were surprised by the big MiG's heavy frame and crude construction. Old valve technology radio and radars in particular inspired much mirth at Soviet backwardness. The NATO scientists stopped laughing when they realized that the old-fashioned electronics were solid proof against EMP and the aeroplane's mysterious and heavy nitrogen tanks were designed to pump inert gas into the fuel tanks to snuff out fires. The fact was that the MiG 25 could fly at Mach 2.5 and *in extremis* run at Mach 3.2, as one did, showing a clean pair of heels to Israeli fighters on one over-flight at 70,000 feet, even outrunning missiles fired from below. The MiG 25 was the product of an alien technology and, with its very long range nuclear-tipped air-to-air missiles, a serious threat to the US and the NATO family of airborne radar and command and control aircraft like the E3 and J Stars.

Similarly, rumours of a new solid titanium-hulled Soviet nuclear submarine were greeted with derision in the west when they first surfaced in the mid-1970s. The 'not invented here' brigade of US manufacturers stoutly assured concerned NATO intelligence officers that such a submarine was absolutely inconceivable. No one could build a large titanium-hulled vessel; it was impossible – why, even the US couldn't do it! It was, therefore, with some surprise and dismay that the US Atlantic fleet detected one of the new Soviet Alfa class boats closing on a NATO exercise. As the noisy Alfa accelerated to over 40 knots, dived to 2,500 feet and shot *directly underneath* the carrier task group, the shocked US anti-submarine sonar operators realized that the Red Navy was, for once, technically a long way ahead.

The Cold War at sea spawned other innovations too, from nuclear depth charges to nuclear mines. Indeed, there is considerable evidence that the war at sea may have been the first to go nuclear. Only a tactical nuclear depth bomb could reach a fast enemy submarine going deep; the temptation to use nuclear depth charges to protect a carrier battle group or to save thousands of lives in an Atlantic reinforcement convoy would have been compelling. Tactical nuclear weapons were every bit as dangerous to peace as any ICBM.

The land battle in the European Central Region naturally attracted these tactical nuclear weapons. By the early 1950s the US Army was fielding its Pentomic divisions designed to fight – and, hopefully, survive – a nuclear exchange on land. Firepower was firepower: the Corporal missile (1954) could throw a 60KT warhead up to 80 miles; and the M-110 203mm howitzer was configured to throw a 'small nuclear shell' a whole 10 miles. The US Army fielded an even more bizarre weapon, an infantry *company* nuclear launcher called the Davy Crockett. The idea that a *small* nuclear explosion across a valley would win the land battle inspired little confidence, especially among West Germans who felt, with some reason, that mini-nukes may have been only tactical to the Americans, but to the citizens of Fulda or Frankfurt were decidedly strategic. The Davy Crockett quickly disappeared from the inventory. The cumbersome and vulnerable Corporal missile (with its six hours of standing still to be fuelled up) was quietly dropped, and the M110 mobile nuclear howitzer joined the American Honest John battlefield missiles under the tight control of the Supreme Allied Commander Europe with Americans guarding the warheads.

All these 'battlefield', or tactical missiles, and their final versions, the American Pershing and the Russian SS 20, were designed for support to the land battle, should it ever break out. The land threat from the east became obvious to the Allies from autumn 1945 onwards. The Red Army's garrison in Europe was over-large, well armed and configured for the attack. In its turn, the Soviet Union was always concerned about NATO's superior airpower. But the real asymmetry in Europe always lay with the presence of the 20,000 main battle tanks that the Soviets could field and to which the NATO allies had no real answer on the ground. Only the nuclear option could be relied on to destroy massed concentrations of armour or neutralize an airbase 300 miles away. Tactical nuclear weapons on land, at sea and in the air were always an essential factor in the Cold War equation.

NBC (Nuclear, Biological, Chemical) Warfare

The Cold War also spawned one other class of weapons, every bit as deadly in their way as any nuclear bomb: biological and chemical weapons. Not for nothing are WMD (weapons of mass destruction) lumped together under the sobriquet of NBC. Chemical weapons have a long and dishonourable history from their first major use by the Germans near Ypres in 1915. This need not necessarily be so: there is a powerful argument that using intoxicating or soporific gases merely to subdue an opponent is a far more humane method of waging war than vaporizing human beings with a nuclear bomb, blowing their limbs off with high explosives, or even disembowelling them with a bayonet. However, the curious logic of war dictates that chemical warfare – CW – is frowned upon. The principal reason nowadays seems to be that the Cold War managed to build new classes of gas weapons on to the grisly researches of Hitler's Nazi scientists, who discovered that any factory that can manufacture a simple fly killer can also be reconfigured to make deadly nerve gases too. The effects are the same: one whiff of Tabun or Sarin, and the vital links between the body's chemicals and electric nerve impulses break down, leaving the victim paralysed, twitching and breathless. Death is not instantaneous.

Such a cheap and readily available weapon can be put in

bombs, shells, mines – or water supplies. Nerve gas offered a deadly alternative to the blister-inducing mustard gas, which can blind and destroy moist tissues, plus the other deadly chemical agents capable of disrupting or stopping the delicate mechanisms of the human body. Well might Saddam Hussein refer derisively to his use of gas against mutinous Kurdish villagers and the invading Iranians as 'using fly killer'.

Biological Warfare

Although chemical weapons were never deployed during the Cold War, both sides were prepared to use them should they have to. For fifty years scientists on both sides of the Iron Curtain devoted their whole working lives to finding new and efficient ways to use gas and chemicals to incapacitate, maim and kill their fellow human beings. In these impressive academic endeavours they were not alone. Either just down the corridor, or in some separate institute somewhere, other groups of equally ambitious and determined scientists were beavering away trying to find an ideal *biological* agent to slaughter their fellow man. From anthrax and bubonic plague to foot-and-mouth and viral-haemorrhagic fever, a variety of top-secret medical establishments hunted for the 'perfect disease', among a myriad of deadly viruses and bacteria. Fortunately the Cold War never gave them the opportunity to check the fruits of their labours in action: but the tiny stockpiles of their deadly products still exist in some laboratory somewhere, 'just in case . . .'

For this we may even be grateful; for every disease needs a cure. We can only hope that the scientific community is as diligent at BW *defence* as they were in looking for the best way to launch a BW attack.

The Secret War

Fortunately the Cold War never became hot enough for the deadly new family of NBC weapons to be used. However, in one area the Cold War never stopped battling – intelligence. Indeed, there is a powerful argument for describing the Cold War as an *Intelligence* War. From the British and Bolsheviks' Secret Services' first clashes in the years immediately after the Revolution to the fall of the Berlin Wall, this intelligence war never stopped. Not for nothing did Stalin refer to the intelligence struggle with friends and foes alike as his 'invisible front' and the effects of this long-running contest between the intelligence services of both sides were fundamental both to the conduct and the understanding of the Cold War.

From the start of what most people think of as the Cold War in 1946, both the Kremlin and the western allies tried to collect intelligence on the other side. In fact this invisible struggle had been going on since the 1920s. The means deployed defined the post-1945 Cold War on the ground – and at sea and in the air as well. Every resource and artifice was employed. The secret services of both sides ran spies and secret agents to determine just what the other side was up to: men like Penkovsky, Gordievski and Reiner Rupp probably did enough to clarify the opposition's intentions at times of crisis as to be legitimately described as 'working for peace'. Certainly Markus Wolf, the DDR's master spy, was unapologetic about the intelligence collection role of his MfS once the wall came down, saying:

I genuinely felt that our main job [in intelligence] was to prevent surprises . . . so that actions or even adventurous actions that could easily have led to escalation, or even to

> war, would have been desisted from . . . I can state that my unit
> contributed to our having the longest period of peacetime in
> European history. I feel that I can justly claim that.

Wolf's claim is not as grandiose as it seems at first glance.
There is a serious element of truth in his thinking. Whatever
damage traitors like Philby, Ames and the Walkers may have
done to the west, they at least revealed the true state of affairs
to the KGB and their masters just as Gordievsky and Penkovsky did for the eastern secret services. Human intelligence
agents may be fallible but they can reveal *intentions*, the 'fuzzy
logic' variables of intelligence. The easiest part of the Cold
War intelligence collection was, however, always to be found
in identifying the potential enemy's *capabilities*. In the Cold
War the intelligence 'bean counters' reigned supreme with
their blood-curdling tales of new technical superiority or vast
numbers on the other side. Numbers of tanks, guns, planes and
ships dominated the intelligence effort. What sort of weapons
systems did the enemy have? How many? Where were they?
What were they doing? The interaction between intelligence
and intelligence collection and operations to collect intelligence controlled the pace and the action of the Cold War.

Thus afloat there was constant probing and collection on
the high seas. Clumsy attempts by divers to inspect the hulls of
visiting warships in foreign harbours were commonplace and
sometimes ended in tragedy as when the Soviet cruiser *Ord-
jonikidze* berthed in Portsmouth on a goodwill visit to Britain
by Khrushchev and Bulganin in 1956. Britain's SIS-MI6 sent
down a diver to see if there was anything of interest underneath the Red Navy ship. Two days later his headless body
was discovered floating nearby. Even getting too close to
enemy ships at sea could sometimes be dangerous. Soviet
naval exercises were routinely shadowed by NATO planes

and *vice versa*. Sometimes irritated captains turned on their laser range finders in a deliberate attempt to blind over-intrusive pilots. Soviet auxiliary intelligence gatherers masquerading as trawlers came close inshore with the fishing fleet. (One report from the Falklands even alleged that a sailor was deputed to throw a bucket of fish off the back of an aerial-festooned 'trawler' occasionally to attract sea birds and keep up the pretence of fishing.) American intelligence collectors lurked off the coasts of communist countries or the world's trouble spots, sometimes with dire results, as the USS *Liberty* (an intelligence collector deliberately shot up by the Israelis during the 1967 war) and USS *Pueblo* incidents showed. Underwater the clashes were even more violent as submarines tried to track each other and record the all-important acoustic signatures, sometimes with disastrous results as they rammed each other in the deep. However, even these near catastrophic incidents had their benefits: according to one admiral, such activity 'obviously provides unparalleled training for war in a "gloves off" environment'. The comment sums up the fundamental truth about how the Cold War was fought and the reality of that silent battle for those who had to fight it.

In the air the unseen war was constant. Photographic reconnaissance flights were either blatant over-flights, as the British Canberra and US U-2 programmes made their dangerous incursions into hostile airspace, or by concealed cameras in Aeroflot airliners as they wandered 'slightly off course' near some interesting new NATO radar site. Radar and electronic warfare aircraft patrolled the fringes of each other's territory, always on the lookout for new radar emissions or the chatter of careless pilots. Massive signals intercept stations around the globe intercepted communications, identified units and sometimes listened to the telephone conversations of the Kremlin leaders as they drove through Moscow in their Zils, or frantic calls for help from some cut-off Spetsnaz unit trapped deep in Afghan's mountains. The signals intelligence war never stopped on land, sea or in the air. It has not stopped since.

Dirty tricks were normal in the intelligence Cold War. American and British 'liaison' missions set up at the end of the German war became ill-concealed fronts for spying on the other side's equipment and manoeuvres. American officers dug through Red Army latrine pits to bring back reeking signal pads used for lavatory paper and tried to follow Russian convoys or even try and break into top-secret barracks, sometimes with fatal results. British Intelligence Corps officers dressed as members of the Royal Corps of Transport hid in East German pine forests for days waiting for the first sight of some new piece of Soviet equipment. (They fooled no one: a glance at the British Army List showed the name and real regiment of every serving and retired officer.) One commander of BRIXMIS (the British C-in-C's Mission to the Soviet Army in Germany) was hauled in and berated, by the Commander of the Group of Soviet Forces Germany, as 'a hooligan' for daring to spy on his men in a restricted area. The British brigadier replied equally robustly that he was doing no more than SOXMIS (the Soviet C-in-C's mission to BAOR) was doing in West Germany, blatantly spying on Briton and German alike. General Zaitsev burst out laughing and invited Brigadier Learmont to have a drink. Like the Cold War itself, the invisible battle of intelligence had certain rules . . .

Perhaps most dangerous of all were the aircraft 'ferret' flights to collect aerial photographs or record radar and electronic signals. Sometimes an intelligence collector got too close to Soviet airspace and paid the ultimate penalty by being shot down, its crew never to be seen again, either dead or rotting for life in some unknown prison. Only the advent of the satellite endlessly orbiting overhead finally took away the danger. By the end of the Cold War, intelligence collection satellites could pick up golf balls on the ground, record the telephone transmissions of government leaders and, using millimetric wavelength radar, see through thick cloud. It became possible to spot an ICBM preparing for launch and relay the information in real time back to the home country. By the end, intelligence was a genuine confidence builder. But, in the dangerous and finely balanced war of intelligence, even the best satellite could never see through a hangar roof or the White House's walls. For that there is only one solution. The ubiquitous spy is ever with us.

The Cold War was fought in many ways: from propaganda to news management, from diplomacy to aid. None of these bloodless exchanges matched the daily confrontations of intelligence gathering, all designed to clarify the main adversary's capabilities and intentions. All was intended to stop a nuclear war erupting and to control events. Sometimes sideshows and proxy wars erupted: but, thanks to good intelligence, cool political heads and sound crisis management, allied to a healthy fear of Armageddon, none of the little wars of the Cold War ever exploded into a nuclear exchange.

In the most fundamental sense, the Cold War was a war that was never actually fought.

NOTES AND FURTHER READING

This book was written primarily for the interested general reader and not as an academic textbook.

On a subject as vast as the history of the Cold War it is only too easy to drown in the flood of authoritative – and some not so authoritative – sources and references. However, if more detail or further reading is required, then I have found the following books and other references to be especially useful or interesting. Many of these sources of information can be found on numerous internet websites. Although I have not listed every site's complete *www.* address in mind-numbing detail, for the dedicated researcher a trawl through any good internet search engine using key words will reveal many of the references below, plus many, many more. The internet archive now includes so many primary source documents that it represents an important research tool and capability. For example, to read in the original *exactly* what the Soviet ambassador said at the height of the Cuban Missile Crisis in his top-secret telegram to the Kremlin is of huge significance when trying to cut through the fog of what *really* went on, whether the telegram in question happens to be on an internet website or in some dusty archive.

I have also included some seminal television productions as primary references. While some in the academic community deride the idea of modern media (and particularly television) as being 'real' sources, it seems perfectly reasonable to me to accept the on-camera testimony of someone recording his or her memories of events as a primary source. Of course, old soldiers do sometimes forget or embellish their stories. But it is not unknown either for politicians to polish their recollections of events in order to reflect themselves in the best light. To maintain, however, that somehow such recordings are inferior to the written word strikes me as a conceit, and a misguided one at that. It implies that written documents are the 'only true record', as if written records of meetings, telegrams, policy documents and position papers are somehow never 'polished' by their authors, or corrupted, or guilty of omissions or embellishments. Anyone who has ever worked in a bureaucracy, military or civilian, will know immediately how unlikely that is. I have myself been guilty of writing up the minutes of the odd senior policy meeting to reflect what the participants *wished* that they had said, rather than exactly what they did say.

Finally, I agree with my colleague Max Hastings that lengthy bibliographies are sometimes more evidence of some kind of 'virility parade' than any real help to those looking for sensible guidance for further reading. For this reason I have confined myself only to those books and sources that I felt had most to offer, rather than every single possible reference.

Life, and the reader's attention span (let alone the reader's budget), are just too short . . .

General Sources on the Cold War

Jeremy Isaacs' *Cold War* TV series (London, 1998), and the Canadian Broadcasting Corporation's Backgrounder Briefs *Spies* and *Cold War*, are extremely useful as summaries. Isaacs' accompanying book is comprehensive, well illustrated and well sourced. CNN's *Cold War Experiences* and *Spies in the Digital Age* are equally valuable for navigating through literally thousands of references and sources. Louis Halle's *The Cold War as History* reads a little dated now but is still a valuable source for the earlier period.

Lawrence Freedman's *The Cold War* (Cassell, 2001) covers the same ground as Isaacs from 1945 but in a more synthesized form. It is

404   NOTES AND FURTHER READING

particularly strong in its dissection of the evolution of strategic thought, crisis management and the broad themes of the post-war period, as one would expect from the Professor of War Studies at King's College London. For a much shorter, but readable and authoritative, gallop through the period, David Painter's *Cold War – an International History* (Routledge, New York and London, 1999) is a model for short, clear texts on complex subjects, packed with solid facts. Crockatt's *The Fifty Years War* (Routledge, 1995) is also a valuable source for the whole sweep of the confrontation, as is Powaski's *Cold War – the US and USSR – 1917 to 1991* (OUP, 1998).

To understand the detail of the military aspects of the Cold War, David Miller's *The Cold War as Military History* (Pimlico, 2001) is unlikely to be bettered, going into great detail on the subject of weapons, technical developments and the changing armouries of the two sides. Although a little dated now, John Hackett's factional *The Third World War* (Sidgwick and Jackson, 1985) is still the very best evocation of how a clash of arms *might* have developed. Collins' *Atlas of Military History* (2004) contains some clear maps that help to illustrate the various clashes and geo-strategic confrontations of the Cold War although, irritatingly, many lack a scale.

On the well-manured subject of *intelligence* there is always a temptation to turn any discussion of the Cold War into a story about spies and little else. It should be resisted. There are more than enough books on intelligence in general, from Ian Fleming to Polmar and Allen's admirable and comprehensive *Encyclopedia of Espionage* (Greenhill, 1997 and 2004) which, as its name implies, is a positive treasure trove of background on a shadowy subject. Along with Professor Richard Aldridge's excellent *The Hidden Hand* (John Murray, 2002), it remains the first port of call for any reader on Cold War intelligence. The chapter on the Cold War in *The Puppet Masters* (Weidenfeld and Nicolson, 2004) is probably the most accessible *condensed* version of the intelligence Cold War.

With the end of the Cold War much of the secrecy enveloping it has slowly drifted away. The Freedom of Information Act has unleashed quite a flood of primary papers and records; many of the dealings of the NSA, the CIA, and the US Joint Chiefs of Staff can now be accessed with surprising ease. The US National Security Archive is a treasure trove. For the British original Cold War documents in cabinet, Whitehall and elsewhere, the National Archive at Kew (formerly the PRO) remains the bedrock.

The diplomatic side of the Cold War is covered in innumerable sources, from serious diplomatic records. Two heavyweight former ambassadors – Michael Alexander in his *Managing the Cold War* (RUSI, 2005), and Rodric Braithwaite – speak frankly of the situations in which their political masters had dropped them. Crucially, not being either Americans or Russians, they seem to take a somewhat more dispassionate tone than many others equally qualified but more involved in the day-to-day struggles of the Cold War at the highest levels.

Soviet sources are, unsurprisingly, more sparse and selective. There is not only the problem of language, there is also the sheer distance involved, plus the deeply ingrained official Russian culture of secrecy (for example, maps of the Moscow subway were at one time considered state secrets). However, there are agreeable surprises to be had. The excellent Library of Congress Soviet Archive is both informative and objective. For the Russian sources themselves there are several useful references in the comprehensive ArcheoBiblioBase. Weinstein (US) and Vassiliev (ex-KGB) wrote *The Haunted Wood* in 1999, but it still remains a powerful insight into the official Soviet mind and balances many western versions of Cold War events. Zubov and Pleshakov's *Inside the Kremlin's Cold War* (Harvard UP, 1996) offers a good account of what drove the USSR during the Cold War, while the Russian Centre for Conservation and Study of Records of Modern History (formerly the Central Party Archive) has much to reveal and can, to a limited extent, be accessed through Yale University.

Head and shoulders above all other sources is the formidable Cold War International History Project (CWIHP) of the Woodrow Wilson Center in Washington DC, which offers extensive and comprehensive lines of enquiry into a wealth of Cold War topics. It has been working since the early 1990s and can be accessed directly on the internet.

The CWIHP is supplemented by the material to be found on the George Washington University Cold War web site and the London School of Economics Cold War Studies Centre. The Harvard Projects on the Cold War are excellent as is the accompanying *Cold War Journal* and the PHP website.

First Frosts

For the early days, E.H. Carr's *The Russian Revolution, From Lenin to Stalin* (Macmillan, 1979) gives a good summary of the period. In a field overstocked with studies and books it is refreshingly concise. Carr gives a good feel for the momentous events following 1917, as does Konstantin Simonov's *Reflections of J V Stalin* (*Znamia* No.3, 1988).

The story of the attempt by King George V to rescue the Czar seems, against all the odds, to have a ring of truth about it. For a full account of this extraordinary exploit, see Michael Occleshaw's *Armour against Fate* (Columbus Books, London, 1989), where the whole gripping story is related in detail, with full references to the primary sources. Daniel Meinertzhagen's *Army Diary* (London, 1960) seems to bear out this remarkable tale.

The convoluted story of the KGB in its various guises from 1918 to the collapse of communism is told in great detail and straight from the horse's mouth in Christopher Andrew's magisterial *Mitrokhin Archive* (Penguin, 1999 and 2005). He and Vassili Mitrokhin have exposed the whole saga of the Soviets' long intelligence war against the west in considerable detail. It does not make for happy reading and its sometimes startling revelations reinforce the point that the real Cold War went on for much longer than the popular view might suggest.

Richard Deacon's *History of the British Secret Service* and *History of the Russian Secret Service* (Frederick Muller) also form useful backgrounds to the undercover struggle of the 1930s.

Protocol II of the Comintern was published on 4 May 1923 and it is easy to forget that the original Comintern meeting of March 1919 expected Marxism to spread like a rash across the developed world. Revolution and class war across international boundaries would replace wars between nation states. Alas for the Marxist theorists, the Soviet delegation hijacked the whole affair in defence of Russian communism, with consequences that we know only too well.

Sidney Reilly's extraordinary career can be followed in R. B. Spence's *Trust No-One* (Feral Books, Los Angeles, 2002). By the end of his long and chequered career the 'Ace of Spies' seems to have lost the plot.

The whole spirit of the Red Menace is hard for us to understand nowadays. It was very real in the 1920s. Christopher Andrew's *Secret Service* covers it very clearly. As is so often the case, the true social history of the time can often be found in popular culture. The reaction of the middle classes of the day to the threat of Bolshevism in Britain is reflected in contemporary *Punch* cartoons of hairy, prognathous Bolshevik anarchists and even the early *Just William* books of Richmal Crompton have references to the 'Reds' and the

'Bolsheviks'. Read about Mr Dimtritch's exploits in *William the Conqueror*, which was published in March 1926, the year of the General Strike.

See *The Political Police in Britain* (Bunyan) for an anti-establishment perspective on the Zinoviev Letter. The balance of evidence seems to indicate that it was a forgery executed by White Russians in the Baltic States and fenced on to Berlin. The mysterious 'Mr Thun' turns out to have been an ex-officer of the British Secret Services. Bennett's *The Crown Jewels* (HarperCollins, 1997) is considered the definitive answer to a long-standing mystery. Bennett was the official Foreign and Commonwealth Office historian who was tasked by an incoming Labour government to nail the truth about what had become an article of faith on the left once and for all. She tracked the letter to its source, a forger called Orlov in Riga. Unfortunately, no original copy now exists.

The stories of the duping of the gullible left-leaning western intellectuals and apologists for Stalin's savageries are recounted with some humour (and mild contempt) in C.N. Parkinson's *Left Luggage*, a dry and witty political critique of the left in the 1930s. Lenin's phrase *useful idiots* seems wholly appropriate.

George Kennan's powerful and well-informed views on the early USSR are to be found in his *Russia and the West* (Hutchinson, 1961).

Klehr & Haynes' *The Secret World of American Communism* (Yale, 1995) gives some insights into the shadowy world of Marxism in the USA, and Leonard Leshuk's *US Intelligence Perceptions of Soviet Power 1921–1946* (Frank Cass, 2003) shows how the US often misunderstood the difference between Socialist rhetoric and reality between the wars.

Hélène d'Encausse's *Staline: L'ordre par le Terreur* (Editions Flammarion, Paris, 1979) looks at the brutal way Stalin ran his communist empire; Simon Sebag-Montefiore's *At the Court of the Red Czar* (Orion, 2004) looks in more detail at the nervous tensions of life in Stalin's court.

Interestingly, James Klugmann's archive with its pamphlets on the pre-war purges still exists in the Sheffield University Archive; the details of the show trials seems to have given even that dedicated Communist pause for thought.

The polymath Desmond Bernal is a good example of the extraordinary hold communist ideology seems to have had on its converts. Bernal was a famous scientist of the period, who seems to have been yet another confused ex-Jewish intellectual, seduced by the lure of the Soviet workers' paradise. Unlike many other fellow travellers, he never saw the light and remained a blind and dogmatic Stalinist to the end, even supporting the Russians' brutal 1956 intervention in Hungary as a move 'to crush an anti-Semitic uprising'! His infamous musings on the conflict between murdering his mistress and betraying the Communist Party of the Soviet Union are contained in Andrew Brown's fascinating *J D Bernal, the Sage of Science* (OUP, 2005), in which the great brain's rapture in finding an absolute – if seriously flawed – belief system are explored in some detail. The truth was that there were two Bernals: the brilliant scientist and the political dupe.

Victor Gollancz and the Left Book Club are well covered in various websites. The 1930s were a time when the left felt that things could only be improved by socialism. The Left Book Club, and its followers like Harold Laski, believed in *improving the world by the struggle for peace, and a new economic and social policy against Fascism*. Its worthy aims read suspiciously like those advocated by the Communist Party. George Orwell was one of its noted authors.

The Second World War

Ian Fleming's accurate forecast of things to come can be found in the National Archives (PRO), (FO)371 2057/485/38 of 19 April 1939. Sir Owen O'Malley's gloomy warning to Anthony Eden about Britain's Soviet ally on 27 February 1943 is in PRO (FO)371/ 34564 (198).

The Second World War and the determined espionage of Stalin's USSR on friend and enemy alike are well covered by Andrew Boyle's *The Climate of Treason* (Hutchinson, 1979) which rips into the Cambridge traitors, as does Christopher Andrew's *Secret Service*. Nigel West looks at the Anthony Blunt story among others in *Seven Spies Who Changed the World* (Mandarin, 1992) and Miranda Carter's *Anthony Blunt – His Lives* (FSB, 2001) is considered by many to be the definitive account of a long-term Soviet Cold War penetration mole.

Sources on the Cambridge spies abound. E. H. Cookridge's *Philby* is a good start, and it is hard to see how Professor Christopher Andrew's books, can be bettered. Philby's own account and *My 5 Cambridge Friends* by Y. Modin (who was for a time the spies' handler) should be treated with caution. Philby's *My Silent War* is pure propaganda and disinformation by a traitor who was not even trusted by his Russian masters after he fled. In fact, one KGB officer observed dryly that the only time Philby ever got into the KGB officers' club in Moscow on his own was for his lying-in-state.

Churchill's well-known quote about being allied to the USSR is taken from Volume VI of Martin Gilbert's magisterial biography *Churchill* (Heinemann, 1983).

Churchill's experiences in peace and war led to his lifelong interest in intelligence. In his 'wilderness years' in the 1930s he built up close links with the British intelligence services. Dr David Stafford's excellent study *Churchill and the Secret Service* (Abacus, 2000) is well worth a read. Larre and Lane's *The Cold War – Essential Readings* (Blackwell, 2001) gives Churchill's views on the conflict.

In *Venona* (HarperCollins, 1999) Nigel West gives the best and most detailed account of this extraordinarily long-running exposure of the USSR's Third Front in the Great Patriotic War – spying on its own allies. There is a Venona website, managed by Nova Online, where texts can be viewed. Haynes & Klehr's *Venona, De-coding Soviet Espionage in America* (Yale, 2000) looks, as its name implies, at the American end of the operation. These both supplement Kahn's *The Codebreakers*, the Bible on the subject of signals intelligence, along with Bamford's *The Puzzle Palace*, which dissects America's NSA. Nigel West's *GCHQ* (Coronet, 1987) gives an account of the Secret Wireless War.

The website *WW2 Index – Soviet Spy Rings* gives a rather alarming list of all known Soviet espionage activities in the Second World War.

The extraordinary story of how the Swiss Intelligence Service operated in the fevered atmosphere of the final Nazi collapse can be found in Jon Kimche's *Spying for Peace* (Weidenfeld and Nicolson, 1961). It explains how the SS actually negotiated for a separate peace directly with the Allies both on Hitler's orders and behind his back.

The Cold War after 1945

The origins of the post-Second World War clash are well set out in Reynold's *The Origins of the Cold War* (Yale, 1994). Gaddis's *The US and the Origins of the Cold War* (Columbia, 1972) is worth a look for the American view, along with numerous references in the

Cold War International History Project. Many of the British official documents of the time are available in the National Archive at Kew.

Espionage and spies are forever associated in the public mind with the Cold War. Orson Welles' cinematic masterpiece *The Third Man*, set in a divided Vienna after the war, catches the flavour of the period beautifully and precedes the well-known spy thrillers of le Carré and Ian Fleming. These are matched in the USSR by Russian versions of 'the spy as hero', the usual steely-eyed square-jawed heroes being KGB undercover operatives.

British SIS attempts to spy on the Russians and destabilize the occupying Soviet forces in the Baltic States between 1946 and 1954 are to be found in Tom Bower's *The Red Web* (Mandarin, 1989). It records a depressing account of the betrayal, capture or execution of brave Balt nationalists at the hands of the KGB after the war. Philby was the prime traitor.

The overall role of the Soviet Secret Service/KGB in the Cold War is set out in great detail in *KGB, The Inside Story* by Christopher Andrew and Oleg Gordievsky (Sceptre, 1990). Gordievsky was a Soviet intelligence officer who defected to the UK. His betrayal of the Soviet system contributed to a better understanding between east and west.

The immediate post-war scene is well covered by Roy Douglas's *From War to Cold War* (Macmillan, 1981), Sanche de Gramont's *The Secret War* (Deutsch, 1962), and J. H. Anderson's *The US-GB and The Cold War* (Univ. of Missouri Press, 1981).

The *Economist*'s scathing judgement on US Secretary of State Byrnes can be found in the issue dated 5 January 1946.

Detailed descriptions of the growing stand-off between west and east across the Inner German Border can be found in R. C. Raack's *Stalin's Drive to the West* (Stanford UP, 1995), and Mike Dennis's *The GDR* (Pinter, London, 1988). Isaac Deutscher's *Stalin* (Pelican, 1949 and 1974) gives a good insight into the Russian dictator's post-war concerns and policies.

Although a work of fiction, Giovanni Guareschi's *Little World of Don Camillo* (Gollancz, 1951) catches the spirit of post-war Europe. With its daily clash in a northern Italian village between the communist mayor Pepino and the Catholic priest Don Camillo, it brings the communist-capitalist clash on the streets to life. And, unlike the politician's records of the time, it has the added virtue of being very funny.

The very real possibility of a communist takeover of western

Europe in the immediate aftermath of the Second World War is often overlooked nowadays. For two or three years, France and Italy genuinely trembled on the brink of civil war. The Italian secret service and the CIA actually squirrelled away caches of arms and ammunition for use by underground stay-behind partisans to resist any Soviet-style takeover by the Reds. Operation Gladio was revealed in all its embarrassing detail in the late 1980s when a cache was accidentally dug up and the whole plan uncovered, much to the embarrassment of NATO's Special Forces cell and the Italian government.

The Marshall Plan and its impact can be found in Milward's *The Reconstruction of Western Europe* (Univ. of California, 1984) and Hogan's *The Marshall Plan* (Cambridge UP, 1947).

For a detailed account of the early Soviet atom bomb programme, see Holloway's *Stalin and the Bomb* (Yale, 1994).

The post-war problems of Berlin, the Russians and their Zone, and the airlift, are described in some detail in John Tusa's *The Berlin Blockade* (Hodder & Stoughton, 1999).

Stalin's life, and his last days, are vividly depicted in Radzinski's *Stalin* (Hodder & Stoughton, 1996) and Dmitri Volkonov's *I. V. Stalin* (Novosti Press, Moscow, 1989). From all accounts, Beria may well have engineered the dictator's final death through his own secret police guards. The testimony of the assistant butler and the housekeeper at the residence are particularly interesting, as is the unusually high mortality rate among those unlucky enough to have been around Stalin in those last hours.

The best account of Beria's death and the circumstances that surrounded it are to be found in three articles in *Krasnia Zvezda* of 18, 19 and 20 March 1988.

Brodie's *The Absolute Weapon* (Harcourt, New York, 1946) gives a clear understanding of how 'nuclear theology' evolved. Kahn and Kissinger have also written extensively on the subject. Professor Lawrence Freedman's *Evolution of Nuclear Strategy* (Macmillan, 1988) gives a much broader overview of an arcane subject.

The Making of the Atom Bomb by R. Rhodes (Simon and Schuster, 1986) and Leffler's *A Preponderance of Power* (Stanford, 1992) examine the origins and consequences of the nuclear age. Glasstone's *The Effects of Nuclear Weapons* (US DoD, 1977) makes grim reading and is best avoided by those of a nervous disposition.

McCarthy's witch-hunt of American Communists can be found in the BBC Radio 4 documentary *Hollywood on Trial* (Spools Out Productions, 16 August 2005).

All the evidence is that J. Edgar Hoover appears to have been a particularly unscrupulous piece of work. His links with the Mafia, his sexual preferences, and his apparent ability to blackmail elected politicians must alter our perception of post-war American policy. For an interesting exposé of the Head of the FBI's true predilections, corruption and lifestyle, see Summers' *Private and Confidential – The Secret Life of J Edgar Hoover* (Putnam, New York, 1993). *Ultimate Source* (Constable & Robinson, 2005) now confirms many of the suspicions about the corrupt FBI chief's power and influence.

Korea is now well covered as a minor war. Max Hastings' *Korean War* (Michael Joseph, 1987) is a good broad account, as is Catchople's more modern *Korean War* (Constable & Robinson, 2000). Carter Malkassian's *The Korean War 1950–1953* (2001) in the Osprey Essential Histories series is excellent, if brief, and MacArthur's vanity and genius are best found in William Manchester's *American Caesar*. The view from the Kremlin can be found in the Cold War International History Project (CWIHP Bulletin #6 & 7, 1995/6). The air war over Korea is graphically portrayed in *Air War over Korea* (Squadron Publications) which also incorporates new and translated Soviet material.

The lives of all American presidents can be accessed on the White House website. Eisenhower's life and career can be followed in Piers Brendon's *Ike – His Life and Times* (Harper & Row, 1986). His travails with the vexed subjects of over-flights can be followed up in the TV interviews *Statewise Interactive* (Net on Line), which features interviews with ex-USAF pilots Hillman and Austin (17 May 1996), and in Paul Lashmar's splendid *Spy Flights of the Cold War* (Sutton, 1998).

The U-2 incident and its effect on future policy can be found in *CIA Future of the Agency's Overflight Capability*, 7 July 1960 (originally top secret) and supporting documents in the Dwight D. Eisenhower Library, USA, plus the CIA's *Debriefing of Francis Gary Powers*, 1 February 1962 (US National Archives, 1988, now declassified).

There is a great deal now available on the internet on the U-2 spy plane and its missions. In one of the early flights the ground crew accidentally put the L (for 'lethal') suicide pill in amongst the pilot's bag of sweets. He sucked it while over the USSR and, realizing that it was not a lemon drop, spat it out.

Wilfred Knapp's *A History of War and Peace 1939–1965* (OUP, 1967) looks at the evolution of the Cold War at its mid-point, and gives a useful perspective on what it felt like *at the time*.

American policy during the Cold War in the 1950s is in Brown &

Mooney's *Cold War to Détente* (Heinemann, 1984) and Hoope's *The Devil and John Foster Dulles* (Andre Deutsch, 1974). Hoope looks critically at the hawkish US Secretary of State and tries to assess what the outcome would have been if Dulles had been a little less confrontational. Richard Immerman's *J F Dulles and the Diplomacy of the Cold War* (Princeton UP, 1990) is a heavyweight look at the 1950s and the era of 'brinkmanship'. The *Dulles Archive* is to be found at Harvard.

The events of 1956 in Hungary are described in some detail in the *CWIHP,* especially Bulletin 2 of 1992.

After Suez the French never really trusted the Americans and the British. John Newhouse's *De Gaulle and the Anglo Saxons* (Viking, New York, 1970) explains why. The evolution and composition of the French nuclear deterrent (de Gaulle famously said that all he wanted to do was to give France 'the ability to rip the arm off an advancing Russian bear') is on the *Nuclear Weapon Archive* and on the FAS website. See also Yost's Adelphi Paper, *France's Deterrent* (IISS Paper 194, 1985).

Khrushchev's views on the position in 1960 are to be found in an interview with Toyanovsky (Khrushchev's foreign policy advisor) for the Washington Press Club on 30 March 1993.

The view from East Germany (the DDR), and especially its hard-line leader Walter Ulbricht, is in Yuli Kvitinsky's *Vor dem Sturm: Errinerungen eines Diplomaten* (Siedler Verlag, Berlin, 1993). He discusses the problems of the open border before the wall went up.

The Chou En-lai quote is taken from Mohamed Heikal's *Sphinx and Commissar* (HarperCollins, 1978), which examines the whole relationship between the Kremlin and the emerging Arab nationalists.

'Lucky Break' was an MI6 spy working for the British in Cairo in 1955–6. He had access to Egypt's military and political elite and warned Eden about Nasser's intentions over the canal. His material was considered so important that SIS actually set up a special case officer in Rome to handle the traffic. It was Lucky Break who alerted London to the various secret deals between Nasser and Moscow over communist support for the Arab Socialist Union, arms supplies and the Aswan Dam. Eden appears to have believed Nasser was a new 'Arab Hitler' and over-reacted with disastrous results. Lucky Break *may* have been a senior Egyptian Air Force officer (private information).

The French and Israeli complicity over the Suez Canal affair of 1956 is sometimes puzzling. However, it should be noted that at the time there were strong business, governmental and military links between France, Avions Dassault and Israel. Marcel Dassault was a Jew who had survived the Holocaust: for a time the Israeli Air Force was mainly equipped with his French-built jets.

Sputnik's story can be found in the huge amount of coverage in the press at the time, from cartoons to thunderous newspaper leader articles and also in Divine's *The Sputnik Challenge* (OUP, 1993).

The 'brinkmanship' era of the 1950s is well documented in Eisenhower's memoirs (Presidential Library) and the RIIA's documents on international affairs. The various CWHIP documents contain much detail.

The emerging Berlin crisis and the full saga of the Berlin Wall can be found on the *AOL Text History* site. Other sources worthy of a look are Troyanovsky's *Nikita Khrushchev and the Making of Foreign Policy* in Moscow's 'Records of the International Department of the Central Committee' (TsKhSd), August 1961, Folio 4; and the exchanges between Khrushchev and Kennedy of 24 September and 16 October 1961 may be found in the US National Security Archive, Washington DC (now unclassified).

Kurt Wiersma and Ben Larson's analysis is on their site on 'aol.com'.

Tom Lehrer's black song 'And We Will All Go Together When We Go' (*An Evening Wasted With Tom Lehrer*, Sanders Theatre, Harvard, 1959) was a genuine sign of the times. This American mathematics don turned satirical singer was a phenomenon and his mocking delivery and dry wit over a very dark subject made his sophisticated audiences roar with laughter. (The urban myth that Lehrer stopped writing political satire on hearing that Henry Kissinger had been awarded the 1973 Nobel Peace Prize is just that: a myth.) Lehrer's songs can still be obtained and are still worth listening to.

Cartoons of the Cold War abounded and caught both the public and the politicians' mood of the time very accurately. *The Great Challenge* (Rothermere Newspapers, 1958) is a collection of Cold War cartoons and captures the western view of the Cold War in the mid-1950s better than any other single source, being brief, visual and topical.

A good biography of the notoriously aggressive USAF General Curtis Le May is on the Strategic Air Command website. An alternative portrayal of SAC's C-in-C as a demented Cold War warrior can be found on the History News Network. Le May was the commander of the fire-bomb raids on Japan in the spring of 1945 which killed far more civilians than either the infamous Dresden raid or the first two atom bombs. He is famously parodied as the bloodthirsty General Jack D. Ripper in Kubrick's film *Dr Strangelove*. It is significant that both Lyndon Johnson and Robert McNamara found Le May an obstacle to prosecution of the Vietnam War.

The evolution of the MLF is described in Rostow's *Basic National Security Policy* (Draft) for the President of 26 May 1962, and the final policy paper is explained in his *The Diffusion of Power* (New York, 1962). The *Kennedy Papers* in NSC Files (Box 212) of 2 March 1961 show JFK's absorption with foreign policy and the principal countries of interest.

Arthur Schlesinger's *A Thousand Days* (Boston, 1965) is in some ways a dangerous source, as it was intended as an admiring look back at the lost glories of the Camelot era at a time when most Americans would hear no criticism of their murdered leader. Schlesinger's later *The Dynamics of World Power, US Foreign Policy* (Chelsea House, NY, 1983) has more to offer.

Details of Khrushchev's policies post-Cuba are in Raymond Garthoff's piece in the *Bulletin of the Cold War International History Project* (CWIHP) #5 of 1995. *Ultimate Sacrifice* by Lamar Waldron with Thom Hartmann (Constable & Robinson, 2005) contains explosive revelations about Khrushchev's 1963 strong warning over US meddling in Cuba after the 1962 missile crisis and its dire outcome.

For a good Soviet/Russian account of the tense days of the Cuban Missile Crisis, see *The Cuban Samba of the Foxtrot Quartet*, translated from Russian by Svetlana Savranskaya (Military Parade Books, Moscow, 2002 – US National Security Archive).

For details of the underwater standoff that so nearly led to war in 1962 see *CINCLANT* cables to AiG 930, the Joint Chiefs of Staff and *CINCCARIB*, *Current Sub-Surface Status*, 26–28 Oct 1962 (top secret – since declassified).

The assassinations of Diem and Kennedy are comprehensively covered by Richard Belfield in his *Assassinations* (Constable & Robinson, 2005). *Ultimate Sacrifice* goes into the Kennedy assassination and its Cold War links in new and unexplored detail. Vietnam is covered by thousands of books and sources. Karnow's *Vietnam* (Viking, New York, 1983) is a solid account of the whole sorry saga. The Earle Wheeler quote comes from Senate Foreign Relations Committee, 1968. The Westmoreland quote is taken from Karnow. Other worthwhile accounts of Vietnam are Herring's *America's Longest War* (Wiley, New York, 1979), Austin's *The President's*

War (Lippincott, Philadelphia, 1971), and Sheehan's *A Bright Shining Lie* (Random House, 1989).

For a good account of Khrushchev's life and career see Taubman's *Khrushchev – The Man and His Era* (Free Press, Simon & Schuster, 2003).

The Tonkin Incident is dissected (1973) in a critical essay by Jay Marolda, an official US Navy historian, in the official *US Navy Archive*.

There is a useful account of Tet in *Military Intelligence Blunders* (Constable & Robinson, 2004), and the convoluted tale of the Pentagon's contribution is unravelled in McMaster's highly critical, but highly convincing, *Dereliction of Duty* (HarperCollins, 1997), which looks closely at the manoeuvring and deceits behind the Tonkin Gulf incident as well as many others. Interestingly, McNamara has since recanted. His interviews in 2004 hinted that he had probably been wrong over America's strategy in Vietnam.

Détente and arms control are examined in depth in Garthoff's *Détente and Confrontation* (Brookings Institute, Washington DC, 1994), which is good on the 1972 ABM Treaty. Enthoven & Smith's *How Much is Enough?* (Harper & Row, 1971) discusses McNamara's attempt to ensure that the US had enough (and just enough) nuclear weapons for 'cost effective' deterrence.

The story of the evolution of Mutual Assured Destruction (MAD) and the precise numbers of nuclear weapons required are in Saga's *The Limits of Safety* (Princeton UP, 1993). The SALT 1 figures were: USSR, 1,168 ICBMs and 850 SLBMs; USA, 1,054 ICBMs and 656 SLBMs.

The effects on the Cold War of the 1973 Arab-Israeli war are examined in Hyland's *Soviet-American Relations: a New Cold War?* published by the RAND Corporation (R–2763–FF/RC RAND Corp, 1981).

The startling rise in the price of oil after the 1973 war is well charted in a historic graph in *Environmental Conflict* edited by Paul Diehl and Nils Petter Gleditsch (Westview Press, Perseus Books, 2001).

A general overview of the rise of Arab and oil power in the 1970s is to be found in *Islam and Colonialism* by Rudolph Peters (Den Haag and New York, 1979) and *The New Arab Order: Oil and Wealth* by Sa'd al-din Ibrahim (Boulder, Colorado, 1982). Détente and the need for nuclear arms limitations are to be found in David Holloway's *The Soviet Union and the Arms Race* (Yale, 1987) and Garthoff's *Détente and Cooperation* (Brookings Institute, 1994). Burlatskii's *The Mod-*

ern State and Politics (Progress Press, Moscow, 1978) is important because it gives a Soviet perspective on the whole issue of Cold War strategy and nuclear policy. The Royal Institute of International Affairs' *Superpower Détente* is a good overview (1998).

The Peace Movement is well covered by its own supporters, by the press records of the period (see the *Guardian* and *Telegraph* accounts to get a feel for the polarization of the time), and to a lesser extent by academic commentators. *The Peace Movements in Europe and the US*, Kaltefleiter (ed.), (Croom Helm, London, 1985) is a good listing, while Driver's *The Disarmers – A Study In Protest* (Hodder & Stoughton, 1964) offers a wider perspective of the movement. It also shows the very different views on peace movements in the Kremlin, highlighted by the story of the UK CND group's abortive visit to Moscow.

The work of Paul Rogers and his Department of Peace Studies at Bradford University is worth a look for a detailed counter-view of the Cold War. Professor Rogers has long resisted the received wisdom of the Cold War warriors and concentrated on the wider aspects of international security rather than on the bi-lateral adversarial aspects. In particular, he has been concerned with the economic, sociological and regional aspects of the global conflict – hence 'Peace Studies'. His work is respected by both hawks and doves. The *Peace and Conflict Studies Journal* and supporting website offer an interesting and thought-provoking alternative view and agenda.

The work of the SIPRI institute, especially their *World Armaments and Disarmament Yearbook* (Stockholm, year by year) gives a good neutral view of the Cold War and the various peace initiatives. 'Peace Studies' are now fashionable in many universities. They tend to be obsessed by war.

As its name implies, Ed Bloed & van Dijk's *Essays on Human Rights & The Helsinki Process* (Mortimus Nijhoff, Dordrecht, 1985) looks in some detail at the whole Helsinki Process. Tony Evans' *US Hegemony & the Project of Universal Human Rights* (Macmillan, 1996) examines some of the wider geostrategic implications of the subject of human rights.

The KGB's exploits in India and Chile are part of *The Mitrokhin Archive* by Christopher Andrew. This not only tells the whole story of Mitrokhin's extraordinary exploit and defection but gives a remarkable insight into the KGB's operations in developing countries. The revelations about the CIA's *non*-involvement in the Allende coup of 1973 comes from the Study Group on Intelligence briefing at Whitehall's Royal United Services Institute of 28 October 2005.

SALT 2 limited each side's armoury to 2,400 missiles but was never ratified by the USA following the Soviets' 1979 invasion of Afghanistan.

Various accounts, including conspiracy and other theories, of the shooting down of Korean Airlines' flight 007 are widely available on the internet. See *The Conspiracy Encyclopedia* (Collins and Brown, 2005) for a cool appraisal of the possibilities, which mostly centre on the fact that a right-wing US congressman was on board as well as the usual spy-flight allegations. The Russian perspective can be found in an article in *Izvestia* by A. Shalnev (1991).

Afghanistan has attracted a wide range of articles and much of interest on the internet archive. Books are slightly rarer. Eric Margolis's *War at the Top of the World* (Routledge, New York, 2001) is useful, as is Galeotti's *Afghanistan – The Soviet Union's Last War* (Frank Cass, 1995). See also *Unholy Wars: Afghanistan, America and International Terrorism* by John K. Cooley (London and Virginia, 2000).

The inside story of Ronald Reagan's deliberate attempt to hasten the demise of the USSR is well set out in Peter Schweizer's *Victory* (Atlantic Press, New York, 1994), which is extensively researched and accurate, relying as it does on first-hand primary source accounts from participants in the political events of the time, both American and Russian. It contains a wealth of previously unreported detail on such matters as the deployment of the US Stinger ground-to-air missiles by the Mujahidin in Afghanistan and the White House's secret diplomatic negotiations to isolate the Soviet Union technically, financially and politically.

The USSR defence chiefs were becoming increasingly alarmed as the 1980s began. NATO's emerging Air Land battle strategy, based on Allied air supremacy and using deep interdiction air-strikes to prevent any Soviet reinforcements reaching the front line, was a particular source of unease. For the first time in forty years the Soviet General Staff began to fear that they might be defeated in a conventional land battle in Europe, and briefed the Politburo accordingly (private information).

The Exercise Able Archer affair of 1983 is well explored in Bernard Fischer's detailed and convincing *A Cold War Conundrum* (Center for Historical Studies, CIA, 1997), which boasts a host of previously unrevealed primary sources. Along with Vojtech Mastny's *Did East German Spies Prevent a Nuclear War?* (PHP website) it provides a fascinating insight into the background of an event which nearly caused the Third World War, and a nuclear one at that.

SDI – Star Wars – is awash with source material from the technical to the political. Wilkening's *Ballistic Missile Defence & Strategic Stability* (International Institute of Strategic Studies, 2000) and Schroeder's *Directed Energy Weapons & Strategic Defence* (Adelphi Paper 2211987) are the most authoritative.

The political implications of SDI are with us to this day, as a trawl through the internet soon reveals. Reiss's *Strategic Defense Initiative* (CUP, 1992) is a good summary. Paterton's *On Every Front* (WW Norton, 1992) examines 'the high frontier', while *Foreign Affairs* Volume 62, 1984, echoes some of the Europeans' misgivings about American plans.

Tizzard's doubts about his fellow scientists and their baleful role in future wars were in *The Times* of 21 January 1980. Ronald Reagan burst into print personally in his pamphlet *US National Security Strategy* (Pergamon, 1988), which sets out the bare bones of his thinking very clearly. The agenda of groups like the Committee for the Present Danger are to be found on the internet, along with their thinking and background.

The French source on technology theft, code-named 'Agent Farewell', worked in the Technical and Scientific Directorate of the KGB. Schweizer's *Victory* goes into some detail on how vital were these illicit transfers of technology to the Soviet economy. Farewell was eventually caught and executed. (Private information).

Gorbachev has, unsurprisingly, generated a wide range of literature and interest. Schmidt-Hauer's *Gorbachev – the Path to Power* (IB Tauris, London, 1986) is a good place to start, as are Lewin's *The Gorbachev Phenomenon* (Hutchinson Radius, 1988) and *The Soviet Union Under Gorbachev* edited by McCauley (Macmillan, 1987).

Gorbachev's economic and other woes are well set out in Strayer's *Why did the USSR Collapse?* (Sharpe, New York, 1988) and *Rebuilding Russia* (Farrar, Straus, New York, 1991). The Russian economists' view is to be found in Tatyana Zaslavskaya's obscure *Scholars' Critique of the Economy of the USSR* (SURVEY, Vol. 28, Novosibirsk, Spring, 1984).

The Russian disaster at Chernobyl closely mirrors the British incident at Windscale (later renamed Sellafield) in many ways. On 10 October 1957 a careless operator allowed the Cumberland coast reactor to overheat. It then caught fire. By the time the alarm was given the nuclear pile was well ablaze. The uranium inside the blazing core began to spew radioactive smoke into the air. Attempts to put the fire out were fruitless. After 24 hours the UKAEA authorities took the risky step of dumping hundreds of thousands of gallons of water on to the pile in a last ditch attempt to extinguish the blaze. It was a desperate manoeuvre, as no one knew if the sudden release of hydrogen from the vaporized water would cause a nuclear explosion. More by luck than by judgement, the fire went out. A huge cloud of radioactive steam and gas blew into the atmosphere, contaminating the area for miles around. Just as at Chernobyl, the government clamped down on news and failed to inform local residents of the real danger. Prime Minister Harold Macmillan declared that 'openness about the incident would damage public confidence'. It took the British authorities twenty-five years to come clean on the whole incident, finally admitting that the radioactivity had caused over 30 deaths and nearly 300 attributable cases of cancer. Non-government sources put the true figure at nearer 1,000 dead overall. Against this background of governmental duplicity the Russians' admissions about Chernobyl compare as a model of fast reporting. See the *Daily Telegraph*, 1 January 1988.

Joseph Persico's *Casey – His Lives and Secrets* (Penguin, New York, 1991) is good on William Casey's extraordinary secret attempts to bring the USSR down.

The CIA's secret briefing paper on the Soviets' economic woes was *USSR – Facing the Hard Currency Shortages* (CIA – Directorate of Intelligence, BP 5/86).

A perceptive analysis of the Disintegration of the Soviet Union can be found in Frank Smitha's essay on that subject in *World of History*. The end of the Cold War and the collapse of communism are to be found in Herrman & Lebow (eds.) *Ending the Cold War* (Palgrave Macmillan, 2004) and in a host of articles and learned discussions.

The contemporary feel of the extraordinary events of 1989–92 and President Bush's fading doubts about the enormity of what was going on can be clearly tracked in the quality reports of the unfolding story in magazines such as *Time, Newsweek* and, best of all, the *Economist* for the period. *Foreign Affairs* is worth a look for a number of snapshot overviews.

The Limits of Soviet Power (Simon and Schuster, 1998) explains just why the USSR got into trouble and *The Second Russian Revolution* tells the story of the heady last days of communism and Yeltsin's rise to power. To share Gorbachev's daily awareness of the explosive climax to his reign see the BBC's *On This Day* series for the events around 19 August 1991.

For a good discussion of the vexed question *Did NATO win the*

Cold War? see Vojtech Mastny's interesting essay in *Foreign Affairs* (Number 78, item 3, 1999).

The Military Aspects

Details of the *military* aspects of the Cold War can be found in hundreds of books, magazines, pamphlets and even modellers' magazines. (For example, the Americans' top-secret Stealth F-117 fighter was the subject of intense speculation and interest among the model-making fraternity long before it impacted on the front pages of the world's newspapers.)

Details of the military strength and the changing armouries of the contestants can be found in *The Military Balance* (IISS, year by year). The US intelligence community's view of the USSR's military posture is charted in their *Soviet Military Power* (DIA, Washington DC, year by year).

A Soviet view of the military situation at a time when the Cold War was turning ugly can be found in Moscow's *Whence the Threat to Peace?* (USSR Military Publishing House, 1982 and 1984).

For the weapons, the various Salamander books cannot be bettered. *Jane's World Aircraft, Ships, Armour and Artillery, Strategic Weapons* etc., chart the evolution of weapons, and magazines like the *RUSI Journal, International Defence Review, NATO's Sixteen Nations* and the like cover a wealth of military subjects.

Spying and intelligence have generated a literary genre of their own thanks to the Cold War. The works on the KGB and the western secret services are too numerous to mention. Bernd Schaefer's *STASI files and GDR Espionage Information Against the West* (IFS Info paper 2/02) gives a dispassionate and rather chilling account of the East Germans' Stasi penetration of the west and the Federal Republic of Germany in particular.

The reality of the Soviets' plans for nuclear war was confirmed in some detail in late 2005 when the incoming Polish Prime Minister publicly revealed his country's copy of a 1979 top-secret Kremlin plan to invade western Europe following a nuclear barrage. Curiously, the plan stopped at the Rhine and there appeared to be no nuclear targets in either France or the United Kingdom. Markus Wolf's reflections on his extraordinary career as East Germany's puppet master are best summarized in his comprehensive CNN interview *The Man Without a Face*. See CNN Interactive *The Cold War – Spies in their own Words*. The excellent *Open Source Intelligence Digest* (Glenmore Trenear-Harvey) furnishes details of western spies, including the obituary and celebration of a Polish officer who spied undetected for the CIA 'in the name of peace' for over twenty years. See OSINT, *Life in the Shadows,* 21 Feb 2004.

The whole Walker story is recounted in some detail on the Crime Library website as *The John Walker Spy Case*. Walker and the CIA spy Richard Ames did as much damage as ever the Cambridge spies did, and probably more. The works of Nigel West, Christopher Andrew, Richard Aldridge, Michael Herman, Percy Cradock and Raymond Garthoff, plus the CIA and NSA Archives, cover the whole sweep of intelligence accurately and in detail.

Details of the underwater intelligence war (which is still going on) are to be found in *Crazy Ivan* by W. Reed (Writers Club Press). Dr Greg Weir's *Deep Ocean Cold War* (in the proceedings of the US Naval Historical Center, Washington DC) is a valuable and informed guide to the secretive world of submarine warfare. For more detail, the Naval Historical Center's *Undersea Warfare* (Vol. 2, #3, Spring 2000) and the *Proceedings of the US Naval Institute* have much to offer.

INDEX